The Other Philadelphia Story

THE CITY IN THE TWENTY-FIRST CENTURY
Eugenie L. Birch and Susan M. Wachter, Series Editors

A complete list of books in the series is available from the publisher.

The Other Philadelphia Story

How Local Congregations Support Quality of Life in Urban America

RAM A. CNAAN
with Stephanie C. Boddie, Charlene C. McGrew, and
Jennifer J. Kang

PENN

University of Pennsylvania Press

Philadelphia

10   9   8   7   6   5   4   3   2   1

Published by
University of Pennsylvania Press
Philadelphia, Pennsylvania 19104-4112

Library of Congress Cataloging-in-Publication Data

Cnaan, Ram A.
  The other Philadelphia story : how local congregations support quality of life in urban America / Ram A. Cnaan ; with Stephanie C. Boddie, Charlene C. McGrew, and Jennifer J. Kang.
      p.   cm. (The city in the twenty-first century)
  ISBN-13: 978-0-8122-3949-2
  ISBN-10: 0-8122-3949-0
  Includes bibliographical references and index.
  1. Church charities—Pennsylvania—Philadelphia.   2. Faith-based human services—Pennsylvania—Philadelphia.   3. Quality of life—Pennsylvania—Philadelphia.   I. Title.   II. Series
HV530.C623   2006
361.7′50974811—dc22   2006046182

This book is dedicated with respect to the many clergy who serve the spiritual, religious, personal, social, and political needs of their members and communities. Collectively, they also serve the City of Philadelphia and make it a city of hope. Your contribution should no longer be a secret.

To Gil N. Cnaan; may you live to be 120 years old.

Contents

Part IV: Area Organizations That Enhance the Congregational Social Service Capacity

Part V: Conclusions and Implications

Illustrations

Preface

Readers of my previous books, *The Newer Deal* and *The Invisible Caring Hand*, may be familiar with some aspects of this introduction. I came to Philadelphia in 1986 as a visiting scholar for one year. My academic interests at the time focused on how best to provide public social services to people in need. In fact, I did not even perceive nonpublic social services as worthy of academic attention. I am still interested in how societies organize themselves to help their needy members, but I am now more aware of complementary modes to the publicly run system.

I was born in Israel and trained as a social worker in the European framework that took for granted the presence of a benevolent government that assumed the responsibility for addressing social ills. It was to the government that citizens came with new social problems, and it was the government that planned and carried out the intervention. When I began working and studying in the United States, I was amazed by the limited role the government plays in civic life and the distrust most citizens felt toward their government. I noticed that in the United States, in the absence of a benevolent government welfare system, thousands of volunteers and voluntary organizations fill this gap and comprise an active civic life. I turned to the Association for Research on Nonprofit Organizations and Voluntary Action (ARNOVA) to find an academic center where the world of voluntarism and nonprofit organizations is best studied and explored. It was there that I was exposed to faith-based organizations as agents of welfare services. Little did I know that in this venue I would also meet my wife!

In ARNOVA, I also met people who studied nontraditional organizations such as volunteer firefighters, alternative schools, self-help groups, and religious congregations. As time passed, I was struck by the significant role congregations play in maintaining social care networks and community life in America. Throughout the late 1990s, I found numerous newspaper articles on the role of the American religious congregations in restoring civic life in our communities, political speeches on the importance of congregations, and legislation encouraging the participation of congregations and other faith communities in the public life of our society. Yet I could not find any serious academic discussion about the nexus between the faith community and social service provision. My observations and those of my students suggested that these faith communities serve as the American "safety net," social arrangements that guarantee that people who are unable to meet basic needs are supported and are able to survive. The paucity of rigorous research in this area both troubled and challenged me. Consequently, I made it my academic mission to study this area rigorously and shed light on this very American institution.

As I began to study faith-based organizations, I realized that most social scientists tend to shy away from faith-based organizations in general—and congregations in particular. In fact, as is discussed in Chapter 1, I could not even find a good working definition of a "congregation" in the social science literature. I am still amazed by the paucity of literature on congregational involvement in social and community service provision. The overwhelming majority of available resources are political, ideological, and if empirical, based on one or two cases. This book is based on a thorough study of one American city: Philadelphia. Through a detailed and painstaking process, my team and I identified 2,120 religious congregations in Philadelphia. As is detailed in the methodological appendix, we managed to interview 1,392 of them. This was the first census of congregations in any American city. Throughout the book we refer to the Philadelphia Census of Congregations as PCC.

Each interview was conducted on the premises of the congregation and lasted at least three hours. The resulting set of data is the first to offer us a broadly representative yet detailed picture of what religious congregations do to enhance the quality of life in one large American city. Readers in other large urban settings will need little help extrapolating to their own cities. It will be clear to them how much of our social capital and civic energy is the result of the quiet work of congregational members.

Like any historic city, Philadelphia has its own special characteristics. It is known as "the city of brotherly love," a translation from Greek that is old enough to be politically incorrect in its gender-exclusivity. The city prides itself for introducing a few items into our national culinary repertoire, such as the Philly cheese steak, soft pretzel, funnel cake, and water ice (aka snow cones). It was at one time the most important city in America, the site where independence was declared and the Constitution was signed. The Liberty Bell still attracts tens of thousands of tourists, and in the historic district one can still find the printing press used by Benjamin Franklin and the place where Betsy Ross made the first American flag.

At one time, Philadelphia was the second-largest English-speaking city in the world. In the late eighteenth century it served as the first capital of the United States. The Philadelphia Stock Exchange (PHLX) was founded in 1790 and was the country's first stock exchange. But in the subsequent two hundred years Philadelphia fell victim to its neighbors' success. Washington, D.C., took over as the center of government; New York took over as the center of finance. The PHLX is still active, but very few stocks are traded solely in the PHLX and it mostly serves as a means to facilitate contact with the New York Stock Exchange and other such outlets. Through the years, Philadelphia became something of a stop between Washington and New York, similar to Baltimore. But Philadelphia is still unique. As a newcomer to the city, one who had previously lived in Pittsburgh and Boston, I thought of myself as an expert in planting roots in new cities and finding friends and contacts. Philadelphia, however, was different.

In Philadelphia, one is a newcomer for the first fifteen years if not for the first generation. This is the city and region with the highest percentage of native-born individuals still living here as adults. People who grow up in Philadelphia tend to stay around or come back after college and start families here. My first personal experience with this phenomenon was when my son's first-grade teacher made an announcement about grandparents' day. When I inquired about it, I was told that most kids have grandparents living in the area. Indeed, two-thirds of the kids in my son's class had at least one grandparent attending, and some had three or four. As a newcomer, I doubled as parent and a grandparent, as did a few other newcomers. To my amazement, Philadelphia grandparents, parents, and children live in the same community without much interruption, unlike much of the United States, where geographical mobility is the norm.

The social networks of most Philadelphians are rich with childhood acquaintances. People who have their grade school and high school friends living alongside them do not usually need new friends. Thus it takes a great deal of energy for newcomers to join in. Stephen Fried, who wrote an insightful book on the selection of a new rabbi by a Philadelphia area synagogue (*The New Rabbi*), found the same difficulties, although he only moved into Philadelphia from Harrisburg, Pennsylvania. He states:

in Philadelphia, where all newcomers are viewed with suspicion for the first, oh, ten to fifteen years. In many metropolitan areas, synagogue and church communities have such a large percentage of mobile newcomers that their diversity becomes their strength. But not here. A rabbi once told me that the problem with Philadelphia synagogues is that they have too many Philadelphians. And I knew exactly what he was talking about. It's a city that welcomes you with folded hands. (31)

Philadelphia is a city of distinct ethnic groups and as such of segregated neighborhoods. In fact, Philadelphia is known as "city of neighborhoods." Walking through the city, one notices where one neighborhood starts and another ends, even though with the years some neighborhoods have become better integrated. The Library Company of Philadelphia published the *Philadelphia Almanac and Citizens' Manual.* The 1995 edition (Finkel 1995) contained 395 different names of neighborhoods throughout the city of Philadelphia from the earliest days of Swedish occupation to the present. Among the best known are Manayunk, Frankford, Port Richmond, Germantown, Fishtown, Mt. Airy, Germantown, and West Oak Lane. In Philadelphia, one can also find numerous community and membership associations. Toll and Gillam (1995) provided a good overview of the many voluntary associations and nonprofit organizations in the city and the region, but they provided very little information regarding the local religious congregations.

I have been in Philadelphia for more than fifteen years, and hence have passed the first test. I now have friends in the area, and I have slowly come to learn about the city and appreciate its offerings. I am now proud to say that I can contribute to the knowledge of this city and allow people to see it in a new light. Like a true Philadelphian, when one of the city sports teams clinches a national title, I am moved and excited. And like the rest of my fellow Philadelphians, I learn to live with annual disappointment, be it with the Sixers, the Eagles, or even a horse named Smarty Jones.

I selected the book's title as a tribute to an old cultural icon of the city. Long before contemplating a life in Philadelphia, I was familiar with the play and later the movie *The Philadelphia Story. The Philadelphia Story* (1940) is a classic romantic comedy taking place on the Main Line, the affluent string of Philadelphia suburbs. It was an adaptation of Philip Barry's Broadway hit play. The inspiration for the lead female character was derived from real-life Philadelphian WASP heiress Hope Montgomery Scott (1905–1995). The setting of the film is among the privileged upper-class society in Philadelphia. The heroine (played by the late Katharine Hepburn) is a self-willed young aristocratic heiress who is on the verge of a second marriage. The Philadelphia socialite has divorced her dashing, colorful, presumably immature husband (played by Cary Grant) and become involved with a calculated, cold, self-made, and somewhat pompous business millionaire who comes from the city itself (played by John Howard). The plot thickens when her irresponsible ex-husband appears on the eve of the wedding, and not surprisingly, with intentions to shield her from an overly ambitious, cynical tabloid newshound (played by James Stewart)—a second male principal who is also vying for her love on the day (and night) leading up to the wedding ceremony. By film's end, she is rescued and persuaded to return to her playful and loving ex-husband. It is indeed a story about the life of the privileged in Philadelphia in the early part of the twentieth century. It is about an elite, not less privileged citizens, who lived lavishly in the outskirts of the city and traveled by train to manage and run it. It made Philadelphia an icon for aristocratic lineage in the democratic United States. It portrayed the social climbers as those who enter a temple to which they do not belong and whose delicacies they can never even properly appreciate. In Philadelphia, with over three hundred years of population stability, the first real American aristocracy could be observed. And yes, as in good old Europe, correct upbringing cannot be mixed with aspirations and class mobility. It made perfect sense that another Philadelphian became the queen of Monaco. After all, this is where American aristocracy belongs.

At the start of the twenty-first century, Philadelphia's population had dispersed. People with means had migrated to the suburbs, and the city was left with the less well-to-do, a high percentage of ethnic minority residents, and a few committed individuals. For example, between 1990 and 2000 Philadelphia lost 4.3 percent of its residents, and in the previous decade it lost 6.1 percent of its residents. Three surrounding counties in Pennsylvania (Bucks, Chester, and Montgomery) each registered an increase in number of residents in both decades. Delaware County registered a decline between 1980 and 1990, but this trend was reversed between 1990 and 2000. Growth in the five Pennsylvania counties as a whole (3.2 percent) is keeping pace with growth statewide (3.4 percent). However, the key statistic is that a growth rate of 8.8 percent in the four suburban Pennsylvania counties occurred simultaneously with a population loss of 4.3 percent in the city of Philadelphia.

A major symbolic blow to the city was announced on May 17, 2004, when the census announced that Phoenix, Arizona, had surpassed Philadelphia as the fifth largest city in the country. In the 2000 census, Philadelphia had kept its status as the nation's fifth largest city (behind Houston), although its official population count had dipped some 10 percent from a decade earlier. Phoenix, meanwhile, surged 34 percent in the 1990s to a count of 1,321,190. The census cut the gap between the two cities even farther, estimating that Philadelphia's population had fallen to 1,492,231 in 2002 and Phoenix's had risen to 1,387,670. So, on May 17, 2004, it was estimated that the Arizona city, with good weather, clean streets, safe neighborhoods, automobile-friendly architecture and roads, and plenty of space for expansion, had overtaken historic Philadelphia as the fifth largest city. A later estimate in mid-June 2004 found that the gap was not closed, but it was due to Phoenix's slower than expected growth, while Philadelphia continued to decline.

It should be noted, however, that Phoenix's growth is in large part through annexation of nearby communities, while Philadelphia's borders are inelastic.

This is not all. The City of Philadelphia is undergoing a major campaign against blight. During Mayor John Street's first year in office, 35,000 abandoned cars were removed from the streets of the city. These cars had no active owners, no one paying registration or insurance for them, facilitated illegal activities, and were a threat to public health. Worse than this, there are currently 20,000 abandoned properties and 10,000 abandoned lots in Philadelphia. The prevalence of urban blight is very real in Philadelphia, and is similar to that in Detroit. Public education is expensive yet failing to meet expectations. In a summary of the Report Card on the Well-Being of Children and Youth in Philadelphia, the *Philadelphia Inquirer* stated:

The number of first-time ninth graders graduating in four years increased from about 49 percent between 1995–1996 to 58 percent in 2000–2001. . . . each day more than 20,000 Philadelphia public school students (14 percent) are missing from school with unexcused absences. . . . In the 2000–1 school year, 28 percent of students missed more than 15 percent of the total school days, and the high school daily attendance rate was just 77.6 percent. (Fitzgerald 2002: B4)

In the 2002–3 school year, 27 schools in Philadelphia were labeled persistently dangerous. The only other school in Pennsylvania on that list is in nearby Chester. While Pennsylvania as a whole compared favorably to other states, Philadelphia alone accounted for almost half of the schools in the country labeled persistently dangerous. While the list was cut in half at the end of the 2003–4 academic year, the district's own report suggests that teacher assaults in 2003–4 went up 20 percent. Clearly, the Philadelphia public school system is still troubled.

At a time when the tax burden is increasing and the local revenues are declining, someone has to chip in and do more of the work needed to maintain quality of life. Religious congregations and other faith communities shoulder a considerable portion of the burden of the care for the needy people in America, and Philadelphia is no exception. This book documents the heroic role that local religious congregations play in improving the quality of life of people in Philadelphia. It is indeed *The Other Philadelphia Story*, a story of quiet heroes who are rarely applauded or even noticed. This other Philadelphia story is quite likely the other American story; it is a story that sheds a new light on Philadelphia and our cities in general, and as such it is worth telling.

The congregations, 2,120 in all, are spread throughout Philadelphia, helping people in need. Most offer informal or formal services that are modest in scope. Some have a small after-school program while others provide homeless shelters. However, taken together, they comprise a massive force, almost a social movement, of doing good locally and beyond. However, the reader should remember that congregations cannot assume the role that government plays in social services provision and caring for needy people. They are collections of regular people willing to help, but they are not professionals. Their resources are limited and their help is totally voluntary. While their story is illuminating, they cannot singlehandedly cure society's ills. They can be an important complementary player alongside the public and the private sectors, but they cannot be viewed as a substitute for our collective social responsibility. In this respect, I concur with Farnsley (2003: 13), who informs us that "Anyone who does not realize how much congregations do both for their members and for the broader community is just not paying attention. Congregations will continue to do great good, but it is not clear which ones will take on the added role of partnering with public institutions in the interest of strengthening civil society." It is clear that none can be a substitute for the role of government in helping the indigent and needy.

As the author, I have opted to use the editorial "we" in grateful acknowledgment of the important contributions of many colleagues and friends. Three wonderful individuals significantly contributed to this book and I happily acknowledge them as co-contributors. Stephanie C. Boddie was, at the time of the study, a doctoral student at the University of Pennsylvania, School of Social Work, and was the research director at the Program for the Study of Organized Religion and Social Work. She conducted many of the interviews, contributed to many chapters, and is responsible for bringing many chapters together into a cohesive whole. She is currently an assistant professor at the George Warren Brown School of Social Work at Washington University, St. Louis. Charlene C. McGrew is a doctoral student at the University of Pennsylvania, School of Social Policy and Practice. Charlene cowrote Chapter 8 and she helped with data analysis as well as in the editing of the book. Jennifer J. Kang is a fellow at the Program for Religion and Social Policy Research at the University of Pennsylvania, School of Social Policy and Practice. She carried out the interviews and wrote the majority of the material presented in Chapters 10 and 11.

As in my previous book, the responsibility for the theses presented here rests solely with me. My arguments represent a synthesis of many years of research on the role of religiously based organizations, and especially congregations, in the provision of social services. Clearly, I was influenced by discussions with the people who helped me write the book and by many knowledgeable colleagues. Although I am indebted to them, they are not responsible for any of the statements made in this book. Similarly, the mistakes are all my responsibility and I apologize for them in advance.

Part I
Introduction to the Field of Studying Congregations

"Here Is the Church, Here Is the Steeple": Defining and Measuring Religious Congregations

Religious congregations have generated great interest among scholars and policy makers for their civic value. Since the passage in 1996 of Charitable Choice, interest in congregations and their contribution to our social capital and civic society has grown exponentially.[1] But a lack of clarity persists. The number of congregations in the United States is unknown, and even the term "congregation" lacks a precise definition. Congregations have been defined as religious entities with a name, a constitution, a building, and a shifting collection of people engaged in complex actions and rhetoric (Ammerman 1997b). This is an acceptable starting point, but to study congregations effectively requires a more precise operational definition. There is little previous work to draw on, since the new wave of academic interest in faith-based organizations follows decades of ignoring them.

Jeavons (2000: 18) reminds us that faith-based organizations are characterized by "a remarkable diversity in character and mission, operating in very different industries; so much so that they really do not represent a 'coherent net' of organizations in any way." They vary in size and, unlike congregations, easily fold when they face financial or other difficulties. Furthermore, even the meaning they ascribe to the terms "faith" or "religion" is not the same. He further notes that congregations are organizations whose core mission and function is worship and whose essential nature is sacerdotal. This may be followed by religious education and, to some extent, organizational maintenance. Being a worshipping community based on a common theology and practice of prayers is the ultimate purpose of virtually all congregations worldwide. People come to congregations for a variety of reasons, but they ultimately expect to find a worshipping community of people sharing their praying practices.

As late as 1983, David Horton Smith lamented that churches are ignored by social scientists and called on us to focus on them. The importance of his call was recognized by two separate journals, both of which published his views on the issue. Interestingly, the distinction between faith-based and secular organizations has garnered more academic interest since 1996 (see Ebaugh et al. 2003; Jeavons 1998; Monsma and Mounts 2002; Unruh and Sider 2005; Smith and Sosin 2001). Meanwhile, congregations have been taken for granted as something we know about, and no corresponding conceptual development has occurred regarding local religious congregations. Hence we still lack good working definitions of congregations.

An operational definition of a concept is one that allows us to decide whether any item is included or excluded from being listed as part of the concept. Our challenge is how to define local religious congregations in a manner that will enable us to distinguish them clearly from other forms of religious expression. It is our aim to define congregations in a manner that will, for example, exclude monasteries but include houses of worship that are not monotheistic. Such a definition is critical if we are to estimate accurately the total number, sizes, types, and locations of congregations in the United States today. In order to draw valid conclusions from congregational studies, we first need to know what they are, and then how many of them exist in our ecological landscape. This chapter examines the difficulties involved in defining and measuring congregations, while seeking to provide a conceptual as well as empirical definition of them.

Defining a Congregation

"Here is the church, here is the steeple. Open the door, see all the people." Like this well-known children's rhyme, the term *congregation* evokes images of beautiful buildings with a steeple, a cross, a Star of David, or a minaret, as well as groups of people frequently praying and worshipping together in such a place. While some definitions emphasize religious buildings, such as cathedrals, mosques, and temples, others identify a congregation as a fellowship of people who may come together not only for religious rituals and services on weekends, but also for religious or secular activities during the week. Congregations vary by political orientation, governance, faith tradition, theology, doctrines, and worship or other spiritual practices. They range in size from "megachurches" with thousands of members to groups with as few as five members. In our census of congregations in Philadelphia, we encountered congregations ranging from seven to 13,000 members. Clearly they differ in all organizational characteristics, yet they are all legitimate local religious congregations.

While the described aspects of religious congregations are limited by their emphasis on congregations as *places* of worship, such organizations have gained the attention of scholars and policy makers also for the civic value they possess, representing a complex role in today's U.S. society (Dionne and DiIulio 2000). This chapter will examine the difficulties in defining and measuring congregations as it seeks to provide a conceptual and empirical definition for the term. A unified and comprehensive definition is established, based upon the premise of the growing similarity between religious congregations in the United States as they have faced similar challenges, in a process known as *institutional isomorphism* (DiMaggio and Powell 1983).

Identifying and counting religious congregations is a complex task. Prior to conducting such a count, the target for measurement must be clear. Surprisingly, no empirical definition of religious congregations existed in related literature. When we started our census we told the interviewers to locate congregations and conduct the interviews. We were amazed to learn that the available definitions included a wide range of religious gatherings that we had not considered congregations. Consequently, in the first month of the study we were provided with interviews at a monastery, a worship hall at a jail, and a home church. Later on we were confronted with the question of student and workplace worship groups and denominational offices as possible congregations.

Therefore, the first and most important question is whether there is a core model for U.S. congregations that can serve as a basis for analysis. Answering this question requires the following three steps:

1. determining characteristics shared by all congregations;
2. identifying the bases for common features among congregations that diminish the various aspects among religious groups;
3. illustrating the significant differences between religious congregations and others of religious affiliation and secular associations.

These steps will lead to an operational definition of the term "congregation." But first we want to demonstrate how loose the study of congregations is, and why we need a sound operational definition.

Measurement and Findings

One can view congregations as the atoms that make up organized religious life in America. Individuals may be driven by their faith, but in organized religion, the first building block is a collective of believers worshipping together through an agreed-upon theology, text, and rituals (or consensus about the lack of such theology). It is the basic social unit to which members come and from which they go. Congregations may dissolve, split, spin off daughter congregations, or merge with others, and their combined efforts create denominations, theological seminaries, and parachurch groups.

The exact number of congregations in the United States is unknown. Estimates range from 200,000 to 450,000 groups. The Glenmary Research Center (2002) reports for 2000 only 265,727 congregations. The *Yearbook of American and Canadian Churches*—formerly *Yearbook of American Churches*—listed 396,000 U.S. congregations in 1992 (Bedell and Jones 1993); however, the same group reports only 321,000 congregations for 2001 (Lindner 2002). A decrease of some 70,000 congregations in a ten-year period cannot be accounted for by a decline in religiosity, and is most likely the result of a change in measurement. These numbers are also problematic because the U.S. Bureau of the Census reported that individuals claiming to be clergy in 1996 filed 354,000 tax returns. The fact that congregations outnumbered clergy may be due to the fact that some congregations do not have paid clergy, some share clergy with other congregations, and some employ more than one clergyperson. Some members of the clergy serve as pastoral counselors or as members of regional or national staffs of large denominations. Yet the discrepancies among the various estimates are too large to enable us an accurate assessment of the scope of congregations in the United States.

It is important to note that the United States is one of the few countries in the world where congregations are not required to register with the state. It is also one of the few countries in which any person can declare him- or herself a clergyperson and start a congregation. Most nonprofit organizations are required to incorporate, and if their income exceeds $25,000 a year, they have to report to the IRS, using Form 990. Congregations of all sizes and incomes, however, are exempted from registering, and reporting to the IRS is optional. As such, there is no central registry of congregations, and their birth, death, locational change, and existence are not necessarily recorded. Consider the following. The Glenmary Research Group (2002) reported about 800 congregations in Philadelphia. We found 2,100 congregations, after canvassing the streets and merging some twenty large congregational lists. When one wants to assess the nature of congregations, their potential for civic work, or their political strength, such variation in estimates precludes valid inferences.

Rural congregations present another example of the difficulty of a more precise count. The 1990 Church Membership Survey (CMS) conducted by the National Council of Churches (cited in Jung et al. 1998) identified 116,872 congregations in nonmetropolitan counties. Jung and her colleagues contended that there were 200,000 congregations in the area surveyed, a contention that was firmly supported. First, some denominations—especially African American ones—were not included in the list compiled by the survey. Second, many suburban congregations that are rural in nature were excluded by the nonmetropolitan definition implemented by the council. Ethridge (1989) also suspected underestimation and, after studying the public tax-assessment records of thirty counties in middle Tennessee, found that, while the survey identified only 2,391 congregations, the records showed 4,039—a difference of 40 percent. Ethridge found that independent churches—especially Pentecostal churches—were consistently undercounted in the CMS.

Obstacles in Defining and Measuring Congregations

Several factors present challenges to accurately identifying and measuring religious congregations in the United States. First, as has been established above, there is no general consensus on the definition of a congregation, and as all social scientists are aware, a loosely defined entity is very difficult to measure.

Second, as noted above, current interpretation of the First Amendment to the U.S. Constitution exempts religious congregations from any registration, including filing IRS Form 990. As a result, no single source exists for data related to the total number, sizes, locations, and organizational structures of religious congregations in the United States. New congregations can emerge of which only the members are aware. Interestingly, beginning in 1850, the U.S. Census provided data about congregations, but these data were provided by the denominations. The compilation ended in 1936, when several denominations failed to provide the necessary data amid growing concerns surrounding inappropriate government involvement in religious affairs.

Third, many congregations do not trust the government or secular scholars and they are reluctant to provide any information that would be helpful to related research. In particular, small charismatic congregations tend to shy away from any contact with secular America.

Fourth, most attempts to measure the number of U.S. congregations have been made either by denominations focusing solely on their own congregations or by researchers asking major denominations for their statistics. It would be easier and more precise to start with an available list of congregations and sample from it. In the absence of a comprehensive list, researchers have settled for studying, say, all Roman Catholic churches or all Presbyterian Church (USA) churches. These denominations are well organized and local churches are required to report to regional and national headquarters. As a result, small mission congregations, less tightly organized denominations, unaffiliated congregations, and unpublicized fringe congregations have been consistently overlooked.

Fifth, congregations, like many other social organizations, can be born, die, or merge with other congregations. Remember that there was not a single Christian, Jewish, or Muslim congregation in America before 1620. In other words, all the hundreds of thousands of local religious congregations, with the exception of Native American ones, were established by people in the past four hundred years.[2] For example, in Philadelphia, during the study time, two new congregations were formed and two others merged.

Congregations are also known to move to different neighborhoods or change their characters to fit the changing environment (Ammerman 1997a). In Philadelphia and Boston, mainline Protestant and Jewish congregations migrated to the suburbs, following their members, and charismatic and independent new churches took their place in the city (Gamm 1999). One of Philadelphia's largest Jewish synagogues, Har Zion, left the city in the mid-1970s and sold its property to Pinn Memorial Baptist Church. This trend is not only characteristic of white congregations but also of black congregations, when their resources improve and members move to the suburbs. Looking at the issue broadly, Loizillon and Hughes (1999) found that by 1999 approximately 60 percent of the historic congregational buildings in North Philadelphia (built before 1940 and designed as places of worship) housed a denomination different from the original congregation. In most cases, ownership by a mainline Protestant congregation had changed to ownership by a non-mainline congregation, including Pentecostal, Apostolic, and Baptist denominations, as well as independent congregations.

Sixth, many congregations are not accessible by telephone, do not respond to mailed questionnaires, and operate only a few hours per week. Identifying such congregations is time-consuming and costly. In the method of overcoming this problem known as the "hyperlink network," researchers phone individuals in their homes and ask them to identify their congregations (Chaves et al. 1999). However, this approach also often misses poor people's and immigrants' congregations, as they focus on English-speaking members who own telephones. As we show later on, congregations tend to be socially and ethnically segregated; poor people tend to join together for worship services as do immigrants from the same country. It is prohibitively costly to have a staff of interviewers who are proficient in the many languages used by immigrants, ranging from Korean to Portuguese. Similarly, to complement the hyperlink network method by going door to door rather than phoning is too costly, so the method is applied to English-speaking people who have access to a landline telephone.

Seventh, as McRoberts (2003) shows, many congregations in urban America are located in structures designed for business or residential purposes. These often small congregations grow out of local people's needs and use whatever buildings are available and the least costly. McRoberts documents how angry residents complained about decline in business activity because of congregations and the parking difficulties they caused. The clergy and leadership of these congregations are often aware of their violations of building codes and prefer to keep a low profile rather than risk being evicted or summoned to court. In a geographical area of 0.6 square miles, McRoberts found 29 congregations, many of which were hardly known. This situation is quite common in many other American cities, where small congregations knowingly use structures not designated for such purposes so as not to be detected.

Finally, the nominal religious affiliation of most U.S. residents is Christianity. Therefore, the topic of congregations seems to consistently turn to churches, excluding mosques, synagogues, temples, and more obscure places of religious worship or spiritual practice, such as Wiccan congregations. The study of new religious movements reports that many nontraditional religious congregations have been gaining popularity, though they are the minority of American congregations. They are often missing from accounts about local religious congregations, as they require a special process of trust building to gain entry and cooperation. Many congregations are overlooked for this reason, especially by researchers and policy makers.

The Religious Congregation

TRADITIONAL DEFINITIONS

Webster's Tenth Collegiate Dictionary defines a congregation as a "religious community [that is] an organized body of believers in a particular locality." Warner (1994: 63) defines a congregation as a voluntary local assembly gathered for religious purposes. He further describes it as "collectively oriented, functionally diffuse, affective, and particularistic." Similarly, Hopewell (1987: 12) defines a congregation as a local organization in which people "regularly gather for what they feel to be religious purpose [and as] a group that possesses a special name and recognized members who assemble regularly to celebrate a more universally practiced worship but who communicate with each other sufficiently to develop intrinsic patterns of conduct, outlook and story." A congregation presents a shared identity along with a religious function.

As noted above, Ammerman (1997b) defines a religious congregation as an entity with a name, a constitution, a building, and a shifting collection of people engaged in complex actions and rhetoric. According to Garland (1997), this entity also commonly owns property where members meet periodically to observe a religious tradition or spiritual practice that, to some extent, dictates their governance and structure. Wuthnow (1994) establishes that a congregation differs from a traditional community group because people can "congregate" without personal familiarity with each other. He suggests that a congregation differs from, for example, a group of people in a park, in that "there is also a sense of corporate identity attached to a congregation" (44).

The study of religious congregations requires a more precise definition if researchers are to clearly distinguish congregations from other forms of religious expression. The characteristics above are insufficient toward the goal of clearly defining what *is* and what *is not* a religious congregation.

The image of the local religious congregation first brings to mind a building with visible community presence and religious symbols, such as crosses, minarets, or Stars of David. Most congregations do indeed have an address and a place where they meet to hold their worship services. However, congregations do exist without a specified building. Some meet as guest congregations in the properties of other religious congregations; others meet in public places such as schools and hotels or move from one location to another. We encountered a few congregations that meet in people's homes; in fact, the entire Amish community pray in people's homes, rotating week by week.

While congregations have never been bound to a specific place or type of spiritual practice, they have certainly been recognized as distinct social organizations by both scholars and the public. Christians in ancient Rome, Jews in Europe, and African American slaves in the United States who were persecuted for their religious beliefs prayed in groups using open fields and people's homes. These groups did not have publicly recognized designated buildings, yet they were religious congregations. In modern times, the idea of the religious congregation as a group of people with a building began to be challenged as early as 1940 as a result of the ministry of Gordon Crosby (O'Connor 1963). In lieu of the traditional church building, Crosby organized religious meetings in coffeehouses and retreat centers. Even earlier, the Salvation Army recruited converts in the city streets. These attempts helped pave the way for contemporary styles of spiritual practice and the nontraditional meeting places of today's congregations. By the late 1960s, the Department of Church Renewal of the National Council of Churches registered more than 350 experimental congregations gathering in apartments, basements, storefronts, racetracks, and coffeehouses (Johnson 1969). The actual number is estimated to be much higher. Many began as small prayer groups or Bible study fellowships meeting at universities and other school facilities. At the beginning of the twenty-first century, the notion of cyber congregations, people who pray and worship jointly not face-to-face but screen-to-screen, is gaining modest interest. Future researchers may have to consider whether these cyber faith groups are congregations.

Consequently, congregations must be viewed as more than simply places where groups of people gather for spiritual practice, and the wide range of religious expression, form, and function must also be considered in any structured definition.

A NEW OPERATIONAL DEFINITION: BEYOND RELIGIOUS GATHERINGS

In seeking an accurate and workable definition for the religious congregation, it is helpful to consider such an entity within the context of a broader term—a *religious gathering*. Religious gatherings constitute all groups where people come together for the purpose of expressing and gaining further knowledge or practice related to their religion, faith, or spirituality. A religious congregation is an organized and specific form of religious gathering; however, not all religious gatherings are congregations. Examples include family devotions, regional/national denominational headquarters, annual meetings, religious rallies, assemblies, pilgrimages, religious-based homeless shelters and hospices, workplace lunch prayers, and religious chautauquas. Similarly, group meetings that include religious expressions such as blessings, convocations, swearings-in of presidents, and readings of religious texts are not viewed as congregations. For example, some faith-based voluntary associations meet at a specific location and have a group name and a regular body of members with a unique identity who meet on an ongoing basis. They may even routinely pray when they start or finish working. Nevertheless, these voluntary associations are not congregations.

Harris (1995) contended that congregations are a unique subset of voluntary associations. Yet, they are so distinct that they should be singularly defined and studied. The religious and spiritual aspects of congregations are what make them unique. Unlike voluntary associations, congregations are composed of people who share a belief in a higher being, whether it be God, gods, or a search for a transcendent experience. As a structured and organized entity, a congregation expresses its beliefs through the shared values, mores, and practices of its members. It is this unique religious faith—this spiritual quality—that renders congregations deserving of special attention in further research. In this chapter, the more inclusive phrase, *religious congregation*, is used in lieu of *churches* and *places of worship* to denote any organized group with a primary purpose of religious or spiritual practice. This includes all religions, denominations, group sizes, and levels of formality.

As mentioned earlier, it is important to identify criteria distinguishing a congregation from other forms of religious gatherings. To facilitate this, the widely accepted definition established by Wind and Lewis (1994: i) will be expanded. Their original definition referred to a congregation as "people who regularly gather to worship at a particular place." This encompassed all religions and denominations and established the first four criteria—(a) a cohesive group; (b) regular, ongoing gatherings; (c) an organization functioning as, and centered on, religious or spiritual practice; and (d) a group bound to a specific location. These four elements were discussed above; Wind and Lewis's (1994) major contribution is in forging them into a working definition. This definition, as broad and inclusive as it is, poses methodological challenges for those studying congregations. For example, convents, monasteries, religious communes, and some religious cults meet all the criteria, but are not generally considered congregations. Therefore, additional criteria are needed.

The first additional criterion deals with members' residences or work arrangements vis-à-vis the congregation. Unlike a convent or monastery that would require members to live together as part of their religious commitment, a congregation is characterized by the coming together of individuals whose work and living arrangements are separate from the congregational setting. When living arrangements or work are part of the religious gathering, participation in worship services is no longer voluntary. In a congregation, members come voluntarily and meet regularly as a group in a prearranged designated location for the sole purpose of spiritual practice. Some members may live or work on the premises of the congregation, but the majority have to come voluntarily in the sense that their attendance decision will not influence their work or living arrangements.

It is interesting to note that, according to the Wind and Lewis definition, a group of people who pray regularly with a designated religious leader but rotate their place of worship or spiritual practice among the homes of group members would not be considered a congregation. Their definition would also call into question religious gatherings in public spaces, coffee shops, schools, or hotels. However, the operational definition introduced in this chapter would consider such group meetings congregations because our operational definition requires only a designated meeting place rather than a particular building such as a church, synagogue, mosque, or temple. Therefore, this study proposes that, in addition to operating as a religious identity, a congregation indeed is based at a specific location, but that it is not necessarily bound by any one geographical or other meeting place. The location is important only to the extent that it enables members to meet regularly and develop a sense of structure, community, and identity.

The next criterion deals with the presence of leadership. Contrary to the common perspective that a congregation has a leader, the definition provided by Wind and Lewis (1994) does not require the presence of a religious leader. Therefore, Quakers, Jehovah's Witnesses, and other religious organizations with no designated clergy can be defined as congregations. The majority of religious congregations in the United States do, however, have a designated leader. Consequently, the presence of a religious leader has been included as the sixth criterion for designation as a congregation. The leader does not necessarily lead the religious service, nor is this individual necessarily considered the supreme religious authority; and even if the leader is not necessarily defined as clergy, as organizations, congregations must have a person or a committee overseeing the affairs of the group and maintaining its property, finances, and records, just as a chief executive officer would manage a secular organization. In congregations there is some type of authority that regulates time of worship and the provision of needed texts or music books for the worship service to take place smoothly. Congregations are not religious communes whose decisions are always reached by consensus. As social organizations, they need some structure with leadership that is either religious or organizational or both.

The final additional criterion is the formal name of the congregation. As Hopewell (1987) notes, congregations are also identified by a special name that conveys a religious or spiritual purpose and implies a shared identity. Shrines, for example, have special names, but do not imply a shared identity among those who make pilgrimages to them. Family devotions, Bible studies, and prayer groups typically have no special name, but they do provide a shared identity. Therefore, a special name and shared purpose and identity is the seventh and final criterion for designation of a congregation.

AN AGGREGATED DEFINITION OF A "RELIGIOUS CONGREGATION"

The following seven criteria, comprised of the four borrowed from Wind and Lewis (1994) and the four added in this study, formulate a working definition for a congregation:

1. A cohesive group with a shared identity as a religious congregation (people may join and leave, but at any given worship meeting most

attendees would know each other and identify themselves as members). In the case of megachurches, cell groups provide the face-to-face interaction and familiarity.

2. A group that meets regularly on an ongoing basis (in contrast with annual or infrequent prayer meetings, or regular prayer meetings by many individuals who do not form a group—such as around holy graves or historic squares).

3. A group that comes together primarily for religious worship or the spiritual practice of accepted religious teachings or rituals (in contrast with people in prison, workplaces that allow prayers, or people who happen to meet in airports and pray together).

4. A group that meets and engages in religious/spiritual practices at a designated place (the place can be one distinct building with a sanctuary and a clear religious sign or it can be a rented space or even a public space, but the group knows where they will meet, and people come to that place knowing that the identified religious community will meet at that place for the purpose of worshipping).

5. A group whose members come voluntarily and there is no requirement of working or living together (family devotions are one example that is excluded by this criterion, but also prisons, convents, and workplaces are excluded).

6. A group with an identifiable leader, group of leaders, or some other formal decision-making mechanism (for the organization of the congregation to take place, there must be a way of determining at what time people will meet to pray, who may lead the worship service, and who will manage the finances and administrative functions of the congregations).

7. A group with an official name and a formal structure that conveys its religious/spiritual purpose and identity (after all, the primary reason for congregations to exist is the mutual manner by which members express their faith. Such a joint effort requires an identity in name, group belonging and an agreed-upon set of rituals and texts by which the faith is collectively expressed).

It is important to note that this new definition does not require that a congregation adhere to a monotheistic tradition. It is, therefore, applicable to Hindu, Buddhist, and Yoruba traditions, as well as to pagan and satanic groups.[3] No moral judgments are imposed as to the type of religious gathering that should be identified as a congregation. As the presence of non-Judeo-Christian faiths remains relatively small in the United States, they are commonly omitted from public and scholarly discussion surrounding religious congregations. Using the operational definition developed in this study to define congregations enables the establishment of a coherent and consistent unit of analysis that clearly excludes non-congregations yet makes no assumptions about particular religious beliefs.

Are Congregations a Unique Entity?

The inconsistencies in measuring the number of U.S. congregations may lead to the assumption that congregations have little in common with each other. Given that they are so diverse in size, structure, and membership, is it possible that they are not the same social organization? This, in turn, calls into question the notion of studying congregations as a unit of analysis. Nevertheless, this study supports the belief that U.S. congregations have much in common and that, over the last 300 years and despite many variations, they have become increasingly similar. As mentioned earlier, institutional isomorphism explains this phenomenon.

ISOMORPHISM AMONG CONGREGATIONS IN THE UNITED STATES

Despite the variation among local religious congregations, each one comprises a single social unit. They are treated collectively in related statistics for two reasons. First, local congregations have essential characteristics in common, as is shown in the operational definition presented here, and, second, congregations differ significantly from other social institutions. Before we discuss these two points, it is important to note that congregations in all faith traditions serve the same function: they are the societal mechanism by which people of faith come together to form a collective that sets organized and accepted means to worship. While anyone can pray and worship on his or her own, the transforming of individuals into a coherent and organized group is the function of the social institution known as a local religious congregation. This is a very important function, as it establishes the rules and rituals accepted by a group of people and allows them to express their faith in a manner that is understood, consistent, and unifying. Congregations take faith from the individual sphere and transform it into an observed and appreciated entity by members and by other people outside the faith. In all congregations, throughout America and the world, people come together to collectively express what is very private and conceptual. Unlike other religious gatherings, congregations are places of worship where worshippers can be viewed as members; that is, they are regular attenders, they feel ownership of the collective and its properties, they come voluntarily, and they share religious practices. As Farnsley (2003: 36) observed:

Perhaps the least-appreciated fact in the movement to involve congregations in civic life is how much congregations, as organizations, vary from one to the next. At some very basic level they are similar. Most have worship weekly or more frequently. Most employ at least a part-time pastor or have someone who is serving a shift as a clerk. Most, though not all, have some sort of musical program related to their worship and some sort of arrangements for teaching their religious stories and values to their children.

American congregations can be treated as a single unit because, over time, they become more alike in their structure and function. This trend of institutional isomorphism occurs when a cluster of organizations, initially quite dissimilar, reacts to various environmental pressures and develops organizational and cultural adaptations that cause them to act very much alike (DiMaggio and Powell 1983). For example, the quest for a worship hall necessitates purchasing properties and registering them in the name of the collective, be it the congregation or the denomination. In America, the faith group solely undertakes this process; no public institution is involved. Once a building has been planned, purchased, or erected, a building committee is established and raising funds from members becomes a required activity even for clergy who work without pay. Biddell (1992: 92) observes a similar trend at the congregational level and explains the phenomenon in the following manner: "When it comes to matters of staffing, raising and handling money, or the day-to-day operations of the church, most congregations of similar size look surprisingly alike, regardless of denomination."

Takayama and Cannon (1979) suggest that even American Protestant denominations have adopted similar organizational structures as a way to cope with the changing environment. They have national and regional headquarters and procedures of ordination and congregation support. While these denominations change over time and differ from each other, when compared with European denominations they are more alike, as they operate in an environment in which numerous denominations exist and compete. In most countries there are only a few strong and widely representative denominations or religions.

Takayama and Cannon (1979) and Biddell (1992) share the view that congregations have become a unique social institution due to both historical and societal forces. The similarities among congregations in the United States go beyond structure and function. Today's congregations, responding to the current pluralistic nature of society in this country, act more like community centers and organized forms of local representation than their counterparts in Europe (Cnaan et al. 2002). For example, in the United States, the clergy serve as representatives in community conflicts and public hearings, as well as within the political system as a whole, much more than in any other post-industrial democracy. Congregations in the United States also assume a significant role as social service providers.

Ethnic and racial groups in the United States have historically used organized religion as a means of creating a sense of community, sharing the adaptation experience, and assisting one another both financially and emotionally (Boddie 2002; Lincoln and Mamiya 1990; Moore 1986; Warner 1993). This same scenario can be observed today among many Southeast Asian immigrants to this country. Many who are neither Christian nor particularly religious have become active members of Christian denominations to partake in the base support and communal life that the church provides and that reaches beyond religious beliefs. In the process, they subscribe to the religious tradition and rituals of the relevant congregation and undergo baptism and other forms of ceremonies required for admission and acceptance. On the other hand, the segregated nature of congregations is quite universal in the United States. Most congregations are attractive to certain ethnic, educational, or income subgroups. Members gravitate toward congregations comprised of people like themselves.

Haddad and Lummis (1987) and Chazanov (1991) found that among Sunni Muslims the imam—traditionally a member elected as a prayer leader—has become a de facto community leader. The imam represents his congregation in public forums such as ecumenical coalitions or negotiations with City Hall, conducting marriages and funerals, visiting the sick, and counseling families. These activities are more typical of religious leaders in the United States than of imams in Islamic countries. In part, imams are undertaking such activities because government, foundations, and the wider community call on them to follow the lead of other religious leaders, and in part, because their members share expectations similar to those of non-Muslims with whom they now have greater contact. As has been the case with other congregations, mosques within the United States have become centers for education, social services, social activities, and cultural events, as well as religious worship.

Catholic churches in the United States also have more communal orientation and more horizontal governance structure than do those in many other countries (Dolan 1985). It is interesting to note that U.S. Catholics, who constitute less than 5 percent of the global Catholic population, account for 75 percent of the marriage annulments granted by the Roman Catholic Church. This indicates that Catholic wedding and religious practices are more similar to those of other religions within the United States, especially Protestant denominations, and less similar to those of Catholics elsewhere in the world (Vasoli 1998). The roles and practices unique to U.S. congregations stem from the fact that the churches, synagogues, mosques, and other religious congregations of this nation are both a source of mutual support and a power base for those who share the same ethnicity, race, socioeconomic status, religious heritage, and spiritual preferences. Dignan (1933/1974: 142) suggested that the "legal policy regarding congregations in the first third of the nineteenth century was based on the idea that 'the civil power' should treat religious organizations alike by doing as little as possible for any of them and forcing all to conform to one procedure."

Dignan further proposed that the courts and towns treat congregations as voluntary associations and address cases of property and rights between the laity and clergy as if they were regular voluntary associations. Consequently, congregations were forced to seek legal advice and incorporate legally to avoid charges of misconduct and costly litigation. This was the case not only for Protestant churches, but also for Catholic churches and Jewish synagogues (Carey 1978). According to Carey, this treatment by the court and public officials strengthened the role of the laity in all congregations within the United States and rendered them more similar to each other than to their counterparts in Europe.

Fried (2002) interviewed a seasoned Jewish rabbi who is revered for his insights and wisdom, David Wolpe. According to Wolpe, when the American rabbinate professionalized it modeled itself after the Christian structure. Fried concludes that this is the reason why rabbis call their work "pulpit work"—a Christian term. Like churches, synagogues have personnel committees and building committees, and they have to maintain a building as well as pay benefits and insurance for employees including the senior clergy.

The issue of social responsibility and related social services has often been cited as a major difference between religious congregations. It has long been argued that, compared with mainline Protestant congregations, conservative congregations have been more insular and more concerned with the spirituality of their members and spreading the gospel, and therefore opposed to social welfare and social service involvement. Recent studies have suggested that this is not the case (Cnaan and Boddie 2001; Mock 1992; Regnerus and Smith 1998). Regnerus and Smith (1998: 1347), for example, concluded that U.S. residents "want religion to speak to social and political issues, and act accordingly. Among religious traditions, conservative movements such as evangelical Protestantism are the most publicly oriented, constituting a reversal of past traditions. Liberal Protestantism, once the most powerful religious voice in public areas, is now much more privatized than conservative traditions."

These findings suggest an erosion of the classic distinction between fundamentalist and liberal congregations that is concurrently causing these U.S. congregations to become more similar in structure and function. The implication is that even the classical distinction between mainline (liberal) congregations and orthodox (conservative/fundamentalist) congregations is fading.

TESTING THE DEFINITIONAL RESULTS

A good way to demonstrate the problem regarding this issue is the Philadelphia Census of Congregations (PCC) (Cnaan and Boddie 2001). After three years of study, the number of congregations in Philadelphia was assessed at 2,120. Prior to this census, estimates from clergy and local experts ranged from 1,500 to 5,000. The original list, compiled from Philadelphia property tax records and the local Yellow Pages, totaled 1,483 congregations. To verify the compilation and attempt to identify the remaining congregations, four methods were applied. Lists were requested from every denomination, interfaith organization, and other faith-based entities, along with polling stations and the local Bureau of the Census. The fifteen or so separate lists we received were manually merged with the master file because congregations often use various names and may provide more than one address or list the residence addresses of their clergy.

In every congregational interview, clergy members or key informants were asked to identify congregations with which they collaborated, along with their telephone numbers and addresses. Given that the interviewers were paid per completed interview, they had an incentive to identify new congregations and add them to the master list. In fact, at least 20 percent of the new names of our list of congregations came from information gathered at these interviews.

We also sought the assistance of the advisory board for the study, which was composed of religious leaders throughout the city. The board members reviewed the merged list of congregations and supplied missing ones known to them. We provided them with copies of our lists, and we frequently got phone calls from them informing us of missing congregations that we should add to the list.

Finally, the research interviewers traveled the local neighborhoods to identify possibly unlisted storefront churches and other congregations not in the master file. Every block of the city was canvassed, and many unknown congregations were discovered, especially ethnic, minority, and nontraditional congregations. For example, block-to-block canvassing increased the number of known congregations in West Philadelphia by 10 percent.

In combination, these approaches yielded a far more complete master list. From the original list of 1,483 congregations, at least 265 did not meet the criteria for a congregation. They were actually parsonages, convents, a video store, private residences of clergy, or simply nonexistent entities. The Yellow Pages and city property tax files together identified only 1,218 (57 percent) of the 2,120 congregations eventually identified. Acknowledging that the list of congregations remained less than complete, we continued to identify new congregations through the third year of the study. Others that no longer existed or no longer met the criteria of a congregation were deleted. As noted above, some of these organizations were convents, student campus ministries, and other religious gatherings that presented challenging decisions for the interviewers in terms of whether to include them in the initial list.

Conclusion

The operational definitions provided the criteria to assist interviewers in the research process. In one case, an interviewer completed a survey for an organization that appeared to meet all the criteria, and yet it was ruled not to be a congregation. This congregation had a specific meeting place, opened daily for religious activities, had a leader in place, had an official name, and presented a solid structure and religious function. However, the group did not identify itself as a congregation. While there was a core group of people that regularly participated in religious activities, the group viewed itself as a mission that provided religious and physical support for those in need of assistance. This mission was considered a religious gathering, not a congregation.

One way to distinguish a congregation from a more general form of religious gathering is to envision three concentric circles representing religious gatherings. The innermost circle represents congregations; the outermost, religious gatherings that are not congregations. The middle circle represents religious gatherings that do not meet all of the study criteria defining congregations, but which may be commonly viewed as congregations. For purposes of this study, these groups will be referred to as quasi-congregations.

Examples of congregations categorized within the middle circle include college students who regularly meet during the school year for religious services and prison ministry prayer meetings and services. In some cases, the latter gatherings have become more structured and are now often referred to as "prison churches," meeting each Sunday and led by a pastor. One such prison church has even established a deacon board, an ushers' board, and a choir. While this church does not carry an independent name, it meets every other criterion and would be classified a quasi-congregation. Groups founded under an egalitarian theology with no identified leaders are also included in this middle circle because they meet all the other study criteria for being defined as congregations. Similarly, religious communes meet most of the criteria for congregations, except that members do live or work in the location where the congregation is housed.

The outermost circle of the model represents the types of religious gatherings this study would not consider congregations because they fail to meet most of the study criteria. For example, religious study groups, social ministries, and campus fellowship groups may be affiliated with larger congregations without independently qualifying as congregations. The same is true for religious crusades and revivals, which have neither a cohesive group of members nor regular ongoing meetings in a specific location. Because visitors do not constitute a cohesive group, shrines and national cathedrals are not defined as congregations unless they also have a regular group of people attending worship services or other spiritual practices.

Other examples of religious gatherings not considered congregations under the operational definition presented in this study include family devotions, regional/national headquarters of religious denominations, annual religious meetings or assemblies, religious-based homeless shelters and hospices, and religious chautauquas. Similarly, group meetings that include religious expressions such as blessings, convocations, and readings of religious texts are not considered congregations in this research. As greater familiarity was gained with the communities of faith within Philadelphia, more organizations that were not true congregations were identified and removed from the master list. Key informants from mosques and other religious groups that were not well represented on the list were also identified and added to the numbers. Three years of data collection demonstrated the importance of an empirically based and operational definition.

The task of defining and measuring religious congregations was selected as the topic of study for this chapter because of the pervasive nature of religious congregations in this country and the paradoxically limited accumulation of empirical knowledge about these organizations and their social and community involvement. At the onset of this research, the "terrain" was expected to be well mapped; however, the wide gaps in related literature posed surprising challenges. While congregations have been the subject of studies conducted by numerous theologians and scholars in the humanities, this institution has been long neglected by social scientists. Therefore, the unique contribution congregations make to civil society within this country has been hidden and rarely discussed, let alone empirically studied and operationally defined. The following description offered by Elazar (1983: 242) is relevant for all congregations: "It is absolutely vital that synagogues cease to be considered the private property of their members and be recognized for what they are—public institutions bearing significant communal responsibilities." Therefore, all religious congregations are local institutions that should be counted and further studied as vital social units within this country.

Chapter 2
The Religious Landscape in Philadelphia

In many ways, Philadelphia is like other old, formerly industrial U.S. cities where once booming economies have declined and blight has crept in (Sugrue 1996). In other regards, including its religious history, Philadelphia is unique. In 1683, William Penn laid out the city of Philadelphia ("Brotherly Love") as part of a quasi-religious utopian experiment (Adams et al. 1991). As a Quaker, Penn envisioned a community in which all religions could live peaceably and justly with one another in a civil society. Yet, in its early years, almost the only religious gathering places in Philadelphia were Quaker meeting houses, and, until the formation of Christ Church at Second and Market Streets, the Society of Friends was the only active religion in town.

As the city developed and became a trading center and increasing numbers of German, Scottish, and Irish immigrants arrived, Philadelphia and the surrounding areas became a major center for Lutheran, German Reformed, and Presbyterian churches. Soon thereafter, Baptists, who advocated religious liberty, that is, the right of all religions to be practiced freely, arrived from Wales. In the mid-1700s, Philadelphia opened its doors to Roman Catholics to conduct services here, although other colonies tried to keep them out. This is not to say that all Philadelphians welcomed and appreciated the newly arrived Roman Catholics; fistfights and church burnings did occur in Philadelphia, but to a lesser degree than in New York, Boston, and other cities. This religiously diverse city also became a major center for Jews in the United States. By the end of the colonial period, the Philadelphia Jewish community had become the largest in the nation, and it later became an important center for Jewish educational and theological life in America. Philadelphia also had a small representation of white Methodists. Furthermore, Philadelphia was a special place for black Methodists, for it was here that Richard Allen and other African Americans started the first independent black Methodist church in America, the forerunner of the African Methodist Episcopal Church (AME) (Gaustad and Schmidt 2002).

Like many American cities, Philadelphia grew rapidly during the nineteenth and the first part of the twentieth centuries. Industrialization created manufacturing firms producing clothing and textiles, machine tools and hardware, shoes and boots, paper and printing, iron and steel, and lumber and wood. Philadelphia absorbed a wave of European immigrants and southern black migrants during and after World War I. As streetcars and automobiles increased people's mobility, a significant portion of the city's population moved out of the city to the suburbs. While the region's population continued to grow through the 1950s, 1960s, and 1970s, the urban center's population peaked around 1950 and dropped sharply in the following decades. Before World War II, the urban center's population was predominantly white, with a black minority; by 2000, the ratio of black to white was nearly one to one in the city, while the suburban areas were overwhelmingly white (U.S. Census 2000). The loss of tens of thousands of industrial jobs increased the concentration of poverty in the city, where low-paying service sector jobs now prevail.

While much is known about the economy and demography of Philadelphia at the beginning of the twenty-first century, less is known about its religious state. In fact, few studies have aimed at understanding and describing the religious state of any one locale. As noted in Chapter 1, there have been very few attempts to make reliable master lists of congregations in any one municipality. It is our aim to provide a broad but accurate picture of religious life in Philadelphia. We focus on issues that contribute to this picture. We start with how many congregations exist and what this means locally and nationally, their denominational distribution, and the denominations most represented in Philadelphia. We discuss the locations of congregations, the distribution of storefront and megachurches, and where and how often people tend to worship. Finally, we analyze life conditions around congregations in Philadelphia. While congregations are the most evenly distributed local social organization, they are also often housed in areas beset by social ills.

Counting Congregations

How many congregations are there in the City of Brotherly Love? Estimates ranged from 600 to 5,000, and no master list existed that we could use. Using numerous methods of data collection, we found 2,120 congregations active in the city.

The 2000 U.S. Census estimate of 1,517,550 people residing in Philadelphia gives, on average, one congregation per 716 residents, or 1.4 congregations per 1,000 persons. If we assume that this ratio holds for the entire country, then the number of local religious congregations in the United States would be around 393,000, an estimate that correlates with many previous estimates by the Independent Sector and the

National Council of Churches (Independent Sector and Urban Institute 2002). This assumption, however, needs to be carefully studied. Bob Edwards from East Carolina University, for example, reported that he and his students identified 380 Christian congregations in a county of roughly 110,000 people (Pitt County, North Carolina), or about 3.5 congregations per 1,000, more than double what we found in Philadelphia.

Given that the average membership of congregations in Philadelphia is 322, we can conclude that 45 percent of the city residents are active members of congregations—people who attend at least monthly and are known to the clergy or other members. Many more people are affiliated with congregations but are not members. For example, in North Philadelphia, we asked a few teens whether they went to church, and they answered yes. However, when we asked when they had last gone to church, they could not recall, nor could they remember the name of the church they attended. Seeing our puzzlement, one of them volunteered that at times he went with his uncle to his church, and that if he needed a church, this was it. For us, however, this constitutes only affiliation, not membership. These are people who go to church very infrequently, mostly on holidays and in times of crisis, and are not regular contributors to their congregations. To capture this looser connection, we asked the congregations in the Philadelphia Census of Congregations (PCC) to report the number of people who are somehow affiliated with them. These are people who are known to be on "the mailing list" or on "the roll." In the Catholic tradition, they are the people who live in the parish and who are expected to come weekly for worship, but who come yearly or less frequently. Still, these people are among those who have their religious needs met through the existing 2,120 congregations in Philadelphia. The mean number of affiliated members is 584 per congregation. This implies a total of 1,238,080 affiliated members in the city, or about 80 percent of the city's residents. This may be an overestimate, given that some people may be affiliated with more than one congregation. Yet it is an indication that most Philadelphians are connected with one or more places of worship.

Denominational Diversity

Congregations in nearly all American cities reflect two main trends. First, they reflect the history of the city with its waves of immigration and religious dominance. Second, they reflect current trends in religious growth. New and revived denominations plant and establish new congregations as a means of recruiting new members, offering their faith to those searching for new spiritual venues. The Southern Baptist Convention, for example, planted some 23 new churches in the Philadelphia area between 2000 and 2003 (Holmes 2003). In our interviews, we found that many congregations were formed specifically so that a particular up-and-coming denomination could have at least one church in Philadelphia. All in all, we found 181 different denominations among the 1,392 congregations interviewed, an average of eight congregations per denomination. The actual distribution, however, is uneven. The Roman Catholic church has the most congregations in Philadelphia (135; 9.7 percent). There are 320 (23 percent) Baptist churches in the city, but they belong to some twenty different denominations.

When we looked at specific denominations without grouping them into larger categories, we found that those with a significant presence in Philadelphia included Roman Catholic (135; 9.7 percent); Presbyterian (USA) (73; 5.2 percent); National Baptist (67; 4.8 percent); Southern Baptist (67; 4.8 percent); United Methodist (58; 4.2 percent); Episcopal (56; 4 percent); American Baptist (National and Philadelphia associations combined; 54; 3.8 percent); Evangelical Lutheran Church of America (39; 2.8 percent); Church of God in Christ (32; 2.3 percent); African Methodist Episcopal (24; 1.7); Progressive National Baptist (21; 1.5 percent); Assembly of God (21; 1.5 percent); and United Church of Christ (15; 1.1 percent).

In addition, we found groups of independent churches that together could comprise a group larger than any above. For example, 128 (9.2 percent) churches defined themselves as independent nondenominational Christian bodies (79; 5.7 percent); independent Pentecostal (79; 5.7 percent); independent Baptist (48; 3.4 percent); and Apostolic (34; 2.4 percent). Among non-Christian congregations, we found 13 mosques (0.7 percent), 35 synagogues (2.5 percent), 10 Buddhist congregations (0.7 percent), 6 Asian non-Judeo-Christian congregations, and 4 congregations of African religions such as Yoruba and Egbe Sankofa.

Geographical Distribution

Botchwey (2003) studied all nonprofits that are active in seven contiguous census tracts in Lower North Philadelphia, an area particularly plagued by urban blight. She found more faith-based organizations and religious congregations than secular nonprofit organizations (NPOs). Of the seventy organizations in the studied area, 10 percent were faith-based organizations, 61 percent were congregations, and only 29 percent were secular NPOs. Clearly, faith-based groups are most present in these parts of the city. Furthermore, while the secular NPOs tended to be located close to major throughways, congregations were distributed throughout the area. Our data suggest the same for the city as a whole.

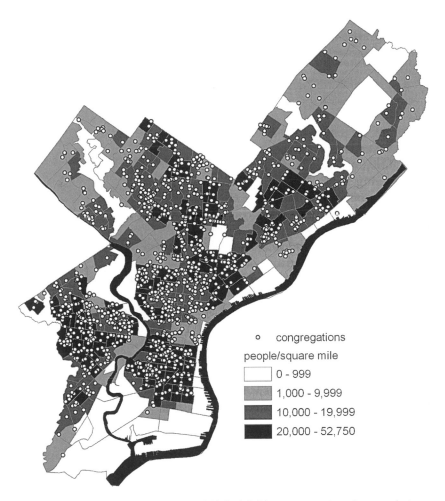

o   congregations

people/square mile

☐ 0 - 999

■ 1,000 - 9,999

■ 10,000 - 19,999

■ 20,000 - 52,750

Figure 2.1. Geographic locations of Philadelphia congregations by population density.

Using Geographical Information System (GIS), we plotted the congregations on the map of the city of Philadelphia. As can be seen in Figure 2.1, the denser an area is, the more populated it is with congregations. Put differently, congregations are located where people are. We calculated the correlation between the density in the 380 census tracts in Philadelphia and the number of congregations in that tract. The result is a strong and significant correlation ($r = .40$, $p < .01$).

We further analyzed the distribution of congregations according to the race (percent blacks) and level of education of residents (percent of those twenty-five and over with a high school diploma) and proximity to a major throughway, and found no significant differences. As shown in Table 2.1 below, congregations are housed in areas that are, on average, confronted with more serious social problems such as crime and poverty. But overall they are evenly distributed across the city. These findings support the claims made by proponents of the faith-based initiative that congregations are community-anchored social organizations that have the widest reach when compared with all other local social organizations. Figure 2.1 strongly demonstrates that congregations are located where the people are living.

Storefront and Megacongregations

One form of congregational life that is quite common is the storefront church (Kostarelos 1995; McRoberts 2003). Most definitions for storefront churches relate to a small number of members, a small budget, and a lack of a traditional building with a steeple and a big sanctuary. Zelinsky (2001: 573) defined a storefront congregation "a house of worship occupying recycled premises—former retail shops, funeral parlors, factories or warehouses (but not former churches)—usually with minimal remodeling. This definition can be stretched to include residences transformed into churches, again with little or no physical modification." Storefront churches are often characterized by a small number of members, many of them relatives or close associates of the pastor. Storefront churches tend to be housed in small facilities in impoverished areas of the city. The economic unattractiveness of the area makes them one of the few groups interested in these properties, and the low rent enables a small group to have exclusive use of the space. Some of these small congregations persist for generations. For others, functioning as a storefront church is a temporary stage. In the PCC, we interviewed 329 congregations that could be called storefront congregations. While some were very old, the average year of incorporation was 1967, and they had been located in their present place for twenty-five years. They are thus, on average, significantly younger than the rest of the city's congregations.

Interestingly, while the majority of these small congregations (61.1 percent) were composed mostly of blacks (75 percent or more of members are blacks), they were not located in predominantly black areas. The implication of these findings is that while many black congregations are small and are in the heart of the black community, storefront churches are near major roads and in areas that are accessible to all people. Similar to McRoberts's (2003) findings in Boston, we found that the storefront congregations are located in areas in which residents have low

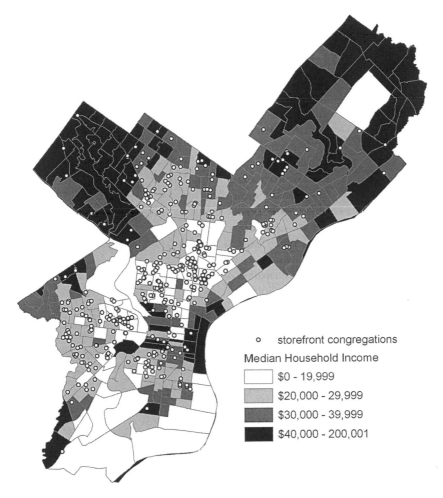

Figure 2.2. Storefront congregations by household median income.

income. As can be seen in Figure 2.2, the majority of storefront congregations are located away from neighborhoods where median household income is $50,000 and above, and more frequent in areas where median household income is below $20,000.

At the opposite end of the continuum is the megachurch. Vaughan (1993) suggested that an average megachurch has a weekly attendance of 2,000 or more people, while total membership can reach 10,000. To accommodate such large numbers requires a structure with a large auditorium, available parking lots, and shopping venues. For the purpose of this study, we defined a megachurch as one boasting 1,000 members and an annual operating budget of over half a million dollars. Most of these churches are also not housed in traditional congregational structures, but have full campuses or own several buildings and hold worship in large auditoriums. Furthermore, all these churches employ more than one clergy member. The best-known megachurches in the United States are Willow Creek Community Church and Saddleback Church, located outside Chicago and Los Angeles respectively.

In Philadelphia, we identified 44 congregations that met these criteria. More than half of the megachurches in Philadelphia (24; 54.5 percent) reported that the majority of their members (75 percent or more) were white. When we looked at the megachurches' locations, we found that they are distributed all over the city and are not correlated with residents' income, race, or other social conditions.

Where Do People Worship?

What do we know about historical relationships between where people live and where they worship? Members of pre-twentieth-century communities were likely to be within walking or carriage-ride distance of a congregation's location. They would likely hear their own church bells or a call to prayer, which helped to regulate daily life, seasons, and community events (Cnaan et al. 2002; Holifield 1994). In the past, then, religious communities were at least partly formed to function within their members' spatial proximity. However, much has worked to change this landscape in the United States. Today, few religious communities prescribe proximity of members' homes as a required part of membership, with the possible exceptions of Orthodox Jewish communities, pre-Vatican II Roman Catholic parishes, or traditional Amish communities.

Personal choice has displaced geographic proximity as a determining factor for where members attend worship. Such choices are often based on shared interests, relationships, or theological preferences over and above location (Farnsley 2003). Today more than ever, people tend to choose a congregation in order to be with like-minded people (Cimino and Lattin 1998; Gallup 1996; Wuthnow 1994). McRoberts (2003) stated that churches are less neighborhood institutions than collections of individuals identifying with one another socially, such as middle-class professionals or the working poor of the same country of origin. He observed that congregations may be drawn together by ethnicity, regional or national origin, class background, political orientation, life stage, or lifestyle. It is less common for a congregation to form around a shared neighborhood identity. Social identity has eclipsed spatial proximity as the dominant factor in worship choice.

Some recent studies, however, suggest that many people still attend congregations near where they live. For example, Woolever and Bruce (2002) found that more than half (55 percent) of persons attending worship reported a commute of ten minutes or less. An additional 21 percent reported a commute of eleven to fifteen minutes, with a total of 88 percent reporting a commute of twenty minutes or less. Few worshippers reported commutes of more than twenty (8 percent) or thirty minutes (4 percent). Similarly, in Philadelphia congregations, according to the PCC, substantial proportions of members were reported to live within walking distance of their place of worship. An average of 42.8 percent were described as residing within a ten-block radius (about a mile) of their congregation. Figure 2.3 shows the distribution of congregations in which at least half the members live within ten blocks of the congregation versus the rest.

"Commuter congregations" are described by Ortiz (1991) as churches in large cities attended by middle-class people who have continued to attend the church even as the neighborhood around it changed and they had moved to the suburbs. This has been suggested as a trend among black middle-class congregations in particular. Trulear (1998) described large inner-city African American congregations as "middle-class churches" in which fewer than 20 percent of the membership still live within walking distance. In fact, there could be two types of commuter city congregations: the congregation in which people live in the city and travel over a mile to reach their congregation and the congregation in which people travel a mile or more from outside the city. When we viewed congregations based on what at least half or more of the members were doing, we found two in five of the congregations (40.9 percent) resident congregations, more than half in-city commuter congregations (57.6 percent), and fewer than one-tenth out-of-city commuter congregation (7.8 percent). The rest were mixed and could not be categorized.

When we tried to find out what determined whether a congregation primarily consists of nearby residents, in-city commuters, or out-of-city commuters, we found that membership, budget, age of congregation, and age of congregation members did relatively little to distinguish them. Denomination, racial composition of the congregation, location of the pastor's home, and stability of the area where the congregation was located contributed most. Most of the Catholic churches and Orthodox Jewish synagogues were predominantly resident congregations. Congregations with clergy residing within a mile also tended to be resident rather than commuting.

As for in-city commuter congregations, Baptist (162; 24 percent), Pentecostal (131; 20 percent), and nondenominational Christian (91; 14 percent) congregations made up more than half. High proportions of

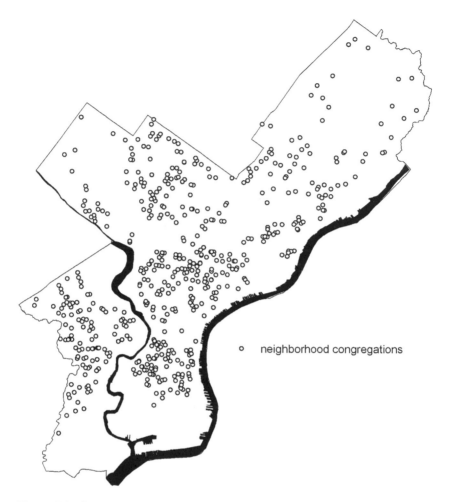

Figure 2.3. Congregations in which at least half the members live nearby.

Apostolic (25 of 33; 76 percent) and Islamic (8 of 11; 73 percent) congregations also fell in this category. In-city commuter congregations were the most likely to have memberships described as "getting younger" and the smallest proportion of members age sixty-five and older. They had a slightly lower percentage of low-income members than resident congregations, but significantly more poor members than suburban (out-of-city) commuter congregations.

Finally, for out-of-city (suburban) commuter congregations, on average, 67 percent of members lived outside the city and 17 percent lived within ten blocks. Suburban commuter congregations had the smallest percentage of poor members and the most members with a family income of $75,000 or more.

Regularity of Meetings

Some congregational buildings stand empty six days a week and are unlocked only on weekends for worship. Other buildings are open seven days a week and serve as community hubs. In Chapter 6, we discuss using space for communal and social purposes. In this section, we focus on the religious use of these properties, the number of meetings directly related to the congregation's main function of being a place where people share and practice religious rituals (Ammerman 2005).

The first question we posed was how many worship services a congregation holds on a weekend. The weekend is defined as Friday afternoon to Sunday night, to include Muslim Friday (Jummah) Khutbah and Salat (preaching and worship) and Jewish Shabbat services. The results show that congregational worship frequency ranged from once a month to 15 times per weekend. The congregation that meets monthly was reported to have only 35 members and not to have a pastor at the time of the interview. The congregation with 15 services was a mosque with more than 1,000 members who meet for prayers five times a day. Interestingly, 18 congregations did not report holding weekend worship services, but reported meeting regularly during the week. In some cases, these were people who met in a workplace; in some cases, the congregations did not own property and had access to a place for worship only in the middle of the week. The average number of weekend services across all Philadelphia congregations is 2.2.

We next asked how many times the congregations meet to worship on weekdays. Fifteen percent of the congregations reported not holding weekday worship services; the rest reported frequencies from once a month to 25 times a week. Almost all those who reported more than 20 worship meetings during the week were mosques, along with a few Roman Catholic churches. Two other churches reported more than 20 weekly worship meetings and had more than an average number (6 and 9) of worship services during weekend. The average number of weekday services across all Philadelphia congregations is 2.9. When we add the two means, we find that, on average, a congregation in Philadelphia meets 5.1 times a week for worship. It should be noted that the same people are not always included; for example, in some cases two weekend worship services are for early and for late risers. Thus 5.1 represents the average number of times a congregation makes itself available for worship services.

A congregation's buildings can also serve members as a site for small group meetings, most notably Bible studies. It is common for small subgroups of members, known in some congregations as cells, to meet regularly to read and discuss religious texts. These are meetings in addition to the children's or adult Sunday classes. Ninety-six congregations (6.9 percent) reported that no such groups meet on congregational property. It should be emphasized that most of these congregations do not own property and hence having such meetings might be impossible. Regrettably, we did not ask about small group meetings outside the congregational building. For example, Tenth Presbyterian Church on Seventeenth Street and Delancey Place reported holding some 100 small-group meetings on its property. But we were also informed that many members live away from the city's center and in the suburbs, and that they hold many more such meetings away from the church building. Among the congregations responding concerning small-group meetings in their buildings, the answers ranged from 1 meeting monthly to 250 meetings weekly. The latter figure is for a mosque with over 1,000 members. On average, among the responding congregations, including those not holding meetings, the congregations host 5.2 small group meetings.

People attending these congregations meet many more times for social programs. As will be detailed in Chapter 6, the space congregations own is a major asset and a service for the community at large. At this stage, we will only note that per month, 10,348 meetings that are not faith- or maintenance-related take place in our studied congregations. This is a mean of 7.4 meetings per congregation monthly or 1.8 per week.

The Environment in Which Congregations Are Housed

In the Preface we mentioned some of Philadelphia's current problems and its struggle against urban blight. Congregations are located throughout the city, and many of them face these social problems daily. Very few congregations have been able to find a location without these urban hardships. In order to assess severity of these problems, we composed a list of 22 social problems and asked interviewees whether they occurred in the area of the city surrounding the congregation's property.

As shown in Table 2.1, the congregations reported locations in areas where social problems are rampant. Very few interviewees reported being confronted with only one problem (1.4 percent); the average was 16 of 22. The most frequently reported problems had to do with drugs and crime as well as unemployment and poverty. In another part of the questionnaire, we asked whether at least 20 percent of the congrega-

TABLE 2.1. SOCIAL PROBLEMS ENCOUNTERED AROUND CONGREGATIONS
(PERCENT REPORTING IT TO BE A PROBLEM, DESCENDING ORDER OF SEVERITY)

Social problem	Frequency
Substance abuse	91.0
Unemployment	84.9
Poverty	84.3
Drug trafficking	84.1
Quality of public education	82.4
Crime	82.2
Teen pregnancy	79.6
Illiteracy	76.3
AIDS/HIV	74.3
Substandard housing/lack of affordable housing	71.8
Homelessness	70.5
Pollution	69.9
Loss of local industries and jobs/limited employment opportunities	69.5
High traffic/traffic accidents	68.1
Family violence	67.7
Lack of affordable health care	67.5
Youth incarceration	67.1
Lack of affordable child care	66.3
Prostitution	63.4
No recreational opportunities	62.5
Gang violence	46.4
Public transportation	32.7

tional members were unemployed; 234 congregations (16.8 percent) responded yes. Not surprisingly, almost all (224 congregations) reported that unemployment is a major problem around their congregational property. Unemployment was also rated as a major problem by 902 of the 1,158 congregations that did not report high levels of unemployment among their members.

Issues pertaining to the public education system and teen pregnancy were a close second. More than three-quarters of the interviewed congregations reported these issues. AIDS, housing, and pollution were also reported to be key problems surrounding the majority of congregations. Given this perceived high level of social stress around their properties, the task of understanding what congregations are doing to improve the quality of life around them is of utmost importance.

The social problems that are least pressing are also of interest. Thanks to the Southeastern Pennsylvania Transit Authority (SEPTA), only about a third (32.7 percent) of the interviewees reported that public transportation is a problem, far less than any other reported problem. This was followed by gang violence, reported by 46.4 percent, and lack of recre-

TABLE 2.2. GIS CORRELATION OF NUMBER OF CONGREGATIONS IN CENSUS
TRACTS AND SOCIAL PROBLEMS, 2000 (ALL SIGNIFICANTLY CORRELATED AT THE
.01 LEVEL)

Social problem	Correlation
Domestic abuse	0.59
Aggravated assaults	0.62
Serious crimes (no rape/murder)	0.47
Serious property crimes	0.39
Median household income	−0.31
Percentage of population in poverty	0.40
Median housing values	−0.20

ational opportunities, reported by almost two-thirds. Only 2 of the 22
problems on the list were not reported to be a problem in the area
around the congregation by more than half the congregations. More
than anything else, these findings testify to the perceived blight that is
pervasive in the City of Brotherly Love, and a challenge to any local organization that cares for the future of the city.

While the data reported above are based on the interviewees' perceptions, we also used the GIS map of Philadelphia to assess the social
problems around the congregations. For the 380 census tracts in Philadelphia, we correlated the number of congregations with a variety of
social problems such as domestic abuse, aggravated assaults, and poverty. As can be seen in Table 2.2, on all accounts the congregations are
located in census tracts where social problems are rampant, so their
assessments of the problems are not just subjective but also empirically
validated.

Conclusion

Although Philadelphia is associated with the Quakers, that group's
impact on the city has drastically diminished. Very few modern Philadelphians are Quakers, and their places of worship are few and far between.
Similar to what Farnsley (2003) reported for Indianapolis, Philadelphia
has a recognizably Protestant culture, but it is broken down into a multi-
tude of individual denominations and independent congregations. Philadelphia also has a strong Jewish base and an even stronger and more
pronounced Catholic one. Both groups have been in the city for centuries and maintain their many congregations and civic organizations.

Philadelphia's considerable black population affects the religious
landscape. The presence of many Baptist, Assembly of God, Apostolic,
and Church of God in Christ churches is noticeable and reflects the

population. The largest two groups of congregations are Roman Catholics and combined Baptists. Many clergy meet weekly over breakfast to coordinate and share experiences and topics of concern, even though they are not theologically or organizationally members of the same group. In fact, there are Monday meetings, Tuesday meetings, and so forth.

We demonstrate that congregations are the most evenly distributed community social organization, and that there are often many wherever people reside. The 2,120 congregations in Philadelphia reach every neighborhood and the majority of census tracts. Congregations are not concentrated around major thoroughfares; rather, they have a strong presence throughout the community. Storefront congregations are also quite well distributed, but they are more prevalent where poor people are. Megachurches are evenly distributed and, because they are often composed of commuting members and need a large space, their location is not essentially relevant to any one neighborhood. It is thus not surprising that, although many people drive to their congregation of choice, still about half go to a congregation less than ten blocks from their home to which they can walk to if they wish.

The congregations' facilities are hubs of community activities (as will be shown in Chapter 6), and many people come to worship and conduct congregational business in them. Many people attend weekend services, and some come during the week for worship, Bible study, and organizational or committee meetings. These buildings are surrounded by decay and blight. The interviewees reported a very high prevalence of social problems, and the same was found when we plotted congregational locations and social problems recorded for relevant census tracts. As we will demonstrate later, the fact that congregations are located in such poverty- and crime-stricken parts of the city leaves them with a challenge to intervene and improve the quality of life in those areas. Congregations and their members are a special feature of the city's landscape, and they rise up again and again to meet the challenges unaddressed by an ineffective and resource-depleted public sector.

Chapter 3

The Organizational Behavior of the Congregations in Our Study

Congregations come in every shape and size. As we discussed in Chapter 1, there is a wide variability in their theological, organizational, ecological, liturgical, and membership characteristics. In that chapter we struggled to find a working definition for the social organization called "local religious congregation." Here we identify the key organizational characteristics of Philadelphia congregations. The Philadelphia Census of Congregations (PCC) allows us to provide a detailed picture of one city's congregations. Because our data come from two-thirds of the city's congregations, they are remarkably representative of those of the entire city. Thus, we can provide a glimpse at how congregations in Philadelphia are structured and compare our findings with some national large-scale samples.

This chapter provides an overview of the key characteristics of the congregations in Philadelphia, focusing on the following issues: theological affiliation and religious strictness, frequency of worship and other meetings, years in existence; membership size, member characteristics, annual budget, sources of income, organizational structure, staff, leadership, and relationships with the wider community. In each category, a full review of the data is compared with various sources. Major sources of comparison are two large-scale national studies: (1) a survey of local churches, mosques, and synagogues representing 41 denominations that participated in the coalition known as Faith Communities Today (FACT), which yielded data on more than 14,000 congregations (Dudley and Roozen 2001); and (2) data obtained from Cynthia Woolever, director of the U.S. Congregational Life Survey (CLS), which surveyed 300,000 worshippers in more than 2,000 congregations (see Bruce 2002). We also use a few other sources with lower levels of coverage to assess how the Philadelphia congregations can be compared to congregations elsewhere. Note that each of these studies relied on denominational lists and did not attempt to provide a census of one metropolitan area. The PCC, however, was designed to access all congregations in

Philadelphia. Its findings portray congregations' organizational behavior in one large American city and beg for a replication other cities to allow us better extrapolation power.

Before we turn to the actual findings and their implications, a word of caution is required. We do not presume that one can treat all congregations alike. We provide this overview of Philadelphia's congregations mostly to show how diverse they are and to emphasize that one cannot approach them collectively and uniformly. Their differences invite us to appreciate their uniqueness and treat them individually and particularly.

Theological and Religious Strictness

Dudley and Roozen (2001: 18) aptly note that "With a survey's aura of scientific objectivity, we may forget that congregations are religious associations and their ultimate source of unity and purpose emanates from their relationship to the transcendent." In the previous chapter we analyzed the denominational affiliation of the congregations in Philadelphia. In this chapter we focus on theological strictness, which we measure, along with the importance of the transcendent, in two key ways. We asked our interviewees to assess first whether their congregation was theologically fundamentalist, conservative, moderate, or liberal, and then whether the majority of members would agree with the statement that the scripture used by their group is the literal and inspired word of God. The emphasis in the second question was on the word *literal*, as implying greater strictness.

More congregations were on the fundamentalist (15.7 percent) and conservative end (39.7 percent) than on the moderate (34.1 percent) and liberal (10.5 percent) end. This finding correlates with the CLS result that 59 percent of congregations were on the conservative side, 29 percent were in the middle, and 11 percent were on the liberal side. Most significant from the PCC data was the fact that the older the congregation, the less likely it was to be theologically fundamentalist. The average year of incorporation of fundamentalist congregations (1958) was more recent, or those congregations were "younger," than conservative congregations (1943), which in turn were significantly younger than moderate (1928) and liberal congregations (1926). Our data do not allow us to determine if the institutional life course of most congregations follows a pattern from a fundamentalist youth to a more moderate-liberal old age, or whether there is a cohort effect in the first part of the twenty-first century that suggests that people are currently seeking modes of worship which are more fundamentalist. Dudley and Roozen found a similar trend in mainline Protestant and Roman Catholic congregations, which are not planting many new churches, while more fundamentalist congregations such as Baha'is, Sunni Muslims, Mormons, and independent churches have been planting many more new congregations in the past twenty years.

About three-quarters of the congregations reported that the majority of their members view their scripture as the *literal* word of God. As expected, the two measures of religious strictness were very strongly associated. The fact that 94 percent of the congregations that labeled themselves fundamentalist (and 81 percent of conservative) answered positively to the question about the "literal word of God" is not surprising. What may come as a surprise is that 60 percent of those defined as liberal (and 68 percent of moderates) also answered positively to the question about the Bible being the "literal word of God." In other words, the perception of the Bible as the "literal word of God" is quite prevalent even among theologically moderate and liberal congregations.

Dudley and Roozen asked a different set of questions regarding sources of religious authority. It is worth mentioning that 82 percent of the congregations in their sample noted that sacred scripture is their source of authority and 60 percent also cited the Holy Spirit. These authors also found that high strictness is associated with growth. It is possible that such relationships are stronger in the suburbs, small towns, and the South, which were sampled in Dudley and Roozen's data, because in Philadelphia these relationships were not found. The level of religious strictness in our sample was unrelated to growth.

We also asked about the congregations' political orientation, whether the majority of members could be viewed as politically conservative, moderate, or liberal. We found that about a third of the congregations are politically conservative (32.9 percent), while about half are moderate (48.4 percent), and only about one-sixth are liberal (18.6 percent). The CLS found that 64 percent of congregations are politically conservative, 26 percent in the middle, and 10 percent liberal. Clearly, political conservativism was strongly associated with fundamentalist theological worldview and vice versa. However, as will be discussed in Chapter 7, this is not the case among black congregations.

Frequency of Worship and Meetings

Although this study focused more on social services and organizational behavior than on religious issues, some aspects of religious activity were ascertained. As discussed in Chapter 2, we asked the interviewees how many times per week, outside holiday seasons, people came to the congregational building for the purpose of prayer and worship. The answer ranged from less than once a week to 42 times a week for one of the city's megachurches. Clearly megachurches, mosques (which may hold five prayer services daily), synagogues (especially Orthodox ones that hold prayer services twice daily), and large-scale Roman Catholic churches that hold masses more than once a day skew the findings. The mean number of worship services per congregation per week was 4.6. When these 61 "frequent worshippers" are omitted from the calculation, this mean dropped to 3.8 worship services per week. Fundamentalist and conservative congregations reported a higher weekly mean number of worship services (4.1 and 4.0 respectively) than moderate and liberal congregations (3.6 and 3.5 respectively). However, an analysis of variance revealed that these differences were not statistically significant. Membership size was the strongest predictor of the number of worship services per week. This suggests that having more members implies a need to offer multiple services on the weekend and to provide services for people who come during the week.

Over a third of the congregations (34.9 percent) hold one weekend service, while a slightly larger percentage (37.8 percent) reported meeting twice and a little over a quarter (26.7 percent) reported meeting more than twice. Predominant among the latter group are megachurches, mosques, Orthodox Jewish synagogues, and large-scale Roman Catholic churches. The other congregations meet less than once a week.

About a sixth of the congregations (17.1 percent) reported no weekday worship services. These congregations were often the very small ones, those that did not own their own place but used a private or public space or were guest congregations on other congregation's property, and those who reported only one weekend worship service.

We also asked about small groups that meet on congregational property outside worship services. Small group meetings included Bible or other study classes as well as committee or youth group meetings. These groups do not necessarily reflect religious activity but include social activities of all kinds. Our aim was to measure the extent to which the congregation property is a place where people meet for any reason that is not worship. During the interviews it became clear that many of these groups are Bible study groups. Seven percent of the congregations reported no weekly meetings of any type; the majority of these did not own their own place of worship. Almost half (47.7 percent) reported 3 or more meetings per week, the number ranging from 3 to 250. In this measure, the larger the budget and the membership size, the more small group meetings were held during the week.

Worship also took place in collaboration with other congregations. Joint worship services were common within and across denominations.

Only 200 congregations (14.4 percent) reported no joint worship with another congregation or faith group. It is our assessment that the actual percentage of congregations that do not worship jointly may be even a bit lower since some congregations did not answer this question. In order to be counted as a valid response, the interviewee had to mention the name of the congregation with whom they worshipped or state that the congregation did not jointly worship with others. Some congregations simply did not answer these questions, and we assumed that they are not engaged in joint worship. For the other congregations, often the "other" congregations validated the response. We allowed reporting of up to 4 joint worship partners and counted the different partners, not the frequency of joint worship. That is, we asked for different worship partners and not how many times they worship jointly with each partner. Two-fifths of the congregations (40.6 percent) reported 4 (or more) worship partners. These findings suggest that congregations in Philadelphia routinely worship with other congregations in the community and share their religious life with others who are not members.

Years in Existence

Congregations came to North America with the first wave of settlers in the 1620s. Ever since, congregations have been forming, changing, merging, and passing out of existence. A census like the PCC could not assess congregations that had disbanded. However, for the active congregations in our census, 34 (2.4 percent) were established before 1800 and 10 (0.7 percent) were established before 1700. In the United States, such old congregations can be found mostly in the Northeast. But, in general, congregations are among the oldest and most stable local social organizations in any city. At the same time, new congregations spring up: 15 percent of the congregations in the PCC study were established in the ten-year span 1991–2001.

The mean year of incorporation of congregations in Philadelphia is 1939, sixty-two years before the study was concluded. The median year of incorporation, however, is 1955, which suggests that many congregations settled quickly, and then stayed in their location for some time. This topic will be further discussed in Chapter 6. It is worth noting here that the median year of incorporation for congregations in the FACT study was 1945 (Dudley and Roozen 2001). Although the dates are fairly close, it is surprising that a national study had a median age older than the median age of congregations in an old northeastern city. The CLS reports an even earlier date of incorporation, 1917. The fact that the PCC mean year of incorporation in a historic city like Philadelphia is more recent than these other studies indicates that the PCC study managed to attract and include new and evolving congregations that other studies often have failed to include.

Among the very old congregations in our sample are Gloria Dei Old Swedes' Church (1677, in its current location for 322 years); Monthly Meeting of Friends in Philadelphia (1681); Unity Monthly Meeting, Frankford (1683); Germantown Mennonite Church (1687, in its location for 309 years); Pennepack Baptist Church (1688); Germantown Friends Meeting (1690); Christ Church (1695, in its location for 301 years); and First Presbyterian Church in Philadelphia (1698). Philadelphia is also home to Mother Bethel African Methodist Episcopal Church, established by Richard Allen, and the African Episcopal Church of St. Thomas, established by Absalom Jones, both founded in 1794, as the first two independent churches of free black people in the nation.

Membership Size

Membership size of American congregations is an important and highly debated statistic. While it would seem that membership should be the simplest organizational characteristic to measure, this is not the case. A variety of studies found out that defining congregational membership is difficult, for several reasons. To begin with, some denominations do not include children as members until a certain age, so that youth (ages thirteen to eighteen) can make a mature decision to join or not. Second, there is no agreed upon method of defining who is a member. Some congregations only define as members people who have gone through a full conversion or confirmation experience. In others, all attenders are viewed as members regardless of their religious education or faith tradition. Third, geographic mobility is more and more common in the United States. The CLS reports that one in three worshippers have attended their current congregation for five years or less. This means that the turnover rate in the average congregation is fairly high.

Often congregations report as members anyone on their mailing list or, as it is known in Baptist circles, everyone "on the roll." This leaves a huge gap between "official" members and those who regularly attend. In many congregations, people are officially members if they are registered with the congregation but may attend only on key holidays and significant family events, such as confirmations or funerals. This phenomenon is particularly common in Roman Catholic churches and non-Orthodox synagogues. For example, every Catholic who lives within the parish boundary of a Roman Catholic church is considered a church member, and in non-Orthodox Jewish synagogues, there may be some fifty members attending on an average Saturday while on high holidays more than five hundred dues-paying members attend. Given these varieties of local congregational experiences, the literature lacks a good working definition for congregational membership.

In the PCC, we distinguished three categories of members. First we asked the interviewees to inform us about their mailing list numbers. The idea was to obtain the largest number possible of people associated with the congregation. There was only one congregation in which the mailing list was smaller than average attendance, the reason being that visitors to Philadelphia came to the church because it is a historical site. For all other congregations the "on the roll" membership was the largest number reported. There were, on average, 575 people on the mailing lists of Philadelphia congregations. No other study has made this differentiation, so we cannot compare this finding with other sources. We used this first measure as a means to set the tone about our other measures of congregational membership.

Our second and third measures of membership size considered people who attend services regularly and are known to the body of the congregation. These measures helped screen out people who come once or twice or who are formally members of one congregation but actually attend another. Individuals who met this more stringent criterion of membership were those who attended the congregation at least once monthly and were known by name to the clergy or some other leader of the congregation. In addition, we separated this measure of membership into two further categories: formal members (meeting the religious criteria if such exist) and regularly attending nonmembers (such as spouses, interested neighbors, and people attracted to the congregation but unwilling to join or still in the process of conversion/confirmation). Combined, these two measures provided us with an estimate of the congregations' active membership. Overall, we found that an average congregation in Philadelphia is composed of 322 members, including children of all ages. We found that the average number of official active members was 276 and of nonofficial active members was 46.

Farnsley (2003: 36–37) reported a somewhat larger congregation size in Indianapolis. In his words, "We found that the mean congregation has roughly 400 members"; however, "fully half of all congregations in Indianapolis have fewer than 150 members." The Philadelphia active membership number (322) is larger than those reported by other national studies. The CLS reported that the average size of a congregation is 244, of whom 73 are children. This number is close to that of official and active members found in Philadelphia (276). The FACT data show that half the congregations (50 percent) have an adult membership less than 100. In fact, these numbers are more similar to those obtained in the PCC. To assess the compatibility of this estimate for the Philadelphia congregations, we omitted the children from our estimates and then looked for the median. We found that an average of 21 percent of the members were children; removing them from the average *active* number of members left 254 adult active members. The median of the adult members is only about 90. In other words, the high mean of active adult members was affected by a few large megachurches, while about half the congregations in Philadelphia have fewer than 90 adult members and 56 percent reported adult membership of below 100. This is another indication that the PCC managed to reach younger and smaller congregations that are often passed over by congregational studies.

Another membership measure is weekly attendance. Average weekly attendance is lower than membership size, as not all members attend every week. We found that on average, and regardless of the number of worship services held over the weekend, 221 people per congregation in Philadelphia attend worship services. This number is larger than the average weekly attendance of 186 people reported by the CLS for 2000. The likelihood that the PCC included new and energetic congregations may explain why relatively more people were reported to attend their congregations on at least a weekly basis.

Another indicator of church attendance, though an indirect one, is the seating capacity of the building. We asked how many people could occupy the worship space when it was full; the average was 438. Seating capacity ranged from 15 to 35,000. Using these averages gives a ratio of seating capacity to average weekly attendance of 221/438, or 0.5. The CLS reported the average seating capacity where worship is held as 258. For the reported 186 people attending a in an average week, the researchers suggested a more efficient capacity use of 186/258, or .72. There are numerous explanations for these differences in seat utilization, among that many Philadelphia congregations are housed in properties that previously served larger congregations, and many remaining mainline churches in Philadelphia have smaller congregations than in the past. Large and growing congregations have often relocated to the suburbs (see Chapter 6), and smaller congregations purchase and use the same large property.

Membership in congregations frequently fluctuates. During the period of our study, some congregations lost so many members that they ceased to exist, while others were just starting out and still others were experiencing an influx of new members. Of 1,392 congregations, nearly half (47.8 percent) reported a rise in membership over the previous three years. For the same period, a third (31.5 percent) reported stable membership and a fifth (20.7 percent) reported a decline.

These findings indicate the strength of Philadelphia congregations in attracting new members and maintaining current membership. These findings correspond very well with Dudley and Roozen, who found that

51 percent of the congregations in their study reported growth in the previous five years. However, unlike some studies, we did not find that religious strictness, political orientation, budget size, or number of active members significantly accounted for growth or decline in membership. We did find that growing congregations were significantly younger and more racially distinct, with more black and fewer white members.

Members' Characteristics

One of the key characteristics of congregational makeup stems from members' quest to worship with like-minded people and consequently to form segregated mini-communities (Cnaan and Boddie 2001). There were two idiosyncratic congregations in our study that were ethnically diverse but very homogeneous in other aspects: all the members were ex-addicts and the congregation served as a support group for those trying to avoid relapse into substance abuse.

Given that congregations are not merely places to worship but also places where community life is formed, it is not surprising that people tend to congregate in homogeneous religious groups. From immigrants to ethnic groups, and from poor to affluent neighborhoods, congregations tend to serve people who find each other's values or worldviews compatible. In this section we will look at three characteristics that describe the makeup of a congregation's membership: household income, race, and age.

Reflective of almost half the households in the city, interviewees reported an average member's household income of below $25,000 (45.2 percent). An additional third of members' income was reported to be between $25,000 and $50,000 (34.2 percent). Combined, 79.6 percent of congregational members were found to have a household income below $50,000. Looking at it differently, in 27.6 percent of the studied congregations, more than three-quarters of members came from households with an income of less then $25,000. In another 10 percent, three-quarters of the members came from a household with an income between $25,000 and $50,000. A clearer picture emerged when we merged these two income categories: 75.4 percent of the studied congregations reported that three-quarters or more of members coming from the under $50,000 income bracket. On the other hand, in 6.8 percent of the congregations at least three-quarters of the members from households had an income above $50,000.

In racial composition of congregations, we also found a great deal of homogeneity. In later chapters we discuss black and Latino congregations in more detail, their unique characteristics and involvement in social services provision (Chapters 7 and 8). In this chapter, we view race only as a characteristic of congregational composition. The majority of congregations in Philadelphia (51.7 percent) reported that at least three-quarters of their members are black. As discussed later in Chapter 7, this is quite representative of the city's population and the American urban scene after World War II. This finding is a major difference between the PCC data and those of FACT and other studies. Dudley and Roozen, for example, reported that 76 percent of their congregations were mostly or all white. This is an identifiable difference between an urban study and one that includes a large share of suburbs, small towns, and rural communities.

The same trend of segregation occurs regarding other ethnic groups. As noted in Chapter 8, less than one-tenth (7.8 percent) of the congregations in Philadelphia are Latino congregations, with three-quarters or more of this ethnic group making up the congregation. About one in twenty congregations (4.6 percent) is composed of at least three-quarters Asian members, and almost all of these are unified along one specific country of origin. Finally, a quarter of the congregations are composed of a majority (three-quarters) of white members (25.1 percent). When these numbers are combined, we find that in nine out of ten congregations (89.2 percent), three-quarters or more of the members are from a single ethnic group. As such, congregations indeed embody homogeneity. Our data support the notion that people, when left to their own devices, choose to congregate with people who are similar to themselves, with the same life experiences and social positions (Wuthnow 1998). Similar findings were reported by Farnsley (2003: 52), who found in Indianapolis that "Of the congregations we visited, 86 percent had membership substantially—90 percent of the members or more—of one race."

Age is a characteristic that was not expected to provide a picture of homogeneity. After all, congregations attract families and stress the importance of intergenerational contact. Even so, not quite one in five congregations (17 percent) reported that more than half the members of their congregations are elderly (defined as people over age sixty-five). A little over a quarter (27.2 percent) of the congregations reported that half or more of their members are between thirty-four and sixty-five. We labeled this category "adults." Only a small portion of the city congregations (6.6 percent) reported having half or more of their members in the young adult range (nineteen to thirty-four). There were also some congregations that clearly catered to children and youth; 6.2 percent of congregations reported that half or more of their members were younger than eighteen. Overall, almost three in five congregations (57

TABLE 3.1. ANNUAL OPERATING BUDGETS OF PHILADELPHIA CONGREGATIONS

Annual operating budget	Percent of congregations	Average congregation membership
Under $50,000	34.9	70
$50,001–$100,000	24.0	145
$100,001–$200,000	20.2	251
$200,001–$500,000	13.0	581
$500,001–$1,000,000	5.5	1,258
Above $1,000,000	2.4	2,251

percent) had one significantly dominant age group, a feature that added a surprising element of homogeneity.

The PCC also asked about the gender composition and marital status of congregation members. As shown in Chapter 9, more women than men are members of local religious congregations. In Philadelphia the ratio of women to men was almost two to one (65.25 percent and 34.75 percent). Dudley and Roozen (2001) and the CLS study found a similar preponderance of women worshippers. As for marital status, we opted to ask, "What percentage of the congregation's members are single (including widows, widowers, divorcees, and single parents)?" We chose this language to bypass tension, given the current ideological war about the definition of marriage, ranging from having same-sex ceremonies to not considering people married in civil ceremonies or remarried divorced people as truly married. Our aim was to get a sense of how many members were not married. The mean percentage of singles in a congregation in Philadelphia was 40 percent—a number very similar to that reported in the FACT study (Dudley and Roozen 2001), where 20 percent of congregations reported that "none or some" of the members were married and 33 percent that "about half" were married.

Annual Budget

For most congregations, issues of finance are often kept confidential. As noted earlier, congregations are exempted from reporting to the Internal Revenue Service (IRS)—even if their annual income exceeds $25,000, the requirement for other nonprofits. Surprisingly, some 90,000 congregations voluntarily submit form I-990 to the IRS, but this number is too small to base an assessment of congregational annual budget. As shown in Table 3.1, in the PCC we used six income categories.

The findings in Table 3.1 show that more than half the congregations were operating on an annual budget of less than $100,000, quite expected, given that half the congregations have fewer than 90 adult members. As the right column of Table 3.1 shows, low-budget congregations are composed of fewer members and vice versa. The two variables, annual operating budget and membership size, are highly statistically correlated.

However, the actual dollar amount of the budget may indicate less about the congregation's perception about its fiscal stability or "bottom line." We asked the interviewees if their last year's budget resulted in a surplus, balance, or deficit and whether the congregation was financially "strong, sound, or struggling." Some 19.1 percent of the congregations reported that in the year before the survey they had a budget surplus, 53.4 percent reported a balanced budget, and 27.1 percent reported a deficit. Regarding financial stability, the CLS found that 29 percent of congregations reported an increasing financial base, 53 percent reported stability, and 19 percent reported financial decline or even threat to their existence. Clearly, in Philadelphia the smaller and evolving congregations presented a less rosy financial picture compared to the CLS findings.

For the measure of financial strength, a similar picture emerged. Fewer interviewees responded that their congregation was financially strong (9.6 percent); a majority reported that it was sound (51.6 percent) or struggling (38.8 percent). Similar findings are reported by Dudley and Roozen. Thus, in our sample, about one-third of the congregations reported facing financial difficulties and less than 10 percent reported being financially strong and viable. While our two measures of fiscal strength were highly associated, some 28 congregations with a surplus also reported they were struggling financially, and 9 congregations reported a deficit but considered themselves financially strong. It may be that in some cases a clergyperson or lay leader used the challenge of a deficit to urge the congregation to achieve a new plateau of giving, while in other cases the small surplus was maintained through hard work and careful saving.

Sources of Income

When we asked the congregations about their major sources of income, it came as no surprise that the primary source of income was members' contributions through pledges (annual commitments or dues) and offerings (usually in a plate). While in the language of congregations both may be considered tithing, the two are quite dissimilar. Pledging is assumed to be more reliable and sustainable, as it demands an advance commitment and allows for planning. Plate offerings rely on people's ongoing willingness and does not allow for advance planning. In Philadelphia, we found that combined pledges and offerings accounted for an average of 80 percent of congregational income: pledges 30.5 percent and plate offerings 49.5 percent.

Congregations in Philadelphia also relied on a variety of other methods to raise money, but these amounted to far less income than pledges and offerings. The most notable fund-raising methods were activities such as bingo, bake sales, car washes, thrift stores, and flea markets (4.2 percent); support from denominations or other such bodies, including suburban churches (3.7 percent); special gifts/bequests (3.7 percent); endowment/trust income (2.9 percent); support from foundations through grants (2.8 percent); rental income from use of property (2.4 percent); support/grants from government (local, state, and federal) (0.5 percent); contracts for service income (0.4 percent); and support from nonprofit organizations (0.3 percent).

Clearly, the most significant sources of income are pledges and offerings. More than half the congregations (55.9 percent) reported that 90 percent or more of their budget came from these sources, and seven in ten (68.8 percent) reported that at least three-quarters of their income came from these two sources. Chaves and Miller (1999) and Kearns (2003) found similar patterns. Kearns found that even among faith-based organizations, higher percentages of the annual budget came from individual donations, congregational sources, and denominational bodies, and less came from corporate and government grants.

The reliance on pledges and offerings was significantly and negatively correlated with year of incorporation. In other words, the longer the congregation had been in existence the more it relied on bequests, investment, rental property, and other forms of income that come with maturity. Surprisingly, membership size also significantly correlated with pledges and offering. The larger the number of members, the more the congregation relied on offerings and the less on pledges. It is possible that large congregations do not need the mechanism of pledges and are assured that their membership will guarantee sufficient financial support. Another reason for this statistical correlation may be that mega-churches, which are known for avoiding pledges and relying on the satisfaction of regular worshippers. Additionally, our data set included some large Roman Catholic churches that rely more heavily on offerings than on pledges.

Staff

Congregations are known to rely heavily on volunteers, with fewer paid staff to run their affairs. For example, Farnsley (2003) reported that in Indianapolis congregation staff sizes were small on average. "Fully

TABLE 3.2. PERSONNEL POSITIONS AND LEVEL OF REIMBURSEMENT (AT LEAST ONE
SUCH POSITION) IN PHILADELPHIA CONGREGATIONS (PERCENT OF
CONGREGATIONS)

Function	Full-time person	Part-time person	Volunteers only
Clergy	61.4	24.6	22.9
Secretary	10.3	6.5	84.5
Administrator	20.5	23.6	58.5
Janitor	8.2	8.9	83.7
Maintenance	13.6	30.7	58.6
Treasurer/bookkeeper	3.6	11.8	84.4
Social program director	9.0	7.8	85.1
Teacher and music director	14.4	26.9	53.7

30 percent of congregations have one full-time, paid staff member, but another 27 percent have none. Another 12 percent have two. This means that nearly 70 percent of congregations have zero, one, or two full-time staff members, yet the mean is 2.75. Again, a relatively small number of congregations with very large staffs are inflating the averages."

In Philadelphia, the PCC found an even larger percent of congregations that did not have a full-time paid clergyperson. More than a third of the congregations (38.6 percent) reported having no full-time clergy. One in five of the congregations without full-time clergy (22.9 percent) had no paid clergy at all, while the rest had part-time paid clergy. We found that one-fourth of the congregations (24.6 percent) employed a part-time clergyperson. In some of these city congregations (15.8 percent), this part-time figure included senior clergy who were bivocational. Such clergy work full- or part-time elsewhere and run the congregation as well. A small number of congregations (6.5 percent) reported two full-time clergy and a similar number (5.3 percent) reported three to twenty-two full-time clergy. The emerging picture, as in Indianapolis, is of a few well-endowed congregations (often Roman Catholic and megachurches) with three or more clergy, while most congregations have only one full- or part-time clergyperson.

Congregations, however, employ many other people in various positions, such as secretaries, administrators, janitors, and the like. About a third of the congregations (32 percent) reported at least one paid full-time position in addition to the clergy. As shown in Table 3.2, the most common positions were administrators, teachers and music directors, maintenance persons, and secretaries. All in all, congregations with other paid positions were significantly larger in membership and budget size. They employed from 1 to 50 full-time staff members, with a mean of 1.9 positions. If we add paid clergy, the average Philadelphia congregation has 2.7 full-time paid positions—remarkably similar to the number reported from Indianapolis.

Congregations also rely to a large extent, however, on part-time employees. It was beyond the scope of this study to assess if the person employed part-time was being paid a small stipend or a fair market wage. As indicated in Table 3.2, part-time positions were occupied mostly by maintenance people, teachers and music directors, and administrators. Assuming that these functions are carried out in all congregations, we calculated in the right column of Table 3.2 the percent of congregations that reported no full- or part-time paid person covering the relevant position. Again, we could not calculate the level of volunteerism, such as whether one person gives one hour a year or a few people give all their time for these functions. We only know that these functions were not covered by paid staff and hence were likely to be covered by volunteers.

The high number of these volunteer-covered positions is an indicator of congregations' key strength: their ability to draw on members to perform tasks for which other organizations must rely on paid staff. One could argue that some of these functions may not be necessary: a congregation that does not own a building does not need a maintenance person. The right column of Table 3.2 includes cases where the function is not needed, but these cases are few. The emerging picture is that many functions are performed by volunteers, especially secretarial, janitorial, treasurer/bookkeeper, and social program director positions. This analysis does not take into account many other volunteer roles that are commonly carried out in a number of congregations, such as usher, flower arranger, and planner and organizer of the weekly fellowship.

The clergy in Philadelphia are quite distinct compared to their national counterparts. To begin with, a relatively high percentage (56.1 percent) live within ten blocks of the congregation site. As such, the clergy are often members of the community who live and work in the same neighborhood. Educationally speaking, 10 percent of the city clergy hold a doctorate (usually in theology), and half have some graduate degree (50.1 percent). Almost three-quarters graduated from a theological seminary (73 percent). The rest (23 percent) have either no formal theological education or only a certificate. This percentage of clergy without theological education is significantly higher than the 12 percent reported by Dudley and Roozen. However, their large sample of 14,301 congregations included only those that are part of organized denominations and excluded the sort of independent and unaffiliated congregations we included in the PCC. Interestingly, these authors also found that clergy education, both general and theological, had a negative impact on the likelihood that the congregation would maintain traditional religious values and its commitment to their specific denomination's heritage. On the flip side, educated clergy were more likely to be employed in congregations with a strong social justice orientation.

Organizational Structure and Leadership

We asked the interviewees about the ultimate authority or bodies of leadership in their congregations, since we wanted to know by whom and how final decisions regarding budgeting and planning are made. In most cases some form of an executive committee composed of elected or appointed members served as the board of the congregation. Like the trustees of nonprofit organizations, this group of people make the final decisions and often approve the congregation budget. Common titles for these leaders included deacons (18.6 percent), executive committee (6.3 percent), elders (5.1 percent), session (4.5 percent), and pastoral council (2.5 percent). An additional 42.6 percent of the congregations called this group of people the board or the trustees. Combined, this type of arrangement was described in almost four out of five congregations (79.6 percent).

This finding suggests that in most congregations there is a form of representative democracy but not of participatory democracy. In most congregations, a group of dedicated members assumes most responsibilities, while most members benefit from the leaders' volunteer efforts. In contrast, in 1.4 percent of the congregations, the final decisions are made by the entire congregation. In these congregations, including most of the Quaker meetings, the members meet, discuss proposals, and come to a collective decision. In 2 percent of the cases, many of them Roman Catholic churches, the ultimate authority rests outside the congregation and in the hands of the denomination or a regional administrator. Finally, and surprisingly, in 17 percent of the congregations the clergy were described as the ultimate authority fully responsible for final decisions. This relatively high percentage of ultimate power by the clergy is different from that in most other nonprofit organizations, a topic that will be developed further in Chapter 13.

Most congregations are large and busy enough to require the use of a committee structure. Only five congregations in our sample reported having no committees, relying solely on the clergyperson and his or her relatives and friends to perform tasks of the congregation. In some cases the interviewees refused to provide detailed information about the committee structure of the congregation. In all, 1,208 (86.8 percent) congregations reported at least one operating committee and 639 con-

TABLE 3.3. PERCENTAGE OF CONGREGATIONS REPORTING TO HAVE A STANDING
COMMITTEE, BY TYPE OF COMMITTEE

Committee type	Number of congregations (percent of all committees)	Percent of congregations reporting having this committee
Leadership (trustees, board, etc.)	722 (14.9)	60.9
Administration (planning, membership, nominations, personnel, etc.)	302 (6.2)	25.1
Building-housing (property, construction, maintenance)	166 (3.4)	13.8
Finance (including fundraising)	377 (7.8)	31.4
Ushering/hospitality	165 (3.4)	13.7
Worship (religion, liturgy, service planning, etc.)	333 (6.9)	27.7
Music (band, choir, performances)	213 (4.4)	17.7
Evangelism/missions/outreach	587 (12.1)	48.8
Fellowship	42 (0.9)	3.5
Education (school, adult education, Bible classes)	417 (8.6)	34.7
Sunday school	210 (4.3)	17.5
Men	121 (2.5)	10.1
Women	226 (4.7)	18.8
Youth	325 (6.7)	27.0
Children	79 (1.6)	6.6
Social welfare programs (all social welfare programs and social action)	554 (11.4)	46.1
Total	4,839	1,202

gregations (45.9 percent) reported five or more committees. As we did
not want to tax our interviewees, we limited the list of active committees
to five. Table 3.3 provides a view of the most frequent committees
reported. It should be noted that in many cases we had to aggregate
various committees by name and function. For example, "property,"
"building," and "housing" committees were assumed to be similar, and
food, clothing, and benevolence committees were listed as social welfare
committees.

The first four committees listed in Table 3.3 are the ones responsible
for management and leadership. Typical in almost all voluntary associations, these committees maintain the daily and weekly needs of the organization and steer decision making. The following types of committees
are quite unique to congregations, responsible for sustaining elements
that are germane to the congregation's faith tradition or spiritual guidance. Such elements include worship, evangelism, ushering, and fellowship. Members of these committees are responsible for guiding religious

practices and socialization as well as attracting new people. The next set of committees relate to special subgroups in the congregations, such as men's and women's fellowship or ministry groups. It is interesting to note that, while youth committees are quite frequent in congregations, there are very few committees focusing on children, with the exception of Sunday school committees. Although programs committed to youth are quite common in congregations, the frequency of "youth committees" in Philadelphia congregations was much smaller than other types of committees. Finally, about half the congregations reported social program/action committees that were in charge of care and helping those in need.

The picture is thus similar to that described by Harris (1995), who noted that congregations are nonprofit/voluntary organizations with some unique characteristics. Most important is a congregation's reliance on and wish to sustain faith—a feature manifested in the preponderance of faith-related committees. The topic of congregations as a unique subtype of nonprofit organization will be further developed in Chapter 13.

In Table 3.3, we report two sets of percentages. In the middle column we report how many congregations reported having a certain committee and the percentage of such committees from all reported committees. In total, 4,839 committees were reported. As such, the 722 leadership committees represent 14.9 percent of all reported committees. However, among the 1,202 congregations that answered this question, 60.9 percent reported a leadership committee, a percentage reported in the right column.

Relationships with the Wider Community

One persistent myth about congregations is their organizational closedness. Organizations can tend to be isolationist and avoid their surroundings, or they can be open and integrated in their environment. Organizational theorists claim that open systems that are vital in their surroundings do better than closed systems, which are subject to entropy (Thompson 1967). It is often claimed that even nearby congregations of the same denomination hardly communicate with each other or are not aware of each other's activities. Congregations are assumed to intentionally do it alone and operate irrespective of what others are doing or thinking—an assumption that is even more warranted with respect to social services, since a congregation's social program may overlap with a program offered by a nearby congregation and few attempts are made for coordination and sharing (Farnsley 2003). However, this is not the picture emerging from our findings. In fact, congregations are surprisingly collaborative and well imbedded in their communities.

Almost all congregations (1,192, 85.6 percent) informed us that they hold worship or prayer services in collaboration with other religious groups. This suggests that congregations are not isolated groups detached from the world. When we analyzed what groups congregations worshipped with, we saw that the most frequent worship collaborations were with other congregations from the same denomination or with nearby congregations. Furthermore, congregations that did not pray with others were not significantly different in budget size, year of incorporation, or membership size, nor in religious strictness or political orientation from congregations that did pray with other groups. What distinguished congregations that prayed with others more often was twofold: the percent of women members (congregations with more women tended to pray more with others), and the racial makeup of the congregation (black congregations tended to pray more with others while white and Asian congregations tended to pray less often with others).

About two-thirds of the congregations collaborated with other faith-based organizations to develop and deliver community service programs (870, 62.5 percent). Organizations that congregations collaborated with included denomination-based groups, local interfaith coalitions, neighboring congregations, suburban congregations, and faith-based organizations such as Catholic Charities. Somewhat surprisingly, more than half of the congregations (781, 56.1 percent) reported collaborating with secular organizations for the purpose of delivering services or running programs. Secular collaborators included government agencies, local universities, hospitals, neighborhood associations, and community organizations. The collaborations often include sharing space, financial resources, or staff and supplies. While one would expect that congregations frequently collaborate for worship purposes, it was quite surprising to find that so many of them also cooperated with both religious and secular partners in order to help people in need. Only 339 congregations (24.4 percent) reported no collaborations with any religious or secular partner for the purpose of helping others.

Summary

The current debate about the role of faith-based organizations in social service provision at times seems to obscure the primary reason for congregations' existence—their faith. However, one should keep in mind that congregations are formed and sustained first and foremost to allow people to collectively express their faith. That is, all congregations hold worship services, and this is the primary and most frequent service they offer members. On average, the congregations we studied held 3.8 worship services per week (this omitted the congregations that met daily or more frequently). If such services were not in place, the organization would no longer be a religious congregation and members with a social service orientation would not be members of a religious organization. In addition, our data show that even among theologically liberal and moderate congregations, about three-quarters believe that their scripture is the *literal* word of God. To sustain congregations, many members contribute their time, labor, and money. Congregations are for members and by members, and they are among the most vital and participatory organizations that operate on the neighborhood level.

Congregations are living social entities. Like any human organism they expand and contract, are born and die. Unlike a living organism, they can almost endlessly regain strength and vitality or be revived into new youth. Given that Philadelphia is among many older and formerly industrial cities and has suffered from the combined factors of serious blight and the flight of capable families to suburban locales, the vitality found in the city's many congregations is amazing. There are many more financially stable or sound and growing congregations than there are congregations that are withering and disintegrating. The emerging picture we obtained is of a vital and active religious life in Philadelphia. Over two thousand congregations continue to attract a subset of individuals and serve their spiritual and social needs. The overwhelming majority of these local organizations are financed by members through pledges and offerings, and they all seem to survive and many flourish. Often, congregations are located side by side; their success and growth stem from the ranks of newcomers to the city as well as from people who were not previously affiliated, rather than at the expense other groups (such as other denominations). Thus, the reported growth in membership and resources cannot be explained by members shifting congregations or by suburban members who commute to worship in the city. This reported growth and vitality is an indication that religion is alive and well in urban America.

Dudley and Roozen (2001) noted that the northeastern United States has shown the least growth in religious activity, especially in northeastern cities, which have lagged behind the traditionally religious South, the awakening West, and the sprawling suburbs. In Philadelphia, however, we found much vitality and growing strength. The congregations in this study are quite stable in their communities. As stated earlier, the average year of incorporation of a congregation in Philadelphia was 1939, or sixty-two years before the study's conclusion. The median year of incorporation, however, was 1955. This figure suggests that the PCC, more than other congregational studies, managed to reach newer and less institutionalized congregations. The presence of younger congregations, many of which have formed within independent traditions, may explain why more clergy in our study did not attain theological seminary education and why median membership size is below the average reported by some large-scale studies.

Since colonial times, denominations and congregations have emerged as segregated communities. Congregations were first described as ethnic groups in which people groups from the old country or heritage bonded together. Later, as shown by Warner and Lunt (1941), denominations continued to attract people from particular ethnic groups and socioeconomic levels. Warner and Lunt also found that socioeconomic attainment was related to changes in people's denominational affiliation and congregational membership. They further found that membership in a religious congregation correlated highly with civic engagement. For example, members of liberal Protestant congregations were more likely to volunteer and serve on the boards of local civic organizations than members of more religiously strict denominations. In Philadelphia, the PCC found congregations to be highly segregated. As Dudley and Roozen (2001) noted, congregations are not much more segregated than the rest of society. But, clearly the majority of congregations show that like-minded people worship together. This is both a strength and a weakness. The level of trust is usually higher in homogeneous social groups, especially for minority groups, where the congregation forms a social hub and links members between the new land and their former home country and culture. Conversely, people who are substantially different from congregation members may find they are unwelcome or seen as unfit to be members. At times the congregation is foreign to its neighbors. Even among white congregations, the congregation represents one ethnic group based on a country of origin, such as Albanian, Macedonian, or Ukrainian churches. As will be elaborated in Chapter 7, socioeconomic status, region of origin, and ethnic background differentiate congregational membership among black congregations as well.

There is an assumption that, because of their segregated nature, congregations are isolated and uninterested in those who are not like themselves. It is claimed that congregations are not aware of what other congregations do on the same street or in the same neighborhood, that they assume they are the only game in town. Farnsley (2003: 16) noted, "In a survey of faith-based youth programs in Indianapolis, for instance, we found that roughly 80 percent of service providers believed that the programs offered by their organization were unique. In fact, most were substantially identical to, but thoroughly detached from, other programs." In Philadelphia, we did not find support for the notion that congregations are isolationists. We found that most congregations worship with other faith groups (85.8 percent) and collaborate with other faith groups (62.5 percent) and with secular groups (56.2 percent) in order to provide social services. This is not a picture of detachment or ignorance, but suggests that congregations are well-embedded organizations that are in touch with other groups in their environment and act collaboratively with others.

To a large extent, congregational membership mimics the city in which the congregation exists. The average annual income and ethnic makeup of congregations is the same as citywide averages. We will discuss Latino and black congregations in Chapters 7 and 8, but for now it is important to note that black neighborhoods show a preponderance of black congregations—as is the case with Latino, white, and Asian neighborhoods. Given the homogeneous nature of city neighborhoods, congregations are a mirror of the city. In addition, very few congregations command wealth, and many, especially center city congregations, face a scarcity of members and resources. Some center city congregations bus members from other parts of the city but this is not a common phenomenon.

Congregations come in all sizes and shapes. While in Chapter 1 we established the unique and special nature of congregations, in fact they are very much a variegated set of social organizations. Some are large and well endowed. These flagship congregations tower over their environment and often have ample financial and volunteer resources with which to carry out impressive projects. Much more common, however, are the more than 50 percent of congregations which have an adult membership of less than 90 and annual incomes less than $100,000. One key mistake that many policy makers and media mavens make is to treat congregations as if they are all alike or are all poised to provide services in their communities. Trying to recruit congregations to provide community services as if they were all alike is futile, given the fact that one congregation may have few members who are busy sustaining the religious function of the organization while another congregation may have hundreds of members who are able and organized to assist when called upon. The strength of congregations is in their diversity. Potential members are attracted to specific characteristics and can find the one congregation that is best suited for their need. Once they are members, they may become contributors to the congregation's well-being and to the social services it offers.

Part II
Congregational Contribution to Quality of Life in Urban America

Chapter 4
Informal Care by Congregations

One common criticism of congregational social programs is that they are small, unsustainable, and limited in scope (Chaves 1999; Farnsley 2003). The accuracy of this specific criticism will be assessed in the next chapter. In this chapter we focus on the importance and scope of informal care and, in so doing, show that these presumed weaknesses are also strengths and assets. Small and informal also mean flexible and adaptable. Our focus in this chapter is on social support that is not organized formally but provided on an as-needed basis. We rely on the literature on social capital and Robert Wuthnow's (1998) concept of "loose connections" between members of the same community that are not mandatory and yet are quite bonding. We argue that the loose connections that bond members to their congregation and to other members are fruitful in many ways that are unique to American congregations, whereas in other societies they may be unnecessary. Congregations are places where many Americans easily acquire social capital (Ammerman 2005; Bane, Coffin, and Higgins 2005). In a society like the United States, where helpful immediate ties to extended family members are scarce and information is costly and rarely available, informal support, referral, and advice are especially valuable. Often, individuals and families confront situations that are stressful and that require expertise that is hard to get. In a congregation one can find a sympathetic ear, readily available expertise, and willingness to help find solutions to individual needs. In this respect, the informality and smallness of congregations make possible an open house for all people, especially members, to offer creative and personal solutions to idiosyncratic problems or, at least, to find connections that can lead to the problems' solution.

Help for human needs can come in many different forms: from personal advice by a relative or a friend to a national program that provides technical or fiscal assistance. While our attention is often focused on formal services and the agencies providing them, most care and support are offered informally and in an ad hoc way. And at times the distinction between formal and informal care is hard to make. The following example from our study may highlight this issue.

Informal care by congregations may take many forms. One small Pentecostal church in West Philadelphia collects money that the pastor gives to poor people who come and ask for help. In addition, the church routinely houses one or two homeless families who are referred by word of mouth. The church property becomes their home for a while, and they use the church kitchen and food supplies for their daily meals. When a family finds a suitable housing situation, a new homeless family may move in. These two modes of assistance, monetary and nonmonetary, have not grown into full-sized or formal modes of help, but rather have remained informal, on an as-needed basis. There has been no congregational meeting to discuss these programs, and help is offered only when a needy individual or family is referred to the church. Yet, at the same time, this church has a food pantry that is a formal program. The food pantry provides groceries on a weekly basis to some twenty needy families. It is planned in detail, and certain members are designated to carry it out. The help for the homeless, meanwhile, does not involve planning; no one in the church is responsible for making sure that a homeless family will live on the church property or that they will leave at a designated date, as is customary in more organized programs that provide housing for the homeless.

Most people feel uncomfortable applying to a formal program; they prefer to be assisted personally and informally. As adults in the United States, we assume that we should be able to solve our problems and needs by ourselves; if this is too difficult, we turn to friends and relatives. The ideology of economic individualism calls on us to be responsible for our needs, to use our informal network to solve problems, and only when everything else has failed, to call upon public services (Cnaan, Hasenfeld, Cnaan, and Rafferty 1993). Also, using public services is associated with a high degree of stigma and failure.

In this chapter, we will show how congregations position themselves to play the role of the extended family and close and trusted friends, serving as informal care providers. We will also discuss the lack of familial support, the need for information in America, and the need for substitute support systems in light of the decline of fraternity organizations and workplaces that used to be arenas for making friends. One of the last bastions of civic engagement and personal bonding, then, is the local religious congregation. What does this mean in terms of helping people solve their ongoing problems? The bulk of the chapter will be devoted to this issue and to findings from the census about informal care provided by local religious congregations in Philadelphia. In the next chapter, we will discuss how congregations attempt to supplement the public welfare system and fill in the role vacated by public retrenchment.

The Culture of Seeking Help in America

In the United States, one of the most powerful ideological and normative foundations is economic individualism. Put simply, this implies that the responsibility for fiscal, social, and human needs and well-being rests ultimately on the person's (or the person's family's) own shoulders. Unlike societies that emphasize familial responsibilities, such as Southeast Asian societies, or those that emphasize a benevolent and often trusted government, such as those in Europe, the American model calls upon the individual's personal responsibility. This is one reason why no strong public welfare state has developed in the United States. A society of immigrants who left their extended families behind and did not see themselves as bonded or able to trust others developed an individualistic stance that called on one to work hard and make it on his (or her) own (Cnaan et al. 1993). Given that throughout American history most Americans have had their extended family in faraway countries and most grown-up children tended to move across the continent, there has been some intergenerational sense of extended family obligation. Furthermore, the distrust of government which the first settlers brought with them as religiously persecuted minorities vis-à-vis the British crown added to Americans' unwillingness to provide government with the power and responsibility to meet many of their needs. In no advanced democracy are distrust of government and the Lockean principle so profoundly characteristic (Brown 2001).

As part of the Protestant work ethic, the early settlers who set the cultural norms of American society sought success by hard work and self-reliance. Needing others was perceived as a last resort from the perspective of both the individual and the community. The person who was poor but nevertheless valued was one who encountered hardships, maintained pride, pretended that he (or she) did not need help, and only acquiesced to be assisted when confronted by the good heart of neighbors who respected his (or her, or their) honorable plight. In numerous books, songs, and movies, the honorable person has been one who did not expect the collective to come to the rescue but rather toughened up and withstood the hardships of life to end up triumphant. In other words, asking for help from others has been ideologically frowned upon and avoided at all costs.

In all societies, to be welfare dependent bears a stigma, but not to the extent that it does in the United States. Consequently, while some welfare programs evolved in the United States after the Great Depression and after World War II, they were never on the scale of European welfare services and never gained widespread public support. Furthermore, the recipients of these programs, with the exception of people on old-age pensions (social security), which were viewed as self-contributing programs and not welfare, were viewed as immoral and shameless burdens on the rest of society.

As we have noted elsewhere, congregations are the places where the most public trust is present and where members expect to provide some form of social care as a means of actualizing their faith (Cnaan et al. 2002; Maryland Association of Nonprofit Organizations 2002). Put differently, in America, people who come to worship expect that clergy or coreligionists will ask them to do good for people in the community. Many clergy are trained to form and establish social ministries and social action projects. The public, from high-level policy makers to the homeless, expect congregations to help out those in need. Furthermore, current social services expect congregations to help people in need, and these services deny help unless applicants first exhaust all available resources in the community—especially resources from local religious congregations. The point is that congregations are places of both worship and public goods.

This is also the case with individual needs. While public agencies are organized along bureaucratic lines, specializing in caring for one issue or a few specific problems, congregations, like families, are open to many different types of needs. Public programs are limited by regulations; every decision must be made within clear guidelines. In fact, many human needs are met through such organized and well-established programs. However, many other needs are met by informal providers such as families and local religious congregations. A congregation may not offer formal ongoing counseling for couples, but when a couple come to the pastor in need of guidance, they are rarely turned away. The pastor will work with them as a trustworthy counselor, a trained member of the congregation will be asked to help, or the couple will be referred to a trusted counseling agency. In all cases, personal preferences for a service are met while stigma is minimized, and this is all done within a supportive and often trusted environment (Miller 1978).

A similar problem exists when one is in need of special information. With the proliferation of knowledge, no one person can possess the answers to most daily living questions, ranging from plumbing to tax return preparation. When, for example, a family move to a new neighborhood, they need information regarding housing, furniture buying, school systems, playgrounds, garbage pickup, best routes for driving to places, and more. While there can be many guides and brochures that may provide some of the needed information, a few knowledgeable neighbors can be of invaluable assistance and reduce the cost of information to almost zero. How then do we find answers to such searches?

Finding Referral and Information

The notion of the power of sociability and getting power through association and contacts with others is an old sociological adage ranging from Durkheim and Marx. "Social capital," the current popular term for such sociability, receives numerous definitions and many uses. Portes (1998: 6), in a review article, suggests that it "stands for the ability of actors to secure benefits by virtue of membership in social networks or other social structures." He sees the rewards of maintaining these networks as manifold: "through social capital, actors can gain direct access to economics resources (subsidized loans, investment tips, protected markets); they can increase their social capital through contacts with experts or individuals of refinement (i.e. embodied cultural capital); or, alternatively, they can affiliate with institutions that confer valued credentials (i.e., institutionalized cultural capital)" (4).

In the United States, the formation of such networks is often difficult, since society is so diverse and geographical mobility is high. School ties, fraternities and sororities of all types, service organizations such as Rotary and Lions, veteran groups, local bars, and clubs serve as places where one can extend one's network and thereby gain access to information and resources. But the institutions that provide face-to-face contact and enhance trust have become less common, and for many they are inaccessible.

For the average person in America, ideological and normative determinants are translated into and manifested as anomie. Many people are isolated, removed from sources of familial support and guidance. People are unaware of how to resolve simple issues such as what to bring to a party or the proper dress code in a new workplace. It is difficult to solve all problems alone. However, in most countries one usually relies on family and friends for advice and support. In America the individual often lives far away from family and friends; hence the plethora of guides, magazines, talk shows, and radio programs that provide information on how to deal with just about everything. We make an industry of that which is widely available in other countries through daily contacts. We buy information as our social networks shrink, and we are educated about health and finance by people we will never see. Given this situation, to give but one example, it is no surprise that Dr. Benjamin Spock's famous bestseller on how to raise babies could be so strongly influential on American childrearing practices a few decades ago.

Many problems people encounter, such as deciding what personal computer to buy, are relatively easy to solve. We usually go by reputation, the advice of the closest guru, or the rating of a given PC magazine. But finding information on purchasing a computer is a relatively easy task.

First, there are numerous other consumers in the same position. Second, the "guru" is most likely not to benefit from his or her giving of advice and hence is less driven by personal interest. And, third, the problem carries no stigma with it. Compare this problem to finding a good therapist for one's child who is found to be using drugs. In this case, the problem is less commonplace, there are fewer available "gurus," and the process of admitting the problem is a stigma-inducing situation itself. The quest for someone who knows what to do or who can refer people to the proper address is paramount.

Thus, the dictum to help as many people as possible is embedded in the culture of congregations. But the help does not have to be formal and organized; it can be informal and personal. A median congregation has at least 90 adult members. In such a place, most attenders feel at home and know many other worshippers. As Ellison and George (1994) and Molm, Takahashi, and Peterson (2000) have shown, congregations generate more informal bonding and communication than any other social and community institution. People choose congregations based on faith and personal sense of comfort. The congregation serves as a surrogate extended family for many members who find within its walls support and readily available information. In a Web site of the Reconstructionist Jewish movement, a member in Media (just outside Philadelphia) states, "I like belonging to a Reconstructionist synagogue, because it means I'm a member of a warm and supportive community. I felt comfortable getting involved right from the beginning. I know that what I say and do makes a difference."

Furthermore, most places of worship provide some form of fellowship where people meet over food and drink, usually after the weekend worship service. The culture of sharing food in fellowship, congregational picnics, or special events forms a sense of family and belonging (Ammerman 2005; Sack 2000). In such occasions, it is quite common for people to raise personal issues that happen to be on their minds. One may ask about a moving company or about applying for a loan. It is likely that a few other members of the congregation will provide the needed information; at times one of them may even be an expert on the subject, who is willing to help free of charge or at a reduced cost. When, for example, families of teens who are bullied in school have an opportunity to meet with other parents who share the same or related experiences, such contacts help alleviate the sense of isolation and provide a safe, empathetic environment in which to express feelings and ask questions. Other parents can offer valuable information on local services and resources and practical advice about most anything, as well as how they or someone they know successfully managed the situation. Another example involves ex-prisoners who are trying to reintegrate into the community. In a church meeting one ex-prisoner mentioned that he had been turned down by the social security office when he asked for a social security card, as he lacked an address and his forms were not properly done. Attendees volunteered to help fill the form in properly, and another attendee knew the director of the local social security office and agreed to talk with him on behalf of the ex-prisoner.

At other times, when the needed information is more personal and sensitive, the person or family will approach the clergy and ask for their guidance. The clergy, in turn, may make an inquiry with other members or fellow clergy and connect the person or family in need with the best source of information.

In an empirical study of people who sought informal help from congregations, Wuthnow, Hackett, and Hsu (2004) found that those who ask for such help are, on average, younger, have more years of education, have more children, have more family problems, seek out other forms of informal help, and attend church regularly. The latter finding is of great importance. The more embedded a person is in the local religious congregation the more likely this person is to ask for help when needed. These authors also found that recipients reported higher levels of trust when help was offered informally, as opposed to formally. In other words, recipients of help perceived that helpers were more trustworthy if friends, relatives, or congregational members informally gave the assistance.

It was thus our hypothesis that a large amount of informal help and sharing of information goes on in our congregations. In this light, we attempted to assess in which areas help is most and least often provided informally by congregations. We also attempted to assess if any particular type of congregation is more likely to offer informal help when compared with other congregations.

Studying Informal Care

Studying informal care is quite difficult. Short of surveying the entire congregation (or even the neighborhood, as was done by Wuthnow, Hackett, and Hsu 2004), asking every member about their experiences with helping or being helped by others in the congregation, we had to rely on knowledge of clergy, which is often comprehensive but at times is limited. As detailed in the methodological appendix, we interviewed clergy and asked them to provide a wide range of information about their congregations.

In our second research instrument, we listed some 215 possible programs and asked the interviewed clergy to assess whether their congregation provided any of them. For each answer in the positive, we asked whether the help given was formal or informal. "Informal help" was defined as help given to someone in the previous twelve months for an issue unaddressed by any organized program. This is an ad hoc response to an unforeseen request for help

We assume that the clergy's knowledge underrepresents the real amount of informal care provided by the congregation; naturally, it is quite possible that during fellowship, people are helped with practical issues that never reach the clergy's attention. However, the clergy response gave us a window into the phenomenon of informal care, and we may assume that clergy bias is constant across the various kinds of help. Hence, even if our numbers represent low levels of informal care, they most likely represent the areas of informal help common in congregations.

Two examples illustrate these types of informal programs. First, when we asked clergy whether their congregations have a program for family counseling, most answered "yes and no." What they meant was that in the previous year (the period covered by the question), there was no official program in place but service was nevertheless rendered. One clergyperson answered, "We do not have a program, but I worked last year on family issues with the Joneses and the Clintons." As such, help came informally and upon direct request, but it was not advertised or preplanned with dates of service. The service too may have been different for each applying family. Even so, it did not lead to the formation of a new program, and any future service this congregation may offer for couples in need of counseling would still be on an informal, case-by-case basis. Second, when we asked if the congregation offers a job-placement program, most congregations responded negatively. However, many of them informed us that, informally, through members' contacts, jobs were often found for members and their relatives. Again, no formal program existed but the service was rendered informally. In both cases, the interviewee's response was, "Yes, we provided such a program, but only upon request, and it is not a formal program."

In cases like these, we asked interviewers to write that the service is offered informally or upon request. The analysis here is based on the answers provided by the 1,392 congregations to questions about 215 social programs. In this chapter, we do not refer to the responses which stated that there were formal programs run by the congregation (see Chapter 5) or that the space of the congregations was used for such programs (see Chapter 6).

Areas of High Level Informal Help

The key service areas in which help is provided informally involve counseling of some kind. For convenience we divided the 215 programs into the following key areas: personal counseling, senior care, children and youth services, health, programs for homeless and poor people, education, art, community security, community organizing, community economic and social development, social issues, housing, and other services for people in need. When we counted areas of help provided informally by at least 10 percent of the congregations, we found 45 such programs. Two-fifths (19 programs, 41.2 percent) are in the area of personal counseling and almost all of them are most frequently reported as informal programs. The most common were couples counseling (73.8 percent), family counseling (70.8 percent), premarriage counseling (63.6 percent), and bereavement counseling (62.5 percent). The other counseling programs were spouse abuse/domestic violence counseling (36 percent), teen pregnancy counseling (34.5 percent), child abuse counseling (33.5 percent), abortion/pro-life issues counseling (33.4 percent), parenting skills counseling (30.7 percent), marriage encounter counseling (29 percent), suicide prevention counseling (27.6 percent), single parent programs and counseling (27 percent), loss of spouse support counseling (25.9 percent), support for divorced parents counseling (25.7 percent), programs and counseling for widows and widowers (23 percent), intergenerational programs and counseling (17.4 percent), crisis hotline counseling (16.9 percent), grandparents support and counseling (13.2 percent), and sex education and counseling (11.1 percent).

It is little surprise that the service most often offered informally (18 of 24 listed areas) is counseling. People seek counseling when they need help with their personal problems and wish for an attentive and sympathetic ear. In the absence of family, clergy and other coreligionists become confidants. It is a key role that most American congregations have always provided for their members, even if members and clergy are unaware of the extent to which it takes place. We heard from almost every clergyperson we interviewed that congregational members often seek help for problems that the clergy may or may not be able to cope with. Many of these clergy, especially the veterans, develop lists of referrals, members with relevant skills who may offer help. But all clergy know that they will be called upon by members to assist in times of personal and family crises; it is part of their pastoral job description. This topic will be discussed further in Chapter 13 when we discuss the role of clergy in America.

The second area in which many programs are offered informally is social action. Many congregations are not formally involved in social action campaigns but informally support such issues. The topic may be discussed in a weekend sermon, or members may ask others to join in a cause, sign a political letter or write in the congregation's newsletter about a social demonstration. Eight social action areas were reported by more than 10 percent of the congregations studied. These areas were family issues (16.2 percent); interfaith/interdenominational collaboration (15.9 percent); social justice (14.7 percent); voter registration (12.9 percent); civil rights (12.9 percent); poverty/welfare rights/advocacy (11.5 percent); peace (11.3 percent); and women's issues (10.9 percent). Similarly, many clergy and congregations reported that they were informally working with the police to bring about peace and quiet in their neighborhood. Given that police often suspect local people of crimes and residents suspect police of intent to incriminate, clergy and congregational settings help bridge divides. We found that cooperation with police and space for police/community meetings were often provided informally (24.9 percent and 14.6 percent of the studied congregations).

There were a few areas of informal care in which technical skills were offered by seasoned and experienced members of the congregations to other members. These areas included financial counseling (30.6 percent), legal assistance (22.1 percent), consumer counseling (19.3 percent), and job counseling and placement (11.9 percent).

There were four programs offered informally by many congregations to the homebound and those with low mobility. It is quite common for congregations to have a group of members or an informal committee to make sure that the sick, the hospitalized, the elderly, and the shut-ins are not left alone but are visited routinely and offered transportation when needed. This is often done informally, the way such arrangements are done in an extended family, when one member is hospitalized or suffers from limited mobility. The key reported areas of social care in this instance were hospital visitation (34.7 percent); transportation for seniors (29.3 percent); visitation/buddy systems (25.4 percent); and sick/homebound visitation (21.8 percent).

A group of informal programs offered by more than 10 percent of the congregations included tangible support for people in need. The beneficiaries of these programs were often indigent neighbors who came to the door of the congregation, when they saw that members or staff were around, and asked for help. The most frequent programs in this category included financial assistance, in the form of giving from clergy discretionary funds (29 percent); food pantries (14.7 percent); day programs for the homeless (mostly by downtown congregations) (14.6 percent), sponsorship for students in need (10.6 percent); and adoption of a welfare family (10 percent). Two tangible programs that were offered informally by more than 10 percent of the congregations, but that did not fit any of the listed categories, were neighborhood cleanup (16.2 percent) and helping people with physical disabilities (10.1 percent).

In a few key areas, no informal program was offered by 10 percent of the congregations, indicating that help in these areas is either formal or nonexistent. These key areas included children and youth services, art, housing, and other services for people in need. Very few areas of help were reported to be offered by less than 1 percent of the congregations. These programs included Sex and Love Addicts Anonymous groups (0.9 percent); Police Athletic League (0.9 percent); before-school care (0.7 percent); translation services (0.6 percent); and neighborhood credit union aid (0.6 percent). What is common in these areas of help is that it is almost impossible to offer informal programs since they can be offered only with the involvement of an external partner such as the police. In special cases, the congregation informally supported programs offered by other congregations and when necessary referred members to these programs, hence indirectly, in effect, offering the service in question.

Which Congregations Are More and Less Involved in Informal Care?

Thirty-eight congregations (2.7 percent) reported that they provide no informal services. Almost all of these also reported no formal programs and were typically very small in size, with a low operating budget, on the brink of extinction, and without full-time clergy. About three-quarters of the congregations (72.3 percent) reported 10 or more areas of informal care, while almost half (46.4 percent) reported 20 or more, a quarter (25.6 percent) more than 30, and 10 percent more than 50. A few congregations (10) reported more than 100 areas of informal care.

A bivariate analysis found that the extent of informal programs offered by a congregation is significantly associated with the annual operating budget, the number of buildings the congregation possesses, the presence of full-time clergy, the number of active members, and the percentage of old people in the congregation (the larger the percentage, the less likely the congregation offered informal care). Surprisingly, theological variables and percentage of members living near the congregation were not associated with the number of informal programs. In other words, conservative and liberal congregations were equally likely to provide informal support. Similarly, whether people live nearby or far away from the congregation did not affect the level of informal support. When we ran all possible explanatory variables in one regression model, only two variables were significant: the percentage of elderly (negative effect) and budget size. Combined, their explanatory power was very weak ($R^2 = .026$), indicating that the provision of informal care is not a function of the congregation's characteristics, but part of its cultural ethos.

Summary

Banks (1997) noted that self-help and mutual aid are flourishing in the United States, and links this phenomenon to the rise of small, community capital-creating groups as opposed to larger self-help organizations (Putnam 2000). Indeed, the local sphere is where people meet each other face-to-face, personal care develops, and informal care flourishes. One of the often forgotten aspects of the American congregation is its function as a surrogate and extended family, a source of informal help. Informal help is significantly different from self-help and mutual-support groups. Informal care does not require that the recipient give back to the care provider. While informal care is the foundation of mutual help, giving back is not a requisite.

Indeed, from the PCC data, we find that the congregation serves as a hub for informal counseling, support skills, and tangible help. When individual members or families have a need at times, they prefer not to approach an existing formal agency; they share their need with clergy or other congregants and thereby often get the help they need. People from the community who are not members also often prefer the friendly support of the congregation. Based on these data, we do not know the efficacy of congregational informal help, how many times a need is expressed and ignored, and how many members of the congregations are involved in the provision of informal care. Given that in most instances our respondents were clergy, it may be assumed that our findings are biased toward clergy's personal involvement in providing informal care. It is also possible that much informal care has not been recorded, as we did not survey members.

For many individuals in Philadelphia, and for that matter across the United States, this type of help from congregations is a preferred one. When the need is perceived to be difficult, and a sympathetic ear is required alongside a trustworthy and solid form of help, the congregation often offers informal care from its collective pool of members, providing a foundational piece for a strong and local civil society. At the core of local relationships is trust in the local congregation and the congregation's central place in offering answers to people's varying needs, be they needs met formally or informally.

As expected, almost all congregations from the PCC had been involved in informal care provision. We have not been able to find good organizational predictors that separate providers of informal care from nonproviders, an indication that informal care is an inherent outcome of people voluntarily congregating for religious reasons on a given property. The decision to offer informal care is not organizationally or theologically based; it is part of the normative expectation in the United States of what a congregation is. Indeed, when congregants offer space and fellowship they become important for forming a caring community. While the chapter opens the discussion on informal care by congregations, formal care by congregations and the space they offer are also of great importance. These issues will be further analyzed in the following chapters.

Chapter 5

Formal Care: Congregations as Social Service Agencies

While all aspects of social care by congregations in Philadelphia are important and worth studying, the tallying of the formal programs offered by congregations is the heart of the present study. As we will show, most congregations in Philadelphia contribute to the city's quality of life, and together they offer a sizeable network of care. With over 2,000 units of care throughout the city, congregations clearly have a profound effect on the quality of life of Philadelphians. Members and non-members of congregations alike in all likelihood feel the efforts of the local religious congregations almost every day of the year.

There are many ways by which we can detail the story of care and actualized compassion offered by local religious congregations. There is not enough space to tell the story of one family from North Philadelphia whose house was built by volunteers from their church and whose son was mentored by a volunteer from another church. Their story could be a chapter in itself. Instead of individual stories, this chapter tallies the congregational-based support in general numbers and in trends. It is less colorful than the detailed stories of real people, but the picture it gives is most telling.

The chapter is arranged as follows. First, we try to put to rest the question of how many congregations are involved in providing social services. By discussing how many congregations are involved in even a modest way, and how many are not, we provide as definite an answer as possible to the debate regarding congregations in urban America. We also analyze and find commonalities among the very few congregations that do not provide even the most modest social service. Once this issue is explored, we describe and analyze who the beneficiaries of the congregational services and what sort of social programs are most likely to be offered by local congregations. While, combined, congregations offer a rich variety of social services, here we focus on the ones that have gradually become the trademark of local religious congregations.

We then describe four sets of specific services that are often less featured in the literature on this subject: health services, arts and culture services, social action services, and programs serving the poor. In the following section we assess the degree to which congregations are isolated from the rest of the community versus the degree to which they are networked and connected with other congregations and secular organizations. Finally, we assess the understanding and involvement of congregations in Charitable Choice and the fiscal contribution and dollar value of congregational social services. We attempt to estimate a value for their contribution by applying a replacement value method.

How Many Shy Away from Providing Social Services, and Why?

The first issue to be explored is what percentage of congregations provide at least one social service. Or put another way, what percentage of congregations do not provide even one, modest social service?

Critics of the faith-based initiatives championed by the 1996 Charitable Choice legislation and President Bush's White House Office of Faith-Based and Community Initiatives often cling to one study that found a relatively small percentage of congregations to be involved in helping the needy. No one study in this area received such coverage as Mark Chaves's analysis of the National Congregations Study (NCS). In a series of publications (Chaves 1999; Chaves et al. 1999; Chaves and Tsitsos 2001) based on a national study of over one thousand congregations, Chaves asserts that most religious congregations are too small and lack the sophistication required for social welfare programs. Chaves found that only 59 percent of U.S. congregations are involved in any social service programs, and that these are often very modest, small-scale, temporary programs. His study is based on the NCS and was conducted in conjunction with the 1998 General Social Survey (GSS). GSS respondents who said they attend religious services were asked to name their congregation and provide contact information. This procedure generated a nationally representative sample of 1,456 congregations. The NCS gathered data via a sixty-minute interview with one key informant—a minister, priest, rabbi, or other leader—from 1,236 of the nominated congregations, a cooperation rate of 85 percent. In most cases, the senior clergy were interviewed over the phone, not face-to-face. The major advantage of this method was that even nonlisted congregations could be accessed via their members. However, the ways the social services questions were asked and measured could have led to an underreporting of congregations offering social services. The language used by the interviewers was not sensitive to terminology used by religious communities, and hence could have led to an underreporting of social service involvement.

While the NCS study was carefully crafted to reach relatively inaccessible congregations, its findings do not match those from numerous other studies all over the country. Other scholars in this field found much higher rates of social service involvement but had weaker sampling methods. Our previous work in *Invisible Caring Hand* yielded much higher rates of social and community involvement, but it was not based on a representative sample. Yet one has to ask, if numerous studies all yield the same result, and a single study yields different results, why the exception gains so much coverage.

In fact, with the exception of Chaves's research, the studies reviewed found that nine out of ten congregations provide at least one social service program that benefits people in the community who are members or nonmembers of the congregation (Cnaan and Boddie 2001; Grettenberger and Hovmand 1997; Hill 1998; Hodgkinson et al. 1993; Jackson et al. 1997; Kinney 2003; Printz 1998; Silverman 2000; Stone 2000; Wuthnow 2000). For example, Nancy Kinney (2003) reported findings from a study of 631 religious congregations across the 12-county St. Louis Metropolitan Statistical Area. She noted that almost all congregations (97.9 percent) reported providing at least one social program. A small group (15.5 percent) reported only one program and the rest reported anywhere from two to eighteen programs. Programs for youth were most frequently cited (59.9 percent), followed by another youth program, summer camps (37.9 percent). Food pantries were reported by 31.1 percent and senior programs by 28.2 percent. Robert Wuthnow (2000) was the only one to study nonmetropolitan congregations. His study concentrated on the Lehigh Valley in Pennsylvania, including the cities of Allentown, Bethlehem, and Easton. Wuthnow found that of a sample of 60 congregations, only two (3.3 percent) did not sponsor any program. This body of knowledge challenged Chaves's most cited study in the field, and we set out to test the discrepancy in such findings, using the Philadelphia Census of Congregations (PCC).

The PCC was unique in that we identified all existing congregations in the city and were able to assess our response rate. No previous study of large magnitude ever sampled two-thirds of all existing congregations. While the National Congregations Study (NCS) is based on some 1,236 from a population of some 350,000–400,000 congregations, the PCC is based on 1,392 congregations from a population of 2,120. Furthermore, as noted in the methodological appendix, our study is based on face-to-face lengthy interviews on congregational premises. As such, the PCC was able to discern services that other studies missed. Finally, we completed three preliminary reports along the way. We reported findings from the first 401 interviewed congregations, then when we had 877, and lastly when we reached 1,211 congregations. In each such analysis the key findings remained practically the same. This is a strong indication for the ability of the studied 1,392 to represent all 2,120 Philadelphia congregations.

In the PCC, only 107 congregations (7.7 percent) reported not to provide even one social service. In other words, about 92.3 percent of the studied congregations in Philadelphia reported to provide at least one social service. This finding from a most representative sample of one urban city lends additional credence to the accumulating number of studies suggesting that the data obtained by the NCS is seriously underrepresentative. While some people wish to see all congregations help the needy, this expectation is unrealistic. In fact, this impressively high percentage of socially involved congregations indicates that helping the needy is a sound congregational norm. As we shall soon document, some congregations provide only a modest type of social service. But this should not confuse the fact that there is no other community-based social institution that has a primary mandate to help the needy and that has so many of its members actively involve in pro-social activities. The amazing story is that so many congregations do anything at all to make life better for a group of people, and many of those not doing so would like to but are unable at present to do so. With the exception of a handful, all interviewed congregations, no matter how impressive their social service offerings, apologized for not doing more and indicated that they wanted to and should do more.

In *Congregations in America,* Chaves (2004) laments that, with some notable exceptions, congregations do not engage in social services as their primary vocations. But this is an unrealistic expectation, akin to wanting our symphony orchestras to hold social services as their primary vocations. The primary reason for the existence of a religious congregation is its religious mission. What Chaves and others miss is that there is no other non-social service organization that has such a significant impact on social services and for which social services are so normatively and practically important in its self-definition. We can understand congregational involvement in social services provision only if nine out of ten libraries, symphonies, galleries, community colleges, and so forth will allocate 10 to 20 percent of their resources to serve the needy and poor. While Chaves and others look at congregations and compare them to social service agencies, they fail to acknowledge that among non-social service institutions, congregations are the most socially generous.

In analyzing which congregations do not provide even one social service, certain factors quickly emerged. The majority of the 107 non-serving congregations (77.5 percent) reported an annual operating budget of less than $50,000, as compared with the congregations that offered at least one program (31.4 percent). Similarly, one-third of the non-serving congregations did not own a building (31.1 percent), as compared with one-sixth of the serving congregations (16.3 percent). About a third of the non-serving congregations were established in the past ten years (30.8 percent), as compared to only one-sixth of the serving congregations (14.6 percent). Among non-serving congregations, three out of five congregations (58.9 percent) had no full-time clergy, as compared with only one-third of the serving congregations (37 percent). The non-serving congregations were visibly smaller in size compared with serving congregations (an average of 70.4 members and 329 members respectively). This set of findings suggests that the non-serving congregations are often the organizationally weakest congregations that struggle the most and focus their organizational energy mostly on survival and growth. A few of these congregations reported that they are engaged in discussions about closing down or merging with another congregation of the same faith tradition in the vicinity. For example, Chambers-Wylie Memorial Presbyterian Church on Broad Street between Spruce and Pine reported that it does not deliver any social programs. A few months later the congregation no longer carried out worship services and its building was rented to the University of the Arts.

The non-serving congregations were also politically significantly more conservative than the serving congregations (50.5 percent and 31.5 percent respectively), and also theologically more fundamentalist-conservative (67.3 percent and 54.4 percent). This difference is typical of newly founded congregations that tend to be more conservative-fundamentalist than veteran congregations. About a third of the non-serving congregations (31.4 percent) reported that in the past three years their membership had grown older as compared with only a quarter of the serving congregations (25.3 percent). Similarly, many more non-serving congregations reported that in the past three years membership had dwindled (30.8 percent and 19.9 percent).

Among the non-serving congregations that reported higher budgets and membership growth, the majority were Asian or Latino congregations that serve first generation immigrants. When we interviewed these congregations, it became clear to us that the majority of the nonreligious energy of these congregations is spent on informal mutual support. In these congregations, it is common for immigrant members to share their needs as newly arrived people in the community, and for other members to share their experience and knowledge or help with tangibles. Among Asian congregations, there was less an expressed desire to help others and form social ministries, while among Latino congregations, most of which are Protestant, there was an expressed desire to form social ministries once the resources became available. It can also be argued that these congregations offer seeds of social services in the form of social support groups and mutual aid organizations for new immigrant congregants and their families.

Interestingly, the percentage of females who are members and the percentage of members who live outside city boundaries were not strong indicators as to whether congregations were non-serving. The gender issue is further discussed in Chapter 9. The findings about members who live outside city limits add to the growing literature that suggests that commuting members and commuting congregations are as concerned about serving inner-city members as are neighborhood congregations whose members live near the congregational property (Chaves 2004; Wright-Smith 2004). These findings stand in contradiction to suggestions made by scholars like Farnsley (2003), who claim that commuting members lack knowledge and concern for the community around the congregational property and hence do not engage in serving these communities. Again, these findings give credence to the hypothesis that cultural norms are the most powerful forces moving congregations to provide social services.

Areas of Social Involvement and Populations Served Among Local Religious Congregations

The findings above suggest that more than 90 percent of the city congregations are engaged in at least one form of social services delivery, modest or comprehensive. However, this statistic just scrapes the surface of the topic. In this section, we will discuss the domains of service offered by Philadelphia congregations, and the populations served by these Philadelphian religious congregations.

Our second research instrument contained some 215 social programs that we expected were carried out by at least some of the congregations. The list was read to the interviewees (see appendix), who noted whether their congregations were engaged in a given program and if so, in what manner (alone, on their property, partnered with others, etc.). Indeed, as expected, each of these programs was carried out by at least one or two congregations. Some programs, however, were more common and may indicate the norm of what local religious congregations are expected to offer their communities. In Table 5.1, we list programs that were offered by 13 percent or more of the congregations. The threshold of 13 percent is arbitrarily chosen to illustrate about 30 of the most commonly offered programs. The far right column gives an estimate of the number of Philadelphia congregations that are likely to provide each of these services. For example, given that in our sample 37.4 percent of congregations reported providing a food pantry, it follows that 793 of the city's 2,120 congregations are likely to offer this program.

TABLE 5.1. MOST COMMON SERVICES PROVIDED BY CONGREGATIONS IN PHILADELPHIA

Type of service	Percent of congregations providing service	Estimated number of congregations
Latchkey programs	13.0	276
Soup kitchens	13.0	276
Parenting skills	13.0	276
Computer training for children	13.4	284
Health education	13.4	284
Organized tours for seniors	13.7	290
Sport activities	13.9	295
Prison ministry	13.9	295
School	14.5	307
Visiting sick and homebound	15.2	322
Scouts troops	15.9	337
Premarriage counseling	16.2	343
Day care (preschool)	17.0	360
Recreational programs for seniors	17.3	367
Neighborhood associations	17.5	371
Community bazaars and fairs	18.6	394
Programs for gang members	19.0	403
After-school care	19.8	420
Educational tutoring	21.3	452
Choral groups	21.3	452
Community holiday celebration	21.4	454
Visitation/buddy program for seniors	22.0	466
Clothing closets	25.0	530
Summer programs for teens	25.5	541
Music performances	27.6	585
Recreational programs for teens	34.1	723
Recreational program for children	34.7	736
Summer day camp	35.8	759
Food pantries	37.4	793

Clearly, feeding the hungry is the most common form of help, where almost one half of the congregations reported maintaining a food pantry and about one-sixth reported offering a soup kitchen. Of the reporting congregations, 37.4 percent offered a food pantry and 13 percent offered a soup kitchen. All in all, 41.2 percent of the congregations offered a food program of one kind or another. The only area close in frequency to serving food to needy people is caring for children (72.3 percent of the congregations). The difference is that programs for children and youth are often limited to the congregation's next generation while programs for poor people are most often designated for nonmembers. The preference for children and youth programs was also found in other studies, such as Kinney's study (2003) of 631 religious congregations across the 12-county St. Louis Metropolitan Statistical Area (59.9 percent). Kinney also found that 31.1 percent of the congregations offered a food pantry.

Among the programs in Table 5.1 are some that can be viewed as part of the regular life of a congregation. For example, choral groups or music performances and holiday celebrations are part of normal congregational functioning. We need to explain their inclusion with a short methodological note. In this case, we asked the interviewees to include these programs only if they have a significant nonreligious aspect. For example, if the choir performs in the community or the holiday celebration is a community event such as on Martin Luther King, Jr., Day, then the programs were to be included. But if the music is for the Sunday service only and Easter or Christmas is celebrated in and for the church members only, then the programs were not to be included. It is very difficult to demarcate where religion starts and social service ends, and consequently it is difficult to determine whether there is a significant social element to the program.

Special attention should be given to services for the elderly. Three programs for the elderly are listed in Table 5.1: "visitation/buddy program" was offered by 22 percent of the congregations, followed by "recreational programs for seniors" (17.3 percent), and "organized tours" (13.7 percent). Given that the elderly often gravitate toward congregations more than any other age group, it is surprising that so few programs for senior adults made it to the table. Transportation support for the elderly is offered by 12.5 percent of the congregations and meals for the elderly came fifth in frequency, reported by 10.3 percent of the congregations. In fact, 55.8 percent of the congregations reported that they do not offer any program for senior adults. Comparing the percentage of senior-serving congregations (44.2 percent) with the many congregations that offer services for children and teens (72.3 percent), it becomes clear that congregations' focus is often on future generations and not on older ones.

Additional findings of interest are programs offered by fewer congregations in the following service areas. In the field of caring for the needy, street outreach for the homeless (11.4 percent), financial support for poor people (5.2 percent), shelter for homeless people (4.2 percent), transitional living for the homeless (3.2 percent), and programs for youth offenders (2.4 percent); in the field of child care, nursery schools (10.1 percent), and before-school care (7.5 percent); in the field of education, scholarships for students in need (11.4 percent), computer training for adults (10.4 percent), adult literacy programs (9.1 percent), sites for Head Start programs (1.9 percent), and GED (General Educational Development) classes (high school equivalency)

TABLE 5.2. BENEFICIARIES OF CONGREGATIONAL SERVICES AND PROGRAMS IN PHILADELPHIA

Beneficiaries	Percent of programs
Children	44.1
Youth	38.2
People with low incomes/poor	34.7
Families	34.1
Adults	23.9
Elderly	21.8
People with addictions	13.8
People with disabilities	12.8
Community residents at large	43.1

(7.5 percent); in the area of community care, international relief (13.9 percent), and space for police/community meetings (9.0 percent); and finally, in the area of community economic development, neighborhood cleanup (11.4 percent), crime watch (8.9 percent), job training (5.3 percent), housing rehabilitation (4.0 percent), recruitment of new business (4.3 percent), new building initiatives (2.6 percent), business incubation (2.4 percent), investment clubs (1.5 percent), and commercial ventures (1.1 percent).

For the third section of our research instrument, we asked congregations to describe in detail up to five of their social programs. We received information regarding 4,287 different programs. That is, on average, each studied congregation reported 3.08 programs. One set of questions in this research instrument was about the population served.

To determine who benefits from congregation programs, we collected data on eight groups of potential beneficiaries. We also took into consideration the fact that a program could serve more than one group, as in the case of a program for young children that also served their older siblings or parents. As Table 5.2 indicates, the major beneficiaries of congregational services and programs are needy children and youth, as well as the community at large. The community-at-large category covers educational, communal, advocacy, and reconciliation programs that do not focus on one specific group, such as "voter registration," "interfaith collaboration" or "neighborhood cleanups." It is a catchall category that implies that a large number of people directly or indirectly may benefit from the program.

Health Services

While congregations are not the natural settings for health care and most often are not equipped with the technical know-how required for health care delivery, there is an ongoing call for utilizing them to reach underserved populations (Sanders 1997; Sutherland, Hale, and Harris 1998). In addition to the traditional parish-nurse that was common in Catholic churches, congregation-based outreach groups are currently providing health education, health screening, and health care. While little is known on the effectiveness of these health programs, DeHaven et al. (2004: 1030) reported, based on a meta-analysis of health care services provided by congregations, that "significant effects reported included reductions in cholesterol and blood pressure levels, weight, and disease symptoms and increases in the use of mammography and breast self-examination."

In *The Invisible Caring Hand* we provided one such example from Germantown, Philadelphia. New Covenant Church of Philadelphia developed a program called Health Team Ministry. The team delivers basic medical assistance, educates the congregation about health/safety issues, and promotes wellness. Their newsletter features brief articles, written in layperson's terms, concerning the use of over-the-counter medications, domestic violence, quitting smoking, and the connection between religion and health care. New Covenant Church became involved in this ministry because many congregants work in the health profession and were willing to use their skills and knowledge to assist members and others in the community. The health care team provides services that complement formal health services, as well as services not available from formal health care providers. In order to be successful and trusted, they use the "African American culture" to communicate with local residents in their own language. In this chapter, we are not focusing on specific case examples, but are interested in assessing the overall involvement of the city's congregations in providing health services.

In our inventory of programs, we included thirty-five different health programs that congregations could provide or host on their property. Almost four in five congregations (79.5 percent) are involved in at least one health service program. As expected, the most commonly reported program was hospital visitation (53.1 percent). Similarly, visiting the sick that are homebound was reported by 15.2 percent of the congregations. This long-held congregational tradition of visiting members, neighbors, and relatives of members who are hospitalized or sick is alive and well in more than half the congregations. If we omitted these programs (hospital visitation and visiting the sick/homebound) from the above analysis, still about two-thirds of the city congregations (65.8 percent) are involved in at least one health program.

Health education is an important area in which congregations are often involved. Given that about half the city's population attends congregations on a regular basis, bringing a health message to the congregation is an efficient means of disseminating knowledge. A variety of specific health education programs were offered by 13.4 percent of the congregations. In addition, drug and alcohol prevention programs were offered by one in ten congregations (10.8 percent), followed closely by sex education (9.4 percent) and nutrition programs (8.8 percent). Fewer offered programs related to quitting smoking (2.3 percent) and maternity (2.1 percent). In addition, 3.5 percent of the congregations reported to offer organ donation education programs. In all, about half the congregations (45.5 percent) reported at least one health education program in the year prior to the interview. It should be noted that some of these programs are ongoing while others are held one weekend a year. However, in all cases these programs reach many people that otherwise are less informed about health.

Direct health services were also common among Philadelphia congregations. One in ten of the congregations were involved in health screening (10.7 percent), most commonly in collaboration with another organization, and in a few cases jointly with other congregations. The traditional parish/regional nurse program was offered by 5.8 percent of the congregations. Wellness programs for adults (4.0 percent) and for babies (2.6 percent) were among the popular ongoing programs offered by congregations. Immunizationwas offered in the previous year by 3.1 percent often as part of the health screening or health education programs. Two direct health programs that were quite popular were diet workshops (5.4 percent) and medical care for people with HIV/AIDS (5.8 percent). Given that AIDS is often associated with gay sex, drug and alcohol abuse, and promiscuous sex, all of which stand against most religious teachings, it is significant that congregations are among the most caring community institutions helping people with this disease. Very few congregations provide full medical or dental services on their premises (1.7 percent each).

Twelve-step support groups traditionally most commonly meet on congregation property. Alcoholics Anonymous (AA) groups were the most commonly reported (11.2 percent), followed by Narcotics Anonymous (NA) (7.7 percent). Al-Anon (spouses and relatives of alcoholics) was reported by 2.4 percent and Alateen (children of alcoholics) by 1.0 percent. Overeaters Anonymous (OA) groups were reported by 1.1 percent and Sex and Love Addicts Anonymous (SLAA) by 1.2 percent. Although we did not include it as a category, nine congregations mentioned Gamblers Anonymous (GA). We have no way to assess how many congregations really host GA groups. In all, one in five congregations (20.6 percent) reported to be engaged in hosting at least one group for people with addictions. Some congregations also offer support groups for congregants or their relatives who suffer from certain diseases. Most frequent is cancer education and support (3.2 percent), followed by Alz heimer's education and support (2.2 percent), and sickle cell anemia education and support (1.8 percent).

In addition to these three groups of programs (health education, direct health services, and support groups), congregations were involved in a few other health-related programs. For example, in the year prior to the study, 8.7 percent of the congregations hosted a blood drive that benefited the region as a whole. Some special populations were assisted by the congregations, such as people in hospice programs (1.6 percent of congregations), with developmental disabilities (2.9 percent), with physical disabilities (3.5 percent), or with mental illness (1.0 percent). Finally, a few congregations were engaged in helping to provide or cam paign for health insurance programs (2.7 percent).

The overall picture is that, in a country where health insurance is often obtained via employment and therefore is something many Americans do not have (or if they do have it, they are only partially covered), congregations offer assistance. Given the complexity and cost involved, congregations can help only marginally. Still, as reported above, their involvement in the health field is quite wide. They cannot and should not serve as hospitals or health clinics, although a few attempt to do so at least one day per week. Their massive involvement, modest as it is, is an indication of the moral bankruptcy of a society that allows so many people, including children, to go uninsured, and the vulnerability of many minority groups when it comes to health education and preven- tion.

Arts and Culture Services

The relationship between the arts and culture and organized religion is viewed largely in terms of two extremes: religion as the bedrock of the arts or as its censor and inhibitor. On the one hand, the church is cred- ited for sustaining and enhancing the arts. Places of worship have histor- ically financed and encouraged the production and consumption of art and culture. In fact, a lot of our cultural capital manifested in music, painting, sculpture, architecture, poetry, and literature has been spon- sored, produced, and consumed through religious institutions. From the paintings of Michelangelo and Giotto to the music of Bach, from the preservation of old manuscripts to the evolution of modern philosophy, we owe the classical masterpieces and the preservation of the arts to organized religion. The Church noticed the power of the arts and harn- essed it to advance religious education, while sponsoring artists, yet it was also viewed as the censor and most vocal critic of arts and culture.

Various religious groups use art and culture in innovative ways to attract new members. Further, Wuthnow (2003: 46) noted, "the presence of musical and artistic programs in congregations is probably beneficial for the spiritual development of church members." Throughout history, the church has attempted to dictate public taste and define morality through control over the arts and culture. Books were censored and banned. Certain musical pieces were forbidden and nude paintings were dressed.

Various religious groups have used art and culture to attract new believers. Yet, religious opposition to exhibits of works by Robert Mapplethorpe or the fiasco of the Brooklyn Museum are just a couple of examples of recent interactions between organized religion and the arts (Cherbo and Wyszomirski 2001). As such, organized religion and the arts and culture in recent times are often seen as having an antagonistic relationship.

However, we contend that the relationship between organized religion and the arts and culture in the United States today is much more complex and rich than these two polar approaches would suggest. It is our view that organized religion in the United States is, to a large extent, the bedrock of arts education and arts appreciation. The cultural capital of many Americans originates in places of worship and is sustained by their tangible and intangible support. Many Americans are first exposed to music, poetry, theater, painting, and sculpture as part of their participation in local religious congregations and through educational programs that take place in these congregations. For example, the annual holiday choir singing that takes place in most churches and synagogues around December of every year involves learning and performing music, which enhances performing arts more than all secular events combined. In December 2005, the Houston Symphony performed at Lakewood Church in Houston in front of 11,000 people. With the exception of an outdoor concert on July 4, this is the largest audience the symphony had reached, and many in the audience got their first symphony experience (Ward 2005).

Wuthnow (1999, 2003) found that 41 percent of Americans reported that they had sung in a choir or assembly at a church while young. Many of America's leading singers, performers, and artists had their first appearances and art education in congregational settings. Furthermore, congregational choirs and music bands often require that their participants read music, be introduced to classical texts, and collaborate with others to produce a quality performance. In this respect both liberal and conservative congregations use music, choirs, and other forms of art to transmit the religious message. From traditional organ playing to electronic guitars, from a cappella choirs to rock bands, from sacred text

TABLE 5.3. TYPES OF ARTS AND CULTURE PROGRAMS OFFERED BY RELIGIOUS CONGREGATIONS IN PHILADELPHIA

Type of program	Percent of congregations providing service	Estimated number of congregations
Musical performances	27.6	585
Choral groups	21.3	452
Music classes	13.1	278
Artistic dance classes	10.2	216
Lecture series	10.1	214
Community theater	9.2	195
Art classes	7.7	163
Film series	6.5	138
Art exhibits	6.5	138
Radio or TV station	6.5	136
Book clubs	6.0	127
Architectural and historical tours	5.8	123
Poetry readings	5.0	106
Neighborhood tours	3.3	70
Artist-in-residence	2.4	51

reading to theater productions, congregations are constantly experimenting and testing artistic means to reach their members and maybe even those who are currently unaffiliated.

In the PCC, we focused on the nonreligious arts and culture programs offered by local religious congregations. Again, the choir can participate in every worship service and yet the service may not be counted in our study as a social program. If, however, the choir also performs in the community, then we listed it as a social program. We therefore reported far less arts and culture events and programs, since many of them were solely religious and were therefore excluded from the PCC. For example, Dudley and Roozen (2001) found that over 80 percent of the congregations have piano or organ music at weekend worship services. This is in addition to the fact that most congregations engage members in singing as part of their devotion. However, the singing of members also penetrates into all other aspects of music consumption, appreciation, and production outside the church (Chaves 2004).

As shown in Table 5.3, we asked about 15 arts and culture services that congregations may provide their members and neighbors. In the right column, we provide an estimate of the number of Philadelphia congregations that are likely to provide each of these services. For example, given that in our sample 10.2 percent of congregations reported providing artistic dance classes, this means that 216 of the city's 2,120 congregations are likely to offer this program.

Clearly the two most common arts and cultural activities are musical performances and choral groups. While most readers will immediately imagine the typical church choir singing and delighting people around Easter and Christmas, our sample has cases in which the musical performance was given by an outside band or troop using the congregation's hall. For example, Tabernacle United Church on the corner of Thirty-Seventh and Chestnut Streets leased part of its building to the University of Pennsylvania. The university developed the space as the Irongate Theater, which is used by student groups and outside performers.

Congregations are also cultural hubs where young people learn dance, music, and arts and where adults hold reading meetings, book clubs, and lectures. Given that such a large segment of the local population frequently participate, such cultural activities are well advertised. People also know that other "consumers" of these activities will most likely be those from churches and neighborhoods (in other words, those considered safe circles), and therefore will most likely participate.

Just as telling are the programs listed in the "other" category, that is, programs mentioned by the interviewees in addition to those from the prearranged list. Some examples will show how congregations select specific arts and culture programs that are tailored to the needs of their members and community. The following are examples: Black History Month programs (mentioned by more than 10 congregations); black history book fair, art camp for children, bookstore, and book sale (mentioned by 8 congregations); library, including being a site for the free library (mentioned by some 20 congregations); outings to the zoo, trips to New York City to attend shows, drama classes (mentioned by 6 congregations); mural painting (mentioned by 3 congregations); martial arts classes (mentioned by 4 congregations); mime or puppet groups (mentioned by 3 congregations); quilt club, and classes teaching the language or the culture of the homeland of congregational members (mentioned by some 30 congregations).

Social Action Services

The third set of services to be discussed in this chapter is generally known as social action. Included are advocacy, economic and community development, lobbying, and political mobilization. These services move from helping alleviate human misery to changing the conditions that bring about the misery. The logic behind congregations as social change agents is rooted in the fundamental purpose for a civil society (Skocpol, 2000). Berger and Neuhaus (1977) were the first to seek out and identify the importance of mediating voluntary associations that could serve independently of the state and be composed of citizens who are interested in protecting their shared interests vis-à-vis the power of the state. These organizations are the foundation of any civil society, necessary for a democracy and the basis for the formation of social capital (Coleman 1990). These associations, although not affiliated with the government, perform many essential societal tasks. There are hardly any other community organizations as well spread out or as well represented as those provided by religious congregations. Indeed, as Smidt (2003) demonstrated, congregations serve in this capacity throughout America (Cnaan, Boddie, and Yancey 2005).

Local religious congregations are vital as organizational networks and community resources. The estimated 350,000 local religious congregations reach about half the American population on an ongoing basis and, as indicated in the previous chapter, are a source of social and community care and concern. Furthermore, as we showed in Chapter 2, congregations are the most widespread community organization. If used effectively, they can bring about change in communities and influence governmental policies. Although some people may see religious groups as oppressive and conservative, many progressive campaigns for social change—from the civil rights movement to liberation theology—originated, in fact, within religious groups (Cnaan, Wineburg, and Boddie 1999). Furthermore, as Kretzman and McKnight (1993) have recognized, congregations have an abundance of resources that can be unleashed in creative ways to improve community relationships and conditions. Congregations command a wealth of resources, including people, space and facilities, materials and equipment, expertise, economic power, relationships, values, and political influence, and they can pool their resources and energies with those of other organizations to meet a variety of community needs (Wineburg, Ahmed, and Sills 1997). Finally, congregations are known to be a potential source of political influence and power, as was demonstrated by Saul Alinsky (1972), who successfully rallied congregations to influence policy making in the Chicago area.

The most frequently noted examples of faith-based community organizing efforts are those by coalitions of urban congregations and community organizations, and by faith-based groups alone. Some such coalitions are formed under the auspices of four national federations—the Industrial Areas Foundation (IAF), the Pacific Institute for Community Organization (PICO), Direct Action and Research Training Centers (DARTC), and Gamaliel. More common, and as outlined in Chapters 10 and 11, are local initiatives of congregations and at times other groups, which form coalitions that in turn influence local policies and practices (Pipes and Ebaugh 2002). Community Development Corporations (CDCs) are considered one of the most effective tools to help people in impoverished and underserved communities participate in the political and economic affairs of their neighborhoods (Harris 1994). Congregations can also get involved in local campaigns to change immigration policies and relationships between ethnic groups, advocate for social justice, and so on.

Cheever (2001) noted in her study of three cities (Chicago, Denver, and San Francisco) that congregations were rarely involved in issues of fair housing or civil rights. Her study joins a long series of studies that suggest that local religious congregations do not find major advocacy campaigns and political struggles to be appealing. In fact, in our interviews, clergy noted that issues such as campaigning for fair housing practices were done by their denominational headquarters and, if needed, they supported these campaigns financially or by letter writing (Ammerman 2005). However, the level of frustration inherent in such activities made it an unpopular topic in congregations, with members preferring to focus on more gratifying and unifying activities. The problem in carrying out social action programs is that they require members to agree politically, be committed to a common vision of change, and work hard before any small and gratifying success is noticeable. Unlike feeding the poor, where the effort is well defined and satisfaction is often immediate, helping in social action is time consuming and often frustrating. Furthermore, in theological terms, many congregations assert that they should not intervene in the political and social structures of society but rather ameliorate the life conditions of the truly needy. Thus, it has been long assumed that congregations are not fast to assume a major role in social action efforts. In the PCC we included quite a few programs, listed in Table 5.4, which can be incorporated under the label "social action." Again, as above, in the right column, we provide an estimate of the number of Philadelphia congregations that are likely to provide each of these services.

The findings support the notion that congregations are much more oriented toward social services provision than toward social change. When one looks at the previous two areas of service (health and arts services), as compared with Table 5.4 (social action), it is clear that the emphasis in Philadelphia congregations is on services rather than changing the causes that created the need for the services. While many congregations (17.5 percent) are involved in their local neighborhood associations and even host them, very few champion causes that used to be major for congregations in the past, such as affirmative action, social justice, welfare rights, environmental action, racism, and peace.

When we asked the interviewees to disclose other areas of social action that were not on our list, some interesting findings emerged. About ten congregations reported that they were engaged in an organized cam-

TABLE 5.4. TYPES OF SOCIAL ACTION PROGRAMS OFFERED BY RELIGIOUS
CONGREGATIONS IN PHILADELPHIA

Type of program	Percent of congregations that provide service	Estimated number of congregations
Neighborhood credit union	2.1	45
Affirmative action	2.2	47
Environmental action	2.8	59
Organize against drug trafficking	3.7	78
Community policing	3.8	81
Civil rights	4.2	89
Suburban-city collaboration	4.5	95
Recruitment of new businesses	4.6	98
Poverty/welfare rights advocacy	5.1	108
Peace	5.9	125
Racism and race reconciliation	6.0	127
Social justice	6.3	134
Interfaith relations	8.9	189
Women's issues	10.8	227
Interfaith collaboration	11.1	235
Voter registration	12.9	273
Neighborhood associations	17.5	371

paign against capital punishment. As noted in the following chapter, many congregations reported that they host polling stations on Election Day and thus enhance, albeit passively, voter registration and political involvement. In fact, voter registration was one of the most frequently cited activities by Philadelphia congregations (12.9 percent), second only to participation in neighborhood associations (17.5 percent).

Although most of our interviews took place before September 2001, four congregations reported protesting the war against Iraq. The following social action activities were each reported by at least one congregation: protest against closing the free library, support for prayers in public schools, support for the National Organization on Disability, support for Promise Keepers, pro-Israel rally, campaign for gun registry, support for transgendered people, campaign against police brutality, and community education against spousal abuse. These issues are very important but also demonstrate the many areas that congregations can undertake to change the wider environment, and the small number of congregations choosing to address these issues.

Matovina (2001) reported a case in Minneapolis where a frustrated Roman Catholic Latino priest organized parishioners to demand police and city help with combating gang violence. A well-managed media campaign along with the parishioners' support brought about the desired change. This priest, encouraged by the success of this campaign, started additional projects, including leadership training for members and a million-dollar, active CDC. While this case is not a typical one, it suggests that persistent leadership and a taste of success are essential ingredients in the quest for larger-scale social change. This success story overshadows the numerous failings unreported by clergy who tried and gave up. This is clearly an area in which our knowledge is too limited and further studying and program development are required.

Poverty-Oriented Services

A large body of the literature on congregational social services assumes that congregations are too weak financially and administratively to care for the poor (Chaves 1999). This claim, however, does not correspond well to the findings from the PCC. In fact, as this chapter and the whole book suggest, congregations are a major support for poor people in the community.

As noted in Table 2.1 above, 84.3 percent of the interviewees reported that poverty is a major social problem in the vicinity of the congregational property. As such it is not surprising that we also found that 34.7 percent of the reported congregational programs deal with poor people and their needs. As seen in Table 5.2, only programs for children and youth were reported to be more popular. As discussed below, we studied the replacement value of congregational social services. While the methods used are outlined below, it is important to note that the average replacement value of a typical congregational program was $3,271.56 (see Table 5.5). The average replacement value of a program serving poor people was somewhat higher, $3,772.56. As such, almost a third of congregational programs are directed toward poor people and, on average, each such program has a replacement value of 115 percent when compared with all other programs. Given that many programs for poor people are not earmarked for members and that they are often not too popular, it is amazing how much care congregations provide to poor people.

Many programs were directed toward poor people alone. Some of these programs were already reported. For example, "poverty/welfare rights advocacy" was carried out by 5.1 percent of the congregations. In Table 5.1, we provide data on the frequency of programs earmarked specifically for poor people. As seen there, food pantries were reported to be the most common social service program offered by congregations (37.4 percent).

Given the many programs directed toward poor people, their replacement value, and the lack of other such programs in the community, it is

TABLE 5.5. MONTHLY REPLACEMENT VALUE OF AN AVERAGE PROGRAM AND
CONGREGATIONAL SOCIAL AND COMMUNITY PROGRAMS IN PHILADELPHIA
($n = 4,287$)

Source	Percent of congregations reporting cost	Average cost per program ($)	Average cost per congregation ($)
Financial support by congregation	59.5	417.86 s.d. = 970.99	1,287.01
Value of in-kind support	67.0	167.22 s.d. = 493.7	515.04
Value of utilities for programs	64.8	166.73 s.d. = 446.4	513.53
Estimated value of space used for programs	75.5	613.33 s.d. = 1057.7	1,889.06
Clergy hours ($20.00 per hour)	69.9	258.40 s.d. = 32.2	795.87
Staff hours ($10.00 per hour)	34.8	187.93 s.d. = 54.6	578.82
Volunteer hours ($17.19 per hour)	83.9	1,517.88 s.d. = 2341.8	4,675.00
Total		3,329.35	10,254.40
Income to congregation	6.3	57.79 s.d. = 144.9	177.99
Total net replacement value		3,271.56	10,076.61

ªSince the congregations studied provide on average 3.08 programs each, we multiplied
3.08 programs by the "average cost per program" to estimate the "average cost per
congregation."

easy to assess that congregations are the local "safety net" of the American social welfare system. One can only imagine what the quality of life of poor people in Philadelphia would be like if congregations and their myriad programs did not exist.

Collaboration for Social Services Delivery

One claim that is often levied against local religious congregations is that they are isolated and unaware of each other's existence or services (Farnsley 2003). As shown in Chapter 2, many congregations are very segregated in nature. Thus, it may be reasonable to assume that indeed they are acting in isolation, without contact with others in their surroundings. This is even more possible when congregants commute to their places of worship and therefore do not necessarily interact much with others who attend neighboring congregations. The reality, however, is significantly different.

As reported in Chapter 3, almost all congregations (1,192, or 85.6 percent) informed us that they hold worship or prayer services in collaboration with other religious groups. A large percentage of congregations collaborated with other faith-based organizations to develop and deliver community service programs (870, 62.5 percent). Somewhat surprisingly, more than half the congregations (781, 56.1 percent) reported collaborating with secular organizations for the purpose of delivering a service or running a program. The collaborating organizations may be government agencies, local universities, neighborhood associations, or community organizations. The purposes of the collaborations often include sharing space, financial resources, or staff and supplies. Interestingly, congregations often elect to worship with others, but also willingly cooperate to help people in need. In other words, the congregations in Philadelphia have an extensive network of religious and social contacts with others, and do not act as islands in the neighborhood. In fact, like congregations everywhere in the United States, they have an active part in the tapestry of community life wherever they are located (Ammerman 2005).

When it comes to the 4,287 reported programs, the majority (83.1 percent) were carried out by the congregations alone. However, it should be noted that congregations with more than five programs tended to report their own programs before reporting those carried out in collaboration with others. Among the 742 programs carried out in collaboration with others, about half (50.7 percent) were carried out jointly with other congregations, and less than a third with the denominational body (31.1 percent). Collaboration with non-faith-based groups was also common. The remaining statistics state that about two-fifths work with human service organizations (39.2 percent), a third with nonprofit organizations (33.6 percent), less than a third with local community groups (29.8 percent), a quarter with a government unit (26.1 percent), and a smaller number with a local university or a college (14.2 percent). It should be emphasized that, in many cases, collaboration involved more than one partner and hence the sum of the reported percentages exceeds one hundred.

In the section of the research instrument in which 215 programs were presented to the interviewees, we included an option to choose a description of a congregation that does not carry out the program or house it but instead helps another organization carry out the program. These are programs not owned by the congregation or carried out on their premises but belonging to others. Congregations often play second fiddle to other organizations in providing cash support or volunteers but do not claim ownership of these programs. Such support has been most common in cases of helping the homeless, and in social action and advocacy. Regarding services for the homeless, the following were reported:

homeless shelter for men (12.9 percent), food pantry (12.7 percent), homeless shelter for women (12.3 percent), job counseling and placement (11.5 percent), soup kitchen (11.1 percent), day missions for the homeless (8.3 percent), and transitional living programs (7.3 percent). Regarding social action, the following were reported: interfaith relations (11.0 percent), racism and race reconciliation (9.6 percent), and social justice (9.3 percent). In addition, international relief (19.0 percent) and marriage encounters (8.2 percent) were also causes that congregations often supported. In all these instances, congregations used their fiscal and human resources to support social programs offered by other larger organizations, including their denominations. Supporting others is another form of organizational connectedness that congregations often embrace and that receives little attention in the academic literature. In order to be able to support an external organization, the congregation must become familiar with the organization and its activities. This type of organizational tie may be labeled a "loose organizational tie" (Wuthnow 1998).

The picture emerging from this analysis is that congregations prefer to provide social services on their own. This makes sense, as the services are a mission of the congregation and a means to bond members around the congregations. However, congregations are also well connected to other congregations and secular organizations in their vicinity, informally connecting and collaborating with such outside groups. More than half the congregations from the PCC are engaged in social care provision with secular organizations, and about two-thirds collaborate with faith-based organizations. Thus, congregations often provide services on their own terms, but they also work with others.

Charitable Choice Utilization

The interviews for the PCC took place from mid-1998 to 2002. At that time, Charitable Choice was in its early stages of implementation and being part of the public discourse. Of the 1,392 congregations we surveyed, 114 (8.2 percent) reported being familiar with Charitable Choice and 109 congregations (7.8 percent) were somewhat familiar. Put differently, 84 percent were not familiar with Charitable Choice.

Thirty-one congregations (2.2 percent) reported holding discussions about whether to apply for grants under its terms, and only two reported having formed a committee or group to draft a grant or contract proposal. However, 50 congregations (3.6 percent) reported that a congregational representative attended a session in which Charitable Choice was explained.

Only 18 congregations (1.3 percent) applied to public sources under the auspices of Charitable Choice. It should be noted that we interviewed during the years in which Charitable Choice was vaguely understood and very few took advantage of it. Eleven of these applicants received funds ranging from $1,500 to $600,000 to provide services such as welfare to work and learning centers. To our knowledge, as of September 2000, only one congregation in Philadelphia and probably in the Commonwealth of Pennsylvania had applied for and received a government grant or contract under the Charitable Choice provision. This congregation, Cookman United Methodist Church in North Philadelphia, provides services for welfare to work transition. All other congregations applied through a faith-based nonprofit organization that is under the auspices of the congregation.

Still, we explained Charitable Choice in our interviews and asked the following question: "If not actively involved with Charitable Choice, would your congregation consider applying for government funds under the provisions of Charitable Choice?" Some 860 congregations (61.8 percent) answered in the affirmative. The implication is that almost two-thirds of the congregations view collaboration with public authority as an option. Among those that answered no, some reported theological reasons. For example, one clergyman explained his refusal by stating, "I will not be able to speak about the Bible." Others refused to consider collaborating with the public sector because of reported negative experiences with government agencies. Yet others are too small and cannot see themselves applying for public money and dealing with the bureaucratic demands that come with such collaboration.

Replacement Value of Congregational Social Care

At this stage, we have documented that congregations are prime contributors to the quality of life for many people in Philadelphia. What is less clear is how valuable this contribution is. It is often difficult to assess the value of public goods that are not traded or purchasable. However, we attempted to find the dollar value of congregational programs in Philadelphia. Often, when economists are faced with the issue of valuation of a public good, they look for an alternative mode of assessment. The one that we have chosen to use is a method called "replacement value." The imputed economic value, that is the replacement value, is used to establish a measure of the congregational contribution to the quality of life of people in Philadelphia, based on the monetary cost of replacing these programs with noncongregational entities. Put simply, replacement value assesses the cost of producing the same public goods produced by local religious congregations in Philadelphia. In this instance, by replacement value, we do not mean the dollar amount it costs for a congregation to run their programs. After all, congregations utilize many available resources such as their property, staff, and recruited volunteers. All this may seem cost-free, but when another, noncongregational organization offers the same service, it must pay for rental space and for salaries for managers and wages for workers. What we therefore mean by replacement value is the amount it would cost others to provide the same services or programs at the level stipulated, if they did not have the congregational property and member volunteers at hand. To illustrate, if a congregation pays a mortgage for a building in which a social program is held, the value of the space is a congregational contribution, which in real terms, has a cost and a financial value. Similarly, if a clergy member invests time in a social program, his or her salary should be recognized as money paid by the congregation, which then allows him or her to spend time providing community-oriented services.

In the PCC, we used seven components that, combined, accounted for the replacement value of congregational services. For each of the 4,287 programs that were reported by the 1,392 congregations in Philadelphia, we asked for seven items of value: (1) the financial support from the congregation (often an actual budget item in the congregation's budget); (2) the value of in-kind support, such as transportation, food, clothing, printing, telephone costs, and postage; (3) the value of utilities, such as heating, cooling, electricity, and cleaning, for programs held on the congregation's property; (4) the estimated cost of renting equivalent space from a commercial vendor for programs held on the congregation's property; (5) the number of clergy hours; (6) the number of staff hours of program directors, secretaries, and other congregation employees; and (7) the number of volunteer hours.

We determined the estimated cost per month for each program (monthly because, based on our previous studies, it was proven the most convenient basis for analysis). When respondents were unable to provide an assessment of program costs, we assigned the value of zero cost. To determine the value of the time spent in providing these programs, we multiplied the number of clergy hours by $20 and the number of staff hours by $10. To determine the value of volunteer hours, we used the standard of $17.19 per hour established by the Independent Sector (2003).[1]

There are many reasons to believe that the estimates obtained using this method are very conservative. First, the number of programs per congregation was limited to five. In order to make the study feasible, we asked the interviews to report a maximum of five programs while many congregations had between six and seventy-two programs; hence, congregations with more than five programs were not fully represented in this report and the value of space, personnel, utilities, and so on of these programs were omitted. Second, informal services performed by congregations, such as one-time rent assistance or ad hoc counseling (see Chapter 4), were not factored into the estimates of congregational programs' replacement values. Third, clergy volunteer hours spent with other community-serving organizations were not counted. Many clergy who are paid at full salary by a congregation also volunteer in hospitals, schools, police departments, community groups, and sit on civic boards, all at the expense of the congregation. Fourth, the externalities of urban churchgoing and community-serving ministries have been linked to lower rates of deviant behavior, higher rates of healthy behavior, lower rates of young male unemployment, and lowered chances for incarceration. Fifth, we truncated the reported values to avoid the inclusion of what may have been outliers, even in cases where the congregation insisted that the numbers were reliable and accurate.[2] Sixth, when any interviewee had difficulties assessing values of service, we assigned the value of zero to that category and as such undervalued the real replacement value. For example, if the interviewee could not assess the market value of renting an equivalent space and declined to answer, even if we assumed the cost to be over $500, we assigned it the value of zero. Finally, this calculation did not count the many spin-off services that started as congregational programs and grew into major social services that serve the city.

As can be seen in Table 5.5, the majority of the replacement value comes from volunteer work and the estimated value of space used for the program. Third in importance, and at about one-eighth of the overall cost, is the actual financial funding of the social programs by their respective congregations. Put differently, for every dollar spent in cash, the congregation provides four dollars in non-cash contributions.

The estimate of $10,076.61 (see Table 5.5) for a monthly replacement value by an average congregation is provided. In order to assess a congregation's replacement value annually, we have to multiply this by 12 months, which amounts to $120,919.32. Again it should be remembered that only about one-fifth of this sum is provided in cash and that the distribution of resources between congregations is vast. In other words, many congregations give modestly while a few give most generously. Now, in order to assess the overall replacement value of the social care provided by congregations in Philadelphia, we have to multiply the latter estimate of an annual contribution by a congregation ($120,919.32) by the number of congregations in the city, including those we did not interview (total = 2,120), and the sum is $256,348,958.40. Put simply, the overall replacement value of the social care provided by congregations in Philadelphia is estimated at a quarter of a billion dollars.

Percentage Allocated to Social Care

Finally, we asked, "What percentage of the annual operating budget is earmarked for social services?" as opposed to operation costs or member development. Of the congregations that answered this question, the mean was 22.7 percent. That is, a little over one-fifth of the congregations' annual budget (excluding capital campaigns and schools) is designated to contribute to the quality of life of people in the community and in the city beyond the cost of maintaining the congregation property and staff.

Summary

The first finding of this chapter is that 92.7 percent of the city congregations are engaged in at least one form of social services delivery, be it very modest or most comprehensive. Furthermore, on average, a Philadelphia congregation is involved in the provision of 3.08 different programs. While the diversity of congregations from the PCC is considerable, this finding stands in contradiction to the findings reported by Mark Chaves from the NCS, but it is in line with every other study of congregations undertaken in the United States. We also learned that those congregations not engaged in social service delivery are often very new, of first generation immigrants, and of very limited means and membership. In other words, as soon as congregations are capable of allocating surplus resources, they start engaging in providing some sort of social and community care.

It is our contention that congregations cannot and should not replace the government as social services providers. Yet they feel responsible for such services and consistently attempt to help and improve the quality of life of needy people among their members and the community at large. In fact, helping the needy rather than trying to transform the social system is a well-ingrained collective norm in American congregational life (Ammerman 2005; Cnaan, Boddie, and Yancey 2005). Clergy are exposed to it in their seminaries, members expect it as part of their service, and needy people know to look for help from their neighboring congregations. When one views all the many services detailed in this chapter for one American city, it is easy to see that many human needs are met through congregations. The problem is that any needy person will have to navigate among the many congregations to find the service that meets his or her specific needs.

Why do congregations get involved in social services provision? It is evident to all who are engaged in congregational care that the motivation is not to recruit new members or convert lost souls into the "proper" faith. At best, sectarian social services can open a crack into a potential client's spiritual journey. Giving food, clothing, after-school program care, or a room to meet in does not transform people from atheism to belief. It is the spirit from within the members that sustains and nourishes the spirit of others. The energy that is produced by doing good with co-religionists is the organizational benefit to the congregation. The congregation further attracts members' commitment and they focus inward to strengthen the collective as a result of their involvement in producing social goods. It is not surprising that Dudley and Roozen (2001) found that 90 percent of the social-serving congregations in their study reported enhanced vitality within their group, as compared with only 46 percent of the non-serving congregations. In other words, rather than saving the souls of the clients by forming social programs, congregations are strengthening their members' religious resolve. This is a win-win situation, where needy people are served and the serving organizations are benefiting. It is this dynamic that can explain the impressive myriad of social services reported in this chapter and the other chapters dealing with social care by congregations.

It is assumed that local religious congregations operate as closed systems deaf to the world around them. Our findings do not support this statement. We found congregations to be well connected to other congregations and secular organizations in their vicinity and to be informally coordinating services. They collaborate and support causes and programs of many groups, and a large number of them are even represented in their respective neighborhood association. Some feel that they are threatened by their surroundings, and hence collaborate only with trusted others. But very few reported to be uninterested in their environment. Clearly congregations can be more engaged in the community and better informed about their neighborhoods, but the assumption that they are isolated from their surroundings is a myth. More than half the congregations from the PCC are engaged in social care provision with secular organizations and about two-thirds work with faith-based organizations.

The replacement value, which is estimated at a quarter of a billion dollars, is just one way to express the immense contribution of the local religious congregations to the quality of life in Philadelphia. Clearly, the city and the state do more than the congregations to help those in need and to enhance the quality of life of residents. The difference is that it is not part of the congregations' mandate to help the needy. No one even really called upon the congregations to move into the domain of welfare, with the exception of their theological stances. They found the way of helping others by themselves, recognizing the many social needs and developing responses. The city and state are obliged to help those in need as part of their civic mandate, but as they have withdrawn, congregations have taken on much of the responsibility. Crowding out in this case involved public sector retrenchment and religious sector expansion. No other Philadelphian voluntary group at the local level has harnessed as many resources and developed as many social services as has the group of local religious congregations.

The service is not necessarily better because it is offered by a faith-based congregation (Voorhees et al. 1996). When a homeless person comes for a hot meal at a soup kitchen, is the food better or more enlightening because it is offered by a congregation rather than by a secular organization? From the point of view of considering the food and its nutritious value, there should be no difference. After all, one comes to such a meal to satisfy hunger. The findings in this chapter only state that congregations, alongside public and other voluntary groups, are very active in meeting human needs. As for efficacy and added advantage of the religious context for services, the verdict is still out.

Chapter 6
Using Space for Good Use

The Landscape

One of the assets congregations can offer their neighbors and cities is building space. As discussed in Chapter 1, most congregations own a building in which they meet to hold their worship functions. Congregations usually aspire to build a place of worship and enlarge it in order to accommodate more people and be noticeable in the community. Often the pride of a faith group is embodied in the edifice it possesses and maintains (Ammerman 1997b). People have been building impressive places of worship since the early days of organized religion. Cathedrals in Europe, grand mosques in the Middle East, Inca and earlier temples in South America, and Hindu and Jain temples in India are all examples of organized religion's pride in its architectural constructions. While pride in the buildings is evident, what is often overlooked is that groups that invest in communal edifices tend to stay within the community and invest in the community's welfare and vitality. The more a religious community invests in its surrounding community, the more it is anchored in it.

Communities in the United States are no exception. Throughout the United States one sees religious structures that are highly visible and demonstrate members' investment, care, and pride. The building of the congregation is not merely a place for meeting, but a symbol of the commitment and strength of the collective faith. Often, when a faith group builds a large and impressive place of worship, other faith groups refuse to be outdone and build even larger edifices to demonstrate their commitment to their faith and, by extension, the strength of their faith tradition.

The urban traveler cannot help but notice the many religious structures with a big cross, Star of David, or minaret on top, showing that they are places of worship. Hindu and Sikh groups in the United States erect large edifices for their temples or gurdwaras that dominate the landscape and demonstrate their presence. But these are examples of only a few types of sacred places. Driving slowly in almost any neighborhood in

America, one can observe the small signs that declare the existence of a faith community. These signs, some worn out by sun and rain, indicate the existence of a place of worship, announce the pastor's name, and invite people to attend worship services at designated times.

Philadelphia is a city of about 133 square miles. This figure includes Fairmount Park, train stations, malls, historic sites, more than twenty universities, and two airports, so the inhabited area is considerably smaller than the total area. The PCC study found 2,120 congregations in the city, so even if we take the high figure of 133 square miles, we can estimate about sixteen congregations per square mile (2,120/133 = 15.94). There is no other social organization as ubiquitous as the local religious congregation.

Buildings can be assets and sources of joy and pride, but at the same time they can be a liability. Financially limited congregations worry about unexpected building expenses, from falling and leaking roofs to malfunctioning boilers. More affluent congregations attempt to maximize their use of their well-kept facilities. However, a large and visible building that is used only on weekends and perhaps once or twice on weekdays is an unused community resource.

In this chapter, we review the available information regarding congregational properties. We provide information on congregational control of space as well as major building problems, and show that most congregations have been in their current locations for a long time and are rarely contemplating relocation. Their facilities are symbols of stability in their neighborhoods. These edifices are central in the community and represent historical and social roles given to and taken on by congregations.

The Logic Behind a Congregational Property

Garrett Hardin, in a series of publications, lamented the "tragedy of the commons" (1968, 2003). The logic for the "tragedy of the commons" is that if anyone can bring his or her cattle to graze in the commons, it is to the advantage of each herder to have as many cattle as possible at present and ignore future consequences. When all herders maximize their utility, the land is overused until nothing grows on it and no one can bring cattle. Put simply, if a property is left for everyone to use and is not properly regulated, it is in the interest of users to abuse it at the expense of other users and bring it to ruin before others do so.

For example, Hardin noted that the first satellite photos of northern Africa showed an irregular dark patch 390 square miles in area. Ground-level investigation revealed a fenced area inside which there was plenty of grass. Outside, the ground cover had been devastated. The dark patch was privately owned land covered with grass, while open spaces (non-owned areas) were overgrazed. Hardin saw this as another example of how people who can use space freely may exploit it.

> The fenced area was private property, subdivided into five portions. Each year the owners moved their animals to a new section. Fallow periods of four years gave the pastures time to recover from the grazing. They did so because the owners had an incentive to take care of their land. But outside the ranch, no one owned the land. It was open to nomads and their herds. (Hardin 2003)

Hardin further gives examples of fishing, use of public roads, and pollution in which public accessibility to goods created misuse and abuse.

While much of Hardin's attention is given to regulation and limitation of personal freedom, he also noted that when private ownership exists, people are more concerned with preserving and maintaining the property, and properties and land are better sustained. Consider fishing. When everyone has access and rights to fish, no one has a real personal interest in making sure that fish will lay eggs, have a chance to mature, and be saved from extinction. However, in the case of a privately owned lake or river, the owner has a lot at stake and will work hard to preserve the sustainability of the fish. Similarly, community parks and schools are often collectively owned and somewhat regulated by the city. However, individuals using the park or school can abuse the property and most often (unless caught in an act of vandalism) will not have to pay for overuse or pure abuse. The repair cost falls on the city as a whole, and nonusers pay for the abuse inflicted by careless users. In such cases, graffiti and broken windows are frequent. In some instances, public regulations and enforcement of these regulations prevent overuse. But, left alone, natural resources and public properties are at high risk of abuse. This is less often the case, however, with congregational property.

Furthermore, as the "broken window" theory goes (Zimbardo 1969), where there are buildings that are not well maintained, blight may follow. Wilson and Kelling (1982: 30) aptly noted that

> if a window in a building is broken and is left unrepaired, all the rest of the windows will soon be broken. This is as true in nice neighborhoods as in run-down ones. Window-breaking does not necessarily occur on a large scale because some areas are inhabited by determined window-breakers whereas others are populated by window-lovers; rather, one unrepaired broken window is a signal that no one cares, and so breaking more windows costs nothing. (It has always been fun.)

In other words, the opposites of an owner's pride and loving care of his or her possessions are the beginnings of blight. The broken window is an invitation to incivility, disorder, and crime. As Wilson and Kelling noted, not every uncared-for building indicates the onset of blight, but it is quite possible that this may be the case. Cared-for buildings, on the other hand, are likely to slow down the process of blight. "Untended property becomes fair game for people out for fun or plunder and even for people who ordinarily would not dream of doing such things and who probably consider themselves law-abiding" (31). That is, damage to property is the outcome of property neglect and not the innate behavior of a few deviants.

The original study "Broken Windows" was carried out by psychologist Philip Zimbardo (1969) in the late 1960s. Zimbardo parked identical automobiles in similar neighborhoods in Palo Alto, California, and Bronx, New York, but removed the license plates from the Bronx vehicle and left the hood open. Within a day, the Bronx car was stripped, while the Palo Alto car went untouched for a week. After Zimbardo broke one of the windows on the Palo Alto car, vandals soon stripped it (Maguire, Foote, and Vespe 1997). In both cases, the people who took advantage of the neglected cars were respectable people and in one case even a whole family with young children. Thus, regardless of the neighborhood's socioeconomic status, when property is left in deteriorated condition, it serves as a catalyst for vandalism and theft. Zimbardo's point, and that of Wilson and Kelling, is that uncared-for properties encourage regular people to destroy them further, starting a process of abandonment and blight. The opposite occurs when public property that is used by many people in the community is well cared for and is part of the local collective pride.

Congregational properties are usually owned by the congregation. The people who use the building pay for its maintenance, and any damage to or problem with the building is the responsibility of the members. Congregational properties are well kept as long as members can afford their maintenance. These buildings are a source of pride and the users take ownership of them, a combination that accounts for the fact that an area can demonstrate a high level of blight yet have sacred properties in it that are well maintained. When a structural problem is observed in a congregation's building, members work to solve it before it worsens and costs more to fix. Often, when a similar problem appears in a public space, often no one assumes responsibility for repairs. Even schools in most American cities are not viewed by students, parents, and neighbors as "their property," but rather as the "city's structure."

Congregational Property

Not all congregations own space. A few congregations rent space for worship meetings from hotels, schools, malls, and clubs. Others share space with a host congregation or meet in private properties. This practice of not owning property was reported by 12.3 percent of the congregations in Philadelphia. Sometimes a "propertyless" congregation asks to be a guest congregation in the building of a larger, more established one (6.8 percent). This arrangement is common for start-up congregations in search of identity and space, and congregations in the aftermath of major crises such as a fire in their previous space or a congregational split. However, congregations without space are the minority. In Philadelphia, we found that four-fifths of the congregations (82.5 percent) own a building. This is a lower estimate than that reported by the U.S. Congregational Life Survey, in which 94 percent of studied congregations were said to own their properties (Bruce 2002). It is an indication that the PCC was able to attract and interview newer and smaller congregations that often go below researchers' radar. Furthermore, given their long stays in their current locations, it is not surprising that only a few congregations (9.9 percent) are paying mortgages for their properties; most are in full possession.

One unique case in this respect is the Jehovah's Witnesses. This denomination builds large, plain buildings, often of one story. In each such "kingdom hall," congregations share space, as few as three or as many as ten. Each group worships separately and holds its own programs, while sharing the building and faith tradition.

Congregations' investment in their sacred property anchors them in the community. In times when many businesses move from the city to the suburbs and from the suburbs to the global market, when arts and culture groups concentrate in city centers, and when fraternal groups are diminishing, congregational commitment to stay in the city is an important community asset. In Philadelphia, only 18.3 percent of the studied congregations reported an interest in leaving their current locations. There was a strong association between wanting to relocate and budget ($\chi^2 = 63.0$, df = 5, $p < .001$). Almost half of the congregations planning to relocate had an annual operating budget of under $50,000, as compared with only 30 percent of the rest of the congregations. In addition, congregations planning to relocate were significantly younger (average year of incorporation 1975), by some forty-five years on average, indicating that a relocating congregation is an evolving one ($t = -17.4$, $p < .001$). When we asked the congregations that are planning to relocate why they were planning to do so, the overwhelming answer was, "We need larger and better space to accommodate our growth and needs." A few answered that their current properties are in such poor condition that repair is too costly. However, the latter explanation was less frequent.

On average, a Philadelphia congregation stays in its current location

for a little under forty-seven years. This is an indication of strong continuity and perseverance on the part of these communities. In fact, congregations stay even when the neighborhood transforms. Often, when
congregations eventually leave for the suburbs or close down their edifices, they sell their property at a nominal cost to another congregation
of a different faith tradition so that the structure keeps serving the spiritual needs of the community. Driving in West Philadelphia, for example,
one can see a large church building adorned with Hebrew words and a
Star of David—the building was a synagogue before it became a black
Baptist church. Similar changes in ownership occur between mainline
Protestant churches and new independent churches, as one can see
while driving north on Broad Street.

The same findings are true for other American cities, such as Indianapolis. Farnsley (2003: 53–54) notes that congregations are often
the community organizations with the longest history in the community.

On average, congregations in Indianapolis have been in their present neighborhood for forty-seven years. In the inner city, the average is close to fifty years.
These fifty years represent two very different countervailing trends in urban congregational life. On the one hand, many of the congregations in what might be
called the downtown, or the inner city, have very long histories that predate the
suburbs. On the other hand, a number of urban congregations have closed or
dislocated to areas far from the city center. As they left, new congregations arose,
related to new residents moving in.

Indianapolis is a young city compared with Philadelphia, and yet the
average stay of a congregation in its location is almost identical. The
most likely explanation is that the PCC reached many more small up-
and-coming congregations that most congregational surveys miss.

Botchwey (2003) studied congregations and other nonprofit organizations in seven contiguous census tracts in Lower North Philadelphia,
an area plagued by urban blight. She found that congregations have the
longest history in this community compared to other nonprofit organizations. Similar findings were reported for New Haven (P. D. Hall 1998)
and Indianapolis (Pirog and Reingold 2002).

Many congregations own more than one building. Of the congregations that own or rent property, exactly half use only one building. The
other half use anywhere between two and thirty-five different buildings,
often for schools, social programs, rental space, or residential places for
people in need. Even congregations that own only one structure report
a great diversity in the buildings they use. Some congregations worship
in storefront properties, which generally consist of one room converted
from a store to a sanctuary. Many of these storefront congregation properties are hardly of any use other than meeting and worshipping. On

the other end of the continuum are congregations that have a large and complex structure with annexes, meeting rooms and classrooms, a large kitchen, a recreation room (often a basketball court), a large auditorium, and grounds that can accommodate bazaars or baseball games. Religious buildings can be both inspirational and functional, focusing worshippers on higher things while also containing necessary rooms like offices, classrooms, fellowship halls, kitchens, and restrooms. These rooms can be translated into educational offices, ESL classes, community theater halls, feeding stations, and meeting spaces, to name a few nonreligious functions often taking place on congregational properties. In fact, Dudley and Roozen (2001) found that inner-city congregations have ample space that can be used for community and social purposes, while suburban congregations are, on average, crowded and in need of space. Indeed, we rarely heard from the interviewees in the inner city that lack of space is a key problem. Parking, however, was often a problem. Many congregations noted that with the exception of Sunday, when parking is free in most of the city (and congregation members can often get placards allowing parking in otherwise restricted areas), parking is scarce and expensive. Some Center City congregations do not hold midweek services or small study groups, as members find it difficult to find parking at a reasonable cost.

We asked the congregations if they had serious problems with their buildings. As expected, some congregations reported such problems. Key among the building problems were roofing (17.2 percent), leaks (13.9 percent), heating or cooling (8.3 percent), stress (6.5 percent), electricity (5.2 percent), and code violations (4.0 percent). These problems overlapped considerably: while 69.4 percent of congregations reported no serious building problems, the other 30.6 percent reported on average more than two. Similar findings were reported by Dudley and Roozen (2001). Similar to these authors, we also found that congregations with small annual budgets and declining membership are more likely to report building problems.

It is most problematic for congregations to maintain old and deteriorating structures. This is especially difficult for Center City congregations when membership dwindles and cost of repair is beyond the reach of current membership. One such case is St. Stephen's Episcopal Church on South Tenth Street. The church, built in 1822, competes with five other Episcopal churches in a Center City area that is no longer a hub for Episcopalians. While the church can meet its ongoing financial obligations, such as clergy salary and utilities, it cannot find the resources needed for cleaning the church façade and repairing its windows. Consequently, St. Stephen's auctioned one of its greatest treasures, a 1902 marble statue by Augustus Saint-Gaudens with an estimated value of about half a million dollars (Salisbury 2004); it is now in the Philadelphia Museum of Art.

A similar problem was faced by First Baptist Church at Seventeenth and Sansom Streets. The building was covered with soot, and membership decline had made it impossible to raise funds for cleanup and restoration. This church joined a small inner city coalition, the Rittenhouse Coalition for the Restoration of Sacred Places, and managed to raise funds and acquire a state grant for the preservation work. (Pennsylvania is among the states that provide funds for the restoration of congregational buildings that are historically significant.) In June 2003, President Bush made federal funds available for such a purpose when visiting the Old North Church in Boston. The Bush administration provided this church restoration with $317,000 in public funds to repair and restore windows and render the building more accessible to the public. Secretary of the Interior Gale Norton announced sweeping changes in other federal guidelines concerning the repair of "historic" churches and other sectarian properties. Norton justified the grant by citing the fact that Old North Church is the oldest church building in Boston, and that Paul Revere spotted two lanterns hung from the church as a signal of the advancing British troops. Another potential source of public money is the Save America's Treasures program launched in 1998 by Bill Clinton. Money was made available for a number of projects involving religious sites, such as a $75,000 grant to the preservation of San Esteban del Rey Mission near Santa Fe, New Mexico. However, such avenues are possible only for congregations with historic value—usually those listed on the National Register of Historic Places. Other congregations facing such restoration tasks are forced to borrow, raise funds, and at times to face the difficult decision of closing.

Regardless of the building condition, most congregations view their places as community hubs. The buildings are often used for worship and religious studies on weekends and a few weekday evenings. These usually well-kept properties are then available for a variety of community functions and bring in people for a variety of nonreligious purposes. As we plan to show, congregational properties are the center of community life, and numerous important activities take place on congregational properties, most often free of charge. The remainder of this chapter provides many accounts of how congregations make public use of their space; just being there to enable the community to use the space contributes greatly to the quality of life of people in the community. Chaves, Giesel, and Tsitsos (2002), based on the NCS, report that most mainline Protestant congregations (85 percent) give or rent space for nonreligious causes, as do 73 percent of Catholics and 55 percent of other Protestant congregations. Similar findings were reported by Wineburg for

Greensboro, North Carolina (Cnaan, Wineburg, and Boddie 1999). Of the 147 responding agencies in Greensboro, 66 percent reported they had used such facilities. Of the agencies using congregational facilities, 73 percent did not pay rent (see also Ammerman 2005).

Sacred Property and Space Consumption

In our study, a large number of the congregations made use of their space to provide or host social programs. Of over 4,287 social programs reported by Philadelphia congregations, the overwhelming majority (89.3 percent) take place at least in part on congregational properties. In other words, most congregations that own or rent a property use this space, regardless of its physical condition, for the provision of social programs.

As shown in Chapter 5, the replacement value of the space allocated by an average congregation in Philadelphia to house social programs is estimated at about $1,889.06 per month. This value is assessed per any studied congregation, including those that have no social programs or do not own space. Thus, we estimate the annual space value per congregation at $22,668.72. For the collective body of congregations ($n = 2,120$), the estimated annual value of space for social and community programs is $48,057,686.40.

In addition to congregations' own social programs, sacred places in Philadelphia are used for numerous other social, civic, and cultural purposes. The following examples show the centrality of congregations in the current urban American way of life. In the following sections, we provide data on various social, community, arts, and developmental programs that find homes in local religious congregations. We provide data using two complementary sources. First, we analyzed data from various organizational Web sites and annual reports, such as the 2002 report by the Committee of Seventy that listed all polling stations in Philadelphia. From this kind of source, we were able to assess what portion of a certain public good is provided using congregational space. Second, we used data from our study to assess what percent of the existing congregations house relevant programs. That is, we assess to what extent Philadelphia congregations accommodate the same public good.

POLLING PLACES

Demonstrating a sense of civic responsibility, congregations provide space for one of the most important democratic activities in America: voting. Although it can be difficult to find an appropriate building for a polling place, the prevalence of churches makes the search a bit easier.

In fact, congregations in Philadelphia provide space for about 18 percent of all the city's polling places. Pennsylvania's election code says that there must be one voting machine per 350–600 registered voters in each of Philadelphia's 1,681 districts. Approximately 300 polling places are located in buildings owned by religious organizations, including churches, synagogues, temples, and mosques.

Housing a polling place requires accommodating a few voting machines for a minimum of three days and having volunteer poll workers and scores of voters walking in and out of the building from 6 a.m. to 9 p.m. In the 2004 presidential election, about 600,000 Philadelphians voted. If the polling places hosted by congregations were used by a representative number of voters, well over 100,000 citizens traipsed through the halls of religious organizations to cast their votes.

The PCC did not ask about housing a polling place, and hence we do not have comparable data. Of the congregations polled, 179 (12.9 percent) reported being involved in voter registration. While the two activities are not identical, we assume that they correlate.

IMMUNIZATION SITES

Every fall, people in the Northeast as elsewhere are concerned with flu that may affect their health in the upcoming months. The City of Philadelphia provides immunizations for residents who are sixty-five or older in October, and those fifty or older and nineteen and under in November. In order to make these shots accessible to all residents, they are offered at eleven health centers in the city, as well as in a variety of community-based sites such as are nursing homes, offices of local politicians, large apartment complexes, and congregational properties.

In 2002, the City of Philadelphia Department of Public Health used 115 community sites to reach residents with flu immunization shots. Of these, 29 (25 percent) were congregational properties; the congregation allocated space, provided the set-up, advertised the service, and cleaned up after the health team left. Forty-three congregations reported being formally involved in immunization (3.1 percent).

AFTER-SCHOOL PROGRAMS

One key problem for many working parents in America is what the children will do after school when parents are still at work. The street is full of temptations and illegal opportunities, and sitting alone at home watching TV and eating junk food is also not a productive solution. One solution to this problem is after-school programming that provides a place where children can go after school and, under supervision, play, eat, and do homework.

The Children's Investment Strategy (CIS) is part of the City of Philadelphia Division of Social Services, aimed at serving children, youth, and their communities during nonschool hours. CIS is an effort to improve the health, safety, and academic outcome for Philadelphia's children and youth through effective and creative youth development and after-school programs. CIS provides support for local groups to provide supervised after-school care. Applicants receive city grants and develop programs that provide a safe haven and quality care. Of the 82 programs in academic year 2002/2003, 24 (30 percent) were faith-based and most of them were in congregations.

Of the studied congregations, 316 (22.7 percent) reported holding an after-school/latchkey program on their premises. The congregations themselves run most of these programs; only 5.4 percent of these programs were reported to be operated by someone else under the congregation's auspices. Clearly, a major portion of the after-school care in Philadelphia depends on the property and volunteers of local religious congregations.

Food Distribution Centers

Philadelphia food pantries are able to serve many clients at little expenditure of financial resources, in large part due to the presence of religious congregations. Many Philadelphia congregations offer food pantries housed in their own facilities, manned by their volunteers, and distributing food they collect or purchase from the Greater Philadelphia Food Bank. Of the 350 food pantries in the city, 220 are run by congregations or faith-based organizations. That is, congregations provide approximately 63 percent of all official food pantries. In addition to space for storage and operations, congregations must provide a great deal of labor to run a food pantry. Besides collecting, preparing, and distributing food, the labor includes keeping records, tracking clients, and making referrals. Members of the religious organizations volunteer their time in the food pantries as part of their contribution to the charitable works of their congregations.

Of the 350 total food cupboards in Philadelphia, 14 are known as Super Cupboards, which, in addition to providing food, also teach life skills with the goal of building self-esteem and self-sufficiency for the clients. Training for these programs is provided by the Pennsylvania State University Cooperative Extension Expanded Food and Nutrition Education Program and includes classes such as nutrition, parenting, job readiness, resume writing, substance abuse, parenting, and self-identity.

Nine of these 14 Super Cupboards are run by congregations, who are able to use the space in their buildings for these classes throughout the week.

In response to our study, we found that 519 congregations have a food pantry. Some have a small food collection while others have daily distribution centers. Put differently, 37.3 percent of Philadelphia congregations provide food pantries on their property. In addition, 168 congregations reported housing a soup kitchen. That is, in 13 percent of the city congregations, a warm meal is provided at least once a week.

WEIGHT WATCHERS

Another well-known organization that uses congregational properties to reach the community, one that we did not include in our research instrument, is Weight Watchers. Weight Watchers is the country's longest-running and best-known diet program. It is a private operation that uses group dynamics and a brand of products to help overweight individuals lose weight. In Philadelphia, there are 31 locations where one can attend a Weight Watchers meeting and attempt to lose weight.

COMMUNITY COLLEGE OF PHILADELPHIA

The Community College of Philadelphia's goal is to build a solid foundation for college transfer, employment, and lifelong learning opportunities. In order to serve its 42,000 enrolled students and make education accessible to potential students, it has a number of neighborhood sites in addition to its four main campuses. Of the Community College's fifteen neighborhood sites throughout the city, four use the facilities of faith-based organizations. These faith-based organizations are able to provide adequate space for several classes at low cost while helping to achieve the goals of the community college by increasing accessibility of education to city residents.

When we asked the congregations about adult education, we found that a large number are involved in housing and offering such programs. One hundred congregations (7.2 percent) house (and most of them also run) General Education Development (GED) test preparation programs. Fifty-four congregations (3.9 percent) reported housing and usually running adult vocational training. Similarly, 58 congregations (4.2 percent) house and often run ESL classes. Finally, we found that 143 congregations (10.3 percent) house adult computer training, and the overwhelming majority (94 percent) run the program themselves.

ALCOHOLICS ANONYMOUS

Alcoholics Anonymous (AA) is a twelve-step program helping alcoholics to remain abstinent. The program applies a buddy system where a veteran helps and mentors a novice. It also applies a spiritual and religious component where a person acknowledges his or her addiction and surrenders himself or herself to God. It is estimated that about three-quarters of all AA meetings are held on congregational properties.

In our study, 156 (11.2 percent) congregations reported hosting an AA group. In some of these congregations more than one AA group meets regularly. In one inner-city church building, up to five AA groups meet every morning, two others meet in the evening.

NARCOTICS ANONYMOUS

Narcotics Anonymous (NA) sprang from the AA program of the late 1940s and is organized on similar lines. Its mission is to provide an environment in which addicts can help one another stop using drugs and find a new way to live.

According to the NA Web site, there are 176 Philadelphia locations and approximately 311 group meetings each week. Faith-based organizations host more than a third of the groups (119) and provide more than half the actual meeting spaces (99). In the PCC, 108 of the studied congregations (7.8 percent) reported housing an NA group, the majority (64.8 percent) run by a group not affiliated with the congregation.

OVEREATERS ANONYMOUS

Overeaters Anonymous (OA) is a worldwide organization that offers free programs using a twelve-step approach, patterned after AA, for those recovering from compulsive overeating. Not merely a dieting program; it addresses physical, emotional, and spiritual well-being. In Philadelphia, 12 of 37 meeting places (37.5 percent) are in faith-based organizations and 20 of 50 meetings (40 percent) are held in the space of faith-based organizations (Philadelphia Area Intergroup of Overeaters Anonymous 2003). Only 13 of the studied congregations (1.3 percent) reported housing an OA group. The majority of these programs (8 of 13) are run by a group not affiliated with the congregation.

AL-ANON

Al-Anon Family Groups, not affiliated with any sect or denomination, has been in existence for over fifty years; based on the twelve-step model, its goal is to provide support to those affected by someone else's drinking. Groups of relatives and friends of alcoholics who share experiences of being in relationship with an alcoholic meet to strengthen each other and give each other hope. Today, there are approximately 30,000 Al-Anon and Alateen groups in 115 countries. Each month, there are a total of 37 Al-Anon meetings in Philadelphia, of which 73 percent (27) meet in congregational space. Of the 31 meeting places, 74 percent (23) are faith-based.

In our survey, 33 of the studied congregations (2 percent) reported housing an Al-Anon group and 12 congregations reported an Alateen group (0.9 percent). Again, the majority of these programs (24 of 33 Al-Anon programs and 8 of 12 Alateen groups) are run by a group not affiliated with the congregation.

Arts and Culture

In the field of the arts, many congregations own or directly sponsor programs. The sacred space is once again used for communal purposes and to serve nonreligious objectives. For example, 72 congregations (5.2 percent) hold art exhibitions on their premises that they themselves organize and which are open to the public. In addition, 15 congregations (1.1 percent) hold art exhibitions organized and managed by an outside source. The walls often display paintings and other decorative arts, and in some cases local artists are featured.

Of the congregations we interviewed, 91 (6.5 percent) hold their own art classes, and an additional 10 (0.7 percent) provide space for external art classes. Similarly, 105 congregations (7.5 percent) hold their own community theater, and an additional 19 (1.4 percent) provide space for an external community theater. In most cases the programs are open to the public and are not limited to congregation members.

Day Care Centers

Many working parents are hampered by the lack of good affordable day care for their children. Often this is the barrier between a mother's career and concern for her children's welfare. Therefore, congregations that offer day care centers help working parents and the economy. In our study, we found that 236 congregations (17 percent) reported housing preschool day care, 140 (10 percent) reported housing a nursery school, and 26 (1.8 percent) reported housing a Head Start program. Naturally there is some overlap between these programs; overall we found out that 278 congregations (20 percent) are housing at least one of them.

HOMELESS SHELTERS

Homeless shelters are in many ways the most taxing programs in terms of space allocation. For a congregation to have its property used as a homeless shelter, it must provide places to sleep, bathrooms, showers, a kitchen, meeting space, and administrative offices. Hosting a homeless shelter involves having people coming every night and at times every day to the building and using it as their sleeping quarters. It requires a cadre of committed volunteers who are willing to cook for and supervise people they do not know on a regular basis (Ogilvie 2004). And these people are frequently the least desirable members of our society, often in need of a shower and suffering from drug addictions or mental illnesses. Yet many congregations are involved in caring for the homeless. Some are part of a coalition (see Chapter 11 for the case of the Northwest Philadelphia Interfaith Hospitality Network) in which the congregation's space is used to house homeless people for three to six weeks a year. Not all homeless shelters are in operation throughout the year; some operate only during the winter months. Our data do not enable us to make a clear distinction in this regard, and we report on all types combined.

Of the congregations in our study, 35 (2.5 percent) reported housing a shelter for men; 31 (2.2 percent) reported housing a shelter for women; 42 (3 percent) reported housing a transitional program for the homeless. These are long-term programs that include vocational and social rehabilitation. Finally, 25 congregations (1.8 percent) reported housing day mission programs for homeless people. Some of these programs overlap, so we calculated the number of congregations that open their doors to homeless people in a systematic way regardless of the type of program. We found that 87 different congregations (6.2 percent) make their space available for programs that are serving homeless people.

SCOUT TROOPS

Scout troops offer programs for boys and girls and for young and older kids. Although mostly secular and nature-related, these programs require the participants to declare their belief in God and as such can be seen as faith-related. However, their curricula and programs indicate that they are mostly educational. In our survey, 222 congregations (16 percent) reported hosting a scout troop. Often this means that a room is entirely designated for scout activities, and that the scouts use the buildings and utilities on evenings and during hours that no one else is using them.

HEALTH CLINICS

With the rising costs of medical and dental care and the spiraling number of people without health insurance, a few groups have organized to provide these services free or at a reduced rate. Such programs require a space large enough for care provision, a waiting area, and accessibility to the community. Of our congregations, 24 (1.7 percent) reported housing a medical clinic and 25 (1.7 percent) reported housing a dental clinic.

COFFEE ROOM FOR TEENS

Warren (2001) described an innovative use of space by a local religious congregation, a Kids' Cafe for children in an after-school program created by St. Phillips United Methodist Community Church in Philadelphia. The program was later adopted by other North Philadelphia United Methodist churches, such as Cookman United Methodist, and serves as a basis for their program of providing alternative high-school education for teens that the education system failed to reach and engage.

Conclusions

Properties are both an asset and a liability for any congregation. Buildings have to be maintained and they are costly. Most congregations reported having to undertake capital campaigns to raise money to restore their properties. In fact, two-fifths of the congregations (545, 39.1 percent) reported undertaking a capital campaign in the five years prior to the interview or at the time of the interview. Clearly the need to raise substantial funds to maintain, upgrade, or expand congregational physical property is on the minds of most clergy and lay leaders. For many of our interviewees, the question is not whether to engage in a capital campaign but rather when. For others with more limited resources, a capital campaign is a dream that cannot be realized at present but that is worth thinking about and hoping for.

The majority of congregations reported their building to be in good shape, and even those that reported structural problems use their properties for some community purposes. Most congregational buildings are used to host some nonreligious programs and activities. Thus, local congregations' buildings are places where people in the community meet even if they are not members. The volume of social and civic programs carried out on congregational properties makes them social hubs. This chapter has provided many examples of sacred properties as vibrant and productive centers of community service that benefit the public at large.

The importance of the social and communal importance of congregational properties has not gone unnoticed. On May 29, 2003, the National Trust for Historic Preservation listed the eleven most endangered historic places in the United States. The list contained six congregational properties, including Acts of the Apostles Church in Jesus Christ in Philadelphia. Partners for Sacred Places (2003) found that in Philadelphia 20 percent of historic (more than fifty years old) properties housing congregations are expected to face partial collapse or worse in the next five years. Many of these urban congregations do not have and cannot acquire the funds to sustain their properties. This presents a special challenge for our society and our government, as these properties are essential community hubs and their decline only will exacerbate urban blight.

The importance of sacred properties to their community goes beyond the programs and activities carried out in these buildings. The fact that these buildings are well cared for sends a signal that is the opposite of "broken windows." In other words, people observe a building that is cared for more than the public and communal buildings around it as a signal that something positive is taking place. If such buildings are preserved, not all is lost, and even private properties should be cared for. Only when congregational buildings collapse is the decline of the neighborhood complete.

In many urban communities, preserving communal sites requires resources that are hard to find. There is a need for money for building maintenance and upgrading, there is a need for people to watch the property, and there is a need for a public image of goodness and relevance. Congregations, throughout Philadelphia, raise funds to preserve and upgrade their properties, are capable of safeguarding their properties, and at times form watch groups to reduce crime and vandalism. They also have the respect and trust of most neighbors. When the members' resources are no longer sufficient for building maintenance, the decline is slow and reversible. Even in the face of financial and membership decline, congregational buildings are still maintained as well as possible, and are the last communal properties to disintegrate. As such, in neighborhoods where old factories are abandoned and vandalized, places of worship are flourishing and still well maintained, and congregations persist.

Part III
Special Congregations and Subgroups

Chapter 7

Black Congregations in the City of Brotherly Love

Religion in the Black Community

Although in Philadelphia there are many important and interesting groups worth attention, we elected to focus on African Americans, Latinos, and women. They are the largest and most interesting groups about whom we could shed new light. We elected not to focus on Muslims as there were too few Masjids within the city limits to generalize. We also elected not to focus on Asian Americans. Although there is a growing body of literature on this community and its religious characteristics (cf. Yang 1999) we felt that our sample is too small to offer any new or definite conclusions.

The African American community is claimed to be the most religious ethnic group in America.[1] Research supports the importance of religious involvement in the lives of African Americans, who are more likely to pray privately, practice religious rituals, attend religious services, and believe that the Bible is the literal word of God (Jacobson, Heaton, and Dennis 1990; Johnson, Matre, and Armbrecht 1991; Taylor, Chatters, and Levin 2003). Taylor and Chatters (1991) found in their analysis of the National Survey of Black Americans (NSBA) that 93 percent of black respondents reported praying several times a month or more, while 74 percent reported reading religious material. These statistics are significantly higher than those of any other ethnic group in America and, as will be shown in the next chapter, set the African American community apart from the Latino community.

Findings from the 1979–80 NSBA showed that black adults predominantly described themselves as Christians. Of the 89 percent of respondents (n = 2,096) who called themselves religiously affiliated, 98.6 percent identified themselves as Christian (Jackson and Gurin 1993). Furthermore, based on the NSBA it was assessed that African Americans turn to prayer frequently when confronting serious personal problems, and that they perceive these religious coping strategies to be satisfying and helpful (Neighbors et al. 1983).

Farnsley (2003: 37) found in Indianapolis that "When asked whether religious beliefs are important in making financial decisions in secular life, 84 percent of African Americans said they were, compared to 52 percent of whites. When asked whether religious beliefs are important in political decision making, 77 percent of African Americans said they were, compared to 65 percent of whites."

Surveys show that more than two-thirds (68.2 percent) of adults in the United States belong to a religious congregation (Barna Research Group 2000; Gallup 2001). African Americans are even more likely to belong to a congregation. In 1997, the black church (Protestant and Catholic) claimed 25 million members in 63,000 congregations (Pinn 2003). African Americans report significantly more congregation membership and attendance than either whites or Hispanics (Markstrom 1999; Social Capital Community Benchmark Survey 2001).

According to Baer and Singer (1992), the black church is more than a place of worship. It is a multifunctional institution that has developed many communal institutions for African Americans, such as schools, credit unions, banks, insurance companies, and low-income housing projects, some of which are discussed below. The first African Methodist Episcopal (AME) church, Mother Bethel African Methodist Episcopal Church, established by Richard Allen in 1794, was an offshoot of the Free African Society, a mutual aid society founded in 1787 in Philadelphia that helped free black people and organized some antislavery campaigns. The two aspects of mutual aid and spiritual enhancement still go hand in hand in most black churches in the United States.

Equally important, black churches and mosques are hubs of political training and political participation. Lincoln and Mamiya (1990), in a survey of black clergy, found that 92 percent advocated church involvement in social and political issues. According to Caldwell, Greene, and Billingsley (1992), the social and political involvement of clergy in black churches is both significant and expected.

E. Lincoln Frazier (1964) called the black church a nation within a nation. His contention was that black churches are agents of political, civic, economic, and social involvement and representation in a racially very hostile United States. Mays and Nicholson (1933) noted that the black church was the only institution wholly owned and operated by African Americans, the local institution most available and willing to provide support services to people in need. The church is a refuge where a black person can be a leader and be protected and served by people he or she can trust (Freedman 1993). Similarly, Ellison and Sherkat (1995) called the black churches in the South "semi-involuntary institutions." They used this term to refer to the fact that race lines are rarely crossed in many places and the black churches are the major communal institution for black people, where they act in parallel to white institutions and have the power of a group with their own leadership. Likewise, the black church building has been referred to as a "haven" (Franklin 1997; Jacobson, Heaton, and Dennis 1990).

The black church served an impressive role in the social and political life of black people in America. It was the only place where African Americans could gather for mutual aid and support. As will be discussed below, in the years prior to the Civil War, when African Americans were held as slaves and forbidden education, church gathering and teaching were the major means for education, organization, and leadership. The black church was the place where slaves experienced communal support, developed a sense of group, and gained spiritual sustenance (Raboteau 1978). White churches would not accept black people as equal members because they considered blacks to be inferior. The black church became a refuge where these oppressed people could learn to read and write and develop a sense of community (Moore 1991). Even today, as Sarfoh (1986) noted, the black church remains the only institution that seeks to foster a sense of personal as well as group unity and solidarity among ghetto residents.

Many empirical and conceptual studies demonstrated the power of religion and spirituality in the prevention or reduction of antisocial and risky behavior and personally harmful activities, particularly for young black people (Hill 1997; Jagers and Mock 1993; Mattis 1997; Potts 1991). Furthermore, Gibson (2004) showed that black grandmothers raising their grandchildren gave faith and spirituality as their major sources of strength. All this indicates the special place religion has within the black community in the United States.

What is often forgotten is that the African slaves who were brought to this continent were not Christians. In fact, although the African religions and spirituality were to some extent vanquished, they are the foundation of African American religion even today. The next section surveys the shift from the African heritage to American black Christianity.

From African Heritage to American Christianity

Since its beginnings, the American black version of Christianity has been infused with African spirituality and practices.[2] Du Bois (1899: 30) suggested that in the late nineteenth century "The church really represented all that was left of African tribal life, and was the sole expression of the organized efforts of the slaves. It was natural that any movement among freedmen should centre about their religious life, the sole remaining element of their former tribal system." The African slaves who were captured and shipped to North America brought with them African religions and spirituality. In many of these societies, there was no word for "God." God was everywhere and did not need to be defined. Furthermore, each geographical area had a different set of worship practices, and slaves were mixed in a way that no one version of African religion could prevail.

In the United States, they found themselves in a most unfavorable situation, one unlike that confronted by other slave groups in the Americas, and hence they lost their spiritual roots. First, they were taken to the only Protestant country in the New World; the future United States was Protestant and was built on the ideas of "one Nation under God." Second, in terms of numbers, the African slaves in British North America were the minority while in the rest of the Americas they were the majority. Where Spanish colonialism prevailed, people came from Spain to work in America, get rich, and return to Spain. Consequently, slaves and their descendants became the numerical majority. British settlers came to stay and they were the majority in both power and number. Third, the African slaves were separated from people of their own country or cultural background and mixed with people from other African traditions, so, no common language and few cultural bonds existed to sustain African religions and spirituality. Fourth, their masters expected them to breed new generations of slaves so that the masters would not have to continually import new slaves from Africa, as was the custom elsewhere in the Americas. Consequently, they found it very difficult to maintain African religions and spirituality; every generation remembered less and less about the African divinities and practices and gradually came to adopt the religion that surrounded them: American Christianity (Raboteau 1978). Finally, slave masters attempted to eradicate all aspects of African religions that seemed dangerous. Drums were forbidden, animal sacrifices were outlawed, and altars for African gods were smashed. All this was in an attempt to break bonds between slaves and make them dependent on their immediate surroundings, without a meaningful past or a promising future. Martin and Martin (2002: 40) noted, "Unlike the situation in Catholic slave countries including Brazil, Jamaica, Trinidad, and Haiti, enslaved Africans in North America during the 16th and 17th centuries found themselves a minority among the growing white Protestant majority that was intent on destroying all but the most harmless features of African spirituality and religion."

In fact, many slave owners resisted teaching their slaves about Christianity, fearing that it would foster resistance and aspirations to freedom. Other slave owners thought the slaves to be innately barbaric and subhuman, so that they could never comprehend Christianity, which would only disrupt the work the slaves were supposed to perform. The Great

Awakening was a time when numerous preachers traveled the country and held revival sermons that allowed Christianity to reach a large number of African slaves throughout the South. Raboteau (1978: 120) claimed that the "The Great Awakening represented 'the dawning of the new day' in the history of the conversion of slaves to Christianity." These evangelical preachers who brought the Christian religion to many slaves were highly spiritual, emotional, and uplifting: the key markers of religion in the black church for generations to come (Mitchell 2004).

Slave owners used Christianity to subdue blacks by focusing on Bible passages that call for submission and loyalty to one's master (e.g., Ephesians 6: 5–9), while avoiding liberation-inducing passages. However, the word of hope did spread. A few blacks started to preach on their own, and "hush harbor" worship became common. "Hush harbor" meetings, held at midnight or in far away, less detectable places, were for blacks only. At these meetings worshippers prayed unsupervised, and so the newly acquired religion started to be a force in their desire for freedom and dignity. The meetings helped the slaves to withstand their humiliation, harsh conditions, endless hard labor, and frequent abuse by their slave masters. It is not surprising that slave owners used religion to justify slavery and blacks' presumed racial inferiority, while the African slaves used it to give them strength for their struggle, find hope, obtain some sense of solidarity, and build their own organizations and leadership. As most sociologists of religion note, religion is a strong power that can be used for death and oppression or for healing and liberation.

Not surprisingly, African American leadership came from people of religion. Underground Railroad leaders such as Josiah Henson, Sojourner Truth, Frederick Douglass, and Harriet Tubman; leaders of black uprisings such as Gabriel Prosser, Denmark Vesey, and Nat Turner; and founders of new churches and mutual associations such as David George, Richard Allen, and Absalom Jones were all people of faith. In the last part of the eighteenth century and throughout the nineteenth, the black church was the source of many of the major organizations advocating for and serving people of color in almost all aspects of life. In fact, the church was the first all-black institution that allowed free expression of aspirations for freedom and dignity and gave sound justification for racial equality. Blacks in the United States adopted Christianity but did not copy their masters' religion. Canda (1997: 300) notes that "during the period of slavery, people of African descent mobilized mutual support and liberation systems inspired by traditional African spirituality and Christian principles under extreme adverse conditions."

Martin and Martin (2002: 1) note that "earlier generations of black lay and professional helpers used spirituality as a basis for distinguishing black people from their oppressors; for critiquing society; for affirming dignity, integrity, and self worth; for promoting interracial cooperation and cultural diversity; and for achieving black sanity, communal solidarity, and social support." Furthermore, "pioneering black social workers at the turn of the 20th century had no problem professing their own spirituality, identifying the spirituality of their clients, and working spiritual paradigms into the intervention process" (3). For Martin and Martin, spirituality among black Americans is interwoven with and indistinguishable from religion.

What is most important about these authors' observations is that the profession of social work at that time took an extreme secular turn and disassociated itself from spirituality and religion. In fact, as Cnaan, Wineburg, and Boddie (1999) and Lubove (1965) note, social work in the twentieth century aimed at a scientific look at people's misery and needs and abandoned religious ties. Black social workers' ties to the community and assessment of people, as well as their motivation to do social work, were rooted in religion and spirituality, and it took them a few decades to catch up with the profession's values and ideologies and secular-scientific approach. Furthermore, as Martin and Martin show, spirituality and religion are still so pervasive in the African American community that contemporary social workers should harness religion into their professional repertoire.

The civil rights movement brought the work and importance of black congregations to the forefront of American consciousness (Morris 1984). Following the civil rights movement, African American congregations became active in urban renewal, black business enterprises, economic redevelopment, and housing projects. DePriest and Jones (1997) noted that Christian capitalism encourages African American Christians to pool their dollars and invest in black-owned enterprises and local communities.

Historical Background: Black People in Philadelphia

To understand the role of black congregations in the life of Philadelphia at the dawn of the twenty-first century, one needs to know something about the history of black people in the city. The first black people in Philadelphia were the 150 Africans who came in shackles in 1684, when the slave ship *Isabella* anchored at Penn's Landing. As in the rest of the United States, waves of slaves followed in the next thirty years. By 1720, approximately 2,500 people of African descent lived in the city, some as slaves and others as free people. In Pennsylvania, with its strong Quaker tradition, there was more opposition to slavery than in the other colonies, with a heavy abolitionist streak in Philadelphia. But slavery was legal and many affluent people owned slaves. In fact, while the Declaration of Independence was being debated and signed, all delegates including George Washington brought an entourage that included slaves.

In 1790 Philadelphia had the largest number of free blacks in the United States. This community included Richard Allen, founder of the AME church, who helped initiate the independent black church movement. Allen's church was a major part of the Abolitionist movement in the region and served as a standard for black churches everywhere. While in many ways Philadelphia was a haven for runaway slaves, and the Underground Railroad saw it as an important destination, slaves were not safe there, as slave hunters, sanctioned by the courts, were free to claim them. It was common for a slave hunter to declare any black person a runaway slave, whereupon the black person would be placed in jail until his or her non-slave status was proven.

After slavery was abolished in Pennsylvania in 1820, circumstances did not immediately improve for African Americans. While they made up 10 percent of the city's population and were free, daily race-based discrimination and the threat of white mob violence were constants. At that time there were six registered black churches, with Bethel AME, the largest, commanding about half the black church attendance in Philadelphia. Du Bois (1899) noted that after the Civil War the growth of black churches in Philadelphia was rapid: there were 25 churches and missions in 1880 and 55 in 1897. A race riot happened in the 1840s when jobs were scarce and whites saw black workers as potentially stealing their jobs. Though kept from large-scale participation in the local economy, African Americans, with assistance in some cases from some European Americans, created their own society-within-a-society with elementary schools, orphanages, and nursing homes (Mitchell 2004). Lincoln University in Oxford, Pennsylvania, was founded in 1854 by John Miller Dickey, a white pastor of the Oxford Presbyterian Church. The first black university in the Philadelphia area, it would serve as a model for many black colleges and universities.

Philadelphia would see a huge increase in the black population in the 1890s, as Southern blacks fled to the city. The *Philadelphia Tribune*, founded in 1884 and still in operation, was their survival guide in the city and a means for understanding their new surroundings. Newcomers also found bustling segregated black communities in North Philly and West Philly.

In the late 1890s the University of Pennsylvania and its Wharton School were approached to carry out a landmark study of blacks in urban America. The idea was to carefully study the living conditions of the people in Philadelphia's Seventh Ward, which contained about

10,000 black people, estimated to be nearly one-fourth of the black population of the city. The work of W. E. B. Du Bois, a young black Ph.D. scholar from Harvard who was invited to join the Wharton School, became legendary and laid the foundation for African American studies and the sociology of race in America. Du Bois's meticulous documentation of the life of people in the Seventh Ward was published in his classic 1899 book *The Philadelphia Negro: A Social Study.* Using the best social-scientific methods of inquiry, Du Bois documented the housing segregation and the racial (and racist) segmenting of urban job markets (Katz and Sugrue 1998).

Du Bois devoted three chapters of his book to the black church. In 1896, he found that, of the 2,441 families in the Seventh Ward, only 741 were unconnected to a church or such a connection was unknown. That is, 70 percent of black families in the Seventh Ward of late nineteenth-century Philadelphia were connected with a church. Du Bois further speculated that probably half of the "unconnected and unknown" habitually attended church. The Methodists were decidedly in the majority, followed by the Baptists and then Episcopalians. Although Du Bois himself was not a man of faith, he was most impressed with the leadership quality of the local clergy, their organizational skills, and their influence over the community.

The black population was booming again by World War II, swelling to 18 percent of Philadelphia's total population, working in factories converted for weapons production. Following World War II, many job opportunities were still available, but African Americans often faced retaliatory economic discrimination in favor of returning European American veterans. Housing segregation became more pronounced as whites started to migrate to the suburbs. Those economic conditions and injustices were a breeding ground for the race riots in the 1960s. Over-eager to control the social unrest, voters elected former police chief Frank Rizzo mayor in 1971. His administration was best known (feared) for squashing the rights of African Americans and using police power to intimidate blacks and other liberal forces in the city. That period (1968–80) also saw the rise in Philadelphia of the self-proclaimed "black mafia," the best-known and most feared group of organized black men, who controlled the crime scene and especially the narcotics trade (Griffin 2003).

The first black mayor, W. Wilson Goode, was elected in 1983 and reelected in 1987. Goode's legacy will always be jeopardized for his authorizing the 1985 bombing of the house inhabited by MOVE, a group of black activists. The bombing killed 11 MOVE members, including children, and started a fire that destroyed two city blocks. Middle class whites continued to leave the city and blacks became more visible and politically active. For example, when journalist and political activist Mumia Abu-Jamal was convicted of killing a white policeman, his internationally notorious death sentence has served as a rallying point for blacks and liberal whites. As this book was being written, John Street, Philadelphia's second black mayor, was in his second term in office.

Blacks are the second largest racial group in the city. According to the 2000 Census, 655,824 (43.2 percent of the 1,517,550 residents) define themselves as black or African American. Only whites (45 percent) are slightly more numerous, and the difference is narrowing. In this distribution, Philadelphia is atypical of the Commonwealth of Pennsylvania as a whole, where 85.4 percent are white and only 10 percent are black. African Americans in Pennsylvania are mostly limited to the two big cities, Philadelphia and Pittsburgh.

The Black Church as a Social Institution

It is estimated that 65,000 to 75,000 black churches of various faith traditions exist in the United States (Billingsley and Caldwell 1991). The links between religion and the provision of social services, and for that matter many other communal services, are especially strong in the African American community (Carlton-LaNay 1999; O'Donnell 1995; Schiele 1996; Taylor et al. 2000). One way to understand the black church is through the eyes of Du Bois:

> As a social group the Negro church may be said to have antedated the Negro family on American soil; as such it has preserved, on the one hand, many functions of tribal organization, and on the other hand, many of the family functions. Its tribal functions are shown in its religious activity, its social authority and general guiding and coordinating work; its family functions are shown by the fact that the church is a centre of social life and intercourse; acts as newspaper and intelligence bureau, is the centre of amusements—indeed, is the world in which the Negro moves and acts. So far-reaching are these functions of the church that its organization is almost political. (201)

Du Bois saw that congregations in general are quite segregated along race lines—one of the key characteristics of black congregations, as we noted in Chapter 3. But he also noted that they are also highly segregated *within* race lines. People are attracted to congregations in which they can share common ethnicity, nationality, regional background, class, political orientation, lifestyle, and worldview with the majority of members. This is also true for black churches. As McRoberts showed, some black churches are home to poor blacks, others to middle-class blacks, still others to rich blacks, northern blacks, southern blacks, non-American blacks, and so on. Each church serves a subgroup within the black community and preserves its niche in the local ecology. People do not go to the church next door, but search for one where they can find others like themselves. Having common attributes and expectations means that no one group will be a dissenting force within the church. McRoberts further suggests that in searching for low rent or cheap property many of these churches are located next to each other yet hardly mix.

The black churches are continually undergoing socioeconomic and ethnic differentiation and class stratification, so much so that it is possible that the division among congregations is deeper by class than by race. But, in fact, there has never existed a homogeneous black community or church in Philadelphia. Du Bois noted this phenomenon, giving the following example: "St. Thomas' has always represented a high grade of intelligence, and to-day it still represents the most cultured and wealthiest of the Negro population and the Philadelphia-born residents. Its membership has consequently always been small, being 246 in 1794, 427 in 1795, 105 in 1860, and 391 in 1897" (203–4). He further noted:

The various churches, too, represent social classes. At St. Thomas' one looks for the well-to-do Philadelphians, largely descendants of favorite mulatto house servants, and consequently well-bred and educated, but rather cold and reserved to strangers or newcomers; at Central Presbyterian one sees the older simpler set of respectable Philadelphians with distinctly Quaker characteristics—pleasant but conservative; at Bethel may be seen the best of the great laboring class—steady, honest people, well dressed and well fed, with church and family traditions; at Wesley will be found the new arrivals, the sight-seers and the strangers to the city—hearty and easy-going people, who welcome all comers and ask few questions; at Union Baptist one may look for the Virginia servant girls and their young men; and so on throughout the city. Each church forms its own social circle, and not many stray beyond its bounds. (203–4)

Clearly the black church of today faces different challenges. However, it is still a major communal institution that merits extensive study. It is not surprising that Musick, Wilson, and Bynum (2000: 1570) found that "for all kinds of volunteering except the entirely secular, black volunteering is more influenced by church attendance than is white volunteering, a reflection of the more prominent role of the black church in its community, while socioeconomic differences have a smaller impact on black volunteering." This finding suggests the centrality of the black church in the life of blacks in the United States. It is the social institution that can best move people to commit time and effort for the formation of public goods.

The study of black congregations is often done while viewing them separately as their own units of analysis. For example, Thomas et al. (1994) studied 635 northern black churches and informed us about their social services provision. They found that 86 percent of the clergy indicated that the role of the church was to serve church members and community alike, and two-thirds (67 percent) of the congregations sponsored at least one community outreach program. Combined, these churches offered 1,804 programs, half of them adult and family support programs. Larger churches and churches with clergy with academic degrees (college degree or higher) were the strongest predictors of church-sponsored community outreach.

Taylor, Jacobson, and Roberts (2000) noted that African American adolescents are likely to live in single-parent families (61 percent) or with grandparents (12 percent), and also more likely to live in large cities (56 percent). Wilson (1991) found that African American youth are more likely to live in urban neighborhoods where at least 40 percent of residents live at or below the poverty level. These findings suggest that communities where African Americans are the majority, and often the overwhelming majority, are poor urban neighborhoods that are likely to be struggling with such conditions as single-parent households, high crime rates, poverty, fewer employment opportunities, and overburdened school systems (Sherman, Solow, and Edelman 1994). Given that congregations are most often located where the people are, it is reasonable to assume that black congregations are more frequent in poor neighborhoods than in affluent ones. Indeed in Philadelphia, black churches are spread throughout the city, but are much more common in North and West Philadelphia, two of the most impoverished sections of the city.

Comparing Black and Other Congregations

So far, only six studies have compared the involvement of black religious congregations in social service delivery with that of white or other types of congregations. These studies all suffer from key methodological weaknesses, yet their findings are quite consistent. Chaves and Higgins (1992) used the Gallup data of 1,587 black and white churches from a 1988 study conducted for the Independent Sector. While the sample size is impressive, sampling limitations and reliance on existing lists made the sample biased toward large and established congregations. These authors found that, although black churches were not more active than white churches in social service activities in general, they were more active in specific activities geared toward the neediest and poorest members of our society. For example, black churches were more involved in civil rights related activities and in feeding and clothing the needy. Chaves and Higgins (425) found "compelling evidence that black congregations are more likely to be involved than white congregations in *certain kinds* of traditionally nonreligious activities: civil rights activities and those activities that are directed at disprivileged segments of their local communities" (425; emphasis in original). They also found that "this race effect is not explainable by the organizational or environmental variables available" (438). Thus, political education and empowerment are by-products of participation in organized religion. One key limitation of this study is that the sample included a very small number of black congregations; as a result, its findings are very tentative.

Losh, Fobes, and Gould (1994) carried out a participant-observation study of 37 black and white churches in northern Florida between 1988 and 1990. The authors became deeply familiar with the congregations, but the sample size combined with the limited geographical coverage make it extremely difficult to generalize from these findings. Similar to Chaves and Higgins, these authors found that blacks and non-blacks are equally involved in nonreligious social activities. However, in contrast to Chaves and Higgins, they found that black churches were more likely to be active in areas such as endorsing political candidates, voter registration, and health education.

Bartkowski and Regis's (1999) in-depth study of 29 congregations in Mississippi's Golden Triangle region found that black churches provide more programs geared toward emergency relief such as cash assistance and temporary shelter than do white churches: 36 percent of black but only 19 percent of white churches did so. Black churches also provided more educational programs targeted at youth, such as tutoring (55 percent versus 13 percent) and after school programs (27 percent versus none). The authors caution us, however, that their sample was drawn for a contextual purpose and was too small for statistical significance.

Cavendish (2000) compared black and white Catholic churches from the first multilevel survey of U.S. Catholic parishes conducted as part of the Notre Dame Study of Catholic Parish Life (CPL). The study aimed to represent 10 percent of parishes and ended up with data from 1,883 parishes, only 29 of which had a majority of black members. Indeed, most blacks in America traditionally are Protestants, fewer are unaffiliated, a slim minority are Catholic, and recently an increasing number have become Muslim. Cavendish reports that "Black churches are significantly more likely than white churches to engage in social service and social action activities independent of a variety of demographic, organizational, and structural factors known-or suspected-to influence activism" (371). This study also suggests that congregations with a less hierarchical structure are more apt to provide social services and be engaged in social activism.

Tsitsos (2003) also compared black and non-black congregations, using the 1998 National Congregations Study, a survey of a representative sample of 1,236 religious congregations that suffers, however, from serious underreporting of social service programs. Tsitsos did not find a difference between black and non-black congregations in social service involvement or in the number of social services offered. He concluded that significant "race effects for African American congregations exist for four types of programs: clothing, substance abuse, tutoring/mentoring, and nonreligious education." These findings, particularly the effect on education and mentoring programs, counter the assertion by Lincoln and Mamiya (1990) that "African-American congregations are not doing enough in areas that are critical to African-American youth" (205). These findings contradict those of Chaves and Higgins in that they did not show black congregations to be more involved in "safety net" services to the poorest members of society. Tsitsos, however, found that black congregations are involved in social programs that require more intensive interaction with the people they help.

Finally, based on the data of Cnaan and his colleagues (2002), Boddie (2003) provided a comparison of black, white, and interracial congregations ($n = 228$). Her key findings suggest that black congregations are more involved in educational services for children and youth and in community development. Along with the interracial congregations, black congregations are also more involved in providing basic needs such as food and clothing. Black congregations also reported more programs available daily or weekly, rather than monthly or sporadically. Black congregations, on average, served fewer people and reported lower budgets and membership size.

Although these six studies provide us with some important insights into the unique social involvement and organizational behavior of black congregations, they are small in scope and suffer from numerous methodological weaknesses. The PCC is a rich and comprehensive source for discerning the unique social involvement and organizational behavior of black congregations. The remainder of this chapter is devoted to findings from the PCC comparing black and non-black congregations. This part of the chapter is divided into three subsections. First, we discuss the organizational characteristics of black congregations as compared with non-black congregations. The emerging picture from this analysis is that black congregations, on average, are smaller and poorer than their counterparts. Second, we compare the social and community involvement of black and non-black congregations. With a few notable exceptions, black and non-black congregations are equally engaged in social and community service provision. In the final part, we discuss these findings to assess the state of black congregations in Philadelphia and draw conclusions that may be nationally relevant for the twenty-first century.

The Organizational Characteristics of Black Congregations in Philadelphia

Congregations remain one of the most segregated institutions in the United States. Regrettably, this is also true in Philadelphia: we found that the city's congregations are segregated according to race and ethnicity. Following the traditions of sociologists of religion, we defined as black any congregation in which at least 75 percent of the members are blacks. In some cases the senior pastor was white but the members were predominantly black. Other scholars use a threshold of 90 percent for defining the congregation as a black congregation, and even using this more stringent criterion, 679 congregations (49 percent) in Philadelphia are black congregations. However, for the remainder of this chapter we shall use the 75 percent criterion. We assessed this to be a critical majority to determine the culture and orientation of the congregation. Of the 1,392 studied congregations the majority (719 congregations, 51.7 percent) were black.

As shown in Figure 7.1, the 719 black congregations are aggregated where black people live. While there are areas where storefront churches are frequent and some black churches are located at the edge of the city, the majority of the black churches are located in black neighborhoods. The map shows convincingly that congregations are most often located where their members reside or in a similar neighborhood. Put differently, in Philadelphia, even the congregational location is segregated. Black congregations are most often housed in black neighborhoods, and Latinos and Asian Americans have their congregations in their own neighborhoods.

According to the U.S. Census figures cited above, blacks' share of the congregations in the city (slightly more than half) is slightly greater than their share in the population. As shown below, blacks in Philadelphia, on average, attend smaller-size congregations and the level of religiosity among blacks is higher than among any other ethnic group.

Farnsley (2003) reports that in Indianapolis African American respondents were more likely than white respondents to describe themselves as "very religious or spiritual"; 52 percent of African Americans offered this self-description, while only 37 percent of whites did. The PCC data showed a similar though not so profound trend. While more black congregations reported themselves to be more religiously fundamentalist (19.9 percent) than non-black congregations (11.3 percent), they were less likely to report themselves as religiously conservative (32.9 percent and 47.0 percent respectively). When we viewed conservative and fundamentalist congregations combined, the difference disappeared (52.8 percent for black, 58.3 percent for non-black). Black congregations also

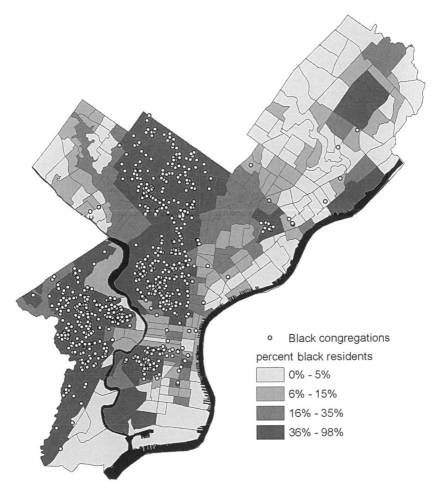

Figure 7.1. Black congregations and locations vis-à-vis residential locations of blacks.

were more likely to define themselves as religiously liberal (12.3 percent versus 8.5 percent). It is interesting that black congregations tend to be more fundamentalist and liberal while non-black congregations are mostly theologically moderate or conservative. In both groups, about a third of the congregations defined themselves religiously as moderate (35.0 percent and 33.2 percent respectively). The PCC data suggest that black congregations are diverse; they should be viewed as a set of diverse social organizations.

Furthermore, Farnsley (2003: 37) found in Indianapolis that African

Americans were more than twice as likely as non-blacks (63 percent versus 30 percent) to say that the Bible was to be taken literally as the Word of God. "They might well have heard this at church, because 64 percent of African Americans reported that in the previous week they had been to church one or more times, while this was true for only 47 percent of whites. Overall, 39 percent of African Americans reported attending church more than once a week over the past year, while only 13 percent of whites said the same." While in our study we did not ask about individual attendance, 90.8 percent of black congregations answered that the Bible is the literal and inerrant word of God, while only 60.9 percent of non-black congregations answered in that manner.

MEMBERSHIP

Among the 719 black congregations in this study, membership ranged from a low of 6 (Lively Stone Temple) to a high of 7,100 (Deliverance Evangelistic Church). Non-black congregations were significantly larger (384 members on average) than black congregations (238 members). Similarly, average weekly attendance per non-black congregation was 278 compared to 164 per black congregation.

These low averages for the black congregations are the result of the existence of many small churches, some of them storefront churches, that are balanced by some twenty-four megachurches, that is, places of worship that attract over 1000 members. About half the black congregations (48.2 percent) reported fewer than 100 members, including children. Two-thirds (67.9 percent) reported fewer than 200 members, including children and youth. In addition to Deliverance Evangelistic Church, large black places of worship include Bethel Deliverance Church, Bible Way Baptist Church, Bright Hope Baptist Church, Christian Stronghold Baptist Church, Church of the Lord Jesus Christ, Fellowship Tabernacle Church, First Corinthian Baptist Church, Freedom Christian Bible Fellowship, Harold O'Davis Memorial Baptist Church, Impacting Your World Christian Center, Mount Airy Church of God in Christ, Mount Carmel Baptist Church, New Covenant Church of Philadelphia, Philadelphia Masjid, Sharon Baptist Church, St. Raymond of Penafort Roman Catholic Church, St. Martin de Porres Roman Catholic Church, St. Matthew African Methodist Episcopal Church, Triumph Baptist Church, Victory Christian Center, Vine Memorial Baptist, White Rock Baptist Church, and Zion Baptist Church.

We asked whether in the past three years membership had gone up, remained the same, or declined. Almost half the black congregations (52.6 percent) reported that membership had risen, higher than the rate reported by the non-black congregations (42.9 percent). Another third (32 percent) reported that membership had remained stable (versus 30.8 percent for non-black congregations), and about one-sixth (15.4 percent) that membership had declined (versus 26.3 percent). This is a statistically significant difference that suggests a trajectory of growth among black congregations. Given, as the next chapter shows, that Latino congregations are also on the rise, it is reasonable to conclude that white congregations are on the decline.

A significant number of people today are choosing to commute to congregations outside their own neighborhood for worship services. In black congregations, significantly more members live within city limits (89.8 percent), but only 39.4 percent within a ten-block radius of the congregation. The remainder (10.2 percent) live outside the city. In non-black congregations, 48 percent live within a ten-block radius, 36.2 percent within city limits, and 15.8 percent outside the city. In other words, black congregations attract more members from within the wider city; non-black congregations attract more members from around the congregation and from outside the city. Put differently, black congregations have more in-city commuters while non-black congregations have more out-of-city commuters. One explanation for non-black congregations' having more people from around the congregational property may be that many non-black congregations are Roman Catholic, churches that traditionally draw members from the local parish.

Black congregations reported a lower percentage of elderly (sixty-five and older) members as compared with non-black congregations (23.7 percent and 27.8 percent respectively), a difference that is not statistically significant. Similarly there were no significant differences regarding the percentage of young members (eighteen and under) (23.7 percent and 19.7 percent). A significant difference, however, was found regarding whether in the past three years the membership of the congregation had, on average, aged, remained the same, or gotten younger. Significantly more non-black congregations reported that membership had aged (30 percent versus 21.8 percent). More black congregations reported that their membership had become younger (42 percent versus 34.4 percent). The rest reported no change.

In black congregations 71 percent of the members are women, while in non-black congregations the percentage is 59.3. That seven of ten members of black congregations are women reflects community issues such as the high rate of male incarceration in the black community and the fact that women throughout the world are more religious then men. It may also reflect the role of black women as single mothers and their search for meaning and order in life (Frederick 2003).

Significantly, more non-black congregations than black congregations (42.1 percent versus 24.2 percent) reported a politically conservative majority. This finding suggests that, as discussed above, blacks on average are more liberal than the general population and see the government as an important player in social policy and services provision.

The findings regarding membership suggest that with a few notable exceptions most black congregations are small in size, have mostly female members, and tend to attract inner-city residents even if they have to commute. Non-black congregations are on average larger in size, gender balanced, and attract more out-of-town members. Those three findings—congregational size, gender, and members' residence—are important as they indicate that, on average, black congregations can assemble fewer resources. Fewer members translate into fewer people who support the congregation financially and carry out missions. Women, on average, have lower incomes and less savings than men. Furthermore, on average, the household income outside the city is significantly higher than in the city, and it is reasonable to assume that out-of-city members bring with them stronger financial support. In sum, we witnessed a large number of black congregations with a lower average membership base and possibly limited financial resources.

FINANCES

Not surprisingly, the average income of members of non-black congregations is higher than that of members of black congregations. Among black congregations, the percentage of members with an annual household income of less than $25,000 was 50.8 percent; among non-black congregations, it was 39.5 percent. Among non-black congregations, the percentage of members with an annual household income of more than $50,000 was 18.5 percent; among black congregations, it was 10 percent. In other words, the financial ability of members of black congregations is limited in comparison to that of non-black congregations. Adding the small congregational size to this finding suggests that black congregations have smaller financial capabilities.

Members' income translates into congregational budget. Based on the data reported above, it is not surprising that almost two in five black congregations (39.4 percent) reported an annual operating budget of less than $50,000, as compared with only 30.1 percent of the non-black congregations. Conversely, 9.6 percent of non-black congregations reported an annual operating budget of over half a million dollars as compared with only 6.3 percent of the black churches.

There were no significant differences between black and non-black congregations regarding the question whether in the year prior to the study their budget ended with a surplus, a balanced budget, or a deficit. In both groups, about one in five reported a surplus, half reported a balanced budget, and the rest a deficit. Whether the actual budget is balanced or not can be misleading. At times, a congregation may purposely work with a deficit budget as a means to encourage members to give more or as a sign of confidence in future donations. In other congregations, a balanced budget may indicate financial worries and avoidance of risks because the leaders know that if they were to "go under" they would not be able to recover. Thus a deficit may indicate financial strength and a balanced budget financial worries. So we asked the congregations whether they are financially strong, sound, or struggling. Almost half the black congregations (44.3 percent) reported themselves to be financially struggling as compared with only a third (33.3 percent) of the non-black congregations. In other words, black congregations, on average, reported lower operating budgets, and while they are just as successful as non-black congregations in ending the year with a budget surplus, they report higher levels of financial woes.

PROPERTIES

On average, a congregation in Philadelphia has been at its present location for forty-eight years. Black congregations, on average, have been at the same location for thirty-three years, non-black congregations for almost twice that time, sixty-four years. Both are stable fixtures in the community, while black congregations are somewhat newer. However, as we showed earlier in this chapter, blacks arrived in Philadelphia after whites were already established in the city and had many places of worship. Furthermore, for quite a while blacks were not allowed to have their own churches. Finally, the demographic trend has been for whites to leave the city and blacks to move in, a trend that helps explain why there are so many new and growing black congregations. Still, Philadelphia has the oldest free all-black churches in the country, and it can be assumed that the longevity of black congregations in Philadelphia is among the greatest in the United States.

When we asked about plans to relocate, significantly more black congregations (20.5 percent) than non-black congregations (16 percent) reported the intention to leave their current place. For both groups, the major reasons for wanting to relocate were insufficient space and lack of parking. However, many more black congregations planning to relocate reported as a motivating factor deteriorating buildings that were too costly to repair.

In both groups, about four in five own their congregational property; most of the rest rent and a few share with others. The differences between black and non-black congregations become evident when we compare the number of buildings available to congregations and the

maintenance needs of congregation properties. Of the black congregations, 44.1 percent reported more than one building at their disposal, as
compared with 53.7 percent of non-black congregations. Put differently,
non-black congregations on average command many more buildings—a
fact that translates into more potential to organize activities and a
greater possibility of financial strength. And the property used by black
congregations, on average, is in greater need of repair. For example,
black congregations reported more roofing problems than did non-
black congregations (19.9 percent and 14.5 percent respectively). This
finding is strongly related to the existence of many storefront black
churches and their quest for low-rent space until they can expand
(McRoberts 2003). This also explains why a large number of black congregations do not own more than one property.

Clergy

Analyzing the data regarding clergy also confirms the fact that the infrastructure of black congregations is weaker than that of non-black congregations. The major difference between the two studied groups is that
19.5 percent of non-black congregations have two or more full-time paid
clergy as compared with only 5.6 percent of black congregations. In
other words, almost a fifth of non-black congregations are strong
enough to have two or more clergy, while only one in twenty black congregations is in that position. Clearly this difference is also the result of
the relatively small size of black congregations.

Furthermore, more clergy in non-black congregations (57 percent)
have completed graduate-level theological seminary training or hold
another graduate degree than in black congregations (28.4 percent). In
other words, professional training is much more common among clergy
in non-black congregations. Part of the difference is due to personal
callings and self-appointments, and part of it is due to the fact that some
major black denominations, such as the Church of God in Christ, do not
have an organized seminary system.

To sum up this part of the analysis, it is clear that the many black congregations in Philadelphia are at a disadvantage compared with non-
black congregations. While there are a few rock-solid large and affluent
black congregations, they are the exception. On average, black congregations are financially and organizationally weaker than non-black congregations. They are smaller, their members possess fewer resources,
they attract mostly women and few men, their budgets are smaller, they
possess fewer buildings and occupy the majority of storefront churches,
their buildings are in greater need of repair, and their clergy have less
formal training. Given this backdrop, the question is to what extent

black congregations can help their members. But before turning to answer this critical question we should compare the needs black congregations face compared with non-black congregations.

Comparing Needs of Black and Non-Black Congregations

In order to assess the reality of life around the congregation, we asked our interviewees whether certain social problems are rampant around the congregational property. It was our assumption that our interviewees knew the key social problems in the area and that these problems are relevant to the members' quality of life even if many of them do not reside nearby. As shown in Chapter 2, the perceptions of clergy are quite accurate and correlate well with the objective measures. Accordingly, we used the interviewees' assessment of the existence of social problems as a proxy for the social needs the congregation faces. After all, when members come to pray and face drug dealers or homeless people, it becomes their issue, their social problem to cope with.

As expected from the income differential reported earlier, significantly more clergy of black congregations reported that their congregations are housed in a poverty-stricken area (91.2 percent) than did clergy of non-black congregations (76.5 percent). The high rate of overall poverty reflects the urban blight that Philadelphians are facing. Similarly, black congregations face more unemployment problems (93.1 percent) as compared with non-black congregations (75.6 percent). This trend is also reflected in the loss of employment opportunities and transfer of jobs to the suburbs and abroad (77.6 percent for black congregations and 60.5 percent for non-black congregations). This income disparity translates into the problem of inadequate or lack of health care, more pronounced in neighborhoods around black congregations (73.6 percent) than around non-black congregations (60.8 percent).

In all the crime-related items, black respondents reported higher rates. Crime in general was reported as a problem for more black congregations (87.8 percent) than non-black congregations (75.9 percent). Gang violence was significantly more problematic around black congregations (52.9 percent) than around non-black congregations (39.2 percent), as was youth incarceration (77.4 percent and 55.7 percent respectively). Many more occurrences of prostitution in the vicinity were reported around black congregations (72.7 percent) as compared with non-black congregations (53.1 percent). Drug trafficking was also more frequent around black congregations than non-black congregations (92.5 percent and 74.6 percent), and drug use was reported as a problem by more black than non-black congregations (94.5 percent and 86.8 percent).

Other quality-of-life issues also were reported as more of a problem around black than around non-black congregations. Issues included public education (86.2 percent of black congregations versus 78.1 percent of non-black congregations reported this as a problem); illiteracy (87.8 percent and 63.6 percent); teen pregnancy (85.5 percent and 72.9 percent); lack of quality affordable housing (82.7 percent and 59.7 percent); lack of recreational opportunities for children and youth (73.2 percent and 50.7 percent); lack of available child care (72.1 percent and 59.8 percent); homelessness (77.8 percent and 62.2 percent); and AIDS/HIV infections (83 percent and 47.7 percent). Even pollution is a larger problem around black congregations (73.8 percent) than around non-black congregations (65.4 percent).

As Massey and Denton (1993) note, most urban neighborhoods are highly segregated; people tend to live in areas where most neighbors are of their own ethnic background. Given that places of worship tend to be near where people live, it is easy to assume that the reported higher rates of social problems reflect a higher level of need. In other words, black congregations are often located in the more difficult segments of the city, such as West and North Philadelphia, and on average they command significantly less resources but are surrounded by greater social needs. This is a bind that black congregations face daily. Given that there are fewer resources and greater needs in black communities, one should ask to what extent black congregations are involved in helping to solve problems in their communities. The next section will answer this question.

Social Services Involvement and Provision

As noted before, of the 1,392 congregations, 1,265 (90.1 percent) reported at least one social program that served the community. Of the 719 black congregations, only 62 (8.6 percent) reported not to provide even one social program. Among the 673 non-black congregations, 66 congregations (9.8 percent) reported not to provide even one social program that served the community. In other words, the percentage of community serving congregations is higher among black congregations than non-black congregations, even though they have fewer resources.

Furthermore, in the city as a whole, the average number of programs per congregation was 3.08. For black congregations, the mean was 3.2 programs per congregation; for non-black congregations, the mean was 2.9. In other words, not only are more black congregations involved in social services provision, but they also, on average, provide a wider array of services.

AREAS OF INVOLVEMENT

As noted in Chapter 5, we introduced a list of 215 possible programs of involvement and asked our interviewees to assess whether their congregation was involved in offering them. In this chapter we limit our analysis to formal programs. That is, we include only programs offered by the congregation on its property or somewhere else, or programs offered on congregational property by someone else (such as AA meetings). We also include active support (in cash or personnel) to assist others who provide this service. In Table 7.1, we have included only service areas reported by at least 15 percent of the congregations. The designation n.s. denotes no statistical difference between black and non-black congregations; the number of asterisks indicates the strength of the difference.

The picture emerging from this analysis is that black congregations are as involved as non-black congregations in serving the social needs of Philadelphians. Of 38 comparisons, black and non-black congregations performed equally in about half (20). Put differently, in these 20 areas of social involvement, the percentages of black and non-black congregations were statistically similar. In 14 other comparisons, black congregations outperformed non-black congregations. Some of these areas are street outreach to homeless people, health education, mentoring/rites of passage, programs for gang members, and scholarships for students in need. In only 4 areas did non-black congregations outperform black congregations: scout troops, homeless shelters, recreational programs for seniors, and international relief. Clearly, black congregations, despite their smaller size and inadequate resources, are committing themselves to help the needs of the urban dwellers at a similar, if not higher, level than non-black congregations. While some scholars have tried to show that black congregations are more committed to poor people or are more concerned with programs that require intensive interaction with clients, we would like to propose that black congregations are more involved in areas that plague the community next to where they are located.

Given the problems with public education in Philadelphia, especially for inner-city black youth, we wondered how much black congregations are involved in providing alternative schooling. Lincoln and Mamiya (1990) suggested that in the face of substandard urban public education, black churches should develop their own private schools. In our PCC data we found 202 schools affiliated with local religious congregations (14.5 percent). The majority of these schools, however, were run by non-black congregations: 135 of the 673 non-black congregations (20.1 percent) provided some form of school as compared to 67 of

TABLE 7.1. EXAMPLES OF SERVICES IN WHICH BLACK AND NON-BLACK
CONGREGATIONS ARE INVOLVED (PERCENT OF CONGREGATIONS PROVIDING
SERVICE)

Type of service	Total	Black	Non-black
Sports activities	15.3 (n.s.)	15.1	15.5
Scholarships for students in need	15.4 ***	18.6	12.0
Mentoring/Rites of passage	15.6 ***	22.6	8.0
Health screening	16.4 **	19.0	13.7
Crime watch	16.5 (n.s.)	15.6	17.5
Music classes	15.0 (n.s.)	15.6	14.4
Organized tours (for the elderly)	15.6 (n.s.)	14.7	16.5
Drug and alcohol prevention programs	15.7 **	18.5	12.8
Neighborhood cleanups	16.1 *	18.5	13.5
Street outreach to homeless people	16.5 ***	19.6	12.9
Parenting skills workshops	17.2 (n.s.)	18.0	16.4
Health education	18.1 ***	21.4	14.6
Scout troops	17.9 ***	13.2	22.9
Interfaith collaboration	18.5 **	21.5	15.7
Visiting sick/homebound people	18.0 **	20.8	15.0
Premarriage counseling	19.2 (n.s.)	20.8	17.4
Hospital visitation	19.5 *	21.8	17.1
Daycare (preschool)	18.2 (n.s.)	17.6	18.7
Homeless shelter	18.8 **	13.5	19.5
Marriage encounters (retreats)	18.2 (n.s.)	18.9	17.4
Recreational programs for seniors	20.2 ***	16.5	24.1
Community bazaars/fairs	21.4 (n.s.)	20.8	22.0
Prison ministry	22.0 **	25.4	18.4
Choral groups	25.3 *	13.8	20.4
After-school care	21.7 (n.s.)	20.7	22.7
Programs for gang members	21.8 ***	28.1	15.2
Neighborhood associations	21.9 (n.s.)	23.1	20.7
Visitation/buddy program (for seniors)	24.2 (n.s.)	28.4	21.5
International relief	23.5 ***	15.4	32.1
Educational tutoring	23.5 (n.s.)	25.1	21.0
Soup kitchens	24.0 (n.s.)	25.1	22.9
Music performances	29.4 (n.s.)	29.4	29.4
Summer programs for teens	29.4 (n.s.)	30.8	27.9
Recreational programs for teens	37.0 (n.s.)	38.1	36.0
Clothing closets	37.0 **	41.0	32.8
Recreational program for children	37.3 (n.s.)	37.5	37.1
Summer day camp	40.6 (n.s.)	42.6	38.3
Food pantries	50 (n.s.)	49.6	50.5

n.s. = not statistically significant; * $p < .05$; ** $p < .01$; *** $p < .001$

the 719 black congregations (9.3 percent). This clearly reflects the resources available to the congregation. However, looking carefully at the data shows that many of the non-black schools were affiliated with Catholic churches and in fact were part of the parochial system offered by the local archdiocese. When we omit these schools from the analysis, non-black congregations still reported more schools (10.6 percent) than black congregations (7.3 percent) but the difference was barely significant. In other words, given lesser resources and without considering Catholic schools, the school offerings of black and non-black congregations were quite similar.

POPULATIONS SERVED

We also were interested in whether there is a difference in the population on which the actual programs are focused. For each of the 4,287 programs offered by the congregations, we asked for the primary population targeted by the program. In many cases answers included more than one population, as many programs serve both children and adults or both poor people and the elderly.

The data reported in Table 7.2 suggest that, with one exception, black congregations target more populations than non-black congregations. Both groups equally serve children, the future generation of most congregations. However, with regard to other age groups, the community at large, and mostly to the disadvantaged in the community, black congregations are more attentive and responsive to their needs. Most notably, black congregations serve poor people, people with addictions, and people with disabilities significantly more than non-black congregations.

TABLE 7.2. BENEFICIARIES OF CONGREGATIONAL SOCIAL PROGRAMS IN BLACK AND NON-BLACK CONGREGATIONS (PERCENT OF PROGRAMS OFFERING SERVICES TO THESE POPULATIONS)

Population served	Total	Black	Non-black
Children	44.1 (n.s.)	44.9	44.3
Youth	38.2 **	40.4	35.7
Poor people	34.7 ***	39.1	29.7
Families	34.1 **	36.1	31.8
Adults	23.9 ***	28.2	19.0
Elderly	21.8 *	23.1	20.3
People with addictions	13.8 ***	17.2	9.9
Disabled people	12.8 ***	14.8	10.5
Community at large	43.1 ***	47.4	38.2

n.s. = not statistically significant; * $p < .05$; ** $p < .01$; *** $p < .001$

Black congregations are situated in neighborhoods where the needs are greater, and the data suggest that they are aware of the needs and make efforts to meet them.

Longest (1991) suggested, based on a study of 41 black churches in Washington, D.C., that assistance in cash usually goes to church members, while in-kind assistance usually goes to nonmembers. We did not study this issue, but based on a few discussions with some of the interviewees this hypothesis cannot be supported. It is possible, however, that cash support requires a higher degree of trust, and that such trust is extended to known members before nonmembers become familiar enough to the congregation to be trusted.

In the next section, we will study who they serve and who they collaborate with in order to provide these services. Finally, we will assess the fiscal value of black congregations' contribution to the quality of life of Philadelphia's residents as compared with that of non-black congregations.

Who Benefits and Who Serves?

On average, each congregation-sponsored program served 41 members of the congregation as well as 80 nonmember community residents. Black congregations, on average, served 36 members of the congregation and 75 nonmember community residents; non-black congregations served 48 members and 85 nonmember community residents. In other words, non-black congregations, true to their size and resources, provide larger numbers of programs but each such program reaches fewer recipients.

Given that most of these programs are run by volunteers, we found that, on average, a program is provided through the labor of twelve congregational members and five people who are not members of the congregations. This last group is composed of people who are involved with the congregation as volunteers and not as members, and also those who use the congregational space for service delivery, such as AA groups. Black congregations, on average, employ ten members and four nonmembers per program. Non-black congregations, on average, employ sixteen members and seven nonmembers per program. Again, these findings are a testimony to the larger membership size and greater resources commanded by non-black congregations.

COLLABORATIONS

Collaborating with other groups is a sign of openness and willingness to cooperate both theologically and socially. Among the black congregations, 92.5 percent reported holding at least one joint worship service with another congregation. Among the non-black congregations 78.3 percent reported doing so. We also asked our interviewees if their congregations collaborate with other faith-based groups (congregations, denominations, local faith-based coalitions, etc.), and if they do so with any secular organization. Among the black congregations, 57.9 percent reported collaborating with another faith-based group and 37.9 percent with a secular organization for social services provision. Among the non-black congregations, 67.5 percent reported collaborating with another faith-based group and 54.4 percent with a secular organization for social services provision. These findings suggest that black congregations are more open to joint worship services but are less open to social service collaborations. One reason may be the lack of resources and thus a sense of inadequacy when approached by external bodies. Black congregations are much more secure when it comes to worship practices than about their ability to offer equal funds and volunteers to a joint social service project.

Among the two studied groups, almost equal percentages of interviewees were familiar with Charitable Choice (17.2 percent of black congregations and 14.7 percent of non-black congregations). While very few congregations actually reported applying for a grant under Charitable Choice provisions, six of the eight that did so were black. The real difference emerged, however, regarding the congregations' willingness to apply for public funds under Charitable Choice provisions once these arrangements were made clear to them: 67.9 percent of the black congregations and 55.3 perceont of the non-black congregations were willing. This finding is compatible with our finding that black congregations are politically more liberal and with the literature that suggests that African Americans are more willing to accept government support and involvement in social services provision (Black, Koopman, and Ryden 2004).

REPLACEMENT VALUE

One question remains: "What is the actual financial value of services offered by black congregations and how does it compare with other congregations in the city?" In Chapter 5, we discussed the concept of replacement value. In this chapter, we use this method to contrast the replacement values of black and non-black congregations. In other words, we compare the fiscal values of the social contributions provided by black and non-black congregations in Philadelphia.

By replacement value, we do not mean solely the dollar cost incurred by congregations in running their programs. (See Chapter 5 for a break-

down of what we mean by replacement value and for how we determined estimated costs of programs.) We aggregated all program income
to the congregation, both cash and in-kind, and deducted this from the
total estimated cost to obtain the total replacement value of the congregation's social services and programs.

The mean monthly replacement value of any congregation in Philadelphia was $3,329.35. Programs offered by black congregations were,
on average, of lower replacement value and amounted to $3,296.37. Pro-
grams offered by non-black congregations were of higher replacement
value, $3,367.29. To determine the average monthly replacement value
of all social services provided by an average congregation, we multiplied
the average cost per program by the average number of programs per
congregation and deducted what the congregation may generate as net
income from the activity. For black congregations, the average monthly
program revenue was $72.00; hence the net replacement value is
$3,224.37. For non-black congregations, the average monthly program
revenue was $78.23; hence the net replacement value is $3,289.06.

Black congregations, on average, reported more programs (3.2) than
did non-black congregations (2.9). Thus, we used these numbers as multipliers when determining the average cost per program and the average
replacement cost for black and non-black congregations, respectively.
Thus the average monthly replacement value of a black congregation is
$3,224.37 times 3.2, or $10,317.98, and the monthly average replacement value of a non-black congregation is $3,289.06 times 2.9, or
$9,538.27. In other words, the contribution of black congregations in
terms of replacement value, on average, is even larger than that of non-
black congregations. Multiplying these numbers by 12 provides an estimated annual replacement value for each group of congregations:
$123,815.76 for black congregations and $114,459.20 for non-black congregations.

Given that there are more black congregations than non-black congregations in Philadelphia, their overall contribution is larger than that
of the non-black congregations. For the 719 black congregations
counted in the PCC, their total annual contribution is estimated at
$89,023,531.44, versus $77,031,041.60 673 for non-black congregations.
In other words, black congregations, collectively, support the quality of
life of Philadelphians to a larger degree than do non-black congregations.

Summary

Black people arrived in Philadelphia more than three hundred years
ago. Given the Quaker spirit of the colony, slavery was not rampant, and

the area was one of the places in America where free black people could live, work, and even own property. This is not to say that they were treated equally and received full citizenship rights. In fact, racism and discrimination are still widespread problems in Philadelphia. Among the clearest manifestations of modern-day racism are the levels of urban blight and segregation in the city. As soon as black Philadelphians became a strong force in the city, whites started to move to the suburbs and blacks were left behind in a few selected neighborhoods known for their high poverty and crime rates and low quality of education available. Many of our interviewees believed that the city has failed its black residents by allowing businesses to relocate away from the city and by not providing high-quality education. The fact that two of the last three mayors have been black did little to change the overall picture of the declining tax base, deteriorating public services, and white residents' flight to the suburbs.

As the literature suggests and our data show, blacks are more religious than any other ethnic group, and black congregations are, on average, smaller in size, command fewer financial resources, and are attended mostly by women. One would expect under these conditions that black congregations would be less inclined to develop and sustain social programs. We know that social service involvement by local religious congregations is strongly correlated with the congregation's financial resources and membership size (Tsitsos 2003); hence black congregations in Philadelphia are expected to provide fewer social services. On the other hand, black congregations are housed in communities where needs are most pressing, and their clergy and members, even those who commute, face a harsher reality than those in non-black congregations.

Verba, Schlozman, and Brady (1993) and Harris (1994) suggest that the more hierarchically structured the denomination, like the Roman Catholic church, the less likely it is to foster civic involvement among congregants, while more decentralized and democratic denominations are more likely to do so. Indeed, most of the black congregations are Protestant and only a few are Catholic (19 churches, 2.7 percent) or Muslim (7 mosques, 1 percent). This may explain why so many black congregations are involved in providing social services and why they offer, on average, more social services than non-black congregations. Working in a nonhierarchical structure and facing so many needs, black clergy, lay leaders, and members are compelled to tackle the social issues that surround them. They are more inclined to take matters into their own hands, and even with insufficient help from municipal resources, black congregations work to meet local needs and improve the quality of life in the community around them. As such, black congregations offer more services and cover all target populations more than non-black congregations, with the exception of services for children, which both groups cover equally. Black congregations offer more programs, however, for needy populations, such as people with addictions, poor people, and the elderly.

The literature has tried to understand the differences between black and non-black congregational social service provision. While the involvement of black congregations, especially historically, is celebrated, the reality of today is most unclear. While some scholars have tried to show that black congregations are more committed to poor people or are more concerned with programs that require intensive interaction with clients, we propose that black congregations are more involved in areas that plague their local community. Because black congregations are often located in areas plagues by poverty, homelessness, and other social ills, they tend to provide social services in these areas.

Commitment and devotion alone, however, may not be sufficient to offer a massive intervention. Black congregations provide programs that are staffed by fewer people and serve fewer people. There is a limit to their ability to compensate for fewer resources, such as their membership pool and available money. Their programs are greater in number and fewer in resources. When one considers their size and limited resources, one realizes that they are doing a commendable job in meeting the needs of Philadelphians. It is not clear how generalizable the findings are, but given the work of other scholars (e.g., Billingsley and Caldwell 1991; Thomas et al. 1994; Tolliver 1993) and the history of the black church in America, it seems that our findings are valid nationwide.

True to the history of blacks in the United States, the government meets very few of their needs. Thanks to affirmative action and equal-opportunity policies a new black middle class has been created. Many more black people are well educated, hold high-level positions, and command sizable salaries. However, they are still the minority among the black community; a visit to any large American metropolis or to any state or federal prison will demonstrate how far we are from real equality and true social and economic integration. As in the past, the black congregation is tackling the social and human needs of black people. With the spirit of compassionate conservatism, we can only expect less direct government support and more expectations that the black congregations will step in to serve as community pillars and the first welfare stop for all those who are in need of help. It is in these local institutions that food is offered and educational support is provided. It is in these congregations that children are cared for and teens are nourished and mentored.

It is imperative for social observers and policy makers to understand that not all black congregations are alike. The flagships of the black religious community are the large congregations that offer lots of social services and frequent solutions to crises; it is to them that politicians appeal in times of unrest (Wood 1997). However, most black congregations are small in size and short of needed resources. These congregations need much technical support and training as well as financial support if they are to be harnessed by any government as a means to alleviate misery in urban America. Johnson (1980) shows that larger congregations and congregations with clergy who graduated from seminary or college were more involved in social service delivery and in social action activities. Yet, as Longest (1991) and Cnaan and his colleagues (2002) show, regardless of denomination and size, black congregations are willing to help the needy. Black clergy take it as part of their spiritual mission to mix the secular with the sacred into a holistic ministry. However, it is important to remember that some can do more than others because they have more access to resources, skills, and conviction.

A few studies summarized earlier in this chapter contrasted and compared the social commitments of black congregations and non-black places of worship. These comparisons were often based on small sample sizes and suffered from major methodological limitations. The present study, in a city where half the residents and half the congregations are black, enables us to provide a sound comparison. Given that the units of comparison are each of more than 600 congregations, the likelihood of error is quite small. And indeed the emerging picture only partially mirrored the work of previous scholars in this field. Our findings, in broad strokes, suggest that black congregations are smaller and less resourced but are eagerly involved in social services provision, and that while some of their programs are of a smaller scope, they provide more programs overall that focus more on the neediest city residents and their neighbors. In other words, black congregations are still a major agent of change and strength for the quality of life in the black community.

One can only imagine how our urban scene would look if these congregations ceased to be providers of care. If such a scenario were to occur, the burden on public services and the social unrest that would follow are hard to imagine. Black congregations are carrying the load of helping that many believe should be the domain of the government. But when the government was not assisting needy people in black neighborhoods, the black churches and mosques stepped in, as was the case historically, and did their best to support their members and their neighbors. In a way, black congregations serve to uphold social order and prevent race-based riots. They substitute for public care and serve the polity with their commitment to people's quality of life. If, however, a process of secularization takes place in the black community, one can expect a major disruption in the social status quo.

Chapter 8

Latino Congregations in the Twenty-First Century

The United States is witnessing a dramatic change in its ethnic composition.[1] From an Anglo-European focus of new immigrants we are now facing an increasingly diverse population (Singer 2002; Kilty and de Haymes 2000; Cerrutti and Massey, 2001). Public discourse is shifting into the future of the United States as a Christian white society. The current debate about the immigration law is an indication of the rise in Latino/Hispanic immigration in all parts of the United States. Mostly Mexican, but also from Central and South America, these legal and illegal immigrants are the fastest growing group of newcomers to the United States and by now the largest minority group.[2]

The Latino population, at 35 million members, is now the largest minority group in the United States (U.S. Census 2000). Between 1990 and 2000 the white, non-Hispanic population, estimated at 196 million, grew by 0.3 percent and the black population grew by 1.5 percent, whereas the Latino population grew by 4.7 percent. This population growth is due to new births and immigration, and the rates of both continue to rise. The Latino population is young, with 35 percent under eighteen. The high birth rate and low median age indicate continued population growth.

Latinos in the United States have a unique history of colonialism and immigration that puts them in different social situations from non-Latino groups. Latinos are too often compared with African Americans, as they are the two largest minority groups in America and have shared the same struggle for a better life and a bigger share of the American dream. However, Espinosa, Elizondo, and Miranda (2003: 12) suggested that "in many ways Latinos represent a kind of *nepantla* racial-ethnic community of in-betweeners in American society. This is not to imply that Latinos are always in-between blacks and whites." While the Latino and African American communities are both characterized by low household incomes, low educational attainment, and high rates of incarceration, the two groups are significantly different in a number of ways.

To begin with, Latinos in the United States have a different primary language from English. Consequently, most Latinos and their children face communication problems in the job market and education. A growing number of communities are organized in Spanish, where business, media, and daily communication occur in Spanish and there is no practical need to speak English. Most of these Latinos have a high school education; there are fewer with a college education (7.5 percent) than among non-Latinos (19.3 percent) (Fry 2002).

Second, Latinos are multi-ethnic. Many people in the United States view Latinos as one group speaking the same language and sharing the same culture. However, Latinos come from many different counties and do not share common norms, cultural heritages, or educational backgrounds (Bean and Tienda 1987). In many of their counties of origin there are even distinct cultural differences among regions.

According to the 2000 Census figures, the 35 million Latinos living in the United States have 22 countries of origin. Most Latinos do not see themselves as Latinos but as, say, Puerto Rican, Salvadoran, or Mexican, and the cultural boundaries can be strong. For example, to many families, a marriage between a Cuban and a Dominican is considered cross-ethnic and is frowned upon by both sides. In summary, a distinctive feature of the Latino community is its lack of homogeneity compared to African American and white non-Hispanic communities. The many subgroups may not necessarily get along or have much in common.

As noted, Latinos often have a country of origin to which they remain connected and to which many of them, if needed, can go back. This creates an issue of dual alliance and dual affiliation. Castex (1994) reports that many Hispanics in the New York City area, especially Dominicans, refuse to become U.S. citizens in alliance with their home country and as a sign of distrust of American foreign policies. This is not to say that Latinos do not wish to be in the country legally or become citizens. But the sentiment highlights the loyalty of some Latinos to their country of origin and the fact that the United States may be in collision with their home country's interests.

The dual alliance of Latinos in the United States gets translated into economic terms. Many Latinos are in the North to support parents or children and wives in their own countries, a commitment that may last a long time. Every month Mexican residents of the United States send "home" to their families over $1 billion. This enormous amount of money comes from the paychecks of low-wage earners who send small sums. Collectively, Latinos from Central and South America annually send home a sum of 30 billion dollars (Suro 2003). This sum is equivalent to the amount that other ethnic groups use to improve their quality of life or to support charitable organizations. The end result is that many

Latinos in the United States are left with little money for their own subsistence. Suro suggests that this generous support to their families at home keeps Latinos in the United States financially strapped.

Finally, the Latino community does not have a common experience that can unify it and set a coordinated course of action for the future, unlike the African American community that collectively suffers and shares the traumatic experience of slavery, or the Jewish community that shares the traumatic experience of the Holocaust. Given all these differences, one cannot simply take knowledge gained from one extensively studied ethnic group, that is, African Americans, and transfer it to Latinos. It is the obligation of researchers to study this group separate from other ethnic groups and appreciate its internal diversity.

Consequently, Latino cultures cannot be reduced to a list of unified, timeless, unchanging values and characteristics. Latino-origin groups are diverse and riddled with internal tensions and conflicts. Their cultures are constantly emerging as they deal with old conflicts in the context of the new realities produced by immigration (Longres and Peterson 2000, 66). Furthermore, Latinos are not well mixed with other ethnic groups. For example, Goode's (1990) study of three Philadelphia neighborhoods reported that attempts at planned integration between local ethnic groups often failed. Goode attributed this failure to ignoring residents' views and preferences. The process of new Latino immigrants entering predominantly Black or Anglo communities was often associated with ethnic tension and increased isolation on all sides.

A few scholars documented the persistent economic disadvantage of Latino residents in the United States (Fix and Passel 1994; Partida 1996). As with many other ethnic groups, Latinos concentrate in homogeneous neighborhoods, where most residents are Latino, the common language is Spanish, and the level of poverty is very high (Massey, Zambrana, and Bell 1995). This may hamper attempts to integrate into mainstream United States. However, other scholars (Padilla 1997; Perlmann and Waldinger, 1997) suggest that this persistent poverty is most common among the first generation of immigrants and is likely to disappear in the second generation. If this trend continues, then Latinos are following the trends set by European and Asian immigrants whose second generations are self-sustaining. However, given the large numbers of illegal immigrants who cannot find entry into the American society or advance into better paying jobs, the process of full integration of Latinos into the American society may be slower than that of previous immigrants (De La Rosa 2000; Mahler 1995).

Both U.S.-born and immigrant Latinos are disadvantaged by the transition from a manufacturing to a service economy (Massey, Zambrana, and Bell 1995; Padilla 1996). As Portes and Rumbaut (1996) suggested and as amplified by Mexico's president Vincente Fox, Latinos in the United States are more often than not stacked at the bottom of the labor market. They are the lowest paid employees of the service and agriculture industries.

The Latinos' unique heritage and characteristics make them stand out as compared to other ethnic groups. Research among Latinos notes strong family and social support systems that surpass those of the Anglo community. However, as Sherraden and Barrea (1996) noted, concentrated poverty coupled with low English proficiency provides little hope for massive Latino social advancement. The U.S. Census (2000) also reports that Latinos in 2000 had a higher percentage of single-parent families than all other ethnic groups (about 30 percent), and this percentage reached over 40 percent for Puerto Ricans, the largest group of Latinos in Philadelphia.

Latinos are also known to be less amenable to formal volunteerism. Based on a secondary analysis of the census data, Michel, Green, and Toppe (2003) report that Latinos exhibit the lowest rates of volunteering (15.7 percent), compared with all other ethnic groups (27.6 percent for the population as a whole). However, when second-generation Latinos are studied alone, while their rates of volunteering were still below the general population, rates for Latino volunteer work were higher than those reported by blacks (22 percent and 19.6 percent respectively). Similarly, Brown and Ferris (2004) reported, based on the Social Capital Benchmark Survey of 29 communities and some 29,000 individuals, that Latinos were the least likely to volunteer or donate money.

Religion and the Latino Community

Religion is an especially prodigious source of Latino identity, cultural cohesiveness, and social organization (Diaz-Stevens and Stevens-Arroyo 1998). As a resource for communities and individuals, religion also serves to strengthen and enrich social programs. Latino religion in America is distinct from that of other ethnic groups in many ways, including language difference, the role of religious faith in daily life, shared traditions, values and symbols, literature, folklore and music, and the concept of government and social responsibility (Diaz-Stevens and Stevens-Arroyo 1998). However, the Social Capital Benchmark Survey (2001) found that Latinos are less religiously involved than other ethnic groups in the United States. This study found that 47 percent of black respondents participated in religious activities other than worship, compared to 41 percent of white and only 31 percent of Latino respondents. As we will show later, other studies also support these findings.

In studying the adaptation of immigrant communities into the United

States, scholars have suggested that local religious congregations play a key role in this in this process (Ebaugh and Chafetz 2000; Warner 1998). As we will further discuss in Chapter 14, congregations are places where face-to-face interactions take place and where social capital is built (Smidt 2003; Wood 2002). Religion offers important psychological and emotional support in times of stress and in situations of transition and shift. However, religious communities are also known to provide tangible social support, advice and instrumental care, and to represent the needs of immigrants in an institutional manner. In the Latino community religious affiliation is associated with cultural identity. At the same time, scholars have also suggested that the immigrant church, while strengthening ties with the home country and home culture (Levitt 2001), may also hinder the process of immigrants' assimilation (Mullins 1987).

Many Latino immigrants, legal and illegal alike, find churches to be among the most familiar, welcoming, and supportive institutions available. Menjivar (2002), who studied Salvadoran immigrants in San Francisco, Washington, D.C., and Phoenix, found that immigrants in the three locales were well aware of church leaders' response to the problems they faced and of churches' help in dealing with issues of adaptation. Levitt (2002: 150–51) summarized the role of religion in helping immigrants, especially Latino immigrants, as follows:

Religious institutions have always helped immigrants integrate into the countries that receive them and enabled them to stay connected to the countries they came from. . . . Religious institutions are extending and expanding their global operations such that migrants can remain active in sending-country religious groups and in the congregation that receives them. Religious participation incorporates migrants into strong transnational institutional networks where they acquire social citizenship and can seek protection, make claims, and articulate their concerns, regardless of their political status. It integrates them into transnational religious civil society that can complement or substitute for partial political membership.

Menjivar (2002) also found that churches provide immigrants with resources that the immigrants themselves deem necessary, such as legal assistance, financial assistance for rent, advice dealing with problems in their neighborhoods, and kind words in desperate moments. Espinosa, Elizondo, and Miranda (2003) found that 74 percent of Latinos in their study wanted their churches to aid undocumented immigrants. Thus, from the point of view of immigrants, religion, as has been the case historically, may continue to provide avenues for groups to improve their lot.

Latinos are usually either Catholics or Protestants. Menjivar (2002) observed more people in a Catholic church than in the two evangelical churches in the same city combined. Our Philadelphia data show an average ratio between members of Catholic and Protestant churches to be almost 16 to 1 (1,581 versus 90), much bigger than that observed by Menjívar. Nationally, 70 percent of U.S. Latinos are Catholic; this number has remained stable for the past decade. More and more Latinos in America are converting to Protestantism, but the percentage of Catholics is kept stable by the prodigious influx of immigrants from predominantly Catholic countries such as Mexico, which has one of the highest rates of Catholicism in Latin America (Espinosa, Elizondo, and Miranda 2003). Espinosa, Elizondo, and Miranda found that the percentage of Latino Catholics drops with each succeeding generation living in America, and the percentage of Protestants rises correspondingly. These authors suggest that "in national perspective, there are now more Latino Protestants in the United States than Jews or Muslims or Episcopalians and Presbyterians combined" (16). Of the non-Catholic Christians, Pentecostals and Evangelicals constitute the majority. Despite these changes, Matovina (2001) found that Latinos are the largest Catholic group in America; due to substantial Latino immigration, they will continue to comprise the majority of Catholics in the first decades of the twenty-first century.

Badillo (2004) interviewed a priest working with Latinos in Chicago who noted that the Mexican population in terms of faith is more conservative than others in the parish. As we will demonstrate, in Philadelphia Latino congregation members are indeed theologically and politically conservative.

Menjívar found that the ethnic compositions of Catholic and evangelical churches differ. Catholic churches tended to be diverse, while evangelical churches tended to be more homogeneous. Catholic churches, based on the local parish principle, not only assemble Latinos from various countries, but also include parishioners from non-Latino countries of origin. In the Philadelphia study, we found that in the seven Latino Catholic churches only 78 percent of the members were Latino; the others were white or African American. Furthermore, 80 of the 139 Catholic churches in Philadelphia had a range of Latino members, from a handful (less than 1 percent) to just under half (45 percent). In these congregations, Latinos were the minority members and the churches were clearly heterogeneous.

In small homogeneous churches, the clergy know all the congregants and are personally involved in members' lives. Programs are tailor-made to meet members' needs or are suggested by active members. In large Catholic churches the approach is more collective, and initiatives come from the clergy or a committee. Either way, the initiatives are often successful. For example, in a nonrandom survey of 427 Protestant Latino churches in 33 states, Amy Sherman (2003) found that seven of ten (69.5 percent) churches provided at least one social and community service.

Church attendance is positively associated with a number of benefits for youth and adults. Religious involvement seems to be related to school attendance. Even though the statistics regarding Latino school attendance in the United States are troubling, at least one study found a relationship between parental religious involvement and children's educational attainment. For example, up to 40 percent of foreign-born school-age Latinos in the United States are not enrolled in school (Hirschman 2001). Hauser, Simmons, and Pager (2000) estimated the school dropout rate for Latinos at 21.6 percent compared with 11.5 percent for non-Latino white students. While some, like Alba and Nee (1997), suggest that second-generation Latino students perform as well as other U.S.-born students, this is yet to be proven. In contrast to these studies, Sikkink and Hernandez (2003) conducted a secondary analysis of three databases that indicated that Latino parents' religious involvement has a strong positive impact on Latino first-graders' educational attainment. Furthermore, Latinos who attend church more frequently also spend more time with their children in such educational activities as reading books and going to the library than do infrequent attenders and nonattenders. Among high school Latino students, the level of religiosity was associated with staying in school but did not explain it.

Latinos in Philadelphia

As noted in the previous chapter, Philadelphia is a typical postindustrial city that lost about a quarter of its population between 1950 and 2000 (U.S. Census 2000). In the decade before the 2000 census, Latinos in Philadelphia grew from 5.5 percent to 8.5 percent of the city population (Bartelt 2001). In many ways, however, this growth does not provide a real picture of Latino immigration in the region. In suburban communities such as Norristown and Kenneth Square, large parts of the local economies are based on Latinos, and they have formed their own mini-communities. Little is known systematically about the life and needs of Latinos in Philadelphia.

In this chapter, we analyze findings regarding the congregational life of Latinos in Philadelphia. As noted above, Philadelphia is not a historically Latino city like Los Angeles and Miami, but Latinos have always been present, and in recent years the city has witnessed a resurgence of Latino immigrants. In this chapter we summarize findings regarding two main areas of interest. First, we summarize the characteristics of the congregations as social organizations and compare Latino and non-Latino congregations in the following areas: religious affiliation, membership size, age of members, income of members, gender distribution, property, budget, sources of income, grant application and income, personnel, clergy information, and governing structure. Second, we provide data on the scope and nature of congregations' social and community outreach to needy neighbors; sources of support for congregations' community-serving work; providers and recipients of congregations' social and community programs; knowledge of government policies such as Charitable Choice; the extent of interfaith, ecumenical, and religious/secular partnerships; and conservative estimates of the monetary "replacement value" of congregations' programs. Following the methodology in this study, we present this information by comparing Latino and non-Latino congregations. Finally, we discuss the implications of our findings and the adequacy of the available literature.

Latino Congregations In Philadelphia

We found 148 documented Latino congregations in Philadelphia,[3] which implies that Latino congregations compose 7 percent of the city's congregations. Put differently, on average, there is one congregation for every 715 city residents overall, while there is one Latino congregation for every 871 Latino residents. As can be seen in Figure 8.1, Latino congregations are not evenly spread throughout the city, but are more prevalent where the concentration of Latino residents is higher. It is possible that any number of Latino congregations went undiscovered. However, we have no reason to believe that these unknown Latino congregations would be located away from the Latino community.

Latinos and Religion in Philadelphia

This chapter focuses on a subsample of 109 Latino congregations, consisting of the interviews we conducted with three-quarters (73.6 percent) of the known Philadelphia Latino congregations. Among the 109 Latino congregations, membership size ranged from 12 to 6,500 members. On average, 186 people attended at least one worship service per month per Latino congregation. Children were included in the average membership size of the congregations in our sample. The median number of members was 68. In other words, half the congregations in our study reported membership of fewer than 68 individuals. Taking the average number of monthly attenders (186) and multiplying it by the known 148 Latino congregations suggests that 27,528 Latino residents of Philadel-

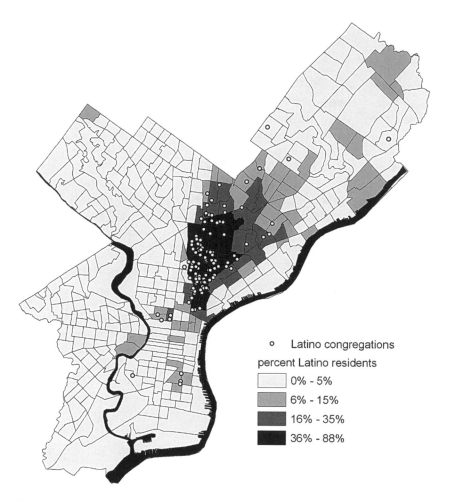

Figure 8.1. Latino congregations and locations vis-à-vis residential locations of Latinos.

phia are congregational members (defined as monthly attenders). An additional 3,852 Latinos were reported to worship in non-Hispanic congregations. Putting these two numbers together suggests that only 24.3 percent of the Latino residents of Philadelphia attend local religious congregations (versus 47 percent of the population as a whole).

Not surprisingly, non-Latino congregations were significantly larger (320 members) than Latino congregations (186 members). Average weekly attendance at non-Latino congregations was 228 people, compared to 112 at Latino congregations. The seven Catholic Latino churches commanded many more members (1,581) than non-Catholic Latino congregations (90), so the difference is even more pronounced in the Protestant churches. Though we did not study it here, it is possible that some Latino Philadelphians worship in congregations outside the city in the surrounding suburban areas. However, other members of city congregations reside outside the city limits and commute into the city to worship, and we assume that these numbers cancel each other out.

However, if we consider all people who were reported to be affiliated with a Latino congregation, including people who attend only on major holidays and major life events (such as baptisms and weddings), the average number rises significantly. This group of people, which includes those discussed above and occasional attenders, averaged 294 per congregation. Put differently, 43,512 Latino residents of Philadelphia were affiliated with the known 148 Latino congregations. This suggests that 33.7 percent of Philadelphia Latino residents are affiliated with a local religious congregation.

A large percentage of the congregations (77 congregations, 71 percent) had a majority of members from Puerto Rican origin; this is congruent with Philadelphia's history. However, it also suggests that even within the Latino community, church attendance is segregated by country of origin and churches are carefully chosen by compatriots.

The number of members in any one congregation changes frequently, so our one-time data collection may have missed trends. Thus, for the sample of 109 Latino congregations, we asked whether membership had gone up, remained the same, or declined in the previous three years. Almost two-thirds of the congregations (63 percent) reported that in the past three years their membership had risen. This was a much higher rate than the rate reported by the overall sample (46.5 percent). Another quarter (25.9 percent) of Latino congregations reported that in the previous three years their membership had remained stable (versus 23 percent for non-Latino congregations). Just over 11 percent reported that membership had declined in the previous three years (versus 21.5 percent for non-Latino congregations). These numbers suggest that Latino people in and around Philadelphia are in the process of joining local religious congregations, and that congregations are witnessing a significant growth in membership. While a smaller percentage of Latinos attend places of worship, Latino congregations are more vibrant than other congregations in their growth and ability to attract new members.

In today's highly mobile and transient society, many people think nothing of driving past local neighborhood stores in order to shop at their favorite mall. The same can be said for congregations. A significant number of people today are choosing to commute to congregations outside their own neighborhood for worship services. We found that in Latino congregations significantly more members lived within city limits (94.9 percent, versus 81.4 percent for non-Latino congregations). The remainder (18.6 percent) lived outside the city. Interestingly, 43.1 percent of members lived within a ten-block radius of their congregations, a similar percentage to non-Latino congregational members. In other words, Latino congregations attract more members from within city limits while non-Latino congregations attract more members from outside the city. One explanation for this difference may be that many Latinos have limited means, so that even if they live in the surrounding counties they pray where they live to save on transportation costs to the city. Another, more plausible explanation is that because Latino-populated neighborhoods in the city are concentrated, people tend to have their churches where they and their compatriots reside. Furthermore, Roman Catholics are most likely to worship in the parish where they reside.

Latinos are often associated with Catholic churches. By virtue of the conquest of Central and South America by Spain and Portugal, Catholicism became the dominant religion in those regions. However, of the 109 Latino congregations we interviewed, only seven were Roman Catholic (6.4 percent), although these seven congregations are the largest: on average each had 1,581 regular attenders and 3,078 affiliated people. Non-Catholic Latino congregations averaged only 90 regular attenders and 100 affiliated people. These differences are quite dramatic; they demonstrate the emergence of small non-Catholic churches alongside large traditional Catholic churches.

The studied congregations consisted of forty different denominations. The denomination with the largest number of Latino congregations was a Pentecostal denomination (63 congregations, 58 percent). Two denominations followed at some distance: seven congregations were a variety of Baptists, and, as noted above, seven Roman Catholic churches were predominantly Latino (6.4 percent). Espinosa, Elizondo, and Miranda (2003) and Greeley (1998) found among second-generation Latino Americans that one in six or seven joins a Protestant church, often a charismatic-evangelical strand rather than a mainline Protestant church.

LONGEVITY AND GEOGRAPHIC STABILITY

The average Latino congregation in Philadelphia is quite young: only 6 congregations were incorporated before 1900, and 73 (68 percent) were incorporated after 1980. The average Latino congregation was established some thirty-five years ago (1974). In comparison, the average year of incorporation for non-Latino congregations is 1936. These averages represent a trend of expansion that parallels the growth of the Latino community in Philadelphia.

On average, a Latino congregation in Philadelphia has been located in its current location for nineteen years. They have been in their present locations from as little as a few weeks to as long as 140 years. Interestingly, given the relatively young age of Latino congregations and their growth trend, they are quite stable in their communities. Most Latino congregations (78, 72.2 percent) own their property and only 11 (10.2 percent) are still paying mortgages for their congregational building. Twenty congregations (18.8 percent) rent space, 7 (6.5 percent) use private space owned by a member of the clergy, and the remainder share space with other congregations.

When asked if they planned to relocate in the foreseeable future, more Latino congregations answered positively (30.3 percent) than did non-Latino congregations (17.2 percent). This may be the result of newer and still-growing Latino congregations that started in basements or storefronts and are now in the process of institutionalization (or "in the process of finding a larger or more permanent home").

CLERGY

Not surprisingly, Latino clergy are the chief executive officers of their congregations and also initiate much of the service activity spawned by congregations. Of the 109 Latino congregations, about two-fifths (only 42, 38.5 percent) had at least one paid, full-time member of the clergy. A much smaller number, six Latino congregations, most of which are Roman Catholic, reported two full-time clergy, and only two congregations reported three full-time clergy. Twelve congregations reported a part-time paid clergyperson (11.1 percent). In contrast, we found that significantly more non-Latino congregations had at least one paid full-time clergyperson (63.2 percent). In other words, three-fifths of the Latino congregations reported not having paid full-time clergy, compared with two-fifths of non-Latino congregations. The most striking finding in this respect is that exactly half the Latino congregations reported that their clergy are not financially reimbursed. Such clergy are truly bivocational, in that they work full-time elsewhere and voluntarily serve as clergy.

Most clergy in Philadelphia are male (87.1 percent), with no significant differences between Latino and non-Latino congregations. About two-thirds of all clergy (722; 67.3 percent) reported graduating from a theological seminary. More clergy in non-Latino congregations graduated from a theological seminary (70 percent) than in Latino congregations (60 percent).

POLITICAL AND THEOLOGICAL ORIENTATION

Latino congregations in Philadelphia are politically diverse. In 50 percent of the Latino congregations our interviewees told us that the majority of members are politically conservative; 31.1 percent were labeled moderate and 18.9 percent liberal. Significantly more Latino congregations (50 percent) reported a conservative majority than did non-Latino congregations (31.6 percent). This is one clear example where Latino congregations are different from African American congregations, who reported more liberal tendencies than the rest of the congregations in Philadelphia, a result that is consistent with Badillo's (2004) findings.

Likewise, in 14.8 percent of the congregations interviewees informed us that the majority of their members are theologically fundamentalist; 61.1 percent described the majority as conservative, 21.3 percent as moderate, and only 2.8 percent liberal. The corresponding percentages for non-Latino congregations were considerably less conservative (13.7, 38, 35.1, and 11.1 percent respectively). These findings were further emphasized when Latino interviewees were asked if the majority of members would agree that the Bible is the literal word of God: 95.1 percent answered positively.

These statistics imply that Latino congregations are rightly described as theologically far more fundamentalist-conservative, and also politically conservative, more often than non-Latino congregations. These two variables were strongly associated ($\chi^2 = 22.75$, df $= 6$, $p < .01$), suggesting that, in the Latino community, congregations with politically conservative members are also theologically conservative or fundamentalist and vice versa. Our findings differ somewhat from those of Espinosa, Elizondo, and Miranda (2003), who found Latinos to be morally and ethically conservative but politically and economically liberal. It is not clear whether our sample was biased or whether church-attending Latinos in Philadelphia, and maybe even nationally, are more likely to be politically conservative than non-church attending Latinos.

MEMBERS' INCOME

Not surprisingly, the average household income of members of non-Latino congregations was higher than that of members of Latino congregations. Among Latino congregations, 77 percent of members had an annual income of less than $25,000; among non-Latino congregations 45.8 percent were reported at this level. Conversely, among non-Latino congregations, members with an annual income of more than $50,000 were reported at 16.1 percent, versus 2.3 percent among Latino congregations. These findings suggest, as our literature review indicated, that Latinos in Philadelphia command fewer financial means and are, on average, in the bottom range of the economic scale.

BUILDING FACILITIES

On average, Latino congregations are less likely to own their meeting places and occupy fewer buildings overall than do non-Latino congregations. Only 72.5 percent of Latino congregations own their space, compared to 83.4 percent of non-Latino congregations. Among Latino congregations, about a third (36.7 percent) occupied more than one building compared to half the non-Latino congregations (50 percent). In addition, many congregational buildings were reported to be in need of repair. More Latino congregations (45 percent) reported building problems such as roof problems, leakages, and stress than did non-Latino congregations (29.5 percent).

ANNUAL BUDGET AND FISCAL STATUS

Congregations in this study identified their annual budget in the following categories: (1) under $50,000; (2) $50,000–100,000; (3) $100,001–200,000; (4) $200,001–500,000; (5) $500,001–1,000,000; and (6) over $1,000,000. Two-thirds of Latino congregations (67.6 percent) reported budgets of less than $50,000, compared to one-third (32.1 percent) of non-Latino congregations. This difference alone suggests that most Latino congregations operate on a very low budget compared to all other Philadelphia congregations. Budgets between $50,000 and $100,000 were reported by 24 percent of the congregations (19 percent of Latino congregations, compared to 24.4 percent of non-Latino congregations). When we combined the other categories into congregations with anannual income of above $100,000, we found that only 13.3 percent of Latino congregations were included, compared to 43.5 percent of non-Latino congregations.

Not surprisingly, significantly more Latino congregations (54.7 percent) perceived themselves to be struggling financially than did non-Latino congregations (37.5 percent). In face-to-face interviews with Latino clergy, it became clear that balancing the budget and avoiding deficits was a priority. With annual budgets of less than $50,000, the congregations could indeed appear to struggling financially.

SOURCES OF INCOME

For all congregations, on average, about a third derived their income from pledges or dues, which included tithes (37.2 percent), while about half the income came from offerings (47.1 percent). Overall, about 16 percent of congregations' finances came from other sources, such as denominational support, special gifts, endowments, contracts with the government, and thrift shops. Overall, 44 Latino congregations (40.4 percent) applied for financial help from an outside source. The majority of Latino congregations that applied for external financial support received at least one grant (43 congregations; 39.4 percent).

Latino Congregational and Social Services Provision

As noted before, of the 1,392 congregations surveyed, 1,270 (91.2 percent) reported that they provided at least one social program that served the community. The average number of community-serving programs per congregation was 3.06.[4] This mean refers to all 1,392 studied congregations and includes the 123 congregations that did not provide any social services. Overall, congregations reported a total of 4,261 programs (often called "social ministries"). Of these, Latino congregations carried out 6.7 percent (289 programs), while 93.6 percent were carried out by non-Latino congregations. We noted that these percentages closely parallel the proportion of Latino versus non-Latino congregations in our sample (6.9 percent versus 93.1 percent). On average, a Latino congregation in Philadelphia provided 2.65 programs whereas a non-Latino congregation provided 3.12 programs. That is, non-Latino congregations were more active in social services provision.

LATINO CONGREGATIONS AND AREAS OF SOCIAL INVOLVEMENT

Our checklist of 215 possible services or "ministries" included programs—whether administered formally by the congregation on its property or elsewhere, or carried out on their property by a third party—which served the needy in Philadelphia. Table 8.1, compares the types of service areas Philadelphia's Latino and non-Latino congregations are involved in. We have included only service areas reported by at least 15 percent of the congregations (n.s. denotes no statistical difference between Latino and non-Latino congregations; the number of asterisks indicates the strength of the difference between the two groups).

As seen in Table 8.1, the key finding is that Latino congregations are less involved in almost every area of social service program. In particular,

TABLE 8.1. EXAMPLES OF SERVICES IN WHICH LATINO AND NON-LATINO CONGREGATIONS ARE INVOLVED (PERCENT OF CONGREGATIONS THAT PROVIDE SERVICE)

Type of service	Total	Latino	Non-Latino
Sports activities	15.3 **	6.4	16.1
Scholarships for students in need	15.4 **	5.5	16.3
Mentoring/Rites of passage	15.6 ***	1.8	16.8
Health screening	16.4 **	7.3	17.2
Crime watch	16.5 ***	4.6	17.5
Music classes	15.0 (n.s.)	12.8	15.2
Organized tours (for the elderly)	15.6 ***	2.8	16.6
Drug and alcohol prevention programs	15.7 (n.s.)	14.7	15.8
Neighborhood cleanups	16.1 (n.s.)	11.9	16.4
Street outreach to homeless people	16.5 (n.s.)	10.1	16.9
Parenting skills	17.2 (n.s.)	11.9	17.6
Health education	18.1 *	10.1	18.8
Scout troops	17.9 **	7.3	18.8
Interfaith collaboration	18.5 *	10.1	19.3
Visiting sick/homebound people	18.0 ***	6.4	19.0
Premarriage counseling	19.2 (n.s.)	14.7	19.6
Hospital visitation	19.5 (n.s.)	14.7	20.0
Day care (preschool)	18.2 **	9.2	18.9
Homeless shelter	18.8 **	19.1	7.9
Marriage encounters (retreats)	18.2 (n.s.)	19.3	18.1
Recreational programs for seniors	20.2 ***	4.6	21.4
Community bazaars/fairs	21.4 **	11.0	22.3
Prison ministry	22 (n.s.)	28.4	21.5
Choral groups	22.9 *	13.8	23.8
After-school care	21.7 *	10.1	22.7
Programs for gang members	21.8 **	10.1	22.8
Neighborhood associations	21.9 ***	4.6	23.4
Visitation/buddy program (for seniors)	24.2 ***	9.2	25.4
International relief	23.5 (n.s.)	18.3	23.9
Educational tutoring	23.5 **	10.1	24.6
Soup kitchens	24.0 ***	10.1	25.3
Music performances	29.4 ***	12.8	30.8
Summer programs for teens	29.4 (n.s.)	28.6	25.7
Recreational programs for teens	37.0 (n.s.)	28.4	37.8
Clothing closets	37.0 **	22.9	38.3
Recreational program for children	37.3 (n.s.)	32.1	37.8
Summer day camp	40.6 *	31.2	41.4
Food pantries	50.0 *	38.5	51.0

n.s. = not statistically significant; * $p < .05$; ** $p < .01$; *** $p < .001$

non-Latino congregations are significantly more involved in helping elderly people and youth. One exception is summer programs for teens, where Latino congregations are proportionally more involved though the difference is not statistically significant. Similarly, Latino congregations provide less sick/homebound visitation. It may be that the extended Latino family supports its elders and children better than those in the rest of the city and hence these services are not needed. However, this proposition needs to be tested by further empirical study. Latino congregations are also significantly less involved in programs for the poor, such as food pantries and soup kitchens, but significantly more engaged in homeless shelters, which may indicate that homelessness is becoming a problem in the Philadelphia Latino community.

CONGREGATION BENEFICIARIES AND VOLUNTEERS

The interviewers were asked to identify the primary beneficiaries of the programs provided by congregations. The data from the 1,392 congregations we surveyed indicate that, on average, each congregation-sponsored program served 43 members of the congregation and 84 non-member community residents. Interestingly, Latino congregations, on average, served fewer church members than did non-Latino congregations (27 versus 44), but more noncongregational members (104 versus 83). This measure suggests that Latino congregations tend to serve their wider community more than their own members in comparison with other congregations.

On the service provider side, the social service delivery staff per Latino congregation averaged 9.7 members (paid staff and volunteers) and 7.8 volunteers who were nonmembers. Among non-Latino congregations, members amounted to 12.8 and nonmembers to 5.2. In other words, Latino congregations rely more on nonmembers while non-Latino congregations rely more on their members and staff.

To determine the beneficiaries of the congregation programs, we collected data on nine groups of potential beneficiaries, taking into consideration the fact that a program could serve more than one group, as in the case of a program for young children that also served their older siblings or parents. As Table 8.2 indicates, the major beneficiaries of congregational services and programs, for both Latino and non-Latino congregations, are needy children and youth.

As seen in Table 8.2, Latino congregations reported lower rates of service to older people and the young. This supports our previous findings and gives credence to the hypothesis that in the Latino community caring for the young and old remains within the bounds of familial responsibility. Latino congregations provide an equal amount of care for the

TABLE 8.2. BENEFICIARIES OF CONGREGATIONAL SOCIAL PROGRAMS IN LATINO AND NON-LATINO CONGREGATIONS (PERCENT OF PROGRAMS OFFERING SERVICES TO THESE POPULATIONS)

Beneficiary	Percent of programs	Latino	Non-Latino
Children	44.1 **	36.6	44.6
Youth	38.2 *	29.7	38.8
People with low incomes/poor people	34.7 (n.s.)	31.5	35.0
Families	34.1 (n.s.)	29.7	34.4
Adults	23.9 *	18.6	24.3
Elderly	21.8 ***	10.0	22.6
People with addictions	13.8 **	8.2	14.2
People with disabilities	12.8 ***	6.5	13.3
Community at large	43.1 (n.s.)	38.0	43.5

n.s. = not statistically significant, * $p < .05$; ** $p < .01$; *** $p < .001$

poor, community members, and families, but provide less care for people with addictions or disabilities than other congregations. This difference may be the result of limited resources rather than a planned priority, but this finding begs for further and more in-depth study.

CONGREGATIONAL COLLABORATIONS

Many congregations collaborate with other congregations, government agencies, or community organizations to provide social and community services. These collaborations often include the sharing of space, financial resources, staff, and supplies. Yet how many congregations, particularly Latino congregations, actually do collaborate with other organizations in the provision of social services?

We found that congregations are inclined to worship with other congregations. Almost all congregations reported that in the past year they had worshipped jointly with other congregations (85.6 percent). Latino congregations are even more inclined to worship together with other congregations (89 percent) than non-Latino congregations (85.3 percent).

Regarding social service collaborations, we asked the interviewees if their congregation collaborated with other faith groups (e.g., a congregation, denomination, parachurch or other faith group) and with secular organizations/groups. Almost two-thirds of the studied congregations (62.5 percent) reported collaborating with faith groups and less than half collaborated with a secular partner (45.7 percent). More non-Latino congregations (63.3 percent) reported social service collaborations with other religious groups than did Latino congregations (53.2

percent). Similarly, significantly fewer Latino congregations (37.6 percent) reported collaborations with secular organizations in social services provision than did non-Latino congregations (57.8 percent). These findings suggest that while Latino congregations tend to worship with other congregations, they are less likely to join other faith-based or secular groups in social service provision. Again, the reason for this may be that many Latino congregations are small and less established and have not yet linked with others for the purpose of providing a social service.

CONGREGATIONS AND CHARITABLE CHOICE

Section 104 of the Personal Responsibility and Work Opportunity Reconciliation Act of 1996, commonly known as Charitable Choice removed the barriers that prohibited congregations without a separate 501(c)(3) tax status from contracting with the government to provide social services.

At the time of our data collection, from 1999 to 2002, the majority of congregations in Philadelphia reported a lack of knowledge about Charitable Choice (84 percent). A small percentage 114 (8.2 percent), reported some knowledge of Charitable Choice and only 109 (7.8 percent) knew clearly what Charitable Choice was. We explained Charitable Choice to respondents who were not familiar with the policy, and we asked whether their congregation would consider applying for government funds under its provisions. Of these congregations, 861 (61.8 percent) answered affirmatively, indicating that they view collaboration with public authority as an option. There was no significant difference between Latino and non-Latino congregations in their willingness to participate in Charitable Choice. This is yet another instance where Latino congregations are quite different from black congregations. The latter are much more likely than other groups to endorse Charitable Choice. This finding is in line with Wuthnow's (2004: 291) findings that "Hispanic respondents were scarcely any more likely to favor government-funded religious programs than white non-Hispanic respondents, despite being about twice as likely to have received welfare benefits themselves." While 50 percent of blacks in Wuthnow's study supported this policy only 26 percent of Hispanics and 23 percent of whites reported such support.

Replacement Value of Congregational Programs

One question remains: "What is the actual financial value of services offered by Latino congregations and how does it compare with other congregations in the city?" In other words, how much would it cost to replace all the social and community services provided by community-serving ministries in Philadelphia, and especially those of the Latino congregations?

By replacement value, as we discussed in Chapters 5 and 7, we do not mean solely the dollar cost incurred by congregations in running their programs. Replacement value also includes how much it would cost others to provide the same level of service when they have neither congregational property nor volunteers at their disposal. Our analysis of replacement value here takes into account the same seven expenses outlined earlier; see Chapter 5. For each program reported, we determined its estimated cost per month. As noted in Chapter 5, these estimates should be regarded as very conservative. In Chapter 5, to determine the average replacement value of the social services provided by an average congregation, we multiplied the average cost per program by 3.08 (the average number of programs per congregation). Because Latino congregations, on average, reported fewer programs (2.56) than did non-Latino congregations (3.12), we used these numbers as multipliers when determining the average cost per program and the average replacement cost for Latino and non-Latino congregations respectively.

Using the formula described above, the average replacement value of a Philadelphia congregation's community and social programs was assessed to be $10,338.13 per month. There were significant differences between Latino and non-Latino congregations in terms of replacement value. Programs run by Latino congregations were, on average, less costly ($2,938.14 compared to $3,410.47 respectively). Because Latino congregations, on average, carried out fewer programs (2.56 compared with 3.12), the total replacement value of social programs by Latino congregations per month ($8,376.63) was lower than that of non-Latino congregations ($10,703.23). Furthermore, Latino congregations invested fewer dollars in their programs and fewer staff hours (indication of relative limited means). However, Latino congregations provided more than their counterparts in in-kind support for their social programs.

Based on the average replacement value of $10,338.13 per program per month, we obtained an annual replacement value of $124,057.56 per program per year. Given that our research to date indicates that there are some 2,120 congregations in Philadelphia, and assuming (as we do) that our sample of 1,392 congregations is highly representative of the city's congregations, we estimated that the replacement value of the community-serving programs of all Philadelphia congregations was $256,348,958.40 per year. Performing the same analysis for the Latino congregations suggests that they annually provide programs worth a replacement value of $100,411.56. Multiplying this number by the known 148 Latino congregations in Philadelphia suggests a collective annual replacement value of $14,860,910.88, or 5 percent of the total citywide annual replacement value. This 5 percent replacement value is somewhat below the percentage of Latino congregations in town, which is 6.9 percent.

Latino Congregations That Are Involved in Social Services Provision

An examination of the association of certain congregational characteristics and the kinds of social services they provide offers a unique lens through which to view Latino service provision, and provides practical information. First, such knowledge enables Latino congregations to compare themselves with and learn from other types of congregations. Accordingly, they will be able to assess their own community involvement and to determine whether change is required to facilitate further social and community involvement. Second, they will have a better understanding of the types of social services for which they are best equipped and capable of providing, whether it be in collaboration with other organizations or independently. Third, understanding the connection between congregational characteristics and their social services provision may help congregational leaders to identify the potential of a congregation whose current involvement is minimal. Lastly, this information allows politicians and civic leaders, as well as community practitioners, who wish to encourage congregational social services provision to make better decisions when deciding whom to partner with, and whether changes are necessary to enhance congregational involvement in social services provision.

A set of variables are proposed in the literature to explain such variability in congregational involvement in social services. These variables can be grouped into four key categories: characteristics of congregational membership, leadership characteristics, financial resources, and congregational characteristics.

We considered five variables which reflect a congregation's membership and demographics: size of congregation (number of members), membership growth (in the past three years had the congregation grown, stayed the same, or declined), percentage of congregants aged sixty-five and over, change in age of congregants in past three years (grew older, stayed the same, or got younger) and percentage of single adults. For leadership characteristics, we used the following key variables: number of paid clergy, number of paid staff, and level of education achieved by the lead pastor. We looked at three variables as measures of a congregation's financial resources: annual operating budget, fiscal status (struggling, stable, or strong), and income level of congregants (percent of households with annual income of $75,000 or more). We also considered five final variables: age of congregation, political orientation of congregation (conservative, moderate, or liberal), theological orientation of congregation (fundamentalist, conservative, moderate, or liberal), and percentage of congregational members who live within a one-mile radius of the congregation.

A related topic is the congregation's denominational affiliation. As noted, only a small number of the congregations are Catholic. However, Catholic congregations are significantly larger in size and contain many non-Latino members. Thus, whether the congregation is Catholic or not is an important overriding factor that can explain social service involvement. Overall, we found fifteen possible explanatory variables in the literature that may account for the Latino congregations' social services involvement. We applied three measures of social services provision by Latino congregations. In the interviews, we gave the interviewees a list of 215 possible areas of social services and asked them to indicate the ones in which their congregation was involved. Note that we did not count the number of programs the congregation offered, since one program might provide services in several areas. For example, a homeless shelter program that provided meals, clothing, and vocational counseling in addition to overnight shelter would count as involvement in four service areas. Aware of the limits of this method, we kept the number of social and community areas of service as one indicator of the congregation's overall level of involvement. Latino congregations reported from 0 to 77 areas of involvement, with a mean of 11.6 and a standard deviation of 15.6.

A second measure demonstrates a congregation's relative commitment to social and community care: the percent of the annual budget allotted for social programs. Six Latino congregations did not answer this question. Of the 102 remaining congregations, 35 (32.1 percent) reported that none of their budget was allocated to social service provision. The mean percentage was 14 percent with a standard deviation of 18.7. This percentage is significantly lower than that reported by non-Latino congregations (23.4 percent; $t = 4.12$, $p < .001$). Finally, as noted above, we calculated the average monthly replacement value of the congregation's social programs. The strength of the average monthly replacement value is that it estimated the gross magnitude of aid provided by a congregation.

Of the 15 possible explanatory variables, 5 were found not to be significant with any of the measures of social service involvement. These five variables were: membership growth in the past three years, percent of seniors (65 +) among members of the congregation, percent of adult members who are single, fiscal status (surplus, balanced, deficit), and percent of members who lived within a mile of the congregation. To assess which of the many variables were of relative predictive value, we ran three separate regression models. These results are presented in Table 8.3. We did not include the 5 variables that were not associated with any of the measures of social service involvement, so our model starts with 10 explanatory variables. The results of the three regression models reveal parsimonious and elegant models of prediction.

Three variables explained participation in more areas of social involvement: higher number of paid staff, clergy with full college education or above, and higher annual operating budget (above $100,000). The percent of the annual budget dedicated to social issues was best explained by one variable, the existence of paid full-time clergy. Finally, the valuation of the congregation social programs (replacement value) was explained by three variables: number of active members, number of paid staff, and being Catholic.

Summary

This is the first attempt to collectively portray Latino local religious congregations in one large city. Many of our findings will require further study in other locales before they can be accepted as representative. Some of our findings raise questions about the Latino community in Philadelphia and its ability to represent the country as a whole. It is important to remember that while Latinos have become the largest minority group in America, their ranks are not unified and their geographic distribution is uneven. While Philadelphia and its suburbs witnessed great growth in its Latino populations and in Latino congregations, it is not a typical Latino city. Traditionally Philadelphia did not attract many Latino immigrants and even now the number of Mexican Americans in the city is relatively small. Regardless, we provide the first baseline data about congregational life for the Latino community in one urban area in the United States.

Latino congregations in Philadelphia are relatively new and mirror the Latino residential pattern. As can be seen in Figure 8.1, wherever Latinos live there are the congregations. It was surprising to find that a significantly smaller percent of Latinos attend places of worship regularly compared with whites or blacks in the city. It is possible that the South and Central American Catholic tradition has led to a common sense of religion and that many feel that participating in a local congregation at Easter and Christmas is enough. Alternatively, it is possible that many Latinos who work in service jobs that are open on Sundays are unable to attend church.

TABLE 8.3. REGRESSION MODELS EXPLAINING LATINO CONGREGATIONAL SOCIAL AND COMMUNITY INVOLVEMENT (BLANKS INDICATE INSIGNIFICANT BETAS)

Variable	Number of programs		Percent of budget		Fiscal value	
	B (st. error)	Beta	B (st. error)	Beta	B (st. error)	Beta
Constant		-5.8		8.6		8,933.3
Number of active attenders (size)					.82	3.73
Change in age (membership got younger past 3 years)						
Number of paid clergy	.42		4.0	.5		
Number of paid staff	2.9	.9			178.0	663.1
Clergy highest education	10.5	9.4				
Annual operating budget		4.1				
Income of members (percent $75,000 +)						
Age of congregation						
Conservative ideology						
Catholic					2,717.6	5,648.4
Variance explained		$R^2 = .45$		$R^2 = .20$		$R^2 = .42$

Interestingly, while most Latinos in our sample attended Catholic churches, there were few of these large churches (only 7) among the 109 Latino churches we studied. This indicates that Protestantism, especially in Pentecostal and Apostolic churches, is emerging and may bring more members of the Latino community to church. The fact that almost a third of the interviewees noted that their congregation was contemplating relocation also suggested their young age, process of growth, and pursuit of institutionalization. When congregations are in earlier stages of organizational formation, resources are still limited and the focus is on recruitment of new members, obtaining needed resources, and gaining legitimacy. Among Latino congregations, then, organizational resources are limited and it is not expected that these congregations would be able to perform in a manner equal to non-Latino congregations.

The confluence of the data available on Latinos and our findings suggests that congregational involvement and the use of congregations for strengthening social capital and civil society is more likely among second- and third-generation Latinos. As was the custom in Mexico and other counties of origin, the first generation is less religiously inclined and focuses on sending money back home while surviving in the United States. The second generation starts to mimic the American culture and norms, which may include a search for spiritual meaning and being socially organized around local religious congregations. Within this trend, we also find that the quest for religious expression is meaningful and separated from the Catholic roots of the country of origin; hence we find many forms of Protestantism among the second and third generations of Latino immigrants. This conclusion, however, is quite tentative and should be more carefully studied before it can be accepted as conclusive.

The low involvement of Latinos in congregations, the relatively smaller-sized congregations, their political and theological conservatism, and their low rate of social service involvement are issues that puzzle us. The needs in the Latino community are quite visible, and churches are called upon to help and also perceive their role as a helping one. It is clear from our interviews that Latino clergy are interested in developing social services; however, their resources are limited. In many cases, congregations had too few resources to have a paid pastor. Clergy volunteered their time and often did not have formal higher education. Over time, it is likely that Latino churches will stabilize, their clergy will become professionalized, and they will expand their role along with other congregations as community servers.

Espinosa, Elizondo, and Miranda (2003) reported that 62 percent of Latinos want their churches to become more involved with social, educational, and political issues. An even larger percentage wanted their churches to help undocumented immigrants. However, only 22 percent reported engagement in activities on behalf of a specific, social, educational, or political issue. These findings support our findings of the low rate of social and communal involvement by the Philadelphia Latino congregations.

The low rate of attendance at congregations may also explain the low level of volunteering found by Michel, Green, and Toppe (2003). The two most common explanations for volunteering are being asked and being a congregational member. And indeed, as congregation members, people are often asked to join service projects. Low levels of congregational attendance, thus, may contribute to Latinos being less involved in volunteer activities. On a larger scale, this may affect their integration into some aspects of the larger society.

Given what we currently know about the Latino community in the United States, it is possible that there are correlations between their relative lower engagement in congregations, congregations' smaller sizes, and low social service involvement and findings about the vulnerability of Latinos. For example, Galea and her colleagues (2002) found that in New York City Hispanics were the group most susceptible to PTSD and depression after 9/11: "Hispanic ethnicity was associated with both PTSD and depression, and the association was independent of other covariates" (986). Similar findings are reported about Hispanic Vietnam veterans (Ortega and Rosenheck 2000). It is possible that stronger faith communities can foster supportive ties and provide personal and social assistance in times of stress. When people face adversity alone they are more prone to suffer long-term effects. The religious congregation in America serves as a buffer against adversities for many people, but least so for Latinos. For now, many Latino congregations are not ready for the task, but with more members and professionalized clergy they will be more than ready.

Given the connection between clergy's level of education and the annual operating budget, along with number of paid staff and congregations' involvement in more areas of social services provision, the implication is that many Latino congregations do not have the critical mass of trained clergy, large membership, sufficient operating budget, and number of staff to enable the congregation to look to needs outside of the congregations with confidence. Simply put, the more a congregation struggles to maintain itself, the fewer resources are available for serving the needy in the community. Latino congregations may need to grow and become more institutionalized before they can provide care for needy people in the community. At this stage, with the exception of the Catholic Latino congregations, most Latino churches will need trained ministers and staff, and growth in membership and budgets.

Chapter 9

Women in Congregations and Social Service Provision

Religion was once a major institutional means to control women and that even today it is sometimes used as such (Neitz 1998). One has only to recall the status of women in Afghanistan under the Taliban regime to appreciate how oppressive religion can be for women. In the name of religion women have been ordered to stay at home, shave their heads, suppress their sexuality, forfeit career aspirations, and be submissive to their fathers, husbands, and sons (Manji 2004; Markkola 2000; Westerkamp 1999). Despite the cross-cultural and historical evidence for the diversity of religious beliefs, there are also some common features of belief systems: gods are usually envisaged as invisible spiritual forces, some with human attributes, who are good and powerful. Most often, god(s) are thought of as male—a concept that has been used to suppress the position of women vis-à-vis men in many societies. The more traditional or fundamentalist groups among the world religions allow women the least freedom of choice, stressing their roles as supporters of their husbands, bound to stay in the marriage no matter how abusive it may be.

Yet women throughout history have also found in religious institutions an opportunity for creating autonomous support groups and social action forums. In fact, before the twentieth century, women in most societies discovered their own voices and interests mostly through religious groups. In eras when women were not allowed to leave home alone, they still could attend women's meetings at the congregation and plan congregational activities, albeit in terms of local norms (Cnaan, Wineburg, and Boddie 1999). Some of the most prominent members of the suffrage movement in the nineteenth century, such as Antoinette Brown Blackwell, Olympia Brown, and Anna Howard Shaw, saw in their convictions about women's rights an extension of their call to religious ministry (Zink-Sawyer 2003). Women in contemporary society, meanwhile, not only form their own groups within congregations, but claim much more equality and assume an active role. On the other hand, many com-

mitted religious women still feel that contemporary religious congregations pay lip service to equality while in practice supporting the old
values of male domination.

Three components are used to measure the role of women in local
organized religion. The first measure is attendance. While almost no
studies have been undertaken to look at differences in religiosity
between the sexes, evidence for consistent differences between women
and men has emerged from data any time researchers have cared to
make a comparison (e.g., Hollinger and Smith 2002). In studies of religious behavior over the past hundred years, the greater religiosity of
women seems to be one of the most consistent findings (Argyle 1958;
Beit-Hallahmi and Argyle 1997). Stark (2002) provides data on levels of
religiosity for men and women in 49 Western and 8 non-Western cultures. In every case, as expected, women were more likely to describe
themselves as religious, as compared with men. Similarly, Gallup and
Lindsay (1999) reported that women in the United States have been
found to be significantly higher than men on all measures of religiosity
used in public opinion polls. While this is nationally the case, it may vary
between congregations, and more proscriptive denominations may
emphasize family life and attract more couples or even more men. The
exception to this rule occurs in traditions where ritual attendance by
women is discouraged or at least not a required element, such as Islam
and Orthodox Judaism. In these faith traditions the majority of those
attending are men (Loewenthal, MacLeod, and Cinnirella 2001).

Many reasons and explanations for women's religiosity have been
offered, but they have rarely been empirically tested. It is argued that
women more than men need religion in their lives, hence they take a
more active part in religious congregations (Davis 1987–88; de Vaus and
McAllister 1987; Ulbrich and Wallace 1984). Similarly, Hollinger and
Smith (2002: 242) suggested "that women's behaviour is more often
directed by sensitivity and intuition, while men are more likely to act
according to rational and logical considerations." Others have suggested that the male tendency for aggression and risk-taking, as compared with women's propensity for collaboration and solidarity, are
reasons for the greater religiosity of women (Geary 1998; Miller and
Hoffman 1995; Stark 2002). Thompson (1991) found that both men
and women who had a feminine self-image on the Bem Sex Role Inventory were more religious, especially as measured by prayer and other
devotional activities. In a study of 411 undergraduates, Mercer and Durham (1999) found that those with a feminine or androgynous orientation, of both sexes, were higher on a mysticism scale. These two findings
suggest that females' high level of religiosity is not physiological but is
more related to personality and social factors.

The psychoanalytical approach to the topic is interesting, though it is given short shrift these days. According to Freud's notions of paternal projection in the Oedipal period (ages three to six), girls should have a positive attachment to fathers but boys should feel ambivalent about them. Freud (1920, 1928) then proposed that God is a fantasy and substitute father figure. By this theory, for women the image of God and attitudes toward God are more similar to those toward their fathers, and for men more similar to those toward their mothers. For women God is seen more often as a healer, and also more often benevolent rather than punitive. If the culture carries an image of God as male, as a father, this image should therefore appeal more to women. However, the main evidence in support of this hypothesis is the finding that images of God are similar to images of parents, particularly one's parent of the opposite sex (Beit-Hallahmi and Argyle 1997).

The second measure of women's participation in organized religion is their membership in congregational councils (executive committees) and various key committees. These roles are important avenues for women to assume nonclerical leadership roles. In most denominations, women can serve as treasurers, committee heads, and members of councils. The hierarchical nature of religion and its long-lasting patriarchal essence suggest that women may not be adequately represented in these roles. Yet, there is a long history of women, in all denominations, running the lay life of the congregation. Women have taught and run Sunday schools, edited bulletins, led choir rehearsals, prepared and organized fellowship and picnics, sold raffle tickets, raised funds, read texts, coordinated outreach to the needy and youth, and managed weddings or funerals. Without the unpaid cooperation of women, important pastoral activities would stop. Furthermore, a fair number of women choose to give their time and efforts to the congregation, rather than to paid employment.

In some traditions, women have been forced to stay solely in "women's auxiliary" groups, where they performed only the social services and care functions of the congregations. Christiano, Swatos, and Kivisto (2002) noted that historically men had dominated the most powerful lay positions, such as finance, building, and personnel, and occupied most of the seats on the congregation council. This was the normal state of affairs even if the denominational doctrine did not call for such practice. Many women led and staffed missionary groups that were formed after the Civil War and lost their independent status in the 1920s, when they were absorbed into male-dominated "parent" mission boards (Yohn 1995).

In Catholic and more fundamentalist religious communities, women are still forbidden from assuming the role of clergy and are allowed, at best, to serve as lay leaders. Until the laws of the Catholic Church were revamped in 1983, only clerics could hold "ecclesiastical office," that is, jobs involving decisions in church governance. Since all Catholic clerics were men, no women could even apply. However, since 1983, as a result of the decline in the number of male priests, women have been allowed to take leadership roles in many more areas of the church. A study of 25 women who serve in leadership roles in the Catholic Church found that Catholic women—married, single, and religious sisters—are already participating in the administration of the Catholic Church by making high-level executive decisions affecting church personnel, property, and policy (Leadership Conference of Women Religious 2002). The study showed, for example, that women in church administration participated in almost all categories of decision making that affected church property, yet their role in policy decisions was more focused on areas affecting people. More than seven of ten respondents said they were responsible for evaluating and hiring personnel. More than 74 percent of the respondents said they had been the first woman to be a chancellor in their diocese; 69 percent the first financial officer; 66.7 percent the first tribunal judge; 55.6 percent the first director of Catholic charities; 52.8 percent the first pastoral director; and 36.4 percent the first vicar/delegate for religious affairs. In other words, even those denominations that forbid women from becoming clergy often and maybe reluctantly use them as key lay leaders.

The third measure of women's participation in organized religion is their serving as clergy. Clergy in most religious congregations is the highest status and honor in the group. Throughout Jewish history it was common practice for theologians to talk about a woman's flawed nature and limited religious capacities, which prevented her from responding to a call to ministry, pursuing theological training, or taking up a leadership position in the family. However, Reform and Reconstructionist traditions have had women rabbis for the past half-century. The Conservative tradition now also allows women to serve as rabbis, but Orthodox Jews still reject women as rabbis. There are some within the Christian fundamentalist movement today who think the same way. They argue that women should not address the audience of men as Jesus intentionally chose 12 men but not even one woman to be the future leaders of the church (Bellville 2000). In fact, at a Promise Keepers rally at Liberty University, the Rev. Jerry Falwell said, "It appears that America's anti-Biblical feminist movement is at last dying, thank God, and it is possibly being replaced by a Christ-centered men's movement" (Clarkson 1997). Similarly, in Islam, an aspect of leadership is the ability of the imam to lead the Muslims in prayer. It is accepted that women are barred from being imams, as they cannot lead men in prayer (Mernissi 1993).

In denominations that require ordination, the debate over ordaining women is ongoing, with liberal denominations having women's ordination, and the more conservative ones prohibiting it. The earliest Christian traditions have been subject to debate and reinterpretation; the first modern Christian denomination in which women led worship was the Quakers in the seventeenth century (Larson 1999). However, this was not "ordination" because Quakers had no clergy. The Congregational Church performed the first official ordination of women in 1853 (Chaves 1997). The first conference on ordination of women took place in Boston in 1882 (Eck and Jain 1987). At present, about half the Christian denominations in the United States ordain women. During the 1950s, only 2.1 percent of the nation's clergy were women. This figure doubled to 4.2 percent in the 1980s and stands now at 9 percent or 50,000 (Nesbitt 1997). Clearly, in this respect modernity and gender equality are in opposition to traditional views of clergy as males representing a male God. For many Christians, also, Jesus ought to be represented in the congregation by a male figure.

Woman seminarians find it difficult to procure a position in large and established congregations and often end up in assistant clergy roles or in small congregations that no other clergy wish to lead. They also receive lower pay (Francis and Robbins 1999; Carroll, Hargrove, and Lummis 1983; Lehman 1993; Nason-Clark 1987; Sullins 2000; Zikmund, Lummis, and Chang 1998). Carpenter (1987) found that the same problem exists in the black church. In fact, half the black women seminary graduates transferred to a different denomination, as they were not welcome in congregations in their own denomination. Even when women serve as clergy, they are found to devote more time to pastoral counseling and hospital visitation as compared with male clergy, who devote more time to administration and maintaining job status (Perl 2002)

Today, there are still strong voices opposing the ordination of women (Ashley 1996; Miller 1995). The three largest denominations that oppose women's ordination are the Catholic Church (the largest religious group in the United States), the Southern Baptist Convention (the largest Protestant denomination in the United States), and the Lutheran Church, Missouri Synod (Chaves 1997). One issue is the preparedness of congregational members to accept women in the role of clergy. Hoffman (1997) studied the attitudes of 399 Christian laity and clergy in various Christian traditions in the United States toward the role of women in church leadership. He found that 75 percent of ELCA Lutherans, Methodists, Episcopalians, and Presbyterians (USA) supported equality in church leadership, as did almost 50 percent of Catholics. However, fewer than 25 percent of Assembly of God, Southern Baptist, and fundamentalist church members supported women as clergy. Respondents who believed in Mary as the virgin mother were less likely to support equality of women in church leadership, suggesting they believed in the role of women as supporters rather than leaders.

Weber (1968) observed that religious movements of the underprivileged gave equality to women at first, but as they became established withdrew it. This observation has been found to be true of American Pentecostal sects in the early twentieth century, some of them African American. At first they had many charismatic women preachers who were sometimes the founders of sects, but their numbers then fell (Barfoot and Sheppard 1980). This is true as well for the female founders of modern religion movements, such as Ellen G. White, Mary Baker Eddy, and Madame Helena Petrovna Blavatsky. The groups they started soon came to be run by men.

Seventh-Day Adventists believe that White was appointed by God as a special messenger to draw the world's attention to the Holy Scriptures and help prepare people for Christ's Second Advent. White wrote more than 5,000 periodical articles and 40 books; today, more than 100 of her titles are available in English. Her official homepage listed her as "the most translated woman writer in the entire history of literature, and the most translated American author of either gender. . . . *Steps to Christ*, has been published in more than 140 languages" (White 2003).

Mary Baker Eddy discovered and established a Bible-based system of spiritual healing which she named Christian Science. Her book *Science and Health with Key to the Scriptures* was translated into many languages and has sold over 10 million copies worldwide. The Church of Christ, Scientist was established in 1879, four years after *Science and Health* was published. It consists of the Mother Church in Boston and about 2,000 churches in 79 countries.

Madame Blavatsky was among the first to introduce knowledge of Eastern religions to the West—including the ideas of karma and reincarnation. She launched the Theosophical Society, calling her message Theosophy.

Women in leadership roles may change the culture of the congregation. Royle (1987) noted that the impact women clergy and leaders have on the congregations they serve is understudied. What we know is that congregations with women clergy tend to be more democratic and the laity tend to feel more empowered (Lummis 1994; Nason-Clark 1987). But we have known very little about which congregations allow women greater participation and how this participation affects the congregational social programs. This chapter addresses these questions.

Research Questions

Based on our literature review, we posed four main questions. The first focuses on the frequency with which women are members, lay leaders, and clergy of congregations. We will find out the mean of each such variable and assess the correlations between these variables. In other words, we will test whether congregations with more women members also have more women lay leaders and clergy.

Our second question focuses on which congregations offer women more opportunities to become lay leaders and serve as clergy. The clergy role is mediated by denominational doctrine, and we expect to find more women clergy in more liberal denominations. However, in both cases, we would like to find out if congregational characteristics (such as percent of women in congregations, percent of members, percent of members who live nearby, membership size, budget size, years of existence, theological perspective, and clergy education) are associated with the practice of having women serve as lay leaders and as clergy.

Third, we want to assess how our three variables of women in the congregation (women as members, as lay leaders, and as clergy) are associated with the congregational involvement in social service provision. Based on the limited literature, we expect that those congregations in which women are allowed greater equality (more lay leaders and women clergy) will be involved in larger areas of social service.

Finally, we wish to examine what most explains the social involvement of the congregation. That is, will issues like size and budget explain social service involvement better than the gender-related variables (percent of women in congregations, women as key leaders, and clergy) or vice versa?

Measurements

In the PCC, with regard to the gender-related questions, we asked the interviewees to assess the percentage of women among the adult members. We then recorded whether the senior clergyperson was a woman (in the few congregations with more than one, we did not record whether any assistant clergy were women). Finally, we asked the interviewees to list the congregation's most important five committees, and for each such committee we asked whether the chairperson was male or female, or if there were co-chairs of the two sexes.

As in the previous chapters, we applied three measures of community involvement. First, we asked for the percentage of the operating budget allocated for helping people in need. Second, we counted the number of areas of service (help) the congregation had been engaged in during the previous year in an organized way (excluding responses to crises and help given on "as needed" basis). Finally, we assessed the replacement value of the social services offered by the congregation, as discussed in Chapters 5, 7, and 8.

We used a set of variables that were expected to explain women's representation as lay leaders and clergy, and also to explain variations in social service involvement. Most of these variables are detailed in Chapter 3. We asked about the congregational operating budget (excluding capital campaign) and used it as a dichotomous variable comparing congregations with an operating budget of under or over $100,000. Membership size was measured as people of all ages who attend at least monthly. Length of congregational existence was measured as the year of the interview minus the year the congregation was established. Due to the fact that the largest group of congregational members by race in Philadelphia was blacks (see Chapter 7), we used the percentage of members who are black as our measure of race distribution in the congregation. Expecting people who live nearby to be more active in congregation activities, we measured the percentage of members who live within a one-mile radius of the congregation building (estimated as ten blocks). We measured clergy education as a dichotomous variable and compared clergy who have a seminary degree or higher versus those with no such level of education.

Finally, given that we obtained more than 200 different denominational affiliations, it was quite difficult to use the denomination as a variable; instead we used "theological strictness," which was measured by asking the interviewee if the majority of the members of the congregation see themselves theologically as fundamentalist, conservative, moderate, or liberal. We checked the reliability of this variable in terms of its association with a question that asked whether the congregational doctrine affirms that the Bible is the intended and literal word of God. The result showed a strong significant association ($\chi^2 = 86.1$, df $=3$, $p <$ .0001). For the regression models, we used this variable as a dichotomous one using fundamentalist and conservative as one group and liberal and moderate as the other group.

Findings

PRESENCE OF WOMEN IN CONGREGATIONS

As expected, more women than men are members of local religious congregations. The PCC found that the ratio of women to men is almost two to one (65.25 percent and 34.75 percent respectively). Farnsley

(2003: 76) also found in Indianapolis that, overall, "about 60 percent of congregational members are women."

Contrary to our expectation, the theological strictness of the congregation was not significantly associated with the percentage of women as members. In other words, the fundamentalist congregations that tend to emphasize family values did not attract a more balanced gender distribution of members. The percentage of black members in the congregation was significantly and positively correlated with the percentage of females ($r = .391$, $p < .001$). Similarly, the size of the congregation's budget was negatively but weakly correlated with the percentage of women in the congregation ($r = -.106$, $p < .001$).

We asked the interviewees to list up to five key congregational committees. As mentioned in earlier chapters, a total of 4,124 committees were reported. We also asked for the gender of the person running the committees. We found that 2,217 (53.8 percent) committees were headed by women, clearly a percentage below membership. Each congregation was allowed to report five committees; hence the chairpersonship could range from none to all five chairs being women. We found that in 13.6 percent of the reporting congregations there was not even one woman serving as a chairperson of any committee. In 20.7 percent of the congregations, there was one committee chaired by a woman, and in 27.9 percent there were two committees chaired by women. In a quarter of the congregations (24.6 percent), three committees were chaired by women, followed by 10.6 percent of four committees and 2.5 percent of all five reported committees.

It is no surprise that the overwhelming percentage of clergy in Philadelphia were male (88.1 percent). Only one in nine congregations (11.9 percent) reported having a woman senior clergyperson. This percentage is higher than the 9 percent reported nationally (Nesbitt, 1997), but significantly below the percentage of women members or lay leaders.

THE CONGREGATIONS THAT ENCOURAGE WOMEN AS LAY LEADERS AND CLERGY

We found that an increase of black members in the congregation is positively though weakly correlated with the number of committees chaired by women ($r = .146$, $p < .001$). We found, however, that black congregations do not have a higher percentage of female clergy when compared to other congregations.

We also found that the theological stance of the congregation is significantly associated with women chairing committees ($\chi^2 = 43.76$, df = 15, $p < .001$). Fundamentalist and conservative congregations reported lower numbers of women chairing key committees. Similarly, the theological strictness of the congregation was also significantly associated with the percentage of women clergy. In other words, fundamentalist and conservative congregations reported fewer women clergy (9.2 percent and 6.5 percent respectively), while moderate and liberal congregations reported higher rates (15 percent and 27.4 percent). This finding accords with what intuitively makes sense and what is known in the literature.

The size of the congregation budget was strongly and significantly associated with the number of women serving as chairs of key committees (χ^2 = 61.36, df = 20, p < .001). Congregations with low budgets reported more cases where no woman served as chair of a committee compared with congregations with a larger budget size. The size of the budget, however, was negatively associated with women serving as senior clergy (X^2 = 15.05, df = 4, p < .001). Most notably, among the 99 congregations reporting an annual income of more than $500,000 a year, only one had a woman as senior clergyperson. Of 710 congregations with an annual income of less than $100,000, 98 (13.8 percent) reported having a woman as senior clergyperson.

The number of years the congregation had existed was significantly associated with the number of women serving as chairs of committees (F = 5.89, p < .001). The post hoc analysis revealed that older congregations had more women as chairs of committees, most notably in the case of four and five women as chairs (of five reported committees). This finding is correlated with the one reported in Chapter 3. We found that older congregations, on average, tend to be theologically liberal, while younger congregations, on average, tend to be theologically strict. Thus, years of existence may mimic theological strictness. The age of the congregational members, however, was not significantly associated with the gender of the clergy.

Membership size was not significantly associated with the number of women serving as chairs of committees. However, membership size was significantly associated with the gender of the clergy (t = 3.22, p < .001). The average size of a congregation employing a male clergyperson was 357, compared with 123 for women-led congregations. Again, large and rich congregations tended to prefer males as senior clergy.

The percentage of members who live nearby (within a one-mile radius) was not significantly associated with either of the two studied variables: women as chairs of key committees and the gender of the clergy.

Congregations with clergy who had not completed a college or a higher academic degree reported a lower number of women serving as chairs of key committees (χ^2 = 11.95, df = 5, p < .05). There was no significant association between the gender and the level of education of the clergy. Put differently, both males and females who felt called stepped forward to become clergy without seminary training.

WOMEN IN THE CONGREGATION AND SOCIAL PROGRAMS

Contrary to our expectation, a higher percentage of women members of the congregations was not correlated with a higher percentage of the operating budget devoted to social programs ($r = -.07, p < .05$). When we tested the association between the number of women lay leaders (heads of committees) and the percent of the budget allocated for social programs, no significant association was observed using one-way ANOVA. When we assessed the gender of senior clergy, however, we found that congregations with women clergy, on average, spent a higher percentage on social programs. Congregations headed by men spent 21.4 percent of their budget on social programs, and those headed by women spent 25.7 percent ($t = -2.22, p < .05$).

Regarding the areas of social program involvement, we counted all the areas (of a possible 215) that the congregation owns and runs on its property. The range was from 0 to 154, with a mean of 11.5 programs per congregation. We correlated the number of areas of involvement with the percentage of women in the congregation and the result indicated no significant correlation ($r = .01, p > .05$). The number of women as chairpersons of key committees was strongly and significantly associated with the number of areas of involvement ($F = 10.3$, df $= 5$, $p < .0001$). Viewing the mean number of areas of social involvement showed a progressive increase with the number of women as key chairpersons of committees. For example, congregations with no women leaders were involved in 8.5 programs, those with one leader in 9.9 programs, those with two leaders in 12.1 programs, those with three leaders in 13.4 programs, and those with four leaders in 17.4 programs; the only decline comes when there are five women leaders in 16.5 programs. A post hoc Scheffe test showed that the "zero women-leader group" was significantly different from all other groups. Additionally, the "four women-leader group" and "five women-leader group" were equally different from all other groups. When we tested the relationship between the gender of the clergy and number of areas of involvement, no significant difference was detected ($t = .236, p > .05$). In fact, the means were almost identical: 11.4 for male-headed congregations and 11.2 for female-headed congregations.

Finally, we assessed the impact of the three variables on the replacement value of congregational social services. The percentage of women in the congregation was not statistically significant when correlated with the replacement value. Similarly, using a one-way ANOVA, the number of women chairing a key committee was not associated with the replacement value. When we tested the association between the gender of the clergy and the replacement value, again, no significant difference was found.

WOMEN, CONGREGATIONAL CHARACTERISTICS, AND SOCIAL SERVICE INVOLVEMENT

In order to assess the overall impact of the gender of members, lay leaders, and clergy, we applied a set of regression analyses. We used seven congregational characteristics variables and the three gender variables and assessed their impact on the variables of social and community involvement. The regression model predicting percent of the operating budget devoted to social programs yielded an R^2 of .022 when the gender variables were not included and .035 when they were included. While both models were significant, they are of weak predictive ability, and so is the improvement in the contribution of the variable measuring the percentage of woman members in the congregation and the gender of the clergy.

The models predicting variability in the number of areas of social programs involvement yielded an R^2 of .118 when gender variables were not included and .137 when they were included. Only one gender-related variable was significant in the latter model, the number of women chairing a key committee.

Finally, the models predicting variation in the replacement value of the congregational social services yielded a very weak R^2 of .017 when the gender variables were not included and .020 when they were included. While both models were significant, they again are of weak predictive ability, and none of the gender-related variables was significant.

In all, the gender-related variables added to the variability of only two of the three dependent variables (percent of female members and gender of clergy in the case of the percent of operating budget devoted to social programs, and the number of women lay leaders in the case of areas of involvement). Thus, knowledge of the gender of members, lay leaders, and clergy did not add much to our ability to explain variations in social and community involvement.

Conclusions

As expected, we found that more women than men belonged to religious congregations, yet their participation among key committee leaders and especially as clergy was significantly smaller. Women often participate as members and serve as volunteers but less as religious leaders. Furthermore, women clergy, on average, were in smaller congregations (an average of 123 members compared to 357 for male clergy). As Eck and Jain (1987: 117) noted, "here again, one confronts an old and pervasive disjunction: the indomitable presence and influence of women at the domestic and grass-roots level, and the virtual absence of women at the public level." The fact that we found 11 percent of congregations headed by women, whereas previous studies found only 9 percent, can be explained in two ways. First, it is possible that with time more congregations and denominations open the door for women to serve as clergy, and that the time span between our study and previous studies explains the increase in the percentage of women clergy. Second, and less optimistically, our study is limited to Philadelphia, a city in the Northeast, where relative liberalism and equality are more accepted than in the Midwest and South. Nevertheless, it remains the case that across the United States the numbers of female clergy compared to women members clearly show that gender equality is far from being the congregational norm.

Our findings about the percentage of women clergy and the characteristics of congregations that tend to employ women clergy were supported by the findings of the National Congregations Study, which was based on the General Social Survey of 1998 (Chaves et al. 1999). For example, their data show that 36.8 percent of male clergy work in congregations with more than 100 adult members, while only 24.6 percent of women clergy work in such congregations. It is still difficult for a rich congregation to accept women clergy but small and poor congregations are forced to accept them, given denominational approval, as they are less costly and more willing to accept a senior clergy position even if it is underpaid. Larger congregations often perceive women as deserving less pay, and their financial strength allows them to find "more suitable" male clergy deserving more pay.

One interesting finding is that among black congregations the percentage of women members is the highest, and women are also often the chairpersons of congregational committees. But in terms of clergy in black congregations, men still comprise the majority. A possible interpretation is that in a community in which about a third of the young male population are in prison or supervised by the justice system, fewer men are available or interested in religion. However, those men keenly interested in religion find the way to leadership more accessible than in other ethnic communities. Alternatively, black women still face double jeopardy, as they are hampered by racism from outside and sexism from inside their community. Yet another explanation is that blacks are more traditionalist than other ethnic groups in terms of religion.

Similarly, as expected, fundamentalist and conservative congregations reported having fewer women clergy and lay leaders, as compared with moderate and liberal congregations. However, these congregations are not attracting more men as members than other congregations. This may imply that, while clergy roles are officially blocked for women, they do not find the congregations any more oppressive and therefore attend them overall just as often as moderate and liberal congregations, in which women can more easily hold leadership positions. In fact, more restrictive congregations are gaining in popularity, and many people who seek strong spiritual experiences prefer them to the more liberal congregations. They accept that the "authentic" religious voice is one that calls for male clergy and they accept conservative values that may oppose gender equality. The problem with this trend is that it blocks the opportunity of women clergy from serving these congregations, and these congregations in turn miss out on the opportunity to employ better-qualified women clergy. Because the pool of candidates in these congregations is more restricted, congregations fail to even interview women who could be excellent religious leaders. Women clergy are left to either give up their clerical aspiration or find a less restrictive denomination.

With regard to social and community involvement, the impact of the gender variable was marginal. In fact, in most areas that we looked at, women-related variables added too little to the variation. One can infer from this that women in congregations are not as concerned with their traditional role as "nurturers." Along this line, one may assume that women clergy are too busy proving themselves to be competent, that they are often acting in the role of male clergy to such a degree that their unique traits are being lost. Another possible explanation is that women clergy and women lay leaders are less influential than their male counterparts in convincing their congregation to invest in helping their communities. Oftentimes, their voices are silenced and their good intentions bypassed. Finally, these findings are most likely related to the persistent norm of social responsibility and community care embedded in all American religious congregations. As Cnaan and his colleagues (2002) showed, in the United States a strong social norm exists for congregations to be highly involved in caring for others in need. This norm is so pervasive that the gender of key lay leaders or the clergy is not powerful enough to mitigate it. As we showed in Chapter 5, 92.3 percent of congregations in Philadelphia are engaged in social services provision. Furthermore, almost all interviewees "apologized" for not being more involved in social services provision. In other words, congregations are using their resources to help others whenever possible, and hence the key variables that were significant in all models were congregation size and budget. Simply put, the bigger and richer the congregation, the more it helps others, regardless of the gender of its key players.

Part IV
Area Organizations That Enhance the Congregational Social Service Capacity

Chapter 10

Interfaith Coalitions: The Story of the Northwest Interfaith Movement

Individuals form groups in order to achieve common goals that are beyond the capacity of individuals or families. But even groups are at times too small and weak to bring about a desired change. In this case, groups gather to form a coalition or an alliance, for what cannot be done by one group can often be done by many.[1] Community organizers and other agents of social improvement have traditionally turned to collaborative arrangements to effect wide-scale change. Barringer and Harrison (2000), examining research on "interorganizational relationships," found them to encompass joint ventures, networks, coalitions, consortia, community development corporations (CDCs), and alliances. These may be defined as "an association between two or more . . . organizations joined together to achieve a common goal that neither alone can accomplish" (Poole 1995: 2). Barringer and Harrison (2000) suggested that the benefits of "interorganizational relationships" are manifold: sharing cost while achieving mutual goals, minimizing financial and political risk, increasing visibility, increasing legitimacy, increasing focus on selected tasks, enabling one another to develop new products or services, and mutual learning.

Congregations are also organizations that possess limited power and can benefit from joint ventures. In every American city, congregations have coexisted for many years. Many share the concern for the quality of life in their communities, yet most are too small and resource-deficient to have a real effect on their environments, so they may elect to form a coalition or alliance. Philadelphia is no exception. In the City of Brotherly Love, religious organizations have participated in alliances and coalitions to achieve larger common goals, including providing social services. The existence of numerous congregations, as we documented in earlier chapters, is the basis on which larger superstructures can exist and work on behalf of the whole community, city, or region.

Much academic work has focused on the extent of religiosity of faith-based organizations rather than their various organizational structures and ways of functioning. Various typologies classify faith-based groups according to their level of religiosity and according to the organizational integration of religious elements. These include works by Goggin and Orth (2002), Jeavons (1998), Monsma and Mounts (2002), Smith and Sosin (2001), Unruh and Sider (2001, 2005), and the Working Group on Human Needs in Faith-Based and Community Initiatives (2002). However, very little research on faith-based organizations distinguishes interorganizational faith collaborations from single-faith organizations. One notable exception is Ebaugh and Pipes (2001), discussed below. Sorely missing in the literature is any in-depth case study of one local faith-based coalition.

Three coalitions/alliances have received attention in the literature. They are Boston's Ten Point Coalition, which worked on reducing gang violence and teen murders in the poorest parts of Boston (Polakow-Suransky 2003); Tying Nashville Together (TNT), a coalition of 43 congregations and other local groups working on community development (Byrd 1997); and the Los Angeles Metropolitan Churches (LAM), an association of small to midsized African American churches that formed in the aftermath of the 1992 South Central Los Angeles riots (Brown 2005). LAM recruited the Rev. Eugene Williams, a Philadelphia pastor and community organizer, to be its leader. LAM has 50 active member churches and is involved in issues ranging from poverty to education, from racism to prison reform (Cnaan and Sinha 2004).

The most common forms of faith-based "interorganizational relationships" are the ecumenical or local clergy alliances. These groups often focus on religious issues and seek to improve relationships between various congregations and the wider community. They rarely focus on social improvement. CDCs, however, are notable exceptions. As Cnaan, Wineburg, and Boddie (1999) noted, CDCs focusing on social improvement are commonly formed by congregations and faith-based groups, and religious CDCs composed a large share of all CDCs. A less discussed form of interorganizational collaboration is the local coalition/alliance. Ebaugh and Pipes (2001) studied faith-based coalitions in Harris County, Texas, and documented coalitions' work in social services since the 1980s, when the economy in Houston plummeted. These coalitions were made up mostly of Protestant and Catholic congregations, which provided the majority of funding and volunteers needed to run the coalitions' services and activities. By contrast, Pipes (2001) examined nine community-based ministries across the United States, observing their structure, staffing, services, and the role of faith. In these nine cases, the groups depended least on congregations and most upon contracts with government. Specifically, interfaith coalitions—collections of congregations of different faiths—accommodate members' different faith traditions and seek out theological commonalities accepted by all partners. For the sake of organizational efficiency and attaining democratic representation among members, spiritual common ground is sought after, such as spiritually oriented care for the needy and indigent.

In a partnership or alliance there are two levels of objectives, the one held by the group and those particular to each member or partner (Byrd 1997). Furthermore, the final partnership/alliance will not be what any single congregation or group expects. It will be a fusion that incorporates objectives of all the participants yet in itself is distinct. As it seeks to form its own identity, a successful coalition may be totally different in its final form and activities from what the founding partners envisioned. Such was the case of the Northwest Interfaith Movement (NIM) in Philadelphia.

NIM exemplifies an organization that was founded as an alliance of faith groups and that evolved into a social service nonprofit agency. Although member congregations are essential for NIM's existence, NIM does not follow any one faith tradition, and staff and clients are free to hold and practice whatever faith they adhere to. The "religious tolerance" can be traced to two sources: (1) the interfaith nature of the organization and (2) the use of professional recommendations in its strategic planning in the 1980s. Religiosity has been expressed in an interfaith fashion through public forums and intercongregational dialogues.[2] This tolerance toward all religions has allowed services to be implicitly religious, in that services by themselves have often been expressions of faith for staff members and understood to be nonverbal manifestations of a religious community's sacred background. In other words, every worker has been allowed to assign religious meaning implicitly, but no public expression of religion has been commonly sought out. Furthermore, the unwieldiness of the coalition's growing board led indirectly to a loosened connection with its original congregation members. An outside consultant from a local theological seminary had recommended that a few representatives from outside the congregations also be elected to the board, which created a somewhat less congregation-based decision-making locus. Yet, without the initial support and legitimacy given by the member congregations and their subsequent support, albeit at times passive, NIM could not have been in operation; its legitimacy and power continued to come from its member congregations.

As will be shown below, NIM's more professional assets bolstered the work of what may be deemed the less professional, grass-roots work of church groups and community-based groups. For example, NIM was able to amass the resources and technical skills to help volunteers educate themselves about issues of elder care or child care. Also, as will be discussed below, NIM's professional staff provided professional training and support for volunteers and staff of other agencies ("technical assistance"). In addition, in its collaborative work, NIM acted as a mediator between government inspectors and congregational day care providers to help providers meet facility standards and defended them against any unfair penalties for failures in compliance with codes.

Standard Characteristics of Coalitions/Alliances

Coalitions have traditionally been valued for their ability to garner resources in order to effect large-scale social change. Such ability depends on cohesion among members and stability through leadership changes. As we will soon show, NIM mastered stability in leadership but did not exemplify membership cohesion.

The formation of coalitions or alliances depends heavily upon their social and political contexts, so understanding any one coalition requires understanding its specific background (Wahba and Lirtzman 1972). Before forming a coalition or an alliance, prospective members often find themselves in an unstable state, whether due to insufficient resources to influence their community or due to threats from outside forces. Coalitions are formed when groups find themselves presented with a crisis and find commonality in mission and openness to combine efforts with other groups. The most ideal condition for congregational collaboration is uniting with proper partners who "match in mission." In times of need, often the mission is what brings congregations to the table and keeps them there, even if they are not 100 percent satisfied.

Often coalitions struggle to maintain cohesion among their members. Members may be lost over time as costs outweigh benefits (Dluhy 1990). To keep members engaged, continual exposure to coalition strategy, activities, and education to issues may be necessary (Dluhy 1981). Ideally, a coalition or alliance ensures that each member's voice is heard and understood and no voice is ignored; dissenting voices are encouraged to speak and then persuaded to cooperate. If members hold different values or they see the coalition as representing challenging perspectives, they may decentralize into subgroups or simply withdraw. Sometimes members accept their membership as given, support the alliance financially and/or with volunteers, but avoid involvement in day-to-day operations or policy issues. Their retention as members requires little effort, but is often without significant impact on either the member or the alliance. Other members expect to have a real voice in the alliance. Their retention can be achieved through granting and assuring members' ownership of the coalition. Overall unity can be achieved by focusing on overarching purposes and allowing members the freedom to carry out tasks according to their cultures. Finally, unity can also be achieved by allowing the alliance to operate independently of its constituent members altogether, although such a scenario begs the question, "Does membership mean anything?"

Coalitions need not only internal consistency but also outside support. Within the community, coalitions often survive based upon their legitimacy. That is, if a coalition loses its credibility as an effective agent for a social need, it will falter (Dluhy 1981).

Some coalitions are ephemeral in nature, because they arise as responses to short-lived interests that surface during a time of crisis. Mirola (2003) studied the Detroit newspaper strike and found four religious coalitions that were formed as a result of the crisis and the burden on the families of the strikers. Although five years of struggle ended with very few tangible gains, clergy and religious coalitions provided the strikers with a moral frame that critiqued the two newspapers and, out of that critique, called people of faith to support the strikers, as was the case in many other labor struggles (Billings 1990; Fantasia 1988; Fuechtmann 1989).

Sometimes coalitions are formed ad hoc but develop into more stable organizations (Boissevain 1974). The process of developing permanency often involves shifts in mission and member involvement. In their study of 28 substance abuse prevention coalitions in Illinois, Hays and colleagues (2000) found that diversity of members, involvement of members in decision making, members' involvement in coalition services, and effective leadership that unifies members and acquires needed resources resulted in greater levels of effectiveness.

What about faith-based and interfaith coalitions? How do faith-based organizations fare in establishing strong coalition/alliances that have strong membership through strong leadership and the involvement of members in decision making?

Research into faith-based coalitions has traced certain facets. In their study of 14 interfaith coalitions in Harris County, Texas, and 9 interfaith coalitions across the country, Ebaugh and Pipes (2001) noted that although named "interfaith," these coalitions involve mostly Christian congregations. They also found that such coalitions also depend heavily on volunteers, often church volunteers. Furthermore, the member congregations also provide the coalition with legitimacy (Hallman 1987). Some interfaith coalitions depend on resale shops and member donations; others rely heavily on government contracts and foundation grants. Groups are often reluctant to receive federal funding available through Charitable Choice, legislation promoting the funding of faith-based services, because of the loss of autonomy and the requirement of paperwork. In other respects, coalitions and alliances vary in size and coalitions in Harris County served mostly blacks (although fewer than half the 14 coalitions studied there could provide client data). Most began with the mission to address emergency needs, such as shortages in food, clothing, transportation, and housing.

There is clearly a scarcity of studies focusing on faith-based coalitions. This chapter provides a case study, a Philadelphia-based one, of a faith-based agency, but hopes to add to the groundwork of literature on faith-based coalitions.

Background

NIM is an interfaith alliance with offices centrally located in Mt. Airy, the geographic center of Northwest Philadelphia. Starting as a religious movement, this alliance began and still is characterized by an implicit religious motive: to ameliorate poor social conditions and emerging blight in the city. The organization has retained its original identity as a collection of congregations; however, as it has grown, NIM has adopted a nonprofit agency framework which is less dependent on congregations. Presently, NIM acts mainly as a source of training and technical assistance to child care agencies and individuals and institutions providing services to vulnerable and aging adults. NIM accomplishes its work through staff and volunteers.

Explicit religious language is largely absent from NIM's organizational structure and services. The traditional coalition provision of ad hoc services has also given way to formalized operations. There is little reliance upon volunteers, save for one program area, and most funding comes from sources other than congregational members. Staff has grown from two in 1980 to about 25 in 2003. It should be noted, however, that NIM was formed not to deal with mere short-term needs, as are most interfaith coalitions, but to address more entrenched issues such as racial divides and other systemic issues in the community. (In fact, in the 1970s addressing "merely" emergency needs like housing actually divided its ruling board.)

Inception and Brief History of NIM

Started in 1969, NIM grew from the efforts of a Presbyterian minister, Bruce Theunissen, in Northwest Philadelphia. Theunissen came to Philadelphia in 1966 to serve as the coordinator of the Germantown Presbyterian Council—a group of 14 Presbyterian churches supported by the Presbytery of Philadelphia, which sought to facilitate effective ministry in Germantown. Theunissen was aware of further ecumenical and interfaith possibilities in Northwest Philadelphia. From 1966 to 1969, he attended trainings to develop plans for the organization and worked to establish what is now NIM. In 1969, the Presbytery allowed Theunissen to shift his roles from the Germantown Presbyterian Council to NIM. Theunissen rallied 13 congregations, including a Jewish congregation, and by 1970, the "Greater Germantown Ecumenical Movement" (now NIM) was granted 501(c)(3) status and had a modest budget and one staff member.

A board was formed with two representatives from each member congregation. Early dialogues included topics of race and Jewish-Christian relations. In 1975, NIM involved itself in housing advocacy work, which divided the board. The third director, the Rev. John Scott, helped form a spin-off community organization, the Central Germantown Council. By 1980, NIM had two full-time staff members, a part-time staff member, and a budget of $62,000. The Rev. Richard (Dick) Fernandez, who had professional experience in interfaith work, assumed leadership at this time. Under Fernandez, the organization grew to 25 staff members with a budget of $2.5 million. Currently, NIM is led by Rabbi George Stern, the only rabbi in America who leads a community-based interfaith coalition.

NIM's alliance of congregations is comprised mostly of Christian churches and is a reflection of the neighborhood. Of its 40 congregations, 34 are Protestant or Catholic, 3 are Jewish, 2 are Unitarian, and 1 is Muslim. From the start, Theunissen had set NIM apart from other interfaith groups by working "through [and] together" with congregations as much as possible.

Mission and Religion

In an interview, the fourth executive director of the organization, Dick Fernandez, indicated that the primary purpose of NIM has been to affect public policy by being a catalyst for change. As NIM was not the outcome of a crisis, it has aimed to be more long-standing and to address systemic needs. NIM also focuses on helping social practitioners in child care and elder adult care improve their services and meet high quality and citywide standards. NIM has intervened with government regulators to assure accurate and fair evaluation of their programs. Through improving aid to children and adults, NIM tries to "build a more just and sensitive community through advocacy and service."

As an interfaith alliance, NIM remains religiously motivated in its advocacy and social services. The current executive director, George Stern, stated that its services grow out of religious teachings. It is the "loving purpose of God" to have agents like NIM transform public life for the betterment of its individuals. The organization is comprised of staff members who have various particular faith traditions and seek to express their commitment through their work at NIM. The presence of such employees contributes to the organization's interfaith character.

As an organization that represents various faiths, NIM builds common missions upon which different religious groups agree. It does not promote one religion over another, in either its daily operations or its social services. It does, however, occasionally sponsor interfaith services that respectfully reflect the diversity of NIM members and the community at large, and invites speakers from different faith traditions. Thus NIM not only advocates for and provides social services, but also promotes interfaith cooperation within the religious community of Philadelphia. Overall, NIM espouses the belief that religious commitment is expressed not simply in rituals or words, but most importantly in action that is "God-like."

Religion is "implicit" in NIM's activities. Staff members are personally committed to a faith, and the coalition's base is a collection of congregations. Some religious references appear in NIM materials, such as "doing God's work on behalf of our neighbors" (Stern, newsletter, 2002) and "transformation of public life consistent with the loving purposes of God" (in NIM's Statement of Purpose). NIM personnel policies provide a generous number of annual leave days so that staff can freely and with encouragement opt to observe religious holidays and holy days.

The driving values of NIM are social, political, and religious. As an alliance, NIM has set itself apart by consistently enlisting the opinions and organizing efforts of community members. While it had the resources to work alone, NIM consistently bridged into the community and worked with the congregations and other organizations in the community. It has hired external consultants to survey the needs of the community, and has created programs to meet them. For example, one study concluded that the community lacked adequate child care facilities and food assistance programs for senior adults, who were also too often victims of violence. In response, NIM created task forces that led to Northwest Meals on Wheels and Northwest Victims Services, both NIM spin-offs, and also established its own child care training program, now the Neighborhood Child Care Resource Program, described below.

Both Fernandez and Stern emphasized the crucial importance of the separation of church and state. They noted that the power inherent in government can corrupt the moral fiber of faith-based organizations that are closely linked with political leaders or financially dependent upon the political process. In the opinion of both Fernandez and Stern, independent faith-based alliances are best equipped to serve as intermediaries between the government and the local community because they reflect the community as a whole and represent a moral voice.

Structure and Management

STRUCTURE

Given NIM's religious history and social motives, we now examine its structure under the influence of its mission. NIM has a formal structure, reflected in its literature and organizational arrangements. The organization has bylaws and stable and transparent funding. Its public face includes newsletters, a Web site, and public advocacy statements. Policy decision making resides in the board, which hires and evaluates the executive director. The executive director issues checks based upon policies set by the board. As Ebaugh and Pipes (2001) noted, interfaith coalitions often have volunteers from member congregations. NIM's bylaws require that its 24 board members must include members of at least 15 of its constituent congregations. In practice, most of the rest are from other faith-based groups. The board elects its own officers, including chairperson, vice chairperson, secretary, and treasurer. Emeritus positions are occasionally granted to those who have contributed significantly to NIM over many years. Board members serve on NIM's various statutory and ad hoc committees, its Racial Justice Dialogue Group, and its Sustaining Creation environmental initiative.

The crucial day-to-day work of running NIM's main programs for younger and older populations belongs to the staff. NIM currently employs a full-time executive director, two full-time program directors (for children and youth and for older adults), and approximately 20 other full- and part-time staff engaged in training, publicity and outreach, grant writing, elder ombudsmen work, and general support of the agency. A full-time office administrator and full-time finance director oversee daily operations.

The role of congregations in the alliance has diminished over time. Over the years, several factors have contributed to difficulties in securing active commitment from its member congregations. One reason has been its growing size; congregations committed more when the coalition was smaller and more immediate. Additionally, NIM has found out that reliance on clergy as points of contact between itself and the congregants is not always efficient. Clergy methods for rallying volunteer support and commitment differ, and on the whole, they have not been able to clearly and completely communicate NIM's needs and expectations to their congregants. More efficient are contacts between NIM board members and the congregational leadership.

As the number of NIM congregations grew and NIM's programs took on a more professional character, a board composed of representatives chosen by the congregations became unwieldy and ineffective. On a consultant's advice in 1989, the board changed its structure. New bylaws mandated that only 15 congregations had to be represented on the board. Moreover, they were to be selected through a nominating process, not appointed, and were therefore free to vote independently, without necessary regard to policies and practices of their congregations. The remaining 9 were to be nominated from the community. As a result, more than half the congregations have no seat on NIM's board. Over the years, the representative and decision-making power of the congregations has diminished, and NIM has grown an independent locus of power in the board. Presently, NIM can be described as an agency independent of its participating congregations, but related to them and open to their input.

Congregations undertake various roles within NIM and value being part of NIM to different degrees. Some maintain a rudimentary association with the movement; the least involved congregations are in alliance through name only. Others become highly involved and provide volunteers or funds. Such congregations are generally more aware of NIM's activities and priorities. NIM tries not to discriminate among members according to their level of activity, and has tried to maintain relations with all clergy, seeking out those from more inactive congregations. A NIM board committee serves as a liaison between NIM and the congregations. It should be emphasized that NIM would like all 40 member congregations to be interested and active. In reality, at any given time, less than half the congregations are actively engaged and financially supportive, very much the same as in most coalitions or alliances, especially those which are interfaith.

Conversely, some nonmember congregations receive services from NIM. For example, those that run child care centers, after-school programs, or programs for senior citizens benefit from the technical assistance offered by NIM staff and have easy access to NIM workshops geared to improvement of their services. NIM also cosponsors some programs with congregations, providing staff knowhow and support. Such programs often come in response to suggestions from congregations, such as the program on peace for which NIM provided speakers and publicity after the outbreak of the Iraq war.

Since most of NIM's budget comes from government contracts and foundation grants, NIM does not need approval from its member congregations when undertaking an effort. Although less cohesive than at its start, NIM has sought to maintain contact with all members. There are some forums in which all members meet and discuss common or particular issues. Member congregations are generally informed about NIM's activities through a newsletter sent four times a year to donors and member congregations, as well as through email notes and hand-sent mail directed specifically to clergy.

NIM is aware that as its operation has become more professional, a disconnect has developed between its programs and its member congregations. As a result of a strategic plan developed in 2004–5, NIM has begun efforts to strengthen its historical base. NIM is establishing a Congregation and Community Council (CCC) through which congregations will share ideas, forge links between each other, and help NIM plan new initiatives which the congregations see as valuable to their own missions. The council will also serve as a means of maximizing the efficiency and effectiveness of an already documented strength of congregations, namely, their pool of activist, caring, and religiously motivated volunteers. NIM would help recruit, train, and supervise the volunteers, and match them up with programs best suited to their interests and expertise. By assisting in congregational volunteer programs, NIM would serve its members and strengthen their ties to NIM—which would in turn allow NIM to recruit volunteers for its own programs.

While NIM has experienced some difficulties in terms of member involvement, recent experience also demonstrates the loyalty of its members. Alliances undergoing changes in leadership often experience loss of members during the transition. This was not the case at NIM, which installed a new executive director, Rabbi George Stern, in 2002. The transition has been smooth, with no marked changes to the programs, staff, or congregational membership. Indeed, Stern has augmented the efforts of the former executive director, Fernandez, to strengthen the roles of congregations within NIM. NIM membership has grown, and the council holds much promise. Fernandez and Stern meet regularly to facilitate the transition. In fact, both read an earlier version of this chapter and jointly met with the senior author to discuss inaccuracies. Their verbal and written comments indicated harmony and shared organizational vision.

One weakness of NIM is the absence of fully engaged African American congregations. In an interview, Fernandez spoke of the reluctance of African American churches during his time at NIM to get involved in the coalition. Day (2001) reported on the reluctance of most African American churches to involve themselves in coalitions or alliances, as these organizations are often too broad in focus, and regional, rather than local, in their impact. It may be that minority or ethnic congregations have a more narrow range of interests and beliefs, which cannot be accommodated by the more broad-ranging system of social interests and theological spectrum of an organization like NIM.

MANAGEMENT

As noted above, as an interfaith alliance, NIM does not promote any specific faith tradition. Faith, in its broader sense, is manifested in the actualization of helping the needy. In addition, NIM does not discriminate in hiring; it neither requires religious commitment among its leadership, nor appeals to religious authorities for its decisions. According to Jeavons (1998), this nonadherence to religious oversight renders NIM "religion tolerant."

Other evidence for NIM's inclusiveness comes from its varied funding sources. NIM does not rely on funding from religious sources. In its early years, NIM had support from congregations, individuals, and one foundation. Currently, funding comes mainly from public sources and foundations. There is no imposed membership fee, and some member congregations do not make regular financial contributions. For the fiscal year 2003–4, NIM received 55 percent of its income from public agency contracts, 37 percent from foundation grants, 4 percent from congregations, religious jurisdictions (especially the Philadelphia Presbytery), individuals, and corporations, and 4 percent from program fees and other sources. Thus, NIM is similar to many coalitions reported by Ebaugh and Pipes (2003) in its dependence on local public contracts for the provision of social services.

At the time of writing, and as is the case with most alliances except those that impose membership fees on member congregations,[3] the specific ways in which NIM delivered services were greatly influenced by the interests and priorities of its funders. For example, NIM closed down its support of congregation-based after-school programs when funders shifted their support to city-based and School District of Philadelphia programs on which NIM had little influence. Resource dependency was evident when, at the suggestion of foundations, NIM's Neighborhood Child Care Resource Program joined with two similar neighborhood-based child care groups to create the Philadelphia Early Childhood Collaborative (PECC). It should be noted, however, that decisions such as those mentioned were consistent with NIM's overall mission. They were changes in focus, not in overall direction.

NIM's nonreliance on donations from congregations leaves NIM free to set its own programs. Thus, NIM reports no programmatic conflicts with member congregations. In addition, NIM avoids religious divisiveness by stressing the commonalities among its various faith groups. Generally NIM takes public stands only on broad issues of public policy, such as child care and senior services. As indicated above, explicit religion is absent from NIM's professional procedures and service practices, while religious values infuse NIM's pursuit of its mission. Still, while programmatic decision making is centralized, NIM encourages member congregations to pursue tasks and activities in ways suitable to their culture and faith. This includes activities NIM has trained them to engage in, such as volunteering to bring activities to personal care (assisted living) homes, where many congregations offer voluntary prayer.

Services

NIM has created and sponsored numerous programs since its inception in 1969. These have included efforts to aid the hungry, runaway youth, latchkey children, low-income families, and the elderly, through providing goods, access to services, or funding. NIM has also provided leadership and support for advocacy efforts, including education, utility costs, and child care. NIM operates on multiple levels—foremost as a resource to other services and as a funder of programs, but also as a leader in advocacy groups and sometimes as a direct services provider.

Currently, NIM has targeted two groups in its services: the elderly and preschool children. In fiscal year 2003–4, 53 percent of NIM's expenditures paid for the work of the Neighborhood Child Care Resource Program, 28 percent on its various Long Term Care Program initiatives, and the rest on administration, fund-raising, and special community programs (antiracism training, an interfaith Thanksgiving Service, a Martin Luther King Day service, and an annual assembly honoring congregational volunteers).

Neighborhood Child Care Resource Program (NCCRP)

A neighborhood-based program, NCCRP offers training and resources to child care teachers and caregivers in Northwest Philadelphia and beyond. The program also provides child care information to low-income families. The NCCRP trains in-home providers of child care, low-wage caregivers, and teacher assistants. NIM believes that by developing the skills and knowledge of such workers, the quality of childcare in the city will be improved. NIM's work in this area has not specifically targeted congregation-based programs or depended upon congregational resources.

NCCRP supports a unique Resource Room equipped with curricular materials, toys, and learning kits which child care centers, after-school teachers, and parents and grandparents of young children can borrow. Materials are multicultural and geared to children with regular and special needs. The Resource Room assists with computers and internet access and provides such services as laminating and book binding. With this material in hand, NCCRP's trained early childhood professionals visit centers and home-based providers to share material and advice on effective care of children. NCCRP offers an annual Child Care Fair, at which dozens of providers share information with neighborhood residents about their programs. NCCRP's Child Care Warm Line offers parents advice on choosing quality child care and referrals to other resources in the city. NCCRP's other services include: support groups for caregivers and teachers, including the Early Childhood Learning Cooperative, a group of teaching professionals who meet to discuss developments in early childhood education; conferences and workshops for child care providers, such as the Northwest Consortium of Directors Conference for child care directors; dozens of training workshops; start-up grants to family child care centers serving up to five children and who are seeking to procure state registration and city licenses; and publication of the *Directory for Children, Youth, and Families*, which details health, educational, social service, and recreational resources located in Northwest Philadelphia.

Some of NCCRP's training and technical assistance is coordinated through PECC. Together they improve the quality, access, and availability of child care and health care in Northwest, North, Northeast, and parts of South Philadelphia, a combined effort reaching 700 child care programs, approximately 60 percent of the child care programs in the city. Through PECC, NNCRP delivers health and safety resources to home-based and "neighbor and relative care" programs, links families with young children to health care and insurance, and trains child care staff to provide health care information and support to children under their supervision. The Early Childhood Training Institute provides training for certification and educational opportunities for child care providers, including first aid, fire safety, and food handling. NCCRP offers college credit-bearing courses that lead to certification as a Child Development Associate. In addition, NCCRP and its partners offer grants of up to $400 under its Quality Enhancement Fund to programs that demonstrate initiatives to improve child care, to renovate their facilities to meet licensing standards, and for limited start-up support.

School Age Ministry Program (SAM)

School Age Ministry began when congregations approached NIM for general technical assistance to meet licensing standards for their after-school programs. From 1995 to 2002 NIM supported 54 congregations (both within and outside NIM's alliance) seeking to establish licensed after-school programs in low-income neighborhoods. SAM provided technical assistance in creating curricula, training in health and safety, child development, nutrition, and discipline, and financial assistance to purchase equipment and work toward licensure. In 2002, SAM started a Summer Care Program to help congregations with licensed after-school programs expand their summer programs from the standard two-week summer camp or Vacation Bible School to five-day-a-week summer-long programs. SAM provided start-up funds for facilities improvement, equipment, and staff development. Finally, for licensed programs SAM mentored staff in meeting the Standards for Quality School-Age Care established by the National School-Age Care Alliance. SAM distributed its *SAMLink* newsletter to over 500 congregations and organizations throughout the Delaware Valley as a means of providing recommendations and connecting faith-based and after-school care communities.

SAM's financial assistance came through several foundations and grants. Even with it, many congregations failed to achieve licensing. That failure, coupled with changes in city and school district programs for latchkey children, caused public agencies and foundations to cease assisting stand-alone congregation-based after-school programs. As a result, NIM began phasing out the SAM program in 2002.

Long Term Care Program (LTCP)

Of all the programs offered by NIM, those for the elderly have most used both NIM and non-NIM congregations and their members, both as volunteers and in leadership roles. The Long Term Care Program formed when NIM approached church volunteers and urged them to connect with long-term care facilities. The support of such congregational volunteers has affected elderly services considerably. As the elder need is general throughout the city, many volunteers come from a variety of congregations, and NIM assists programs geared to seniors living at home in member and nonmember congregations.

The Neighbor to Neighbor Program serves elderly living in nursing homes and personal care (assisted living) facilities. It began when a congregational member noticed a senior citizen at such a home who needed additional care. NIM professionals track resident needs, train staff, and assist in recruiting and training congregational, community, and student volunteers sent out as "neighbors" to visit the elderly. The trainings are the crux of this project, enabling volunteers to improve the care they give. Workshops such as "The Many Shapes of Care-Giving and Care-Receiving" focus volunteers on building relationships through one-on-one activities and group interactions. It is interesting to note that some volunteers bring voluntary Bible study and worship services to the facilities and invite residents to their congregations' social and spiritual activities. This infusion of religious content is done by individual congregations, with NIM's knowledge but not its involvement.

Many long-term care facilities struggle to assure high-quality service because of low staff numbers and minimal training. LTCP responds in three ways. First, with minimal funds LTCP trains direct service staff in an attempt to improve their ability to serve the residents. Second, through its Caring Community Luncheon, NIM has provided appreciation "parties" for residents and staff at nursing and personal care homes.

Third, NIM contracts with Philadelphia Corporation for Aging to provide mandated ombudsmen for half of the long-term care facilities in the city. NIM's Ombudsmen respond to complaints from residents and others involved in the care of both vulnerable and elderly adults. Staff deal with over 500 complaints annually and have handled 1,400 requests regarding placement and community services. They visit seniors in transition from one caregiver to another and provide information to nursing and personal care homes on quality of care, abuse prevention, and residents' rights. As part of this program, NIM trains volunteer ombudsmen to act as supplementary "eyes and ears" in the facilities.

Seniors and Partnership Across the Northwest (SPAN) also uses congregational volunteers and community volunteers as key workers in reaching out to older adults living in their own homes, often isolated. SPAN is actually a coalition of several agencies who send volunteers to work with NIM to serve this growing at-home elderly population. SPAN organizes volunteer outreach efforts among congregational members. It encourages social activities for the elderly, including a weekly lunch called ElderDiner, held at nine congregations and launched by a pastor on the SPAN board. The lunches provide a venue for informational sessions on health, insurance, and other topics, for blood pressure checks and exercise programs. SPAN volunteers also provide home repair, train congregational and community members, and distribute literature of value to seniors. SPAN has published a 100-page directory of senior services in Northwest Philadelphia. Finally, SPAN has organized conferences and workshops for volunteers and seniors, and their families on salient issues in elder care. Many workshops involve spiritual and religious dimensions that can vastly improve older adults' ability to deal with their changing health, mobility, and social situations. Such workshops, focused on adjusting to and accepting the aging process and exploring one's own spiritual approach to aging and dying, are the most explicit religious elements in NIM's services.

SPAN has actually grown in response to requests from congregations. In fact, NIM has assisted congregations beyond its usual catchment area to start programs for the elderly. This NIM role is especially significant in that it encourages congregations to serve this growing but often ignored portion of their membership.

ADDITIONAL ACTIVITIES

In addition to the above key areas of involvement, NIM is active in various smaller projects. NIM has regularly recognized civic leaders. At its Annual Assembly, it gives Community Services Awards to recognize "people who have been a sign of hope in our midst." Through its H. John Heinz, III, award, it commends notable contributors to elderly services. NIM also grants the Neighbor to Neighbor Volunteer of the Year Award for outstanding work with aging adults.

NIM sponsors community discussions and conferences on social issues. Every year, NIM sponsors the Martin Luther King Interfaith Celebration, a gathering of people from different faiths, choirs, and religious and community leaders who speak on King and social issues. Occasionally NIM sponsors or cosponsors other community forums, such as "Religion: A Source of Peace or a Source of Violence?" (Spring 2001), "Islam" (Fall 2002, cosponsored with First United Methodist Church of Germantown), a workshop on race issues (September 2003), and "Religious Approaches to Peace" (Fall 2004, cosponsored with St. Paul's Episcopal Church).

Since 2001, NIM has been a cosponsor of Good Schools Pennsylvania, a movement seeking adequate and equitable funding of public schools. In 2005 NIM joined the Northwest Philadelphia Hospitality Network (which houses homeless families in congregations) to cosponsor Interfaith Advocates Philadelphia, to mobilize faith groups in support of efforts to bring about systemic change in homelessness and poverty.

Relations with Other Organizations

NIM regularly seeks to partner with agencies and organizations whose missions parallel and complement its own. Many have been mentioned above, such as Philadelphia Early Childcare Collaborative and Good Schools Pennsylvania. Others include Anti-Violence Partnership, Please Touch Museum (for children), Interfaith Community Ministry Network, North American Interfaith Network, National Association of Young Children, Children's Defense Fund, Women's Business Development Center, Vermont Center for the Book, Chestnut Hill Hospital, Temple University, and the Albert Einstein Hospital Care Center. NIM seeks collaborations wherever they can enhance its provision of services.

Assessing Success: Models to Offer Social Service Providers

An interfaith alliance is successful when it impacts public policy and secures more adequate distribution of services within a community. NIM has been often recognized as such by the Philadelphia community. Its ElderDiner was recognized by the Philadelphia Corporation for Aging (PCA) as a cost-effective way for congregations to serve the elderly. LTCP trainings also received commendation from PCA. LTCP also received the 2003 Rev. Francis Shearer Award from the Emergency Fund Coalition for Older Philadelphians, a program of PCA. USA Toy Library Association awarded PECC the 1999 Player of the Year award. More recently, the director of NIM's NCCRP was elected president of the USA Toy Library Association in recognition of her work in this area. In 2001 the Unitarian Universalist Church of the Restoration in 2001 honored executive director Richard Fernandez with the Rudolf Gelsey Award for his community service, social justice, civil rights, and religious leadership work.

NIM's success is also demonstrated by the interest of new congregations to join its alliance. For many years it has provided services beyond its original geographic area. In mid-2005 NIM launched a broad-based effort to enlist the support of congregations and other faith institutions within zip codes surrounding its original base. Preliminary evidence points to a significant positive response, attributable to the reputation for service which NIM enjoys.

Summary

In the context of this book, the key lesson from NIM's story is that congregations in Philadelphia and in other cities can serve as building blocks to create alliances that aim at meeting social needs at a level beyond the reach of most individual congregations. The level of congregational influence over and financial commitment to the coalition superstructure may vary significantly. In most cases, these alliances and coalitions have to obtain funds elsewhere. But, most important, the congregations are the entities which provide community imprimatur for the work of the coalition and serve as the moral foundation for the activities of the alliance. Clergy may be active and highly involved in alliances like NIM or silent inactive partners, but their tacit support is necessary for congregational involvement. The alliance superstructure sometimes addresses pressing problems affecting certain congregations and at other times engages them in activities of community import that do not directly impact given congregations. But overall, interfaith coalitions serve as guardians of civil society and catalysts for social changes which individual congregations would be unable to effect. The congregations and the alliance superstructure develop a symbiotic relationship: the alliance takes advantage of the resources and prestige of the congregations; the congregations rely on the alliance to better fulfill their missions.

While a wide body of literature has been devoted to categorizing faith-based organizations in terms of their level of religiosity, we suggest that an important way to look at faith-based organizations is by their structure and organizational dynamics. As indicated above, coalitions depend on congregations for legitimacy and support. It is not surprising, therefore, that Kearns (2003) found that more than half of the faith-based organizations in Pittsburgh were established by either a single congregation or a group of congregations. But until now neither mono-faith nor interfaith alliances and coalitions have received much scholarly attention.

This chapter examined the complex effects of interfaith status on the operations of an alliance. Researchers need to consider the specific effects of interfaith cooperation on social services, including the goals for unity and the diminished role of explicit sectarian religiosity in service provision. NIM has managed for over thirty years to respect all faith traditions. In true interfaith spirit, its churches, synagogues, and mosques are all equally valued and respected. Service to the community is itself seen as an expression of religious values by NIM's board, staff, and member congregations. NIM focuses on the core religious teaching "Love your neighbor" and encourages congregations and their congregants to act out their faith in the public sphere.

Warren and Wood (2001) found 133 faith-based social change organizations in the United States in a national review of faith-based community organizing. Matovina (2001) listed over 150 such groups along with their location. These studies took note of the Eastern Pennsylvania Organizing Project and Philadelphia Interfaith Action (PIA), which organize political action for social change by using congregations as their resource base. But they did not include congregation-based coalitions like NIM, though they are arguably essential components of civil society that provide civic outlets for people who would otherwise be underrepresented or marginalized. If these national studies missed a highly visible organization like NIM, one can only assume that many more such alliances have been overlooked.

NIM has developed over the years from a collection of congregations whose representatives on the NIM board set action goals to an alliance of congregations that looks to NIM's independent board and professional staff for direction. The alliance represents the member congregations but acts independent of them. NIM is not a collection of fee-paying congregations but a nonprofit superstructure that relies on its member congregations more for legitimacy than for resources. It is linked directly to some of its member congregations through programs initiated by NIM and held within them or with the involvement of congregational volunteers. But not all member congregations are so engaged. NIM's ties to allied congregations are not as strong as they were at the time of NIM's founding in 1969, a change we have examined above and which, as of this writing, is being addressed by NIM itself.

Intentionally, there is little explicit religion in NIM's services, except within congregation-based programs in which volunteers, once trained, are free to deliver services which may include specific religious content. From these teachings, NIM's leaders strongly believe that Americans drawing on their diverse religious traditions can work together to improve public life. As such, NIM represents a long-standing example of a coalition or an alliance effectively pooling resources and expertise to address social ills.

NIM is a coalition/alliance that has survived and adapted to environmental changes. Starting with one employee, NIM developed into an essentially professional agency with two dozen paid employees who are responsible for most of NIM's service delivery. It is well recognized in the social service arena and in the community. NIM maintains its status as a bridge between religious groups themselves and between government, secular, and sectarian institutions. Both its expertise in the delivering of social services and the respect with which the community views NIM are signs of its success. Yet while not dependent upon its members for the day-to-day programs it administers, NIM would not be as successful standing alone. It exemplifies the potential in congregations to provide a basis for more effective social services impacting Philadelphians and improving their quality of life.

Chapter 11

Using Congregational Capacity to Help the Homeless: The NPIHN Story

In a climate in which there are more partnerships among community organizations, it behooves scholars of nonprofit groups to examine the organization and success of interfaith networks (Cnaan, Wineburg, and Boddie 1999). How do they operate, and what marked characteristics do they exhibit in their social service efforts? Some interfaith collaborations are comprised of organizations coming together to form an alliance or a coalition. In other instances, several groups in an area are asked to help support another organization that aims at solving a particular social problem. This chapter examines one such program, The Northwest Philadelphia Interfaith Hospitality Network (NPIHN), whose primary mission is to provide food, shelter, and transitional assistance to homeless individuals and families in the Germantown area of Philadelphia by utilizing congregational resources.

NPIHN has only a few staff members, but has been able to mobilize and coordinate the extensive resources latent in local religious congregations to provide an impressive array of services to Philadelphia's homeless population. In a sense, NPIHN is like a company which designs, markets, and sells, but outsources production. Nevertheless, NPIHN directors are closely involved in service provision, and the values of the organization permeate all of its outsourced operations. All this leads to an interesting parallel with a much more well-known values-driven company: Newman's Own brand of salad dressings and pasta sauces.

In *Shameless Exploitation in Pursuit of the Common Good* (2003), actor Paul Newman and author A. E. Hotchner describe the formation of Newman's Own. No doubt many readers have seen their products on the grocer's shelf if not in their own kitchens. But not all users know that the company pours its entire profit into charitable giving, most of which goes to various summer camps for sick children. In twenty years of operation, Newman's Own has earned and contributed some $150 million.

Though the tone of their story is light—they claim to have accidentally flouted every known sound business principle and attribute all their success to luck—Newman and Hotchner are clearly proud of their close personal involvement. The story starts with Newman and Hotchner stirring a batch of salad dressing in Newman's basement, and goes on to highlight their perpetual commitment to quality ingredients, freshness, and high standards. They point out that their brand is genuinely their business, not merely celebrity name-licensing. They do what they feel is right, not necessarily what's calculated to bring the most profit—and then of course they give any profits away.

With such pride one might expect them to operate their own factories. However, as they clearly state: "We even toyed with the notion of setting up our own bottling plant in a nearby vacant facility that had once housed a bottler, but the prospect of hiring workers and running such a plant was too daunting" (19). Instead they contracted with existing bottling plants to produce the dressings and sauces according to their specifications. They defined this operating mechanism "shameless exploitation" because they used the manufacturing resources of others.

NPIHN is like Newman's Own in several key ways, all of which will be apparent in the more detailed description below. First, NPIHN serves primarily as a designer and facilitator, and outsources everything from facilities to labor. Second, the NPIHN staff demonstrates intense and ideologically driven involvement with every aspect of the service. Third, NPIHN explicitly attributes success not to business acumen but to a combination of external forces and the inherent good of their core values. Newman's Own says they got lucky; NPIHN says God answered their prayers. Fourth, Newman's Own is unswervingly committed to freshness and quality ingredients; NPIHN is committed to combining personal, respectful holistic provision of immediate food and shelter needs with motivation and skills training toward lasting life change. In essence, both produce much-needed public goods by harnessing resources that they do not command and do not intend to command.

Social Service Delivery to Religious Congregations

Outsourcing is nothing new to government and business. Businesses contract out services to able parties, and foundations seek expertise on issues from university scholars; government contracts with the private sector for many things up to and including war fighting. What is relatively new is the trend toward enlisting the services and resources of civil society (Salamon 1987), including religious groups, as outlined in the most recent welfare legislation, Charitable Choice. And as we have seen, groups like NPIHN even subcontract work to congregations. But how has this outsourcing of labor or enlisting of expertise fared?

A survey in Indiana concluded that congregations involved in human services and organized into a network, on average, do not secure needed resources as successfully as secular nonprofit organizations, or faith-based organizations involved in human services and operating within a network (Clerkin and Grønbjerg 2003). These findings, however, need to be corroborated, and scholars are calling for (and conducting) research on religious networks (Cnaan et al. 2002; Pipes and Ebaugh 2002). In that vein, this chapter focuses on NPIHN's procurement and disbursement of resources to meet the housing, food, and life skills needs of the homeless in the city.

Chaves and Tistsos (2001) described the types of services offered by congregations and the methods and structural arrangements by which they secured resources. In their study of a nationally representative sample of congregations, they found that congregations tended to attend to emergency needs for food, shelter, or clothing. Only 10 percent of congregations (comprising 20 percent of attenders) are involved in the "more personal" kinds of programs involving "holistic, long-term, or face-to-face" services. They also noted that congregational involvement in homeless services often takes the form of providing money and/or volunteers to shelters administered by other organizations. Congregations may also provide food to a shelter on a rotating basis with other congregations, provide food on a regular basis to the homeless, or provide shelter in their buildings. Congregations depend upon volunteers organized for regular, specific tasks, but often the group of volunteers is small. Of congregations that involved themselves in social service activities, 80 percent had used fewer than thirty volunteers. Chaves and Tsitsos recommend that programs desiring to successfully engage congregational volunteers should conform themselves to these models.

Congregations that have effectively reached out to their communities also exhibit the nontraditional organizational approach of relying upon church members to lead the process. Lay members held one-on-one meetings with community members, held house meetings, and helped pastors announce events during worship or through key news venues (Wood 1997).

When seeking to document their religious nature, a researcher can determine the religiousness of the structure and operations of an organization. Jeavons (1998) suggests several facets to examine, and qualities in those facets such as religious commitment of participants or referral to religious sources for decision making. Scholars in past years have combined the two methods of organizational analysis and identification of religiosity by seeking to determine the dictation and incorporation of religious values and psychologies in organizational practices of religious organizations (Ebaugh and Pipes 2003; Jeavons 1998; Smith and Sosin 2001; Unruh and Sider 2001).

A marked finding among studies tracing more religious features of faith-based or religious services has been the personalized approach of faith-based organizations and congregations in their social services (Monsma and Mounts 2002). Chaves and Tistsos (2001) particularly locate such personal care in programs that require longer contact with clients, such as job training or drug abuse treatment. NPIHN service is both religious and long-term, and prides itself on being personal.

Cnaan and his colleagues (2002) observed a coalition of churches in New Orleans, and found its social motives to be rooted in religious commitment and its organizational cohesion to depend on religious experiences. Examining the Greater New Orleans Federation of Churches, a network that provides primarily recreation and summer programs, they found that the Federation assumed the standard role assumed by a network in relation to government and local citizens: mediating between government and citizens by representing and "protecting" the needs of local residents. Such work was the Federation's act of "witnessing" one's faith. Faith was purposed to not only be practiced privately but also publicly toward those outside the community of believers. Such witnessing required cohesion among members of the organization, achieved through the collective involvement in religious experiences. Members over time produced relations of trust and knowledge of one another. Charismatic leadership held groups under a common cause, while a pluralistic lay membership reached out effectively to community members of different backgrounds.

Berrien and Winship (1999) documented Boston's Ten Point Coalition as taking the same type of mediating role to help curb youth violence in the city. In this case, a religious group of churches, led by clergy, partnered with police in a citywide effort to promote interagency control of youth violence. Clergy granted police—who in incidents of alleged capriciousness and racism had lost a notable degree of authority in the community—legitimacy in the community with their moral authority and proven commitment to community youth. As a result, police forces were more effective in their interagency law enforcement in Boston, while youth built positive relationships with clergy. If it follows these patterns, a network like NPIHN could be expected to be a mediating force in the community, perhaps less efficient because of its lower level of professionalism but more personal than comparable public services.

Methodology

Few scholars have produced literature on faith-based networks. As a result, there are few established methods by which to study them. Byrd (1997) and Hall (1998) have suggested the new sector movement theory (NSM) as a way to understand small religious nonprofits (SRNPs), as compared to the more traditional resource mobilization (RM) theory. In NSM, researchers are encouraged to examine the less studied aspects of values and social psychologies. Sources of information for these variables can be mission statements, explanations of reasons for service, and anything else that gives clues about the organization's sense of identity.

With RM, the researcher can observe the conventional organizational facets of the studied organization. The parameters for this kind of organizational analysis include members of the organization, resources held, types of services delivered, management of finances, and size and qualifications of staff and services (Jeavons 1998). Reingold, Pirog, and Brady (2000) have also recommended evaluating indicators of faith-based organizations' "agency performance," fields including management of finances (how monies are dispersed across services) and management of services (how they are delivered, coordinated, and chosen). Services fall into the categories of human-social, food and health, child care and youth services, counseling, employment and training, housing and community development, legal aid/advocacy, funding/source of revenue, transportation, and interorganizational services and funding. Scholars in recent years have focused on documenting staff, resources, funding sources, services, and sociodemographic variations of congregations or religious organizations (Cnaan, Wineburg, and Boddie 1999; Cnaan and Boddie 2000; Cnaan et al. 2002; Chaves and Tistsos 2001; Monsma and Mounts 2002; Ebaugh and Pipes 2003). We aim in this chapter to offer a combination of RM and NSM.

Data were gathered via interviews with directors and staff, study of documents, and observation of activities in the spring of 2001 and the fall of 2003. These data were analyzed according to both organizational structure and values (employing RM and NSM as described above).

The NPIHN story

NPIHN's mission is to provide short-term resources and offer long-term direction to the homeless in Northwest Philadelphia. In addition to providing food and shelter, the network connects clients to services that address emotional, health, educational and job-preparation needs. Service is not time-limited, and unlike many other shelters, NPIHN encourages clients to stay as long as necessary.

FORMATION AND DEVELOPMENT

NPIHN began in 1990 as a nonprofit coalition of congregations and was incorporated as a 501(c)(3) organization in 1991. The founder and first president, Carol Young, was a member of one of the original participating congregations, a fact consistent with the finding that most congregational services are founded by congregation members (Cnaan et al. 2002). After observing that networks for Interfaith Hospitality Network (IHN) were often located in the suburbs, but not in the city, Young wanted to form a network of providers for the homeless in the city and especially in Northwest Philadelphia. Unable to establish an IHN subsidiary for the city at her own church in Chestnut Hill, she secured the help of a suburban church. The church's clergy approached other ministers in the area and the national parent, IHN, to begin forming NPIHN.

MEMBERS OF THE ORGANIZATION

Sheltering the homeless is a work that is often demanding in that space is needed for a long period of time and a cadre of committed though under or unpaid workers is needed (Ogilvie 2004). Most congregations cannot afford to offer their grounds as permanent homeless shelters; their space is devoted to their primary activities. While they can offer many volunteers, they can offer these volunteers only for a limited amount of time. By networking, the congregations can meet year-round needs by each providing space and volunteers from two to four weeks at a time. Noncongregational groups are tied into this network through their provision of needed services or resources, such as food or transportation. Other interfaith coalitions have provided shelter in much the same way NPIHN does (Pipes and Ebaugh 2002), and NPIHN is one of many IHN organizations.

NPIHN's member congregations are recruited by the executive director. Originally, NPIHN's founder went from one congregation to another and recruited them to be partners with her new homeless serving organization. There are 12 primary congregations that provide space, food, and volunteers.[1] In addition, 8 buddy congregations provide additional volunteers.[2] One of the 12 primary congregations is Jewish; the rest are Christian.

SERVICES AND SERVICE MANAGEMENT

Again, recruitment of clientele began informally. Young stood by Philadelphia's trademark LOVE sculpture in Center City, seeking families interested in the program, and transported them to the NPIHN center in Northeast Philadelphia. NPIHN also received referrals from the Office of Services to the Homeless and Adults (now Office of Emergency Shelter and Services), the city system of Philadelphia. Since then, however, most referrals have come from former guests, ministers, and social services that receive information on NPIHN through city services and churches. There is no systematic data on the number of recipients or their last geographic "home" before going to NPIHN. Besides the streets, guests tend to come to NPIHN from living with relatives, overcrowded housing, and city shelters.

The NPIHN staff and board supervise the 12 congregations who share the work of providing resources and services to the homeless in Philadelphia. All the congregations are eager to help, and none can provide a year-round shelter. Each congregation hosts the guests for two to four weeks, and then the guests are shifted to another congregation. Thus each congregation is faced with the challenge of hosting the guests for a total of about one month each year, which can be broken into two subperiods. There are occasional problems when congregations have unexpected inabilities to host. For example, when one congregation had to leave the network because of asbestos problems, NPIHN lost six weeks of annual hosting.

NPIHN provides two main categories of service: the provision of basic services to the homeless, including overnight shelter and meals, and the provision of more advanced family services, such as transportation, child care, training in the basic skills of parenting and budgeting, and services to prepare clientele for life beyond NPIHN, such as aid in finding permanent housing and in transitioning from welfare to work. It also provides mentoring services to help clients' transition out from the program to their next stage of more independence, and has maintained informal contact with clients to provide supportive relationships after guests leave NPIHN.

On average, in 2001, guests stayed with NPIHN for three months, and were encouraged to find more permanent housing within that time period. Since 2001, under the new executive director, NPIHN has been releasing guests in six months, however, when needed guests can stay even longer. Congregations provide storage space and food for lunches, but adults must fix these themselves. This is done to minimize the burden on member congregations but also to avoid the institutional atmosphere of most homeless shelters and to provide the guests with feelings of dignity, normalcy, and responsibility while they prepare their own food the way they would like it.

NPIHN prioritizes comfort, privacy, and safety. Staff members assess each congregation as to whether it is safe and clean for its guests. The services have been advertised as "private" and culturally sensitive. Hatry

(1999) mentions time insensitivity as one barrier for clients in using a service, and NPIHN's client-centered ethos extends to time sensitivity as well. According to Young, NPIHN's sensitivity to the schedules of its clients positively distinguishes it from city services. For example, whereas a city service would have mothers arrive for a meal at 6:00 P.M. since it is difficult to keep staff much later than that, NPIHN serves dinner at 6:45 P.M., a little later and more convenient for working mothers, and a time which is possible because volunteer staff members are willing to work later. Furthermore, as mentioned above, when clients are settled into the shelter they are encouraged to make their own meals whenever convenient.

When not at a congregational shelter, guests may work on securing permanent housing and employment at the participating YWCA in Germantown. Transportation to and from the YWCA is provided by NPIHN. Various additional services were initiated by the former program director, Sharon Hollingsworth. Hollingsworth assessed guests' needs beyond shelter and food, such as assistance in parenting, budgeting, and securing a job and housing after time at NPIHN. Attention by Hollingsworth was frequent and intimate. She met with guests regularly, two times a month, in one-on-one meetings, to discuss goals and deadlines.

Long-term planning was stressed in family services sessions, particularly for financial and job-preparation management. Budgeting was stressed heavily, with a goal to save 50 to 55 percent of monies to ease the process of moving into new housing after NPIHN. Guests had to show Hollingsworth how much they had saved. They also had to submit bank receipts, housing applications, and progress reports as to where they had gone to apply for work.

Alongside budgeting, the coordinator stressed education. Finally, self-confidence and motivational training were key components of family services. Guests were told to fight the "giving up," and "uncertainty" of being able to "make it" and "do it" in their situation. They were also told to think of their children. Hollingsworth told guests that she did not want them to ever return to the shelter system. In all her services, the coordinator repeated her message consistently to the guests. To a large extent, the success of NPIHN's services has been attributed to Hollingsworth.

The mentoring program is designed to help transition guest clientele into sustainable living conditions. Mentors establish a one-year personal relationship with the mentee and act as "family," much in the same spirit staff members relate to guests in the program (as "friends" or "advocates, " and "bridges to the community" maintaining "trust and respect"). The mentor and mentee meet weekly, and maintain contact by phone. Mentors instill daily living skills, such as managing the home by securing home insurance and safety, managing finances and vehicles, and managing personal lives, such as one's emotional health. The main NPIHN values encouraged are independence, rather than dependence on the mentor. Mentors evaluate former clients for health problems, and social or financial violations, such as drug use, psychiatrically dangerous behavior, abuse or criminal activity, or giving of gifts between mentor and mentee. Recently, staff members have considered expanding the base of volunteer mentors, because one mentor cannot handle a former guest's needs alone. It remains to be seen whether the change in arrangement will diminish the personal nature of the mentor-mentee relationship.

NPIHN also works with area universities to promote education in low-income households. For example, it has participated in a program offering classes to area college students on social change and advocacy, at which clients and former clients have spoken about being impoverished and receiving welfare and social services.

RESOURCES

In general, most resources for NPIHN services come from the member congregations, which provide the food and shelter, and the bulk of the volunteers. Monetary support has come largely from foundations. NPIHN also receives food from a local franchise owned by a congregational member.

NPIHN is highly dependent upon the group of volunteers from each congregation to provide food, volunteer supervision of guests during the night, and other as-needed items such as bedding or medicine. This accords with the study by Ebaugh et al. (2003), on the high dependence of faith-based agencies on congregations for in-kind support and with Ogilvie's (2004) account of congregational homeless shelters in New York City.

Volunteers number at about 1,000 and come mostly from member congregations as well as area universities. The overwhelmingly large number of volunteers, compared to paid staff, employed by NPIHN confirms findings on religious congregations (Cnaan and Boddie 2000; Ebaugh and Pipes 2003). Other volunteers who lead and organize each congregation's responsibilities coordinate volunteers within each congregation. Volunteers include church members and employees who may be called upon for on-the-spot services, most often church secretaries and custodians, who help to move equipment, set up rooms for lodging with beds and dividers, and clean bathrooms. Volunteers from nearby Arcadia College mainly help out with child care. Students have also aided with art therapy, a new activity undertaken by NPIHN. A pediatrician volunteered her services in 2001, linking guests to local physicians. The current director, Rachel Falkove, has marveled at the amount of work accomplished by a cadre of dedicated volunteers.

The congregations also provide resources whenever and whatever guests need. For example, one evening in September 2003, volunteers from St. Paul's Episcopal Church in Chestnut Hill were short on bedding for the guests. Calls were made on the spot to members of various congregations, four of whom in turn provided blankets that same evening, dropping them off at the church fellowship hall. When a guest needed medicine, one volunteer purchased it at the request of the executive director.

NPIHN partners with a broad range of groups beyond its member congregations, but it increasingly depends on public agencies for funding. This may reflect a trend of professionalization. With the arrival of the new executive director, who has directed her efforts at expanding NPIHN's funding base and increasing its visibility, NPIHN has been gaining more formal recognition and support from the public sector. In late September 2003, the city of Philadelphia awarded the network 12 housing vouchers that clients can use once exiting the shelter, but only if accompanied by NPIHN case management staff. NPIHN has chosen to participate in such a partnership not at the social service level but only at the volunteer level.

Previously, NPIHN had expressed even less willingness to work with government. Congregations did not seem to want to partner with government, fearing changes or restrictions to their programs. Philadelphia's homeless office, for example, changed NPIHN's proposed program substantially when it applied for city funds, asking that NPIHN act as emergency housing, and offered a third of the amount NPIHN had requested. Ebaugh and Pipes (2003) found that while faith-based agencies prefer religious sources rather than government funding, many still solicit nonreligious sources. Interfaith coalitions in particular have expressed little interest in governmental funding under the welfare clause which promotes faith-based organizations by offering support and protection of groups' religious characters (Cnaan and Boddie 2002; Pipes and Ebaugh 2002). Recently, however, NPIHN has raised money from the city. A Philadelphia city agency in 2004 gave NPIHN a "shelter fee" of $14 per night per person. As such, the city recognized NPIHN formally as a shelter program in the city. The city also granted NPIHN subsidies in the form of vouchers for low-income housing, which guests could use on exiting NPIHN. Also Senator Rick Santorum provided the organization a grant of $15,000.

Studies of faith-based coalitions have found that the largest amounts of funds have come from congregants (Chaves 1999; Pipes and Ebaugh

2002). In 2001, the largest amount of funds to NPIHN came from foundations (55 percent). The next largest funding sector was congregational members. The remaining funding came primarily from local institutions, such as universities, from NPIHN's fund-raising efforts (such as the sale of "house pins" and community dinners), and from individual donors, including individuals from participating churches, boards, and staff. Donations have been facilitated by NPIHN's affiliation with United Way, by which the most funds enter (Leary 2005).

Local organizations have also provided NPIHN with technical information and resources. The Northwest Interfaith Movement (NIM), which involves congregations belonging to NPIHN, has granted ideas and guidance as to child care, and Germantown Avenue Crisis Ministry has granted food and money. Other ties are to groups who help grant guests job referrals and housing. Finally, NPIHN works with others in a coalition of housing and homeless providers, comprising Greater Philadelphia Urban Affairs Coalition, the Family Service Committee, and the Housing Committee. It also appeals to African American sororities and social circles for volunteers and monetary support.

As a subgroup of the national IHN, NPIHN contributes a small portion of its funding to it (1 percent of its budget). IHN provides its members with technical assistance and information on nonprofit skills management and current legislation such as the current climate set by government for involving more faith-based groups in programs.

The main shortages felt by NPIHN are space and transportation. In strategic planning meetings, staff members have discussed goals of expanding space and granting every family a room. Clients need room for sleep, showering, and changing into clothing for work, and kitchen space for food preparation. Churches and synagogues are not designed as living quarters, so bathrooms and showers are in short supply. Often the bathroom is the only private space, making it inconvenient for guests to change clothes.

In 2001, the Germantown YWCA leased three rooms to NPIHN on its third floor for recreation and personal use by guests and office space for staff. A dayroom provided children of clients a place to go after school to do homework and to play. The dayroom also served as a place where guests could receive phone calls and mail. The two other rooms were office space for the executive director and the program director. NPIHN also secured warehouse space at the Sedgwick Theatre, in which it stored donations. Currently, NPHN offices are at Mt. Airy Presbyterian Church.

Transportation had also been in short supply. It was therefore difficult to move beds and other supplies between congregations. NPIHN had worked hard to try to facilitate this process as best as possible through the use of U-Haul trucks.

EXCEPTIONAL MODES FOR RESOURCE MOBILIZATION: PRAYER AND TIGHT CONGREGATIONAL NETWORKS

Staff members have attributed much provision of resources to prayer—having prayed to God for housing or supplies. They have seen clients receive these resources in phenomenal ways. They tell stories like that of a father with children who needed housing and furniture, which were provided within perfect time frames.

Networking among congregational members and their contacts has also eased the procurement of resources, monetary as well as informational. Information can be particularly helpful in connecting possible member congregations and clientele to NPIHN. Congregations in themselves, being the main providers of resources, are crucial to the operations of NPIHN, and any additional members are most welcomed by NPIHN. Networking in NPIHN is highly localized and not too heavily planned, creating immediate and informal flow of resources. Congregational members may, for example, refer other congregational members to NPIHN as staff or volunteers, or groups in the immediate area to NPIHN, creating a network that is narrow in geographic span and formed rapidly because of the immediate links between congregational members and area groups. These "short" links also allow quick transfer of resources from one contact to the next. As mentioned above, the need for blankets at an area congregation was great, but within two hours, a stack had been formed by the lending of a handful of volunteers reached by telephone. These characteristics have been found in other networks, such as the Greater New Orleans Federation of Churches (Cnaan et al. 2002).

As for providing more intangible resources beyond food and transportation, NPIHN staff can provide crucial social resources, such as access to institutions. The executive director has stressed the place of personal connections in helping guests out of a "bad cycle." For example, the current director has offered her personal connections with the city school system in placing one of the guest high school boys in a better school, which could challenge him more and provide him more opportunities for advancement.

STAFF AND BOARD OF DIRECTORS: SUPERVISION

In 2001, staff included the executive director and the program director, formerly the family services coordinator, both of whom were part-time and paid. The executive director handled admissions and exits, while the program director handled clients' needs and donations for guests once they left the program. In the fall of 2003, the director had undertaken considerable efforts in fund-raising and strategic planning. In 2001, both directors worked approximately 20 to 25 hours per week, not including volunteer hours. There was also a paid professional job-training and parenting-training specialist and a paid van driver, taking clientele between the YWCA in Germantown and the lodging sites on an ad hoc basis.

Congregations provide the staff at NPIHN with valuable information regarding future contacts and clients. Staff members have often been recruited from member congregations. For example, the staff member for parenting and job skills was recruited at a meeting at the church by the former executive director. The director knew the woman was a job career counselor and believed that she could meet the needs of NPIHN. The current executive director is a member of the Jewish congregation in NPIHN and sat on the board for five years before serving as director.

The board of directors is comprised of participating congregations' members as well as members from the local university, Arcadia College. There are also the offices of president, vice president, treasurer, secretary, and corresponding secretary. Committees include those for board leadership development, financial development and fund-raising, programming (especially mentoring clients on and after their exit), professional advising, host recruiting, public relations, advocacy, and personnel. Most decision making power resides in the board. The current director has particularly noted the civility of the board, and attributes this to the faith-based nature of the group.

MANAGEMENT AND STRATEGIC PLANNING: FROM AD HOC TO FORMALIZED STRUCTURE

In 2001, there was no formal strategic plan for NPIHN. The executive director evaluated guests as to whether they could be admitted into the program, and the program director managed a plan for each guest. The method for accessing resources had been to assess what was needed and to meet those needs on an ad hoc basis.

In mid-February 2001, strengths and weaknesses of NPIHN were discussed among volunteer coordinators from different congregations. The main conclusions were that NPIHN needed to recruit more volunteers, provide more concrete roles for them, and better satisfy clients' preferences for food. More weekend volunteers were needed to stay overnight with guests, prepare meals, and call clientele. Strategically, coordinators considered gathering more volunteers through enlisting more member congregations, or asking the congregational buddies to provide more volunteers.

By 2003, NPIHN had begun developing a strategic plan and undertaking many new practices that wee more formalized and professionally informed. For example, the budgeting and banking classes, while offered before, were not on a strict schedule; by the fall of 2003 the staff members were now working to provide these weekly. The same had been true for the mentoring program. The executive director in 2003 was working to build up communicative networks through email among congregations, and among potential donors to raise money. She abandoned other methods of contacting people such as the phone, which she regarded as slower. Also, she worked to enlarge the donor base.

FINANCES

According to financial statements for 1998 and 1999, most finances went toward salaries. Two staff members were paid $21,000 per year, or $14.00/hour plus health care benefits; a professional job trainer and parenting specialist were paid with grants; and a van driver from the YMCA was compensated at $8.00/hour. The same expenditure structure was in place in 2003–4.

VALUES AND SOCIAL PSYCHOLOGIES

In 2001, NPIHN was explicitly religious in its culture and services.[3] Religious motives have informed its work since its beginnings. The Judeo-Christian tenet to love your neighbor as yourself guides NIPHN services. Past directors and presidents have attributed much of NPIHN's ability to raise resources and funds to divine intervention and answers to prayer.

Harris (1995) noted that one feature of congregational welfare services is the special motivations of those who provide the care. In congregations, often people offer religious and theological explanations for their welfare work. As an interfaith organization, NPIHN has stressed the importance of faith in its services. In the past, NPIHN has embraced its work as not its own, but God's work. In that vein, the staff members wish to create a more personable environment in which there is communication of unconditional love, in which services are given in a nurturing and caring manner, and in which services are less institutionalized.

The staff members expressed a faith in God not only through working at NPIHN, but through joint religious practices among themselves and on behalf of clients. Thus, NPIHN would be regarded as religious in nature (Jeavons 1998; Ebaugh and Pipes 2003). Board members held devotions before board meetings involving prayer and study of religious texts. NPIHN also distributed formal documents such as thanksgiving reports expressing faith-based appreciation for staff members. Staff resorted to prayer and looked to God to provide resources and to sustain members and clients in their efforts to bring clients to a place of stability. Staff members guided clients to follow religious values rather than a strict job description, a practice particular to some faith-based organizations (Sider, Olson, and Unruh 2002; Unruh and Sider 2005; Monsma and Mounts 2002). Young, NPIHN's founder, argued that invoking such values inculcated more independence and hope in the guests. For example, to follow the rules demanded obedience, but to follow values required more initiative and creativity from the clients. Young also stated that focusing on values allowed staff members and clients to discuss such concepts as hope, whereas fulfilling tasks did not demand as much consideration of such motivating factors. Cnaan and Milofsky (1997) noted this method of faith-based organizations to motivate its members as their strength.

Staff members expressed "care" toward their guests through strong personal attention. There wass one-on-one attention from caseworkers. The helping process was therefore "more personal and less alienating" (Cnaan, Wineburg, and Boddie 1999). Sherman (2001) stated that such attitudes from staff contributed to the success of faith-based organizations in helping clients. NPIHN approached the homeless with respect for the clientele. Staff members communicated this respect through the practice of hospitality toward their "guests," and through their efforts to build up their state of independence. Staff members were expected to treat their guests in the most welcoming and personable environment possible. NPIHN participants explicitly linked this one-on-one attention to the religious motives of the organization, and that link is not surprising. Jeavons (1998), for example, identified two types of mercy explained from theological texts, one that is more corporal, offering physical aid, and one that is more spiritual, offering personal care and counseling for the soul and spirit. Social services from a religious organization, therefore, have attempted to include not only delivery of resources, but also attention to the inner conditions of the people being served. NPIHN stresses such attendance to the soul and spirit of guests in its services; to nurture these parts of an individual is to reach the essence of that person.

Helping clients build a more independent lifestyle is also a high priority for NPIHN. The notion of individual responsibility prevails in this organization. NPIHN and transitional housing agencies are seen as helpers but not docrs for the guest, a role often coded in the phrase "planter of the seed." They prioritize guests' finding opportunities for housing, for in doing so, guests must create their own plans and strategies. Guests are encouraged to move on from their transitional state at NPIHN to a state of independence. They are encouraged to take initiative and take care of their belongings. Dinner foods are provided by NPIHN, but guests are asked to clean up after themselves—they must wash their dishes, and are advised to prepare lunches for themselves or their children during the week. Cleanup is especially encouraged during the weekends, when guests have more free time.

NPIHN practices hospitality and upholds the notion of "family." Staff members assume responsibilities that family members would take on behalf of their relatives, such as researching sources of medical coverage and accompanying guests as they survey housing they need after they leave NPIHN. Clients are also provided with attentive counseling throughout their stay. In addition, family and a healthy social life are encouraged as a positive growth experience for guests. In its literature and brochures, NPIHN stresses its aspect of providing a home environment. Safety and privacy are also stressed as being assured within their services. Guests are given an opportunity to have more "private" aspects to their lives, such as an address at the YWCA to use as a permanent home contact, and a private phone line. Finally, they are encouraged to spend time with families on weekends and visit community events such as annual Christmas lightings. This creation of a more safe and hospitable environment to attend to the social and possible spiritual needs of guests is an approach to homeless shelters that Jeavons argues may be particular to religious organizations (1998).

In 2003, staff members did not characterize their services as explicitly religious in nature. No religious activities were required or practiced, save prayer or conversation about spiritual issues, should clients wish to speak about such matters. However, the service was unmistakably offered in sacred spaces.

Other interfaith coalitions in Houston have followed such standards of not actively promoting religious content in their services (Pipes and Ebaugh 2002).

SUCCESS MEASURED BY CLIENT SATISFACTION

Has NPIHN been effective in its services? In terms of client satisfaction, it has. Clients express great satisfaction with NPIHN. They feel the staff treats them better than they are treated at city shelters. This is in accord with findings by other scholars, who have shown that clients have been more satisfied with the "personal touch" of religious organizations than with the bureaucratic "impersonal" services of the state (Shapiro and Wright 1996). Not only has NPIHN succeeded in providing a family-like atmosphere, where there is a personal "touch" to its services, but NPIHN maintains this connection with former guests after they leave. Many former guests keep in touch with the executive director.

According to stories from clients who have been in other shelter systems, personable aspects are much appreciated at NPIHN. There is a clear link in their minds between cleanliness and personal respect: They find NPIHN more clean and respectful. In contrast, they described city shelters as dirty and degrading. Families were not treated with respect, and were even treated as "dirt." There was less care, less space, and overall "nasty" conditions. Clients report more positive outcomes from being treated like family at NPIHN; they are able to trust, renew faith in people, renew faith in God, and have hope to continue beyond barriers.

OTHER CONTRASTS WITH NON-FAITH-BASED SERVICES

Pirog and Reingold (2002) claimed that faith-based organizations have stricter eligibility criteria than secular nonprofit groups. They may require higher work requirements or evidence of religious affiliation. In contrast, Ebaugh et al. (2003) found in their study of homeless services of faith-based organizations in Houston that faith-based groups did not necessarily maintain stricter eligibility requirements. NPIHN, however, falls in line with Pirog and Reingold's findings—it does enforce stricter criteria than local government programs and secular nonprofit groups. NPIHN's programs for the homeless involve more strict criteria in that adult clients must exhibit higher motivation to gain self-sufficiency, through gaining education and employment after leaving, and must be in good mental and physical health, showing no psychiatric problems or use of drugs or alcohol. This selection criteria enable NPIHN to cater its services to clients they believe they are most likely to help effectively. This is in contradiction to public services that are mandated to care for all clients and are not allowed to select for "suitable clients."

Compared to public shelters, NPIHN has sought to provide shorter, less permanent shelter and seeks longer-term working solutions. On the continuum of homeless services, NPIHN is a long-term multiservice organization that aims at resolving homelessness rather than merely providing a bed for the night (Johnson and Cnaan 1995). Young stressed its goal of instilling independence and aiming to move clientele into housing within 90 days, although it has extended its services beyond this time frame. Falkove stated that it has taken an average of six to ten months for clients to successfully leave NPIHN. The difficulty is finding subsidized housing or housing for which they have saved enough money.

Conclusion

In this chapter, we provided the case of NPIHN as an example of "shameless exploitation" (Paul Newman's phrase). In addition to the services urban congregations provide directly, they also serve as bedrock for larger overarching structures that use congregational resources. NPIHN is an organization that links 12 congregations and uses their resources to provide services to homeless people in Philadelphia. Acknowledging that housing homeless people on an ongoing basis can be too taxing for any one congregation, NPIHN moves the group of homeless people from one congregation to another every two to four weeks, and each congregation gets a breath before turning again to host the homeless. In addition, NPIHN developed a host of day services helping homeless people retain permanent housing and gain full employment. These pro-social congregations in one neighborhood of the city enable such "shameless" use of congregational facilities and members for producing much-needed public goods. It is the ecology of congregations in the city, their many and varied resources, and their strong norm of helping the needy that make them desire to assist such social entrepreneurial endeavors. This way is yet another mode by which congregations contribute to improving quality of life for people in Philadelphia.

NPIHN has exhibited the social psychologies of creating a family-like, hospitable environment for its guests as a reflection of divine care and the belief in a supernatural being who will provide resources. NPIHN stresses client dignity, and in its actions and language treats its guests as valuable human beings. This is especially difficult to attain when clients are rotated among 12 member congregations and cared for by new congregational volunteers every few weeks. NPIHN is unabashedly religious, providing its services through and on the premises of religious congregations and calling its services faith-based. But clients are not pushed toward religion, and they are free not to participate in any religious activities. The staff members, the places of service delivery, and the spirit of care make NPIHN a faith-based organization.

These attitudes have created an informal aspect to NPIHN's services, and what could be criticized as unstable patterns. Yet, throughout the years, hundreds of homeless families have come to NPIHN, and many have been helped for a long period of time and eventually transitioned to permanent housing and stable employment as well as a healthier family lifestyle. NPIHN has survived and been effective in satisfying clientele, attributing this largely to its attentiveness to guests' needs and to the religious elements of faith and prayer, whereby it has seen resources and staff provided on behalf of the organization and former guests.

Chapter 12

Using Congregational Volunteers: The Stories of Amachi and REST Philly

In the previous two chapters, we presented the case of two umbrella groups that used the willingness and capability of local religious congregations to produce much needed public goods. NIM is an umbrella organization that was formed by a pastor, aiming to resolve neighborhood and city problems. Member congregations in NIM are loosely represented and, combined, they form an alliance that aims to tackle a variety of social issues ranging from interfaith tolerance to care for the elderly. NPIHN, on the other hand, was the idea of one person, a congregational member, who came to a group of area congregations with an idea of helping one specific group of people in need, the homeless. In this chapter, the last in this section of the book, we introduce two organizations that also positively and successfully capitalize on local religious congregations' willingness and capacity, but in a different and innovative way. While NIM is an alliance of congregations and NPIHN is part of the Interfaith Hospitality Network (IHN), Amachi and REST Philly (Rational Emotive Spiritual Therapy) originated in Philadelphia and have been replicated in many other cities.

Amachi and REST Philly both center on the impact of over-incarceration in America, and both recruit cadres of volunteers from participating congregations. Utilizing the principles of group dynamics and faith commitment, the organizations recruit not a congregational representative but a group of members, usually eight to ten, each of whom is trained to provide mentoring and support services and equip his or her peers to provide services to prisoners or children of prisoners.

In this chapter, we discuss these two programs and highlight them as models for "shamelessly" exploiting local religious congregations to "do good" for the city. Both capitalize on the faith factor of people who attend congregations and harness their compassion to assist needy people. While REST Philly was conceptualized and developed years before Amachi, the idea originated (though it is not yet implemented) outside Philadelphia. REST Philly president and founder Dr. Rick McKinney came to Philadelphia only at the invitation of John Street after Street was elected mayor in 2000. At that time, Amachi was already underway under the leadership of former mayor W. Wilson Goode. Accordingly, we introduce first Amachi and then REST Philly. We will then summarize their contribution to the quality of life in the City of Brotherly Love and generalize as to the ability of local religious congregations to generate positive power that can transform the lives of some of the neediest people in America.

Amachi

BACKGROUND

The statistics about incarceration in America over the past twenty years indicate soaring numbers of people in prisons and jails. In 1999, state prisons housed 1,200,000 individuals, while local jails housed 605,000 individuals and federal prisons housed 135,000. During almost any day in 1998, 1 in every 200 residents of the United States was incarcerated (478 individuals for every 100,000 residents). Given that many Americans have been incarcerated only before or after 1998, the proportion of Americans who have been incarcerated at least once in their lifetime is greater than 1 in 50. To put it differently, when one observes a bus or train car, there is a strong likelihood that at least one passenger has been previously incarcerated. More relevant to our project is the fact that at any given time, about 1 in 284 residents of the United States has been released from incarceration within the previous year (Blumenstein and Beck 1999; Roman, Kane, and Turner 2005).

Nearly one and a half million children under age eighteen have a parent incarcerated in a state or federal prison. Over half these children are under ten, and more than 20 percent are younger than five. In addition, more children than ever before experience a parent's incarceration, at least for a short period of time. Children's psychological well-being is jeopardized both when a parent is incarcerated and when the parent returns. Many of these children suffer the grief, guilt, shame, and loss of seeing their parent arrested and taken away, sometimes with neighbors watching. Anger, sadness, and depression are the inevitable emotional results (Bates, Archibald, and Wills 2001; Beatty 1997; Gabel and Johnston 1995; Hariston 1998; Hungerford 1996; Mumola 2000; U.S. Department of Justice 2000).

These children might have to live with a grandparent, aunt, the other parent, or a foster home or facility. Some are separated from their siblings. Many experience unstable housing arrangements that result in frequent changes in care-giving arrangements.

Disproportionately, young men of certain ethnic groups (mostly African Americans and Latinos) go in and out of prisons. Their communities experience recidivism as well, and lose an important part of their local mix of people. Marriages and family lives are significantly interrupted, as well as the wage-earning and economic potential of families. The children of an incarcerated individual miss a source of strength and stability. These "functionally orphaned" children also often face violence, poverty, limited opportunities for an adequate education, and a future that appears to hold very little promise. Anger and powerlessness take hold, and the children too often follow the footsteps of the incarcerated parent and find themselves under the control of the criminal justice system. According to a U.S. Senate report, children of prisoners are six times more likely than other children to be incarcerated at some point in their lives (U.S. Senate 2000: 56)

Given this reality, a few organizations such as Public/Private Ventures (P/PV), the University of Pennsylvania, Pew Charitable Trusts, and Prison Fellowship started negotiations about how to help children of prisoners do well in the community and stay out of jail. John J. DiIulio, Jr., former senior advisor and board member of P/PV, as well as the first director of the White House Office of Faith-Based and Community Initiatives, was the initial force behind Amachi. His insight and vision led to the creation of this innovative program. In hindsight, the idea was simple and brilliant. Given that these children were missing a positive guiding force in their lives, that Big Brothers/Big Sisters (BBBS) was proven to be an effective interaction modality (Tierney, Grossman, and Resch 1995), and that congregations were full of untapped volunteers, the question was, why not ask congregations to provide BBBS mentors for children of prisoners?

When the idea of Amachi was born, many long and cumbersome names were proposed until the word "Amachi" was introduced. Amachi is a West African word meaning "Who knows what God has brought us through this child." It is a statement of hope and understanding that every child has great potential from God and it is our communal responsibility to cultivate every child regardless of his or her parents' debt to society. Consequently, Amachi adopted the motto "People of faith mentoring children of promise."

RATIONALE

It is clear that children of prisoners are a special at-risk population. These children indeed need a warm, steady, reliable adult to guide them. It is well established in developmental psychology that a consistent, nurturing relationship with a dependable adult is essential for the proper development of any child. In the case of a child with an incarcerated parent, a substitute role model is essential. In America, the best agency for providing such services is the BBBS, which is most effective when carried out for a year of weekly contacts between the adult mentor and the child mentee (Tierney, Grossman, and Resch 1995). The problem, however, is that this agency has more needy children to serve than it has volunteers. This is where religious congregations enter the picture.

As Cnaan and his colleagues (2002) noted, congregations in America are composed of groups of people who hold common beliefs and enjoy being together, and thus are likely to join forces and commit to a cause with which they empathize. Members of congregations believe that they and other congregations should be benevolent and offer their space for volunteer and charitable activities. As Wuthnow (1994b: 236) summarized, the congregants in his study were expected to be charitable: "Our culture sees helping the needy as a religious virtue and expects religious organizations to be engaged in service activities." These norms do not themselves generate active participation; they must be considered with other factors such as the congregation's pro-social leadership, committed financial resources, and available resources and other characteristics of the congregation (Cnaan et al. 2002; Dudley and Van Eck 1992; Iannaccone, Olson, and Stark 1995).

As we have shown in previous chapters, volunteers from local congregations have carried out numerous social projects all over Philadelphia, and it has been assumed that, given a new challenge, they will rise to the occasion. The same groups that help provide services to the homeless, carry out numerous summer camps, and provide food for the hungry would be willing to expand the scope of their volunteer activities. Furthermore, as we showed earlier, congregations are the most widespread community social institution in Philadelphia and they enjoy high levels of public trust. Many children are familiar with churches in their communities, and their guardians may even know local clergy on a personal basis.

An ingenious aspect of Amachi is that each participating congregation commits not one or two but a group of ten volunteers. A cadre of volunteers from the same congregation serves as a committed and somewhat self-managed group of mentors who support one another. After the ten or so members of the congregation go through formal screening and training provided by BBBS, they observe, support, share information with, and supervise each other. In other words, in addition to the BBBS investment in these volunteers, the volunteers check on one another, compare notes, carry out shared activities, and substitute for each other if needed. Such group dynamics are absent from regular

BBBS services. Furthermore, they are associated with a faith and belief in God that guides the mentoring process and gives volunteers a sense of mission and ability to ground their labor and impact on children in religious terms.

FROM IDEAS TO IMPLEMENTATION

As with many good ideas, the key challenge is implementation. Through a generous grant from the Pew Charitable Trusts, implementation became possible. Under the auspices of Public/Private Ventures, the Amachi program emerged. In November 2000, recruitment of congregations started. When a congregation signed on, it provided a list of 10 or more committed members who were then referred to BBBS for screening and training. The actual match with a child then followed. Each member volunteer had to commit for at least one weekly hour of personal contact with a child for a full year. By April 2001, the first mentors were meeting with their mentees. A year later, Amachi had 42 churches committed to its work and some 556 matches arranged.

Like all BBBS volunteers, Amachi volunteers meet with the children weekly, talk with them, and offer them fun activities such as visiting the zoo, reading a book, eating in a restaurant, or watching a movie. Amachi volunteers, in addition, sometimes take mentees to church weekend services or to youth activities at their congregations, including church trips, choir practice, and special performances. During these events, mentees may meet other children who are like them and who themselves have mentors, a fact that makes their relationship with the mentor more "normal."

Each congregation is also responsible for collecting and submitting monthly data on how often mentors are meeting with children. Participating clergy are asked to name a church volunteer coordinator (CVC), who is responsible for overseeing and coordinating Amachi within that particular congregation. They generally check with mentors on a weekly basis, through regularly scheduled meetings, phone calls, or informal conversations after weekend worship services. Given the administrative burden placed on the congregation by the program, each congregation is entitled to an annual stipend of $1,500 for incurred costs and $5,000 to support the part-time CVC position.

Since it was unclear how to recruit congregations for this undertaking, a highly visible and respectable individual was invited to head Amachi, former Philadelphia mayor and now Rev. Dr. W. Wilson Goode. On visiting many local churches, he managed to recruit about fifty local and a few suburban congregations to join Amachi. Consequently, the number of mentor volunteers was so large that it overburdened the BBBS capacity to provide screening, training, and matching services, forming a bottleneck. While this was a problem at the time, it also represented a successful "exploitation" of congregations' resources and people for the service of the city. The justification for exploitation of resources, as discussed in previous chapters, is absence of personal gain, especially monetary personal gain. Newman and Hotchner (2003) coined the phrase "shameless exploitation" to describe a scenario where for-profit resources are used for the formation of free public goods, as indeed is the case with Amachi.

BBBS of eastern Pennsylvania was recruited to provide technical support and process the information and training of congregational volunteers. BBBS mentor support coordinators (MSCs) were responsible for screening the volunteers, training them to become good mentors, arranging the matches, and providing supervision and support. Jucovy (2003: 9) noted that "Amachi is a program for BBBS and a ministry for the churches." Volunteer mentors have two supervisors: the mentor support coordinator from BBBS and the volunteer coordinator from the church.

Finally, P/PV staff had to identify children who were eligible for Amachi (children of prisoners), and to obtain permission from their parents or caregivers to participate in the program.

AMACHI IN ACTION

The data reported by the CVC is processed by P/PV and summaries are sent to the congregations. Pastors and CVCs receive a monthly report about their volunteers and information about volunteers from other participating congregations. These reports are used to congratulate volunteers and churches, and to alert congregations when volunteers are underperforming.

Given Philadelphia's size and the many children eligible for Amachi's services, four neighborhoods were selected for the project. These neighborhoods—Southwest Philadelphia, West Kensington, North Philadelphia, and South Philadelphia—were chosen because of their higher rates of poverty and crime. In each of these catchment areas, a community impact director (CID) was hired. CIDs were individuals with experience with relevant communities and familiarity with the local congregations. They were responsible for the day-to-day management of Amachi in their given areas and collaborated with both the CVCs and the BBBS MSCs.

The recruitment of children of prisoners who were not registered in any given master list was done through prisons' social workers. These social workers, who are in daily contact with inmates, knew many of the family situations. Posters were posted in local prisons offering Amachi services, and talks were held in local prisons, explaining and offering Amachi services. Once a prisoner signed up for the program, children needed to be identified, and other parents or legal guardians had to be found in order to obtain their written consent as the ones legally responsible for the children. Contact was made by letters and phone calls.

In the first two years of operation, 42 congregations were recruited, all of which were Protestant churches and many of which were black, with half of the latter being Baptist churches. In fact, about half the mentor volunteers were African American and an additional 8 percent were Latinos, serving mostly children of African Americans and Latinos. This ethnic characteristic of Amachi volunteers is commonly missing in most BBBS programs, where often white mentors work with black mentees.

INDICATIONS OF SUCCESS

Regrettably, there was no outcome evaluation attached to Amachi. While the program is still strong and expanding, its effectiveness has never been studied. In the absence of a rigorous evaluation study, an alternative assessment is to assume that Amachi volunteers have been at least as good as other BBBS volunteers, and to rely on the studies showing that BBBS volunteers were most effective in changing the lives of at-risk children. The assumption is that Amachi volunteers are more effective since they have built-in group-control mechanisms to assure continuity and quality of service. However, this assumption should be carefully studied.

While an outcome evaluation was not part of Amachi in its first few years, a solid process evaluation was subsequently carried out. Jucovy (2003) performed such an evaluation and found that solid accountability was part of the program. As in all BBBS programs, a mentor and child have to meet regularly, usually at least weekly. In each congregation, the CVC collected data every month from each volunteer to evaluate how often, and for how many hours, he or she met with her or his mentee, what activities they did together, and how often they spoke on the telephone. This data collection system, which was different from that for regular BBBS employees, became part of congregations' regular data collection. The results suggested that congregational mentors invested more hours, on average, than regular BBBS volunteers.

According to the *Amachi Year Longitudinal Report, April 1, 2001–March 31, 2003* (Farley 2004), in the first two years of operation, 517 mentees were served. About half were boys (47 percent), ranging from ages five to eighteen. This can be viewed as a small number considering the millions of adults in prisons and the 20,000 Philadelphia children eligible for the program, but it can also be considered a success since it doubled the number of children cared for by BBBS volunteers in the Philadelphia area. A relatively high percentage of the matches lasted for over 12 months (62 percent), the period noted as relevant for a program's successful impact on children.

Furthermore, the program as a whole was adopted by BBBS in other parts of the country. Jucovy (2003) reports that the program was also adopted in nearby Chester, Pennsylvania, and as a partnership with BBBS in southeastern Pennsylvania. A third Amachi project, in Brooklyn, started under the support of Senator Hillary Rodham Clinton. In an Internet search conducted in January 2004, we found twelve additional Amachi replications in various parts of the country, including Hartford; Atlanta; Boston (two separate programs); Baltimore; Lanham, Maryland; St. Louis; Jackson, Missouri; Charlotte, North Carolina; Columbus, Ohio; Dallas; and Milwaukee. Such a rapid pace of replication is quite unparalleled in social services delivery and most likely means that the program is deemed successful by BBBS professionals nationwide. As such, Amachi is not a fluke, but an example of the bridging of secular methods (BBBS) with important resources from places deemed sacred (congregational volunteers and congregational support) in order to assist needy children. It is also an example of a practice replicable in other cities.

REST Philly

Rational Emotive Spiritual Therapy (REST) is a counseling modality that combines cognitive counseling with eight faith-based interventions such as meditation and scripture reading. Its three basic tenets are (1) unwanted behavior is changed by changing the beliefs and thoughts that support the unwanted behavior; (2) in order to sustain behaviors that are new, new beliefs and thoughts must be identified and adopted; and (3) spiritual (faith-based) thoughts best replace the beliefs and thoughts that have supported the unwanted behavior.

The use of a faith-based cognitive behavioral intervention, consisting of the integration of a cognitive behavioral therapy approach called Rational Emotive Therapy and a spiritual or faith-based component (based on the work of Albert Ellis), is cited in the literature as a promising approach (Ellis 2000; Hatcher and McGuire 2001; Steinfeld 1999). In this model, the spiritual component is fully integrated in all aspects of cognitive-behavioral intervention. The literature suggests that both the cognitive-behavioral and faith-based aspects of this intervention, which focuses on emotional healing, have the potential to reduce criminal recidivism and improve problem-solving skills and psychological well-being (O'Connor 2002).

REST Philly is the brainchild of Dr. Rick McKinney, who combines his lifelong experience of working with inmates and hardcore criminals with his formal education in psychology and deep religious convictions. The counseling modality was developed in Las Vegas, where counseling was provided to residents of public housing funded by a Housing and Urban Development demonstration grant for drug elimination. In 1999, McKinney accepted Mayor John Street's invitation to come to Philadelphia to develop a new program to care for ex-prisoners, prevent their reincarceration, and assure their integration into their home communities.

While REST Philly is less celebrated and less funded than Amachi, it offers great hope to those working with prisoners, also "shamelessly exploiting" the spirit of volunteerism and care for others so strongly exhibited by local religious congregations. As the sections below will discuss, REST Philly focuses on adults in both pre-release and post-release prison programs. It provides comprehensive training for volunteer faith counselors. Slowly, REST Philly's work has become more known, and in Pennsylvania, it has expanded to serve additional prisons outside the city of Philadelphia.

REST AS FAITH-BASED INTERVENTION

The spiritual component of REST is regarded as faith-based, in that the faith of the individual client (of any faith tradition) is utilized in the REST clinical/rational process. This intervention can work only with clients who freely and willingly choose their faith as a means to overcome their addictions or criminal ideology. First, it is the client's identified faith-based belief that actually overcomes and abandons the unwanted behavior and its supporting belief and thoughts. Therefore, faith-based or spiritual-therapy encompasses a wide range of moral and religious thoughts appropriate to each counseling issue. Second, in REST, the eight spiritual interventions are process rather than content oriented. In other words, although scripture or religious reading is used, the client must focus on using the literature of his or her faith or belief. Therefore, the religious affiliation of the client, be it Protestant, Catholic, Muslim, or Jew, does not matter. What does matter is the use of the faith-based thoughts and teachings. This spiritual intervention process is thus a very personal and internal activity. Third, in the use of spiritual or faith-based thoughts to replace self-destructive thoughts supporting unwanted behavior, it is the client's faith-related thoughts that are identified and utilized for "replacement thinking." If a client does not wish to work on his or her faith, this approach cannot be used.

To that end, prisoners who are soon to be released are approached and offered to attend sessions run by REST Philly trained staff. These are 13 weekly sessions in which prisoners learn different subjects that pertain to constructive living in the community. Each subject focuses on a personal deficit and addiction-related, negative emotions. The subjects are approached through ways encouraging spiritual enhancement and personal understanding. The 12 subjects are as follows:

1. Understanding and managing fear
2. Understanding and releasing stress
3. Understanding and controlling anger
4. Understanding and reducing anxiety
5. Understanding and unlearning depression
6. Understanding and cleansing guilt
7. Understanding and healing shame
8. Understanding and eliminating false pride
9. Understanding and replacing empty feelings
10. Understanding and mending relationships
11. Understanding and overcoming addictions
12. Understanding and fulfilling your life's purpose

In each of these 12 topics, clients learn the following:

1. the role played by each emotion in his or her addiction and in other related personal problems;
2. how to analyze and rethink incidents related to this subject;
3. how to rehearse new thinking (spiritually based) patterns related to dealing with this specific addiction-related emotion;
4. how to rehearse new faith-based interventions and strategies for dealing with addiction and related problems.

REST as Religious Support

Religion plays an integral role in Rational Emotive Spiritual Therapy, as religious beliefs are usually the strongest set of beliefs that make up each individual's unique belief system. (If not the strongest, they are among the strongest.) They are often the rationale for life-or-death choices and afterlife beliefs. Often, in their conflict with other nonreligious beliefs, feelings of guilt, shame, and stress are often produced. These emotions are the foundation and support for many personal maladies including a host of anxiety-related illnesses. Clients' cognitive conflicts often support their use of drugs and alcohol in an act of obtaining relief known as self-medication (for the Christian part of the program, see McKinney 2003).

Research has demonstrated that religion has a great impact on the healing of drug and alcohol addictions. There are two components of religion that are responsible for its success as a means to cope with addictive behavior: the religious beliefs and the religious involvement of the individual. In the REST process, religious beliefs are addressed throughout. The "religious involvement" of the client is accomplished in the support services mediated by the case manager through collaboration with the client's personal faith institution. Clients are requested to identify a faith institution. If they do not know one, the case manager will help them identify an appropriate faith institution (based on faith tradition, geographical proximity, and the faith institution's willingness to help). The identified faith institution is asked to become a sponsor of this requesting client and provide the means for the client's involvement in religious education, worship, and volunteer services. The selected faith institution is also requested to identify a lay member who could be trained to serve as a faith mentor for this client.

Thus, because it uses faith-based interventions—spiritually based thinking and faith institutions' involvement—REST is identified as a faith-based counseling modality for both institutional counseling and after release from prison care support services. This pre-release process is generally six months in length, which appears sufficient to diminish unwanted behaviors such as drug and alcohol addictions and other antisocial behaviors among many REST graduates, while establishing new behaviors that result in health, happiness, and productive lifestyles.

STRUCTURE

Initially, the program recruited groups of eight volunteers from local religious congregations. Based on the same logic as Amachi, the idea is that civic engagement of congregation members is the highest among any community organizations, and that the small group serves as its own control. In 2003, there were 103 congregations that had committed volunteers to REST Philly. These congregations must not only be committed to supplying volunteers but be willing to accept and support ex-prisoners. As Cnaan and Sinha (2002) showed, although many faith-based providers and congregations are eager to visit prisoners in prison, the majority of them shy away from post-release support. Many congregations find themselves on waiting lists to do prison ministry but would not work with the same people upon release into the community. REST Philly mandates from congregations the willingness to accept the ex-prisoner in the congregation, and the congregation has to develop resource lists to help ex-prisoners with referrals, contacts, and information. Finally, it is expected that the ex-prisoners will join the congregation's social missions.

Some volunteers are trained to become faith-based counselors and interns. These individuals take a 60-hour training program, and, upon completion, have to pass a 370-question exam to qualify as faith-based counselors for an interim. In 2003, there were 340 volunteers, all congregational members, who were trained to understand the world of the prisoner and be able to serve as volunteer lay counselors in each of the city's five prisons. These 340 individuals were trained to provide the 13-week curriculum to inmates who are close to being released.

Clients are recruited through flyers, social workers, volunteers, word-of-mouth efforts, and prison chaplains. When an inmate volunteers to be in the program, he or she is committing to twelve sessions and accepts the faith-based nature of the program. His or her spouse and children also become eligible for counseling by the REST Philly program and are served by other community faith counselors.

Another group of volunteers complete a 36-hour training program that qualifies them to become faith-based mentors and partners. This group of people is trained with exprisoner rehabilitation and each is trained to help their mentees with such problems as housing, substance abuse, vocational training, family reconciliation, and legal affairs. In 2003, there were 51 trained faith-based mentors who had completed training and were assigned offenders. Additionally, there were nearly 50 counselors who doubled as mentors and who could advise on thematic issues of housing, addiction, and so on. At the time of this writing, there is a pool of 200 faith mentors who have completed the initial 13-week program. These volunteers work with ex-prisoners who ask for support during their post-release period. Often, prisoners are people who finished the 13-session program while in jail and were thus assigned to mentors, but sometimes ex-prisoners approach REST Philly and its volunteers while the ex-prisoners are on parole or during their post-release period. Ex-prisoners who are engaged with REST Philly during their post-release period are expected to be assisted and supported for 12 months. The faith-based mentor/partner meets the client while he or she is still in prison at least twice in their pre-release period. After the release, the mentor and ex-prisoner meet regularly and the mentor supervises and supports the ex-prisoner as he or she struggles to be reintegrated into the community and, if possible, into his or her family of origin.

Every Friday evening, six different support groups are held for ex-prisoners across the city in participating congregations. One is in a Catholic church and one is in a Hispanic church, while the others are in black Protestant churches. These support groups are mandated for REST mentees and open to people in the community who feel a need for spiritual counseling, and they are also open to homeless people who are now helped by REST Philly.

REST Philly, whose offices are in the main Philadelphia prison, works collaboratively with the criminal justice system, including thirteen city judges who assign clients directly to the program. REST Philly is also consulted by and used by the city Public Defenders Association and by the Parole and Probation Services. The city criminal justice system views REST Philly as a good alternative to incarceration and a most promising method to reduce recidivism. As such, a new work model was introduced in 2004, wherein judges may release people directly to REST care in lieu of prison time. At the time of this writing, the program was in its initial stages and 46 people were referred to the program, 30 were then accepted by REST Philly, and there were 16 who were already in their care.

One key finding of REST Philly is that, despite the spiritual care and personal willingness of the mentors and counselors, two key barriers to prisoners' successful reentry are successful job training and job placement. Accordingly, at the time of writing, REST Philly planned to venture into this field and develop special training and placement programs that will be helpful to ex-prisoners in the real world. This new venture indicates that REST Philly is flexible and attentive to the real needs of its clients and ready to develop new programs as needs became evident.

INDICATIONS OF SUCCESS

Similar to Amachi, there are no evaluation studies to assess the effectiveness of REST Philly. From the literature, we know that prisoners who participate in religious programming receive fewer disciplinary infractions than those who do not (Johnson, Larson, and Pitts 1997). However, the field of study of ex-prisoners' reentry is sorely in need of systematic documentation of how extensive these services are, their effectiveness, and whether they have the capacity to meet the needs of reintegrating prisoners and their families (McRoberts 2002).

While it is disheartening that such studies are missing, for the purpose of this chapter we will concern ourselves more with the process than the outcome. REST Philly managed to reach 71 congregations in 2003 and recruit some 800 volunteers to its various programs. As there is no systematized arrangement for public or foundation support for the program, the volunteers and congregations pay for the training. This does not, however, seem to be a major deterrent in finding volunteers. Put differently, people are willing to pay to become counselors or mentors.

The program has graduated over 800 inmates from the 13-session program. It is expected that every year, 900 inmates from the five city jails
will be enrolled. Of these enrollees, more than 60 percent requested to
be assisted by a faith-based mentor/partner from REST Philly as a means
for successfully reintegrating into society. Participation in the program
and successful completion of the 13 sessions is now a formal program
for ex-prisoners released early through the Public Defenders Association.

The program has been officially adopted, although not funded, by the
local prison system and the city criminal justice system. Its potential is
evident to the state, and Dr. McKinney, the founder and president of
REST Philly, was asked to extend the program to the state prison system.
At the time of this writing, REST Philly has been implemented in two
state prisons in Pennsylvania. In addition, the REST program was
approved in 2003 as a city subcontractor to provide REST counseling,
faith institution sponsorship, and mentoring for 200 homeless persons
living in a major Philadelphia shelter. In 2004, REST Philly was asked to
offer one-day training to parole and probation officers in the Philadelphia area. There were many more officers applying for the training than
available space could accommodate, so many were turned down. The
great interest of these officers could indicate that they see the REST program as promising and relevant.

In a study of prisoners' preparation for reentry to the community conducted by the Urban Institute, six Philadelphia prison programs were
compared. Among the 200 subjects who participated, REST got the
highest consumer satisfaction rating, as 84 percent of its participants
rated it very useful. Furthermore, participants of REST rated it higher
than participants of all other programs in its being helpful for them
after they were released from the Philadelphia prison system (Roman,
Kane, and Turner 2005).

In 2004, McKinney was asked to visit Trinidad and Tobago to advise
the local government about prisoners' reentry using spiritual cognitive
counseling. After he had presented the model to state officials, prison
officials, criminal justice social workers, and religious leaders, the model
was adopted by the relevant governmental bodies, and its implementation is now in process.

Again, in the absence of a systematic impact evaluation, the program's
success can be assessed only by evaluating its implementation, by consumer satisfaction, and by the reputation it holds in groups outside its
immediate scope. It should be emphasized that REST Philly is one of
the very few programs that help ex-prisoners from the inside out. A few
studies have indicated a better prognosis for ex-prisoners when they
have previously participated in pre-release programming and then followed up in the community. One study in particular highlights the bet-

ter chances of remaining drug free for ex-prisoners who completed both in-prison and post-prison drug rehabilitation programs (Wexler et al. 1999). REST Philly is one program that provides inside and outside support and care for ex-prisoners and that shows great potential for efficacy.

Conclusions

The two organizations discussed in this chapter both use "shameless exploitation" in the sense intended by Newman and Hotchner. Amachi and REST Philly "take advantage" of congregational structures and cultures. Congregations are community institutions that are commonly available and that have pro-social attitudes of serving the those in need. The two programs therefore attach themselves to these congregations and recruit groups of volunteers from over 150 congregations in Philadelphia. Thus they exploit the resources available to a group as opposed to the more limited resources of individuals working alone. By recruiting groups, training them together, and having them work in concert, the congregational volunteers become a support group for each other and a means of social control for their members. A typical volunteer in these programs gets emotional and practical support from his or her peers.

Both programs tackle a seriously problematic group of clients. Amachi reaches children of prisoners and attempts to break the intergenerational cycle of incarceration. REST Philly is aimed at preparing prisoners for successful reentry into the community. Both programs serve difficult, often neglected and feared client populations. Although none of these programs have been followed by a systematic independent evaluation, there are signs that the programs are successful. Both programs are now being expanded outside Philadelphia and are poised to become national models of faith-based intervention with prisoners and their children.

Even though these programs use volunteers in innovative ways, they are not cost-free. They are both training-intensive and require a great deal of monitoring and record keeping. Amachi was supported by a large grant, and REST is supported by donations from member congregations and small grants. Their services cost money, but they offer ways to tap into the generous resources available in congregations and their committed volunteers. It can be safely assumed that other innovative programs will capitalize on this approach, recruiting groups of congregational members to carry out joint tasks that are most challenging for individual volunteers. One can try to seek volunteers in schools or workplaces, but these organizations are not normatively geared to serve the needy, and their social bonds are not as strong as those of local religious congregations.

Part V
Conclusions and Implications

Chapter 13

The World of the Clergy: Contextual Necessities and Leadership Challenges

As a result of the institutionalized separation of church and state in the United States, local religious congregations are not publicly assisted; their operation is distinct from that of the state (Cnaan et al. 2002). In fact, unlike other nonprofit organizations, they are barred from accepting public grants or contracts for supporting their core mission: religious activities. Consequently, clergy salary, building maintenance, program costs, and, as shown above, social ministries are funded primarily by members. Furthermore, the role of clergy, as compared to the leadership of other nonprofit organizations, is more diffuse and challenging.

Clergy responsibilities may range from leading worship services to fixing leaks, from running social ministries to managing the accounts of the congregation, and from counseling a wide range of human needs to representing the community on political platforms. This fuzzy role definition poses organizational challenges that are uniquely American and uniquely congregational. However, these contextual differences and organizational challenges are not widely discussed in the literature.

Religion's Role in Society

Organized religion in the United States is conducted differently from the way it is in most other advanced democracies. To begin with, there is no predominant denominational group in America. There are more than a thousand different religions and denominations that are distinct from and often in competition with one another. Most notably, the United States is the only country to be established as a Protestant country, yet the only one in which no one denomination can claim to comprise a majority. Two large groups make up approximately 20 percent of the American population: Roman Catholics and Southern Baptists. Other groups are even smaller. This sets the stage for denominations to coexist, yet none assumes hegemony and dominance or would be expected to reach such a stage. Most denominations share the desire for equality among religions, which means no government support of any one religion. In the United States, there are no religious political parties equivalent to the Christian Democratic parties common in Europe. The state is barred from acting in any manner that might promote or inhibit any type of religious practice. Furthermore, the burden of maintaining and financing religious activities falls solely on members of religious organizations.

In Philadelphia, we found that 30 percent of congregational finances come from pledges and dues and 47 percent from offerings. That is, 77 percent of all income that reaches congregations comes directly from members. The rest come from various sources, including special events, endowments, and denominational support. Less than 1 percent comes from government. The money from government pays for specifically contracted public work carried out by the congregation and in no way finances the congregation's religious activities. This means that clergy must encourage members to voluntarily support the finances of the congregations. There is no obligation (tax) that can mandate such expenses, and hence clergy must be relevant and meaningful so that people will be willing to financially support their congregations.

The practice of separating state and church is the result of the disestablishment of churches, beginning in colonial times. Between 1776 and 1830, the original thirteen colonies each abandoned the English legal custom of recognizing one church to which all residents paid taxes and in which all public office holders were members (Cnaan, Wineburg, and Boddie 1999; Holifield 1994; Warner 1993). Since 1830, religious life in America has continued in this autonomous direction that sets American congregations apart from those in most countries. Even before independence, two trends were noticeable: the quest for more evangelical and less scholarly religion and the right of taxpayers to participate in decision making about church leadership (Gough 1995).

Given the decline of public support for religious activities, the reliance on individuals' support, and the advances in science and technology, many scholars have predicted the end of religious affiliations and beliefs. Secularization theory, most clearly articulated by Peter Berger (1967), suggests that in modern and democratic societies, religion will become, at best, ancillary. Secularization is based on Max Weber's notion that bureaucracy and technology may lead to the demise of spirituality and belief in the transcendental power of the human spirit. Further, the theory predicts that in modern societies, and especially in America, religion will continue to weaken and society will become secular. Secularization theory also holds that cities in particular are inimical to religion, and that with urbanization the impact and followers of religions will diminish (Wind and Lewis 1994). Proponents of this theory believe that religion is a marginal force in modern society and need not be included in public policy, social services, and research agenda. Indeed, in Europe the secularization trend continues and is attested by the loss of authority of the Catholic Church and the decline in personal religiosity (Voye 1999). However, secularization theory has failed to capture the religious character of the United States. Its proponents attempted a few times to modify it, but ultimately acknowledged that secularization is more European than American (Stark 1999). Indeed, the United States is the most religious of all modern democracies. According to the World Value Survey conducted from 1990 to 1993, more people in the United States (82 percent) defined themselves as religious than did those in any other country (*Economist* 1995). In a 1993 CNN/USA Today/Gallup poll, 71 percent of Americans reported membership in a church or synagogue, and 41 percent reported attendance at a church or synagogue in the seven days prior to the poll (McAneny and Saad 1993). Thus, the most technologically advanced democracy is also the country in which more people seek organized religion. Americans find something important in religion, which is independent of the state, and for which they are willing to pay.

Clergy as Leaders

In theory, many religions, such as Buddhism, Judaism, and Islam, do not expect the senior clergyperson to be a community leader or a good administrator. In these and many other faith traditions the clergy are the most knowledgeable individuals, the ones who can explicate sacred texts, teach the religion, answer difficult questions, perform the religious rituals, and serve as role models in their dignified and virtuous behavior. It is quite common for such an individual to have spent years in theological education and then be approved as a religious authority. But most often this line of training only partially prepares clergy for the role expectations of American worshippers.

Clergy in the United States can be viewed also as the leaders of the voluntary group called the congregation. They are operating in an environment that is significantly different from that of their counterparts in Europe, and under unique conditions, even when compared with leaders of secular nonprofit organizations and small voluntary associations. Harris (1998a, b), who studied British congregations, found many similarities between voluntary organizations and congregations, but also two important differences. First, congregational leaders are regarded not as "hired hands" but as representatives of a higher authority with its attendant traditional and theological power. Unlike the case for nonprofit organizations, these leaders are chosen not only for their administrative skills, but for their ability to represent the sacred for the members. Second, members, who in fact pay the bills and perform much of the labor, cannot alter the mission or the key tenets that govern the collective worship. They can alter what hymn will be sung or what flowers displayed, but they cannot decide on changing the credo of the congregation. These two distinctions are unique to congregations and distinguish all congregations, regardless of denomination. However, as we will show below, American congregations are also distinct from voluntary organizations in other ways that pose unique managerial and leadership challenges to their clergy.

It is our contention that it takes more to be a good clergyperson than the spirit of faith that makes it unique. We argue that certain contextual factors foster a special environment that poses certain leadership challenges that are unique to American clergy. Furthermore, we argue that these differences can be observed most clearly when American clergy are compared with European clergy and with leaders of secular non-profit organizations.

In writing a chapter like this, trying to identify the unique managerial world of American clergy vis-à-vis leaders of other voluntary organizations and vis-à-vis clergy in other advanced democracies, we must utilize gross generalizations. The world of congregations is quite diverse and rich. What may hold true for a small congregation with a bivocational clergyperson (one who works full-time elsewhere and volunteers as clergy) may be irrelevant for congregations with twenty or more full-time positions. Similarly, what may hold true for a grassroots organization may be irrelevant for an established organization with a large staff and well-developed administrative procedures. We use broad strokes with full recognition that some clergy will be puzzled by our assertions. What we aim to do is demonstrate that the challenges American clergy face are sufficiently distinct from those faced by leaders of voluntary organizations in the United States and clergy outside the United States. Based on these distinctions, we then discuss the managerial and leadership practices identified in our study of American local religious congregations. It should be emphasized that we do not focus on successful clergy work in general or on religious leadership. Our focus here is limited to the comparative nature of the chapter: "What unique contextual factors shape the work of American clergy and what unique leadership challenges have emerged that guide their work?" Thus, we focus on the unique and comparative aspects of clergy work rather than on the full spectrum of clergy leadership functions and styles.

Contextual Necessities

In this section, we discuss a set of contextual variables that makes the job of running the American congregation so unique. We list each of these topics and then explain its impact on the congregations. It is our contention that when combined, these contextual factors influence the job characteristics of clergy to an extent that sets them apart from leaders of secular nonprofit organizations.

THE RELIGIOUS FOCUS

As every person knows, and as Harris (2005) noted, the mission of a congregation is mostly stable and unchangeable. Most religions are predicated on texts and practices that were written and sealed thousands of years ago, and deviation is considered heresy. At times, groups argue over the correct interpretation of the original scriptures and the correct way to worship. These arguments, as serious as they may seem, do not usually shift the focus of congregational missions in any major way. Furthermore, given that religion is based on the scriptures, it is not feasible for a congregation to change its mission or change its goals. For example, when a secular voluntary organization faces declining activity or a low demand for its mission, it often rewrites its mission and changes its goals rather than close down. The mission of congregations, however, is more robust, and as we noted above, the options are to stay open or close down but basically with the same mission and same practices (known as goal displacement). This is not to say that congregations do not change. They do, but more slowly and mostly in the margins.

The basic premise of religion is not only conformity with past traditions and rules, but uniformity and consistency. Some members of congregations grew up with certain religious rituals and traditions and elect to join the congregation in order to maintain this part of their lives. Other people join a congregation by selecting a place that will meet their religious and social needs. After joining, however, they do not wish for its core mission to change. Attempts to challenge the core mission often result in bitter conflict and a possible rift (Becker 1998).

In this respect, then, clergy operate in a narrower field than managers of secular voluntary organizations. In voluntary organizations, the leaders can persuade the board to take action and revise the organizational mission. If the organization's core mission is literacy and there is a public call and resources to work in crime prevention, it is not inconceivable for the organization to shift priorities and add this area to its mission. In congregations, if the clergy or board notice that there is a market for new religious practices, they cannot change the mission without losing the trust of current members and their denomination. Hence, congregational leadership functions within the boundaries of a stricter mission that often was devised long ago and allows only limited degrees of freedom, while the mission of secular nonprofit leadership allows innovations and changes within the mission and also in the entire mission itself.

Personal Beliefs

There is no other role in which the leader must persuade people of his or her beliefs. Members expect a clergyperson assuming pastoral responsibilities to be a true adherent to the faith. While members and lay leaders may waver in their faith from time to time, no one is as visible and as expected to demonstrate the "faith." There is no room to share doubts in the existence of God or in the truth of the faith creed. For most clergy in America, the creed comes from the Bible. The first commandment, which is the most sacred of all, calls upon the believer to "love God with all your heart and with all your soul, and with all your strength, and with all your mind." Such a commitment is expected to fluctuate over the course of a lifetime. However, a clergyperson cannot normally share or express this doubt with the same people whom he or she is expected to shepherd in their faith.

While CEOs of nonprofit organizations can challenge their organizations' raison d'être and their personal commitment to the organization's cause, clergy are not allowed to do so. Clergy often are the embodiment of faith and as such cannot exhibit personal doubt or spiritual weakness.

Key Constituencies

In many voluntary organizations, the president/CEO/leader has three key sets of constituencies: board members who supervise and lead the organization, employees who carry out the mission of the organization and who are supervised directly or indirectly by the leader, and consumers of what the organization offers. While there are attempts to have consumers on boards and have board members volunteer as service providers, in most organizations the three key constituencies are separate and often have little in common. The older and larger the voluntary organization, the higher the likelihood that the three constituencies will not meet at all.

In most American congregations, the pastor or rector is the spiritual leader of the congregants, who can be considered consumers. We use the term "consumers" here for academic purposes only, as congregation members generally term themselves "members," "congregants," or "participants." But for the purpose of comparing the people who benefit from the product of the organization, we choose the term consumers both for congregants and clients of nonprofit organizations. As noted above, congregants pay for the maintenance of the congregation, often through pledges or offerings, and many of them view themselves as mere consumers, that is, they come to participate in the religious service and nothing more. However, some of these congregants also serve on the board of the congregation. Hence, every member of the board is also a de facto consumer. By "board," we refer to any of the various organizational forms and committees that run the life of the congregation and maintain its daily functions (see Chapter 2). In many congregations, the staff is small and plays a small role in the dynamics of the congregation's life. For example, in the Philadelphia sample of 1,392 congregations, three-quarters (73.9 percent) reported that they do not have paid full-time administrative/secretarial support. Similarly, four-fifths (95.2 percent) reported that they do not have a full-time bookkeeper/treasurer. The majority use member volunteers, with fewer using part-time paid staff or hiring professional companies. Most congregations have employed one or two people who are in constant contact with the clergy.

The picture that emerges for American clergy encompasses the same people in all three circles: board members, consumers (members), and volunteer supporting staff. This creates ambiguity as to when one is a board member with an executive function and when one (the same person) is a congregant in need of pastoral counseling and spiritual uplifting. The same person who listens to the sermon on the weekend may be determining the pastor's salary on Thursday, calling upon the clergy for bereavement counseling on Wednesday, and helping in the congregation's soup kitchen on Friday. The overlap of congregants' roles and functions creates an environment in which active members are frequently in contact with the clergy and roles are constantly shifting. In other words, the clergy are involved with members of the congregation in ways that are more intimate and personal than those of secular voluntary organization leaders with their volunteers. In the American congregation, many members can be viewed as active participants who assume the triple role of beneficiaries, volunteer staff members, and board members. This active participation of congregational members, which is typically American and typically congregational, puts the clergy in an ambiguous position vis-à-vis many members of the congregation. Fried (2002: 9) followed a rabbi employment search and noted the imbalance in the following manner: "Rabbis are employees, religion workers, with unions and contracts and job-related injuries. They have to negotiate dental benefits with the very congregants they must inspire."

RELEVANT LEGISLATION

In the United States, the principle of separation of church and state is cherished and plays out in many aspects of life. Historically, when the colonies were first populated, each, with the exception of Quaker Pennsylvania and small Rhode Island, had an established church. These churches were approved by the states as the only formal religion in the colony and they were supported by taxes levied on all residents regardless of their religious affiliation or level of participation in religious activities. In the fifty years that followed the Declaration of Independence, the new states played with the notion of allowing more than one church per state. Eventually, all states, Massachusetts being the last, in 1830, legislated the "disestablishment of churches." Accordingly, the state did not officially support any religion and all religions were free to practice and establish their congregations in each state. This principle made its way into the Bill of Rights to the Constitution, passed by Congress on September 25, 1789. The first amendment states the following: "Congress shall make no law respecting an establishment of religion, or prohibiting the free exercise thereof; or abridging the freedom of speech, or of the press, or the right of the people peaceably to assemble, and to petition the Government for a redress of grievances."

What is less well known is that later legislation exempted religious congregations from practices that apply to other nonprofit organizations. To begin with, local religious congregations are not required to register with any public authority (their building may be registered locally for property tax purposes even though in some parts of the country they are fully exempted from property taxes). Congregations are the only organized groups that are exempted from reporting to the Internal Revenue Service and filing tax Form 990 (used for nonprofit entities). Even when their income is significant, reporting is optional, not required. This changes if the congregation holds a for-profit or nonprofit arm such as a printing house, store, or any other business. The majority of clergy are working in congregations that do not report their congregations' financial affairs to local or national governments.

Later legislative practices exempted local religious congregations from other practices applicable to all other voluntary and nonprofit organizations. The passage of Title 7 of the Civil Rights Act of 1964, which prohibits employment discrimination based on race, color, religion, sex, or national origin, and the Equal Pay Act of 1963 (EPA), which protects men and women who perform substantially equal work in the same establishment from sex-based wage discrimination, as well as legislation to prevent age-based discrimination (1967), are not applicable to religious congregations. In a planned effort not to intervene in religious issues, the American legislature purposely exempts religious groups from having to hire people from all walks of life, and this enables congregations to hire only people who share the faith tradition of the congregation. Based on Title 7, congregations are also exempted from the Civil Rights Act of 1991, which provides monetary damages in cases of intentional employment discrimination.

Similarly, congregations are exempted from Title 1 of the Americans with Disabilities Act of 1990 (ADA), which prohibits employment discrimination, in the private sector and in state and local government, against qualified individuals with disabilities. Furthermore, congregations, under the same law, are exempted from the need to make their property accessible for people with disabilities.

The strong separation between church and state and its manifestation in the various laws distinguishes hiring practices of congregations from those of other nonprofit organizations. Board members of congregations tend to hire from within as a means of assuring that their faith perspective will be preserved, keeping the money in-house, being able to pay more modest salaries while asking the workers to give more, and supporting members of the congregation who are in need. Inside-hiring practices keep congregations more segregated than secular organizations; indeed, they are the last bastion of segregation in America. Hiring from within can prevent the congregation from hiring the most qualified people and may limit openness. When congregations do bring in clergy from outside, the new employees are typically expected to join the congregation after they are hired. The clergyperson is, thus, often the more transient member of the congregation, as other staff members are also members of the congregation and often have relatives attending the congregation. In large congregations, new clergy may be allowed and expected to replace the staff to better fit their work style, but this is uncommon, as many staff members are considered part of the congregational family. Leaders of secular nonprofit organizations, even very small ones, can hire staff from the outside, and soon after they are on the job can replace the staff to meet their leadership style and vision and thus gain control over the organization. Clergy, on the other hand, are for a long time a minority from the outside. The exceptions to this rule are clergy who form new congregations and basically own the congregation organizationally, culturally, and legally. Clergy, however, can use theology and shared destiny as means of motivation more than leaders of voluntary organizations.

JOB BOUNDARIES

One of the key characteristics of the clergy's job that is different from that of other leaders of voluntary organizations is the lack of clearcut boundaries. The leader of a nonprofit organization is in charge of the finances, operation, maintenance, and productivity of employees. Good leaders of voluntary organizations also are involved in the quality of life of their employees and may work to foster a familylike spirit in the workplace. However, the boundaries of the job are clear and the board usually makes it clear if the leader steps outside them. If a leader of a nonprofit organization were to spend much time in informal chats with employees or consumers, the board would step in and suggest redirecting priorities. Furthermore, while leaders of nonprofit organizations report that they work long hours and often bring work home, their personal lives and their families are considered outside the limits of their work.

Such rules do not apply to clergy. What rules there are vary from one congregation to another, and there is a lack of well-defined boundaries. Most congregations operate out of one of four polities: authoritative, where the pastor is the founder or the charismatic leader that makes most decisions; congregational, where rules of governance are set by majority vote; Presbyterian, where a board of elders sets policy; or Episcopal, where primary power resides in the hand of a bishop. But, even in the last two forms of church governance, the process of governing has been modified in U.S. congregations by democratic process, in which congregants have varying degrees of input in the decision-making processes.

The clergyperson is the key leader and often the sole full-time employee. Thus, clergy are expected first and foremost to be religious leaders who spiritually uplift the congregation while serving as moral models. As moral and spiritual leaders, they have to set examples with their personal lives. Thus, they and their families are part of the job, and spouses are often expected to contribute to the life of the congregation. It is therefore critical that clergy include care of self and family as part of the expectations of the job itself (Oden 1988; Shawchuck and Hauser 1993). A clergyperson's personal problem with spouse or children is a congregational issue. A clergyperson who has an affair may find his or her personal life the focus of congregational debates and doubts as to his or her ability to lead the congregation (Fortune and Poling 1994). When a leader of a nonprofit organization undergoes a similar personal change or crisis, it is not expected to affect his or her professional life.

Even regular family life is constrained by the role of clergy. The family do not have a traditional weekend in which they can do what they want, as all members are expected to attend services. The worship service is attended and evaluated by family members, and there is no clear separation between home and work. There are very few other jobs in which children and spouses are constantly observing the worker's role performance. Even working spouses are expected to attend services and be active in the congregation. The clergy's children meet and play with children of members, and the clergy's performance and work is too visible to be ignored.

In smaller congregations, which are the majority, clergy deal with building maintenance issues such as leaks and heating or cooling systems. They are responsible for insurance and the financial life of the congregation personally, by hiring firms professionals, or by recruiting volunteers to do the job. Clergy also represent the congregation in denominational, ecumenical, neighborhood, and citywide coalitions and forums. They are the ambassadors of the congregation to the outer world and the link between the congregation and the rest of the world. If the congregation has additional paid staff, it is often the clergy's role to supervise the staff and pay their salaries (in larger congregations this role is designated to committees or to an administrative aide). In other words, clergy, compared to leaders of other similarly sized nonprofit organizations, have smaller staff, and the structure is such that often they are the only people in the congregational building during the week and must personally carry out most functions.

The role diffusion is a sign not only of size but of a culture. Netting et al. (2005: 179) studied the organizational style of faith-based social services. They reported that "the roles played by participants, volunteers, and paid staff reveal the wearing of multiple hats, facilitated by a tendency toward cross-training, role diffusion, and doing what is needed. Boundaries created by roles appear to be less important than pragmatically responding to the human needs."

Furthermore, even the counseling part of clergy work has no boundaries. Most professional counselors specialize in one area of need and deal with consumers who are screened to match their expertise. Clergy who meet with people as needed in their offices in effect have no such screening. A congregant may have a religious crisis or be in the midst of family violence. A congregant may seek advice about how to interact with a child who is associating with gang members or may have just lost his or her job. From alcohol abuse problems to health issues, from mental health to the concerns of the elderly, clergy are expected to meet the personal needs of congregants as they evolve over time. No one person can specialize in all these issues. Even counselors who apply a generalist approach cannot provide religious guidance, spiritual encouragement, or executive oversight of their organization. Clergy ought also to know when and how to refer people for professional assistance and, thus, need to know the network of services and resources more than the typical leader of a nonprofit organization.

One irony about the role of the clergy as counselors is that they are expected to provide numerous hours of free pastoral counseling/therapy. Many clergy are not trained for counseling, and those with some training are expected to counsel in many and diverse areas of life. The public expectation that clergy be able to counsel has brought about an interesting parallel system. The American Association of Pastoral Counselors (2003), headquartered in Fairfax, Virginia, reports that some 3,000 clergy provide this service for full pay at therapists' prices.

Our review so far clearly indicates that while many leaders of secular nonprofit organizations deal with people's social and personal needs, they have a clear separation between clients/consumers with needs and others with whom the manager deals on a daily basis. In congregations, the person who is the chair of the board may also be a participant in a Bible class and may ask the clergyperson to officiate at a wedding ceremony. In essence, the life of a congregation is very intimate and bounded, and clergy have to satisfy the expectations of the same people in various capacities. Furthermore, while they are not allowed to change the mission of the congregation, they are expected to hire and retain members as employees. These constraints pose some challenges that are quite unique to the role of clergy in America.

Leadership Challenges

As noted above, the pastor is not merely a spiritual guide but also the de facto CEO of the congregation. A small fraction of congregations are rich enough to exempt the clergy from running the affairs of the congregation and employ a full-time building manager or administrator. Most clergy are required to carry the burden of running their congregation's financial and property affairs as well as religious affairs.

In the section above, we presented some contextual factors that, in our view, set the world of American clergy quite apart from that of leaders of secular nonprofit organizations or clergy in other advanced democracies. These differences create unique managerial and leadership challenges. Yet, there is no one style that could be recommended for all congregations. Differences in polity, size, ethnicity, and demography impact the ways in which clergy leadership is exercised. The diversity of congregations demands a diversity of work styles for clergy and congregations.

In this section we address a number of factors clergy face in leadership. The topics, based on our empirical work in the past few years, can be divided into two parts: recommendations that work for all congregations with varied manner or intensity and recommendations that are unique to different subgroups of congregations.

THE SELECTION PROCESS

A perspective to consider when discussing the congregational leader as a representative of a higher authority is the importance of the call and congregational office of clergy. For example, in traditional Protestant denominations pastoral leadership is understood in spiritual terms as a "calling." Most religious communities recognize that the person who has received a call to congregational leadership has been assigned from above to a special office within the church. In much of the Protestant tradition, which includes more than three-quarters of congregations in the United States, the pastor may be considered the "shepherd of the deity" or an "under-shepherd to Jesus." In Weberian terms the pastorate can be interpreted as an office with spiritual authority where the authority is attached to the office and not to the mere individual. If this is the case, then in many religious contexts the office of pastor is accepted as the official point of contact between God and the congregation.

From the Protestant perspective, the call to pastor a congregation first begins as a process within a particular congregational setting where the person is considered a member of the congregation either by denominational affiliation or local membership. The process of becoming the head of a congregation differs from that of an executive in a nonprofit organization who can become trained in community service and then transfer those skills to other contextually related nonprofit fields. Each faith tradition invests in potential leaders by nurturing their sense of calling and supporting their eventual appointment to the pastorate. The scope and depth of in-house traditional training, which may be accompanied by theological education from an outside institution, prepares the person for ministry within his or her denomination. Although some congregational leaders move from one denomination to another based on career opportunities or because of disagreement or dissatisfaction with denominational polity or theological stance, the desire of the congregation when training and accepting the person into a leadership capacity within the denomination is that he or she will remain loyal. To become a congregational leader the person must be proficient in the denomination's requirements for membership in that faith community. In independent congregations, however, especially in black churches, a pastor can recruit members and start a different style of worship. Those individuals are even more restricted to one congregation, and it may be difficult to apply their skills to other congregations.

No such demands are placed on an up-and-coming executive being groomed for management in a secular organization. Eventually an executive is given authority to manage the nonprofit organization by the Board of Directors, and the demands placed on the person in this position generally dictate that the person will take the skill-sets developed from one job to another regardless of the field of interest of the organization. One can move from leading a housing agency to leading an art school and so forth.

Indeed, the tenure of clergy in Philadelphia is an interesting finding. The PCC reveals that some clergy are longstanding and others are very new. The oldest-serving clergyman in our sample, the Rev. Timothy C. Turner, began his appointment in August 1945, and when we visited the congregation, Firm Hope Baptist Church, in mid-2000, he was still the senior pastor. Herman N. Thompson of Garden of Prayer Church started a few months later and was still at the helm in May 2001 when we visited the church. However, the average pastor serves in the role of senior pastor less than six years, and 29.7 percent of the clergy are in a post for less than three years. Even when we consider the many new start-up congregations, clergy turnover and replacement are quite common in Philadelphia congregations.

A STRONG PULPIT

One should not forget that, regardless of the many educational, social, welfare, and political functions of a congregation, its primary function is religious. People come to congregations to fulfill their spiritual aspirations in a collective and organized manner. The time that all members meet together is usually during a weekend worship service, Bible classes, and study groups. Clergy are usually active in leading worship through prayer, preaching, and pronouncing God's blessing on the congregation. This is when people expect to be spiritually nurtured, challenged, and possibly entertained. At its best, the preaching event should be charismatic and convey a strong message to help shape the congregation into a distinct whole. Critical to the worship experience is the idea that worship provides a means to interpret life events. Worship is the most meaningful activity of the congregation, and the clergy plays the primary role in its orchestration (Trulear 1985). A successful clergyperson is both a performer and a messenger of words from a higher being. The clergy and members we interviewed stressed this point. It is not surprising that Fried (2002: 295) reported that "When the search committee first did a huge survey, being able to deliver an inspiring sermon was the number-one priority."

People come to a place of worship with unique expectations. In attending worship, people expect to be uplifted and attain new awareness. Clergy who are able to provide a meaningful worship service to which people return have conveyed a strong message and have been successful in their primary role. When members willingly return week after week and are assured of having a meaningful experience, the congregation becomes stronger.

This principle is quite generic. Its application may vary from congregation to congregation. The expectations of members are not unified across all congregations. In fundamentalist congregations, members may expect emphasis on doctrine and personal morality and piety. In mainline Protestant congregations, members expect words of wisdom, commentary on daily events, and a theology of justice. In contemporary churches, members may expect what is now termed "seeker-friendly" worship that is entertaining and includes a deep religious message they can take with them throughout the week. No matter what the niche, the clergyperson presides in the main worship and is expected to excel and demonstrate strong performance skills as well as serious religious leadership. No other leaders of nonprofit organizations are expected to carry out weekly eloquent and uplifting sermons each week and encourage members to contemplate and feel spiritually and personally fulfilled after listening to a sermon and participating in a religious worship service.

SELF-DISCIPLINE

Self-discipline is the ability to have self control over one's personal behavior in a variety of circumstances in association with a variety of individuals and groups. The word *discipline* is derived from *disciple*, or a follower of a master's teaching. The concept of self-discipline implies respect and attempts to understand other human beings without imposing one's personal views and attitudes. While clergy can easily be an authority figure, successful clergy show self-discipline, restraint, and respect to all others. Only with self-discipline as the background can clergy assert themselves and demand respect and trust.

A typical clergyperson spends many hours with people of the congregation and becomes an integral part of the congregation. He or she meets with members all day long and sits in various committees as well as visiting with people. Due to such constant contact with the same people, clergy cannot maintain a public persona at all times. They must develop relationships of trust with congregants over time, "earning the right to be heard" on issues. A willingness to hear and respect what others say can be much more effective in such an environment than imposing one's view.

An approach based on self-control and trust is also likely to be helpful to managers of secular nonprofit organizations. However, a manager in a voluntary organization has less contact with all members of the organization, and therefore can be somewhat less disciplined in speech and thus more expressive of unprocessed ideas and feelings. A clergyperson, by nature of the position, is expected to be more patient and to deal with the same people over and over, and is thus required to be more circumspect in his or her response to situations. Clergy must exercise respect and an ability to listen, process, reflect, and then comment. They therefore may experience tension between the charismatic leadership style that characterizes their role in worship and the empathetic relational styles needed in response to individual congregants. Often, a congregation expects the clergy to literally and dynamically represent the ultimate meaning system for the congregation. The clergy may also be expected to be less quick to speak in order to model listening and the valuing of other perspectives, slowly contemplating and gently responding (Trulear 1985). Possibly as a response to these polar expectations, some charismatic leaders quickly burn out, leaving followers disillusioned in the long run. Other leaders develop staff, both paid and volunteer, that complement their charismatic style with the more personal and therapeutic skills necessary for organizational health.

Empowering Versus Running the Show

The clergyperson is often the newest member of the congregation and may be the next to leave. In many Protestant denominations, clergy are hired by the board. In denominations where pastors are appointed, the congregations often can select among a list of candidates and they may be able to fire the clergyperson with or without consultation with the denominational office. In African American denominations, a bishop's appointment of a pastor to a congregation is less, if at all, informed by congregational preference or desire.

When a congregation is healthy and has longevity beyond the current clergy, it is wise that members feel empowered to do the work rather than have the clergy do it for them. There is the old dilemma of "doing for" versus "doing with," but in this case the ideal situation is to encourage, set directions and expectations, and allow the members to own their congregation. A clergyperson might be viewed as the one who ought to consider the future of the congregation and equip members with the skills and encouragement for service and leadership. As such, the clergyperson does not commit the congregation to an activity, such as a protest or a social program, but offers it to the congregation, encourages members to lead the activity, and supports them in carrying out their work. It is often more difficult to empower than to do, but when a doer leaves, the structure may collapse. When one who empowers leaves, the congregation continues to function smoothly.

In secular organizations, it is common for executives to have training in conflict management, but clergy training may not include such specialization. Conflicts occur within both organizational structures, but the way conflict is handled differs significantly. In secular organizations there is usually a system in place for employees and members to express their dissatisfaction with policies and procedures, such as grievance procedures. This may not be the case in a congregation's polity. The difficulty of a pastor who becomes a mediator is that the pastor fulfills other roles as well. The pastor's professional identity also includes his or her personal identity and religious faith wrapped up in a single package (Rediger 1997).

Forming a Community

A key task for clergy is to form a sense of solidarity and belonging among the members of the congregation. Unlike the situation in European congregations, where the congregation is financed from the outside, American clergy have to gain members' commitment and support. Members want to feel bonded and related to each other and to the congregation. Ammerman (1997a: 57) wrote in this respect, "congregations also engage in activities explicitly designed to strengthen the bonds of members, what many congregations call 'fellowship.' Both in shared tasks, where a sense of kinship is the by-product, and in small groups intentionally formed for fellowship, the congregation's members forge bonds of mutual identification and obligation."

Andrew Greeley (1972) noted that people join congregations to satisfy their religious, social, and psychological needs. He labels these basic needs as the need for meaning (religious), belongingness (social), and comfort (psychological). Ellison (1995) found that people have many motivations for joining a congregation. In addition to expressing their faith, other benefits may motivate people to join a congregation. Some join because they seek a place to socialize their children according to what they view as moral, appropriate, and just. Others do so for the child care available to members or to gain access to opportunities to sing, find a suitable mate, or benefit from counseling services. Regardless of one's reason for joining, the best way to become involved in the life of the congregation is through social relationships with others and small group participation.

As noted, people join congregations to satisfy social as well as spiritual needs. In the United States, many people change their denominational affiliation as adults. "Religious switching" is on the increase, as people choose their congregations for reasons other than family tradition. Furthermore, as Miller (1997) points out, many of today's congregations and denominations did not exist some twenty to thirty years ago. Miller studied the new, very large "paradigm churches" and discovered that for their members, the church is the center of their lives. It represents a refuge from the perceived violence and decay of the secular society. Miller suggested that the dramatic success of these churches is attributable to a sense of community that members cannot find in secular American society. Congregations are excellent suppliers of rich communal life.

Thus, the clergy are required to enable bonding between subgroups of members. One common practice is to have fellowship meetings after religious services in which people have a meal or refreshments while chatting informally. In other congregations, members are divided into small groups that meet weekly and form social relationships parallel to the congregation. In yet others, members are encouraged to participate in picnics, tours, or bingo. No matter what the practice is, clergy in the United States must foster and preserve the group identity and social bonds between members.

THE NATURE OF AUTHORITY

Authority involves power and the ability to impose one's preferences and practices on another. It is obvious that the power of clergy originates both in tradition and in respect (charisma), while the authority of leaders of nonprofit organizations is rooted in bureaucratic structure, control over resources, and to a lesser extent personal charisma. A clergyperson who wishes the group to move from point A to point B often lacks the organizational status to command or require such action. In a nonprofit organization one can change the policies or rules, but in a congregation the authority is superhuman and therefore less amenable to one person's authority. In a congregation, there are no hierarchical structures for a member's performance review. The authority lies in the tradition of respect to the one who keeps the religious tenets of the group and who has dedicated his or her life to holy matters, often at the expense of more financially or materially rewarding vocations.

In bureaucratic organizations authority is delegated by existing procedures, and is delegated from the top down. Clearly, in many voluntary organizations the practice of power and responsibility is informal and quite participatory. However, in congregations the transfer of authority is more often than not traditional and based on symbols and consensus, or out of respect for the clergy's standing.

MONEY MANAGEMENT

As noted previously, many view pastoral leadership and financial management as two separate entities. However, clergy often are required to handle the finances of the congregation. There is no theological or biblical mandate that discourages clergy from managing money. Some people, however, interpret certain verses to mean that doing so is not biblical, notably 1 Timothy 6:10: "For the love of money is a root of all kinds of evil, and in their eagerness to be rich some have wandered away from the faith and pierced themselves with many pains" (NRSV). The verse is often misquoted as "money is the root of all evil." As the executive, the congregational leader oversees all financial functions to develop and advance the church's mission. In the American context the pastor is generally not hindered from doing so. Many clergy moderate finance committees, initiate building campaigns, manage collection plate, and pay debts as long as they do not violate the congregation's constitution. Some congregations write employment contracts that place restrictions on the new pastor's ability to handle finances. This method is employed on a case-by-case basis and is not the normal mode of functioning throughout congregational communities. In contrast, the executive of the nonprofit faces similar challenges in that he or she must maximize the use of funds, generate funds, and control fiscal demands placed on the organization. Comparatively, congregational leaders, like nonprofit executives, must meet fiscal goals or eventually close the doors of the organization.

Summary and Conclusions

In this chapter, we argued that the environment of local religious congregations in the United States is sufficiently unique to warrant special attention. We presented four contextual factors that necessitate special practices by local religious congregations. We said that the religious focus, key constituencies, relevant legislation, and job boundaries combined pose managerial and leadership expectations for American clergy that are different from those of clergy in other modern democracies and are different than the expectations placed on leaders of nonprofit organizations in the United States. After demonstrating our claim, we listed leadership challenges and characteristics that are unique to American clergy. While it is impossible to write about each of the hundreds of thousands of congregations in the United States, we attempted to draw some relevant generalities. These general themes are: a strong pulpit, self-discipline, empowering versus running the show, forming a community, and the nature of authority. Every congregation aspires to hire that one person who will excel in all these domains and will be the unforgettable superclergy. All congregations want to hire similar superclergy. As Fried (2002: 33) found, all synagogues look for "someone who attends every meeting and is at his desk working until midnight, someone who is twenty-eight years old but has preached for thirty years, someone who has a burning desire to work with teenagers but spends all his time with senior citizens, basically someone who does *everything* well and will stay with the congregation forever."

Clearly, not every function carried out by U.S. clergy is significantly different or markedly unique compared with European clergy or American nonprofit organization leaders. As the list of qualities of successful clergy in America proposed by Jackson Carroll (1991) and discussed above indicates, most qualities of successful clergy apply across the board. Clergy everywhere are serving a higher power and thus work with their faith as the leading motive. But American clergy are additionally expected to capture a niche in the religious market and sustain a community of worshippers outside the public sector. It is not our contention that the requirements of successful clergy and running nonprofit organizations are totally distinct. In fact, successful managers of voluntary organizations who receive a religious calling and training would likely be able to adjust their skills to the role of clergy. Similarly, clergy who shift careers to run nonprofit organizations would probably find the transition feasible. Our aim in this chapter is to emphasize that religious life in America is sufficiently unique and poses additional and slightly different leadership challenges to the role of clergy. We did not provide the reader with a guide for successful religious leadership, but attempted to outline the specific contextual factors and challenges facing American clergy as compared with leaders of secular nonprofit organizations and clergy in other advanced democracies.

What can be done to help clergy? Many of the constraints we presented are inherent in the role of a clergy and cannot be transformed. But one way to retain clergy and not drive them to exhaustion is to offer them sabbaticals. Teachers have summers off, and every few years professors can go on sabbatical, but clergy are often in the trenches for decades. Large and resourceful denominations attempt to renew their clergy energy by rotating them and allowing them some time between posts. But, the majority of clergy do not even dream about such an opportunity to renew their spiritual and physical batteries. Since 2000, the Lilly Endowment has enabled some 650 American clergy to step away from their jobs for a few months in order to engage in renewal and reflection. At a pace of about two hundred a year, it may seem like a drop in a bucket, but it is an important and novel beginning that may continue a trend for the future. If more foundations and denominations will continue with this trend, many qualified clergy will not be lost to their vocation, and their commitment to their congregants and the community will be sustained.

Chapter 14

Policy Recommendations: What Have We Learned?

This book contains a wide range of information regarding the social service involvement of local religious congregations in Philadelphia, based on the Philadelphia Census of Congregations (PCC). It is somewhat difficult to summarize and discuss this rich body of knowledge in one chapter. It is even more difficult to draw national conclusions based on these data. The reader may come up with many interesting and relevant conclusions that we have missed. It is, however, impossible to not discuss the findings from this book in light of two key issues that are currently the primary focus of social science research and public policy. The various conclusions drawn in this chapter thus focus mainly on the contributions of local religious congregations to the formation of social capital and civil society, and on their role in the currently tested and debated faith-based initiative.

While we recognize congregations as perhaps the most important social organization for sustaining civil society and producing social capital in urban America, we share many concerns regarding the faith-based initiative. It is our firm belief, as well as our objective assessment, that the faith-based initiative can succeed only if the government increases the funding for social services, and gradually and carefully contracts with local religious congregations and faith-based nonprofit organizations. We cannot see how transferring responsibilities to the faith-based community without sufficient funding will produce a more humane and compassionate society. As we have unequivocally documented, local religious congregations are currently providing an important array of services without public support. Thus, they should be encouraged to keep doing so and not to be expected to save the entire American welfare system. We need to remember that their success and operation are based on their own free will and resources. An attempt to make religious congregations social service units partnered with the U.S. government can occur only if generous funding is attached, and even then congregations may need to consider carefully whether the soul of their activities would be lost.

We also contend that the liberal opposition to the faith-based initiative, at least as far as congregations' involvement in social services is concerned, is faulty. Instead of celebrating the contributions of local religious congregations and recognizing their unique role in society, many liberals and liberal organizations tend to adopt the one study (by Mark Chaves) that found congregations to be less socially involved. In fact, the liberal agenda would be enhanced by acknowledging the many studies showing congregations' notable involvement in social services provision. It would be more sensible to acknowledge that congregations are doing much, but also that, as a sector of society, they cannot bear the hope of welfare on their shoulders. Sadly, the rift between liberals and the presumed conservative religion in America is so wide that, for many liberals, regarding congregations as positive pro-social agents is difficult.

Finally, as the White House Office of Faith-Based and Community Initiatives implements its goals, we offer suggestions as to how the government may best cooperate with local religious congregations. These community-based organizations are quite varied and are different from all other organizations with which the government collaborates. Finally, we offer suggestions as to how the government can be sensitive to congregational culture and how congregations can be sensitive to the public sector.

Social Capital and Civil Society

Our findings in this book should help answer a fundamental question facing social science: whether congregations in America are saving civil society and producing social capital. It is very difficult to answer this question with a simple yes or no. Each individual congregation is a source of both trust and social capital and a group somehow protected from the rest of society. But what is clear is that, combined, the local religious congregations in Philadelphia contribute greatly to civil society and social capital.

A civil society is one where people meet face to face and develop trust relationships that lead to a willingness to do good for their communities and to voluntarily cooperate with the government. Such dynamics require the formation of local organizations that will assemble and represent people of various backgrounds and interests. Berger and Neuhaus (1977) were the first to call our attention to the importance of local groups that mediate between citizens and the powers that have an impact on the local community, such as the government. Many other researchers encouraged the formation of civic organizations and voluntary groups that would allow people to share ideas and interact in ways that would enhance trust and allow residents to elect trusted representatives. The process by which face-to-face interactions lead to solidarity and shared interest is sometimes referred to as the formation of social capital. James Coleman (1990) developed this concept, showing how it is the foundation of mutual care and trust, and Robert Putnam (2000) found that social capital is the foundation for economic development and democracy.

Over two thousand local religious congregations in Philadelphia have some common structural and functional features. They are more frequently found and spread throughout the city than any other mediating organization Berger and Neuhaus (1977) could have envisioned. Every weekend, in almost all these institutions, tens if not thousands of people gather together to pray, listen to a sermon, and participate in a fellowship. Often they picnic together or team up to perform a collective task. People find new friends who are like-minded and engaged in civic work through the social programs offered by the congregations. When a member of the congregation or his or her family members are in need, it is only expected that the group will pull its resources together and help. Every member knows that such help is available when needed, and that private matters will be kept confidential. They also know that they will be respected and trusted when asking for help as a last resort because others have witnessed their plight. This source of social capital is available to the almost half the residents in Philadelphia who are regular members of congregations, that is, those attending at least monthly and known to others in the congregation.

There are very few places where adults can meet others who are of the same mindset and who will not reject or abuse them. Other traditional settings for making friends are becoming less attractive. The workplace nowadays is a competitive environment, where today's friend could become tomorrow's adversary. Neighbors are often strangers engaged in their own social networks. Those with young children are likely to befriend parents of their children's friends. Fraternal organizations and local pubs are no longer attractive to most Americans as a place for socializing. For the most part, in an alienating and mobile society, the congregation is a safe place to meet people who share values, worldviews, and political orientations. They are less likely to abuse one another since they are accountable for their actions in the closed community and since repeated interactions are the key to forming trust and mutual care. Out of the members, one can pick persons who are close in age and life experience and build a network of close friendships.

Only about half the residents in Philadelphia are active members of congregations. One could conclude that congregations' contributions to the building of social capital are limited to congregation members

alone. Three points should be made in response. First, there are few
other social institutions in the city that can claim access to half the population on an ongoing basis. People who go to baseball games or bars are
fewer in number and are probably not meeting the people from those
places regularly. Second, each member of the congregation comes with
his or her personal network of friends and acquaintances. When a member needs help or information, other members may access persons or
agencies with the relevant skills or information from their outside social
networks. Finally, many of the beneficiaries of congregational programs
are not members of the congregation. Therefore, it may well be that the
outreach of congregations and the processes of forming social capital
reach 50 percent or more of Philadelphia's residents.

The offering of social capital may also explain a small but significant
phenomenon we found in some personal interviews of "belonging without believing." In some congregations, especially those with liberal orientations or those that are ethnic, we were told about and met members
who said they are not "very religious if at all." Yet these people attend
services regularly and at times assume leadership roles in the congregation. In these instances, the member wants to belong to the group he or
she feels closest to, finding in it social support and personal acceptance.
Individuals also seek a place in which they can maintain their family's
religious heritage for its own sake. In the end, then, they join even
though their religious commitment is in doubt. Such people recognize
that congregations are hubs of social capital. In a few Jewish Reform synagogues, for example, we were told that some members barely knew the
religious tenets but came to the synagogue to be with their "brothers."
Similarly, in Korean churches, we were told of members who were not
Christians in Korea but wanted to join the Korean church for social
gatherings, Sunday Korean school classes for children, and camaraderie
(Oh 1989).

One argument against local religious congregations as hubs for the
formation of social capital is that they supposedly tend to be isolated and
distrustful of other faith traditions and secular society. To some extent,
this is true. However, we should remember that most congregations do
collaborate with others, for worship and for social reasons. Furthermore,
it is within small cohesive groups that repeated interactions occur in
such a way that mutual support is encouraged and trust can be tested.
In small congregations, people often choose all members as their fel-
lows, while in large congregations, members are assigned to groups, or
choose a Bible study group or similar subdivision that produces a small
circle of trusted friends. Our findings support those of Ellison and
George (1994) and Molm, Takahashi, and Peterson (2000), who found
that congregations generate more informal bonding and communica-

tion than any other social and community institution. What congregations do less of is forming "bridging social capital." While congregations collaborate and engage in cross-congregational activities, trust and face-to-face interactions are often internally oriented, leaving out members of other congregations.

Clearly, there are other institutions in Philadelphia that support the formation of social capital and civil society. The many universities in the area are one such example. The social clubs, neighborhood associations, arts groups, and other groups are all key players in this regard. But, if one tries to look at the picture reversed—that is, how Philadelphia's social capital and civil society would fare if congregations somehow disappeared overnight—a stronger case for congregations as key players emerges. A significant segment of the city's social capital and civil society would be lost in such a situation. And it is doubtful whether congregants, who through their congregations carry strong prosocial attitudes in the company of coreligionists, would have had such values without the local religious congregation.

The Congregation as a Social Service Unit

The key picture emerging from this study is that congregations in Philadelphia add tremendously to the social service system in the city. They are local units that, as a rule, attempt to "do good" in their communities and ameliorate misery. For a country that, unlike most advanced democracies, has no infrastructure of public social services, congregations are a de facto substitute for a safety net. As our findings show, congregations feed and clothe the poor, provide after-school programs, serve as community hubs for people with various addictions, and help couples and families with numerous services and counseling. The wide gamut of services, direct and indirect, has been portrayed in Chapters 3, 4, and 5, and the overall replacement value of these services is conservatively estimated at a quarter billion dollars (see Chapter 5).

Chaves (2004), among other critics of the faith-based initiatives, claims that congregation-based social services do not present us with a meaningful alternative to the services already provided by our community welfare systems. In practice, however, that is an inaccurate assertion. Congregations routinely provide so much to our network of social services that only withholding what they do could demonstrate how important their contribution is. Most basic needs such as food and immediate shelter are provided by congregations. They may not be able to replace public mental health or child welfare services that are outside their domain. However, their services, which are often short-term, emergency-based, and segmented, taken together are a major part of the American welfare system. To be a needy person in America without access to local congregations is a most frightening prospect. One needs to look at what congregations are giving and not at what they can provide in order to appreciate the magnitude of congregation-based care.

Many programs run by congregations are small in scale and limited in coverage. For a needy person or family to get a full response to their needs may mean having to approach several congregations and secular nonprofit organizations. In the United States, there is no one-stop service unit where a needy person or family can come, be assessed, and be served comprehensively. The service system is fragmented and rarely coordinated in its parts. Local religious congregations fit very well into this picture. As formal public services are few and far between, the congregations in Philadelphia, and most likely nationwide, fill the gaps as best they can. This process, known as crowding out, was expected to come as soon as the U.S. government began to withdraw from social services. What was not expected was that congregations would almost exclusively fill the void. It is not surprising that congregations in the United States are very active in many aspects of health care, whereas congregations in Canada are hardly involved in this domain (Cnaan and Handy 2000). In Canada the government provides these services, while in the United States services are privately administered, out of the reach of many people. Hence congregations aim to supply what members observe to be missing.

Crowding out does not happen by itself; it requires intent. When a key player relinquishes its presence someone has to take over the lost service. In the case of social services at the start of the twenty-first century, it is not secular organizations but local religious congregations and other faith-based groups who are stepping in. If nothing else, American congregations should be celebrated for their contribution to the quality of life, when all others have turned their backs to the plight of the poor and needy.

It is crucial for us to understand that, at the community level, congregations are the foundational blocks for social care. Their response is nowhere near as comprehensive and complete as that of public services in other advanced democracies. As a whole, in America, we do not show much compassion to our poor and needy fellow citizens. As a society, we happily relegate social welfare to the congregations, to do it as generously as they may wish, allowing ourselves to spend little on such efforts, keeping the poor and needy at arm's length. But for a needy person such a system as ours means that there is no regularity or assurance of continual care. Also, it is not honorable to American society that congregations must shoulder so much of the burden of social welfare relative to the American public as a whole; it weakens our overall sense of solidarity. In light of the government's avoidance of developing a compre-hensive public welfare system, and the public's lack of sympathy to the plight of the poor, congregations are the key source of help for the needy in our communities.

On Recruitment of Congregations for Social Service Provision

Congregations, as this study shows, are a major part of the welfare arena, providing assistance to the poorest members of our society. The impres-sive welfare and community work done by congregations is not man-dated by anyone, nor is it funded by external sources. This begs the following question: could congregations do more if the state contracted or encouraged them? As we demonstrated with the cases of Amachi, REST Philly, and NPIHN, the capacity for such collaborations is enor-mous and mostly untapped, but there are still many unanswered ques-tions.

First, our culture often expects congregations to carry out their minis-tries alone. While we found that two-thirds of the congregations in Phila-delphia collaborate with other faith-based organizations in serving the needy, and more than half do so with secular organizations, we also found that nine out of ten of the reported programs are carried out solely by congregations acting alone. As such, congregations tend to serve the needy independently, on their own terms. As Cnaan and his colleagues (2002) found, congregations do not view themselves as an arm of the state or any other group, but rather as an independent body that acts on its own assessment of situations. Most often, a congrega-tional program evolves when a member of the congregation, usually a clergy or a lay leader, observes a need and shares his or her observations with the congregation. What follows is mostly a discussion about the problem and the congregation's ability to help. While many such initia-tives and testimonials go nowhere, a few materialize into programs designed to help those in need. But as the initiative comes from within the congregation, it is unlikely that those engaged in delivering the ser-vice will attempt to find partners. Congregations like to own their social programs and to help those in need as a collective spiritual endeavor. The idea of calling upon or responding to an outside organization to share in program delivery is perceived as detracting from the spirit of congregational ministry and service. As such, even when it is obvious to the local faith communities that the needs are greater than what avail-able resources can handle, there is an initial proclivity to go it alone and a resistance to call upon other groups to share in the programs. Often when congregations realize that a program is too large for them to han-dle, they would rather give it up and allow it to become a secular nonprofit organization rather than share it with others. Indeed, in the PCC, 372 (26.7 percent) congregations reported that such organizations had formed when the programs grew too large. This cultural handicap may take a long time to change, and any government agency that wants to collaborate with congregations needs to be aware of it and be accommodating to congregations' ways of doing things.

Local religious congregations, with few notable exceptions, have limited resources and operate at maximum capacity. That is, the budget is maximized and resources are utilized as far as they will go. Programs are operated precariously; a copy machine breakdown can cancel an afternoon event. This stretching of financial and technical means puts the congregation in a vulnerable situation. Collaborating with others, especially under public contracts, exposes vulnerabilities and limits the congregation's flexibility to deal with crises as they come.

Members of faith communities, especially clergy, are frequently suspicious of the intentions of public officials. Often, commitment is limited to the duration of a budget cycle, yet the needs are ongoing and the congregation is left with a promise to the community far beyond its capacity to carry out. People in the local community will have seen many public initiatives come and go; consequently they are inclined to distrust initiatives' staying power. Whether this suspicion is justified is not the issue; the important point here is that this perception makes congregations less likely to collaborate with government.

As such, congregations, based on their impressive social service provision, may seem like the most natural partner for the state to contract out with, for the purpose of helping the poor, but their idiosyncratic nature must first be understood. Some congregations can do way more than they do now, for the capacity for expansion is evident, but, we also need to remember that people do not join congregations to help the needy. They join congregations to practice their faith collectively. And if the expression of faith is compromised or the stability of the congregation as an organization is threatened, the social service component may be last priority. Social services are meant to express faith and to be a mechanism to solidify the ranks from within. Unlike nonprofit organizations that are formed primarily to serve the needy, congregations often have a social norm of helping the poor that is well and alive, but not primary and not a necessary component for its endurance and continued existence. For congregations, social service provision is a norm, but its actualization is an internal affair.

Policy Recommendations for Liberals in America

Since congregations are so involved in social service delivery, many policy questions can be asked and answered. Unfortunately, to a large extent, policies often represent ideologies and are devoid of empirical knowledge. But even more problematic is policy makers' reliance on doubtful data as the basis for their decisions. As we clearly indicated at the beginning of this book, we are liberals who believe in the government's responsibility to help the needy in a coordinated manner and a respectable fashion. We also know that the likelihood of that happening soon in the United States is extremely low. We believe that it will happen eventually, and probably in this century, but not in the near future. So, when public sentiments are anti-welfare and the government wants to wash itself of any welfare program that does not cater to middle-class voters, faith-based voluntary social care is the only approach left. How can liberals reconcile the impressive welfare work done by religious congregations and their ideology of the state's responsibility for social service involvement?

Many liberals are troubled to find out that charity and philanthropy are strongly associated with organized religion. Anyone holding secular humanistic values would rather see a strong and rational public welfare state. However, the conservative-capitalist ideology is currently dominant as its many proponents are controlling affairs in America. Secular humanistic values are not finished but they are held by the minority. In the 1960s, the liberal agenda shaped public policy and was very important for bringing key changes in our social service systems, such as the Equal Opportunity Amendment and the Great Society. Liberals such as us would love to see the return of some of the values that underpinned federal social programs. However, we cannot let our beliefs make us unrealistic about the actual situation, wherein religious congregations have taken on so much of the social burden abandoned by government.

Fearing the expansion of the faith-based initiative as it is advocated by President George W. Bush, many liberals cling to the one study that has shown that only a little over half the congregations are active in offering social services. Ten different studies, including the Philadelphia Census of Congregations, show that, at least in urban America, the rate of congregations' involvement is nine in ten, a fact that makes no impression on our colleagues in the liberal camp, who despite these findings continue to claim that only about half the congregations offer social services and therefore must be apathetic for the most part. In this light, congregations and, by extension, all other faith-based organizations would be incapable of collaborating with the state to deliver social services. We dare to challenge this notion and we suggest a new liberal viewpoint.

The liberal agenda we propose is focused on claiming that so much is being done voluntarily by local religious congregations that it is unrealistic to expect them to do much more. The question should be, given that nine in ten congregations are already offering at least one social service, as modest as it may be, how much more can they expand? Although there is room for increased capacity, one should ask what will happen to the current impressive voluntary care if public funds stream inward. If congregations are called upon to do more, using public funds, will it not be at the expense of the wonderful social services they are offering now? Can they keep this impressive rate of free social service provision and develop new, government-sponsored services all at once? Once money comes in, the amount of voluntary and self-financed services will decline, and one of the most impressive American social organizations, the congregation, will lose its appeal and exclusivity. We should hail local religious congregations for what they are currently doing on their own initiative with their own resources, contracting mostly, if not only, with faith-based organizations that are incorporated as 501(c)(3) organizations. The religious nonprofits should be the target of faith-based initiatives, while congregations should be encouraged to do what they do best without the government interfering. The counterargument— that only a little more than half the congregations are engaged in social service provision—is simply inaccurate and does not serve any liberal agenda.

Another liberal line of argument is that providing social services by congregations and faith-based organizations will violate the principle of uniformity in society. According to this thinking, services should be delivered by various branches of a uniform American public, and congregations and other faith-based organizations are too unique and diverse to mold into a uniform structure.

Robert Wuthnow, in his excellent book *Saving America? Faith-Based Services and the Future of Civil Society* (2004), suggests that, because congregations try to distinguish themselves in terms of membership, loyalty, and internal friendships, they are economically and racially bound, and hence unfit to provide uniform services. As social workers, we argue that this is an advantage. A one-type-fits-all service is known to be mediocre in its effectiveness. What is needed is a variety of care options that people can choose from to find the one best suited to them. Still, Wuthnow's words are most apt: "The challenge is for religious organizations to do their part alongside other private organizations and for the government to continue its part" (310).

Respecting the contribution of congregations will enable liberals to join forces with many in the religious camp who are worried that public funding will weaken the scope and spirit of help. As McDaniel, Davis, and Neff (2005) show, religious people are concerned with the First Amendment, as the nature of volunteerism and generosity may be hampered if programs that are now run freely will be partially or fully subsidized by the public sector.

It is disappointing to be a secular liberal in America and to realize that only the religious community has formed thousands of voluntary organizations that care for the needy and indigent. The secular human-ist movement failed to form similar organizations and pales in compari-son. There is no liberal-secular parallel to the role of congregations in America. Some liberals justify this with the claim that welfare is the responsibility of the government and not of the voluntary sector.

As such, the liberal camp can pressure the government to do its part in assisting the needy and ameliorating misery. No one else in America today can guarantee that the government will continue to fund welfare at an adequate level. By focusing on the faith-based initiative, the gov-ernment is able to further withdraw its commitment to people's welfare. Both liberals and faith-based groups should collaborate to pressure gov-ernment not to abdicate its role in welfare and quality of life.

In the Name of God or Not

The critics of the faith-based initiative, such as the Anti-Defamation League (ADL), rightly worry that serving the needy through faith-based groups will amount to legal proselytization (Farnsley 2003). This is an important point and one that should never be taken lightly. The separa-tion of church and state has been found to be good both for the reli-gious groups in America and for the state. Any coercion to participate in religious activities or to profess faith is unconstitutional and counter-productive to any attempts to build civil society. In fact, government avoidance of any support for religion has made religious groups in America stronger and more wide reaching. We therefore have to be inspect the evidence regarding faith-based proselytization. If the faith-based initiative prevails, it must monitor faith-based programs and ensure that no pressure is put on clients to act religiously.

Before we turn to discuss this issue more carefully, two issues should be articulated. First, anecdotal evidence of faith-based coercion or the lack thereof is insufficient. Clearly, there will always be some fanatics who will try to use public funds to their advantage. Conversely, there are secular service providers who embezzle and abuse clients. No one will suggest, based on these few cases, that we stop contracting with secular service providers. We do not shift policies because a few bad apples spoil the intention of that policy. A few abusers of any program or policy should not set the tone for public discourse, although they comprise the evidence used by news reporters and the media. Just as if one hospice were found to abuse its residents, the whole respite care system would not be cast in doubt, so a few isolated cases of proselytization should not jeopardize the faith-based initiative. What needs to be found is the frequency of proselytization, knowledge that could serve as a basis for a shift in policy. Second, it should be remembered that the congregations in our study, with very few exceptions, provide services on their own volition and at their own expense. These congregations are not part of the faith-based initiative, as almost all of them are unaware of Charitable Choice, government legislation allowing more access to federal funding, and as they were in the business of care long before it became politically fashionable. As such, they can legally and actively proselytize and bring as many souls into their midst as possible. Thus, the amount of proselytization going on in the Philadelphia congregations may serve as a test case for potential proselytization by all faith-based organizations.

First, let us review the scant available literature in this field. Green and Sherman (2002) found that even when ostensibly faith-based organizations provide social services under public funding, three-quarters of them give very little indication that faith elements are present. In fact, very few organizations incorporate any religious components in their service delivery. Emphasis on professionalism and bureaucratic procedures by faith-based organizations contracting with the state were also reported by Chambre (2001), regarding AIDS services in New York City, and by Smith and Sosin (2001), regarding a host of social services in Seattle and Chicago.

In North Philadelphia, Jill Sinha (2004) followed a consortium of six United Methodist black churches that contracted with the city to offer educational services to teenagers who dropped out from traditional school programs. Sinha followed this program for a year and attended numerous meetings, classes, team meetings, and leisure-time activities, as well as interviewing the staff and clients individually and in focus groups. One of the key findings of her study was that the teenagers reported no pressure whatsoever regarding religion. They noted no religious content in the educational program and no attempts to recruit them to attend worship services. Staff members prayed regularly but not with clients, and teens reported no indication of their wanting them to become religious. This is an especially important account, as the service providers are small black churches that are considered in the literature as groups highly prone to evangelize. The fact that these Philadelphia churches, caring for teens as a last resort for the city's educational system, did not attempt to proselytize clients indicates that the fear of this devil is overrated.

As we already noted in *The Invisible Caring Hand* (2002), and as was reiterated in this study, congregations are not getting engaged in social services provision for the sake of evangelism or proselytization. In the many interviews we conducted in Philadelphia, clergy and lay leaders alike reiterated that their motive for providing social services is purely religious. They are following Jesus (for Christians) or other religious persons or dicta, or a founder's vision, and this is how they are practicing their faith in full. We were told of the actualization of faith by serving the needy, and we were told of using one's wealth as stewardship for God as reasons for service provision. But religious motivations were not found to involve clients. Rarely were we informed of even a wish for clients to become members of a faith group. In most instances, we were told that it is impossible to change clients' souls by giving them soup to eat or a bed to sleep on. Most clergy know that it is unrealistic to expect people to find God by helping them with clothing or donations. In many instances, the people served are different in all relevant socioeconomic characteristics from the helpers, and the latter do not want them to become coreligionists. The most they hope for is that the clients may come one step closer to finding their own spirituality. Igniting some hidden flame or planting the seed for later growth is all that our interviewees hoped for. In this time and place, they all know that forcing religious participation makes people more averse to religion, and they do not want that to happen. In many ways, the zeal for proselytization is an artifact of the Great Depression era that is much less prevalent today.

What this says for public policy is that the fear of proselytization is a bad excuse for opposing the faith-based initiative. Fear of proselytization may be good for public relations, but there is no evidence to support it. In fact, very few instances of faith being included in service delivery were reported. And there were even fewer cases of clients complaining or recalling that faith was incorporated in service delivery, which suggests that congregations and most faith-based organizations draw a line between service and proselytization. There are and will be a few exceptions that should be punished, but they should not be used as an excuse to oppose the initiative. If the congregations that are not bound by government rules when providing services and that are funding programs with their own resources do not proselytize, it is quite unlikely that with public funding they will try to do so and endanger their precarious stronghold with the public coiffeur. In fact, liberals can use many better arguments to oppose the faith-based initiative, such as the organizations' right to hire based on whether persons adhere to a faith.

The Role of Religion

Many people in congregations claimed that theology matters. For them, the social activities of their faith community are not an act of social work but a means to actualize their faith. The social programs are theology put into practice, and that is the main purpose of their community work. Put differently, the same people may not be willing to develop and staff a social program if it is not spiritually and theologically anchored in the faith of them and their co-religionists. When asked why they provide social services, many clergy or lay leaders cited biblical verses that call upon the believer to do so. As Cnaan and his colleagues (2002) found, helping the needy is a congregational norm that is an expression of religious teaching and a means to unify the religious group, and that is how it became a pronounced American norm.

Often public providers and state authorities do not grasp the important role that faith plays in the establishment and delivery of social programs. But, in any case, congregations are not social service agencies. They are gatherings where faith is practiced, and as long as serving people is perceived as part of this faith, congregations can provide social services. For religious communities, in the end, the higher authority of a deity or God supersedes the authority of an agency. If there is a conflict between the social program and theology, most often theology prevails. When conflicts arise some innovative solutions are found. For example, when congregation members help people whose behavior is opposed to the congregation, they often stress that "one should love the sinner and hate the sin."

State policy makers and supervisors are expected to be faith-neutral and to disregard the congregation's faith and theology. This gap in religion can be a source of discomfort for both sides. Congregational members are used to having people in their building who are theologically like-minded and with whom they can discuss faith and God even when they clean the building or prepare a meal. Government representatives often feel that when a prayer is part of a meeting (usually to ask God to bless the meeting or to thank him when the meeting is over), or when God is thanked while discussing compliance with budgetary rules, their privacy is violated. At times, these public officials are members of a different faith group, and their religious sensibilities may be different. These two cultures are not easy to integrate.

Faith has no boundaries in the congregation. One interviewee made the following analogy about understanding religion in the context of a congregation: "For us religion is everywhere. When you make a pancake, you see an egg next to the flour, margarine, and sugar. Focus on this egg. When the pancake is done, the egg is in it, but you do not see it. So, for us, this is religion. It is everywhere, and yet you can't see it, but know it is there, respect it, and know that without it, there is no pancake." Congregations are in existence first and foremost to enable their members to actualize their faith. Social services are only one component of actualizing faith and, as such, should be respected and understood as part of the mix. This is not a license for congregations to impose their faith on others or to expect society to accept their theology. Rather, it is an imperative for anyone who wishes to harness congregations to become more active in the social services arena. By being so, he or she can understand how important and relevant faith is for congregations, and to assess if a workable coexistence of religion and social service can be achieved.

We would like to stress that, while forcing religion on clients is often not a real threat, it may indeed happen and state officials have to be on guard to make sure it does not. Secular nonprofit organizations often violate state rules, and inspectors must monitor and sanction them—it should do likewise for congregations that may use public money to provide social care and will attempt to proselytize.

A more subtle issue of faith and social service is having religion within the servicing unit. Such a situation will probably not violate any aspect of the constitution, but in cultural terms it will be at odds with the public service culture. At times, the tradition and nature of the serving organization (the religious congregation) are at stake, and at times respect for the state representatives is the main issue. We do not have enough data to assess the level of conflict that may arise from this issue, but attention to it and mutual respect is clearly required.

Congregational Diversity

One mistake that is currently rampant in many circles is to talk of the "faith-based community." Many scholars such as Thomas Jeavons warn us repeatedly that this community is composed of a variety of organizational types only some of which are congregations. Furthermore, even among congregations, this variety is so rich that many attempts at generalizing about them fall short of capturing their essence. In Chapter 1 we discussed the similarities that make congregations a coherent social institution and also emphasized their many differences.

Policy makers should not lump all congregations into a single social and communal institution. Congregations come in every size and shape, and some are locally oriented while others attract a host of commuters. Some are more this-world oriented and some are more other-world oriented. Some are rich and some are poor. Some own mortgage-free properties and some rent space or use a storefront. Assuming that understanding or working with one congregation is a key to understanding all other congregations is a grave mistake. As documented in Chapters 2 and 3, the PCC reveals this diversity in location, size, resources, level of commitment to the congregation, connection to the community, and social orientation. Some are extremely suspicious and distrustful of secular authorities while other trust them more and are willing to cooperate with public entities. Given that almost half of the city residents attend congregations regularly, one should expect their congregations to be as diverse as the city itself. The challenge for policy makers and city officials is to learn how to work with congregations in their own cultures and to accept their diversity. Congregations as a whole are committed to improving the quality of life, but each of them is poised to contribute differently. None can ever hope to "save the city," but most would like to give a hand in that endeavor, in their own way.

One notable way in which local religious congregations are diverse is with regard to ethnicity. In the United States, most forms of ethnic segregation are frowned upon as if they were outright illegal. As Massey and Denton (1993) show, housing and neighborhoods in America are highly segregated. People either choose or are forced to live in neighborhoods where most of their neighbors are of the same ethnic group. In many cases, this housing segregation is part of the racist spirit of the country. Massey and Denton went so far as to label it "American apartheid." In congregations, however, people choose freely to congregate with people who are similar to themselves. People are free to choose their place of worship, and a large share of the people attending any congregation in Philadelphia does not live within ten blocks of it. The 55 percent who do not live nearby travel some distance to go to their congregation of choice. And given that Orthodox Jewish synagogues and Roman Catholic churches demand that members be local neighbors, the proportion of the commuters among those who are eligible to commute is even higher. Again, these numbers are not unique to Philadelphia. For example, Farnsley (2003: 49) noted that, "In Indianapolis, we know that the average Catholic parish can expect that about 60 percent of its members live within the official parish boundaries. By contrast, only about 40 percent of the members of an urban Protestant congregation live in the immediate neighborhood."

Most often, people commute to an ethnic congregation. Indeed, we found in the PCC that in nine out of ten congregations (89.2 percent), three-quarters or more of the members are from a single ethnic group. It is among people of the same race that a sense of safety, trust, and familiarity reside. This gives many Philadelphians a once-a-week chance to meet people who face the same problems and go through similar experiences as themselves, and to be able to freely express complaint against the rest of society, as well as get and give advice, and commiserate in fellowship meetings. Chapters 7 and 8 provided a detailed review of the unique characteristics of two special ethnic groups, Latinos and African Americans, and their involvement in social services provision.

While people are commuting to their place of worship, these places of worship are often located in neighborhoods in which a majority of the residents are of the same ethnic group. We showed that Latino congregations are most frequently housed in Latino neighborhoods, as is the case for African American and Asian American congregations. Often the commuting is from one black neighborhood to another or one ethnic neighborhood to another. This implies that many congregations are purposely ethnically segregated, located in neighborhoods where most inhabitants are of the same ethnic makeup. As such these congregations are inclined to be concerned with the welfare of the local residents and their social and human needs. The combination of theological quests to "do good" along with ethnic affiliations with local residents makes the congregations caring and involved. But, their various missions are diverse, based on geographical location, local needs, ethnic culture and heritage, and available human and material resources. It is the role of policy makers to understand these dynamics and help congregations fulfill their unique missions rather than try to make them all to do work without regard to their natural propensities and interests.

On the Dynamic Nature of Congregations

Congregations are social institutions that are most viable and capable for birth, death, adaptation, and reemergence. We were reminded of this early in our study when we received an invitation to celebrate the joining of two existing congregations in West Philadelphia. One congregation had many members but no facility, while the other had a facility but a rapidly declining membership and no pastor. The two merged into a new, stronger congregation and changed their names to a single new name. As another example, one of our interviewers, a recent graduate of a local theological seminary, started a new church and, at the time of this writing, his church was still active, though it had not reached a state of being stable and safe. The range of dynamics among congregations also comes from the different denominational headquarters. Denominations and various religious bodies aim to grow and plant new congregations. For example, Holmes (2003) reported that the Southern Baptist Convention had planted some 23 new churches in the Philadelphia area from 2000 to 2003. Many of these new churches are ethnic churches, and not all of them will survive beyond five years. At the same time, the Roman Catholic archdiocese had to close down parishes, merge them with nearby parishes, and open new churches in the suburbs.

Congregations are also undergoing major growth or decline. While the trends can be reversed, they pose a major challenge to those aiming to work with congregations. Any collaboration or recruitment of congregations has to be sensitive to the congregation's life cycle and its current strength. Again, one cannot lump all congregations together, since their stage of evolution is extremely important in understanding their capacity and willingness to engage in collaborative efforts.

Summary

The Other Philadelphia Story is a tale of modern-day America. In a city that witnesses blight and population decline many people are living with a variety of needs. The current political climate does not favor those people who are economically and socially left behind. If it were not for the impressive collective effort of some 2,120 some local religious congregations, life in Philadelphia would have become extremely harsh. Their attempts to alleviate misery and improve the quality of life throughout the city have made the city more deserving of its nickname, "the city of brotherly love." Together, the 2,120 congregations in Philadelphia present a tapestry of rich and variegated care. While individually they are different and require special attention, viewed as a whole they provide the city with much-needed care and compassion. They are telling another Philadelphia story, the one about care and compassion and the strengthening of civil society. If one wants to estimate the financial contribution of religious congregations in Philadelphia, their replacement value is quarter of a million dollars annually.

In order to imagine congregations' contribution to the city, we need to imagine the city as if all the congregations had disappeared. Imagine that one morning you wake up in Philadelphia, and all 2,120 congregations have vanished. In many neighborhoods, the most pristine structures would probably have been replaced with rundown apartment complexes. Many of the scout troops, 12-step programs, and day care centers would be missing and their clients would be unserved. Hungry and homeless people would be roaming the streets and knocking on doors to ask for food and clothing. Children would have many fewer after-school programs or summer camps to attend, and would have become latchkey children, at risk of truancy and juvenile delinquency. Residents of the city would not attend religious worship services on weekends; instead, many would be indulging in television watching and being isolated in their own homes or in malls. We could continue with this scenario, although the picture is clear. Life without religious congregations and their collective contribution to the quality of life would mean either a major burden on the public sector or major deterioration in the quality of life in the city of Philadelphia. Much more study is needed before the full story of congregations in urban America can be fully understood. But the Philadelphia story is a major step along the way.

In the context of the faith-based initiatives, congregations and other faith-based organizations unwittingly have become key players in the public debates. It is evident that the capacity for enhanced social service production is there and the know-how can be easily obtained. Whether it is good for the congregations, the clients, and the government is a different question. It is our belief that if wisely done, and if the public resources were available, those congregations and other faith-based organizations could further enhance the quality of life of Americans. However, to use congregations as an excuse for further cutting public welfare expenditure would be a tragedy. The simplest course of action would be to celebrate congregations' many contributions to social welfare and let them be. The wisest, but very complicated, course of action would be to collaborate with them in increasing care for the needy and indigent.

Appendix: Methods

In this study of Philadelphia congregations and their social services, we used the following methods: in-depth interviews with clergy and lay leaders, structured surveys, and document analysis. When we began this study, we discovered that there was no comprehensive list of Philadelphia congregations from which to draw our sample of congregations. While no one knows the exact number of congregations in the United States, estimates range from a low of 200,000 to a high of 450,000. According to the *Yearbook of American and Canadian Churches*, there were 396,000 congregations in the United States in1992 (Bedell and Jones, 1993).

After three years of study, we estimate the number of congregations in Philadelphia to be approximately 2120. The term *congregation*, as used here, includes all organized faith-based groups, whether church, synagogue, mosque, temple, ashram, or other. To develop a working list of congregations, we originally merged two data files: the City of Philadelphia Property Tax list and the Yellow Pages list of congregations. In order to identify the unlisted congregations, we applied three methods. First, we requested lists from every denomination and interfaith organization in the region. We received about fifteen different lists. We merged these with our master file manually since congregations often use various names and may give more than one address or list the clergy residence, for example. Second, in every interview, we asked clergy members or key informants to identify congregations with which they collaborate along with their telephone numbers and addresses. Given that the interviewers were paid per completed interview, they had an incentive to identify new congregations and add them to the master list. We also enlisted the assistance of our advisory board, which is composed of religious leaders throughout the city. Advisory board members reviewed the list and supplied missing congregations that are part of their groups or known to them. Finally, our research interviewers traveled block-by-block through neighborhoods to identify possibly unlisted storefront churches and other congregations not on our master file. We canvassed every block of the city and discovered many storefront congregations, especially ethnic and minority ones that were unlisted. This combination of the approaches brought us closer to a complete master list.

INSTRUMENTS

We used three research instruments. The first part of the interview (the General Form) gathered background information about the congregation, its history, membership, financial information, staff, governing structure, and relations with the wider community. The second part (the Inventory of Programs) compiled information about the congregation's social services. The interviewers covered 215 areas of possible social and community involvement, with numerous follow-up questions concerning the formal or informal nature of the program, where it was provided, and so on. We asked respondents to identify those services that had been offered in the past twelve months and to omit any that were no longer available. We used a twelve-month time frame to ensure that seasonal programs such as summer camps and heating assistance programs would be included and that responses would reflect the current social program agenda of the congregation.

The third part of the interview (the Specific Program Form) was used to gather information about the most important social programs provided by the congregation, up to a maximum of five programs. With regard to these five programs, the interviewee was asked detailed questions about the program's history, legal status, staffing, who benefits, how many times a week/month/year it is offered, cost to the congregation, and much more. Due to the length of interviewing time, congregations with more than five social programs were asked to choose only the five "most representative of their work." We asked respondents to start with those programs that have budgets and paid staff.

DATA COLLECTION

We spent 3–10 hours in each of the 1,392 congregations we studied. The questions we used were prepared and piloted. Many of the questions were close-ended, but others were open-ended and the responses were verified with documentation provided by the congregations. The interviews and collection of congregation documents were performed by a group of (20–30) well-trained interviewers. A face-to-face interview was selected not only to increase the response rate but also to assist interviewees with confusing questions, to probe when necessary, and to make use of additional information that can be observed while visiting the congregation.

All interviewers received both a lengthy orientation and weekly group in-service training that included the history and an overview of the study, its benefit to the congregations and broader community, ways to use and disseminate data, and an introduction to the survey instruments. Each interviewer was also given a training manual documenting the information outlined above with specifications and clarification for the survey instruments. For more in-depth training, interviewers observed an interview conducted by a trained researcher followed by a question and answer session. The interviewers were closely supervised and observed for the first three interviews and provided with feedback after each session. Interviewers received ongoing training and supervision through weekly meetings where questions were answered and the survey instrument was routinely reviewed. This training and supervision was to ensure that interviewers were familiar with the survey instrument, understood the intent of questions, learned to phrase questions properly, recorded responses accurately and completely, learned to probe interviewees for more complete responses, and addressed issues of confidentiality. Interviewers were also trained to be sensitive to the religious customs and language of the particular congregation being interviewed.

We interviewed one key informant in most congregations. One can ask whether a clergy or key lay leader will not be biased in his or her responses. In a previous study we interviewed one clergyperson and one lay leader; if there was a discrepancy between them, a third leader was to be interviewed. In only one of 50 cases was there a discrepancy. Furthermore, one of our interviewers mistakenly interviewed a clergyperson and four lay leaders for 11 congregations. The level of compatibility between these respondents was very high and it became clear that clergy or lay leaders can provide accurate data regarding the congregation. Similarly, McPherson and Rotolo (1995) measured four different characteristics (size, sex composition, age composition, and educational composition) by three different methods (reports from group official, reports from a randomly chosen respondent to a survey, and direct observation of a group meeting). They found very high correlations (between .8 and .9) among all three logged measures of size and sex composition, and only slightly smaller correlations between the leader report and direct observation for age and educational composition (.73 and .77 respectively). They conclude that, for these four variables, "reports from an officer are just as reliable as direct-canvass measures and could reasonably be substituted for the latter" (McPherson and Rotolo 1995: 1114).

Notes

Chapter 1. "Here Is the Church, Here Is the Steeple": Defining and Measuring Religious Congregations

1. The Personal Responsibility and Work Opportunity Reconciliation Act of 1996 contains Section 104, also known as Charitable Choice. This section encourages states to involve community and religious-based organizations in providing federally funded welfare services. Most human service professionals and scholars are unfamiliar with this part of the legislation and its far-reaching implications for society as a whole, and for the human service administration as it opens the door for mixing religion and publicly supported social services provision (see Cnaan and Boddie 2001).

2. It should be noted that there were earlier nonnative religious endeavors in America, though they had minimal influence on the future religious landscape of the United States. For example, Virginia was settled by the English in 1607, and the Virginia colony had Anglican Christianity and clergy (sporadically). Furthermore, the Spaniards were in America from 1492, and there were Catholic churches in America a century before the English came, many in what is now the United States (Florida, California, Louisiana, and New Mexico). However, in the colonial period and the first half-century of independence these territories were not part of the United States, nor were they influential decades later.

3. It is known that there are many such groups in the United States (Berger, Leach, and Shaffer 2003), but we failed to find or access such groups in Philadelphia. We were offered access to such groups in the surrounding counties, but our focus was on Philadelphia alone and hence we declined these invitations.

Chapter 5. Formal Care: Congregations as Social Service Agencies

1. The value of volunteer time is based on the average hourly earnings of all production and nonsupervisory workers on private non-farm payrolls (as determined by the Bureau of Labor Statistics). Independent Sector takes this figure and increases it by 12 percent to estimate for fringe benefits (Brown 1999; Independent Sector 2003).

2. A few congregations reported fiscal support and value of support in tens of thousands which are true outliers. To correct for these outliers, we set a maximum value (ceiling) acceptable and lowered all such reporting to a reasonable level. For congregational support and value of space, we limited the maximum monthly to $5,000, even though some programs were reported to be valued or cost more. Clergy and staff hours were truncated at 250 hours monthly. Finally, value of in-kind support and estimated cost of utilities was again truncated at $5,000 each. Second, in the case of clergy hours, staff hours, and volunteer

hours, the original values were multiplied by their hourly dollar value: $20 for a clergy hour, $17.19 for a volunteer hour, and $10 for a staff hour.

Chapter 7. Black Congregations in the City of Brotherly Love

1. Throughout this chapter, the term "black" and "African American" are used interchangeably. Although not all black people in the United States are African American, and members of the former group are usually not descendants of slaves, for the purpose of this study we do not distinguish these terms unless otherwise mentioned.

2. We are aware that not all black congregations are Christian. In this census we identified four black mosques, three congregations of African religions, and two non-Christian congregations that are religiously independent. But the overwhelming majority of black congregations, as discussed below, are Christian.

Chapter 8. Latino Congregations in the Twenty-First Century

1. The authors wish to thank Michele Belliveau for sharing her dissertation in progress and generously allowing us to use it in our literature review for this chapter. We would also like to express our thanks to the Rev. Luis Cortez, who served on our advisory board, helped us identify missing congregations, and provided letters of introduction to the Latino community. Our real breakthrough in contacting and interviewing Latino congregations came when we hired four Latino interviewers some of whom are local clergy and who managed to access so many of the otherwise hard-to-reach smaller Latino congregations. We want especially to thank: Ana Marixa Rios-Orlandi, Carmen and Miguel A. Diaz, and Evelyn Echevarria.

2. Based on Oboler (1995), we use the terms "Latino" and "Hispanic" interchangeably. While no term captures the full dimensions of this population, these are the most commonly used. The Hispanic/Latino group was constructed for census purposes by a federal order on May 4, 1978 that stated that a Latino person is "a person of Mexican, Puerto Rican, Cuban, Central or South American or other Spanish culture or origin, regardless of race" (Office of Management and Budget 1978: 19269).

3. For purposes of this study, we defined a Latino congregation as one whose membership was at least 51 percent Latino or whose name was reported solely or also in Spanish. We validated the latter group with members of the Latino clergy and obtained a list of 148 Latino congregations.

4. The averages of 3.12 programs for non-Latino congregations and 2.56 programs for Latino congregation must be considered an undercount because we did not collect data on more than five programs per congregation. The reason was that we did not wish to overtax the patience of respondents who were kind enough to submit to what was already a complex and time-consuming survey.

Chapter 10. Interfaith Coalitions: The Story of the Northwest Interfaith Movement

1. While there are differences between coalitions and alliances (the former is often comprised of actively sharing members the latter of an outside organization maintaining relationships to all member groups but independent of them), here we treat them interchangeably. In the congregational world we discuss all

types of umbrella organizations that are "above" congregations and in which the congregations are members. By the terms religious "coalitions" and "alliances" we do not include social movements where religion was a catalyst to impact activists (Smith 1996). We also do not focus on national coalitions but on local attempts to improve quality of life or eradicate local injustice.

2. We define religiosity of a social services organization as explicitness in religious beliefs in its services, and take such a definition from recent work by Sider and Unruh (2002) and Ebaugh and Pipes (2003).

3. In 1992, a local affiliate of the Industrial Areas Foundation was organized, Philadelphia Interfaith Action (PIA). This type of organization typically charges member congregations annual fees, which pay the salary of a small staff of community organizers. Although we did not study PIA, we can report that this organization helped force the city of Philadelphia to support vocational training programs and a neighborhood blight initiative. In recent years PIA has been relatively inactive.

Chapter 11. Using Congregational Capacity to Help the Homeless: The NPIHN Story

1. Host Congregations include the following: Chestnut Hill Friends Meeting, First Presbyterian Church in Germantown, First United Methodist Church in Germantown (FUMCOG), Germantown Community Presbyterian Church, Germantown Jewish Centre, Germantown Mennonite Church, Mishkan Shalom, New Covenant Church, Oak Lane Presbyterian Church, St. Paul's Episcopal Church, Second Baptist Church of Germantown, and Unitarian Society of Germantown. Additionally, 11 other congregations serve as co-host congregations and provide volunteers, food, and fiscal support. These congregations support the host congregations on a regular basis. Five other congregations provide material support when needed. Two theological seminaries, Lutheran Theological Seminary and the Reconstructionist Rabbinical College are also regularly assisting NPIHN.

2. These are Christ Church and St. Michaels, First Presbyterian Church in Springfield (Flourtown), Janes Memorial United Methodist Church, Our Mother of Consolation, Unitarian Universalist Church of the Restoration, Germantown Mennonite Church, Reformation Lutheran Church, Mt. Airy Presbyterian Church, and New Covenant Presbyterian Church.

3. Under a new director, it is undergoing different forms of professionalization and adopting a more implicit religiosity in its culture and managerial practices. As a network of congregations, NPIHN has obtained resources adequately in the past, but it is being restructured to enlist more congregational involvement and raise more funds, changing its field of ties to outside organizations for partnerships and funding. Despite shifting priorities in its strategic plan, NPIHN intends to maintain its dependence on volunteers.

References

Adams, C., D. E. Bartelt, D. Elesh, I. Goldstein, N. Kleniewski, and W. Yancey (1991). *Philadelphia: Neighborhoods, Division, and Conflict in a Postindustrial City.* Philadelphia: Temple University Press.

Alba, R. and V. Nee (1997). Rethinking assimilation theory for a new era of immigration. *International Migration Review* 31: 826–74.

Alinsky, S. D. (1972) *Rules for Radicals: A Practical Primer for Realistic Radicals.* New York: Vintage Books.

American Association of Pastoral Counselors (2003). *About Pastoral Counseling.* Retrieved September 25, 2003 from http://www.aapc.org/about.htm

Ammerman, N. T. (1997a). *Congregation and Community.* New Brunswick, N.J.: Rutgers University Press.

——— (1997b). Organized religion in a voluntaristic society. *Sociology of Religion* 58: 203–15.

Applied Research Center (2002). *Mapping the Immigrant Infrastructure: An Executive Summary.* Oakland, Calif.: Applied Research Center. Retrieved October, 14, 2002 from http://www.arc.org/Pages/pubs/mapping2002.html.

Argyle, M. (1958). *Religious Behaviour.* London: Routledge and Kegan Paul.

Ashley, B. (1996). *Justice in the Church: Gender and Participation.* Washington, D.C.: Catholic University of America Press.

Ashley, B. (1996). *Justice in the Church: Gender and Participation.* Washington, D.C.: Catholic University of America Press.

Badillo, D. (2004). Mexican and suburban parish communities: Religion, space, and identity in contemporary Chicago. *Journal of Urban History* 31: 23–46.

Baer, H. A. and M. Singer (1992). *African-American Religion in the Twentieth Century.* Nashville: University of Tennessee Press.

Bane, M. J., B. Coffin, and R. Higgins (2005). *Taking Faith Seriously.* Cambridge, Mass.: Harvard University Press.

Banks, E. (1997). The social capital of self-help mutual aid groups. *Social Policy* 28: 30–39.

Barfoot, C. H. and G. T. Sheppard (1980). Prophetic vs. priestly religion: The changing role of women clergy in classical Pentecostal churches. *Review of Religious Research* 22: 2–17.

Barringer, B. R. and J. S. Harrison (2000). Walking a tightrope: Creating value through interorganizational relationships. *Journal of Management* 26: 367–403.

Barna Research Group (2000). *Church Attending.* Ventura, Calif.: Barna Research Group.

Bartelt, D. W. (2001). *Latino Philadelphia: A Report to the Latino Workforce Development Taskforce, Executive Summary.* Philadelphia: Latino Workforce Development Taskforce.

Bartkowski, J. P. and H. A. Regis (1999). *"Charitable Choice" and the Feasibility of*

Faith-Based Welfare Reform in Mississippi. Report submitted to the Joint Center for Poverty Research, University of Chicago and Northwestern University. Also available at http://www.jcpr.org/wp/wpprofile.cfm?id = 98

Bates, R., J. Archibald, and S. Wills (2001). *Improving Outcomes for Children and Families of Incarcerated Parents.* Chicago: University of Illinois at Chicago, Jane Addams School of Social Work, Center for Social Policy and Research and Chicago Legal Aid to Incarcerated Mothers.

Bean, F. D., R. Corona, R. Tuiran, K. A. Woodrow-Lafield, and J. Van Hook (2001). Circular, invisible, and ambiguous migrants: Components of difference in estimates of the number of unauthorized Mexican migrants in the United States. *Demography* 38: 411–22.

Bean, F. D. and M. Tienda (1987). *The Hispanic Population of the United States.* New York: Russell Sage Foundation.

Beatty, C. (1997). *Parents in Prison: Children in Crisis.* Washington, D.C.: Child Welfare League of America.

Becker, P. E. (1998). Congregational models and conflict: A study of how institutions shape organizational process. In N. J. Demerath, III, P. D. Hall, T. Schmitt, and R. H. Williams, eds., *Sacred Companies: Organizational Aspects of Religion and Religious Aspects of organizations.* New York: Oxford University Press. 231–55.

Bedell, K. B. and A. M. Jones, eds. (1993). *Yearbook of Americans and Canadian Churches.* Nashville, Tenn.: Abingdon.

Beit-Hallahmi, B. and M. Argyle (1997). *Religious behavior, belief and experience.* New York: Routledge.

Belleville, L. (2000). *Women Leaders and the Church: Three Crucial Questions.* Grand Rapids, Mich.: Baker Books.

Berger, H. A., E. A. Leach, and L. S. Shaffer (2003). *Voices from the Pagan Census: A National Survey of Witches and Neo-Pagans in the United States.* Columbia: University of South Carolina Press.

Berger, P. L. (1967). *The Sacred Canopy: Elements of Sociological Theory of Religion.* Garden City, N.Y.: Doubleday.

Berger, P. L. and R. J. Neuhaus (1977). *To Empower People: The Role of Mediating Structures in Public Policy.* Washington, D.C.: American Enterprise Institute for Public Policy Research.

Berrien, J. and C. Winship (1999). *Should We Have Faith in the Churches? Ten-Point Coalition's Effect on Boston's Youth Violence.* Philadelphia: Public/Private Venture.

Biddell, J. E. (1992). Religious organizations. In C. T. Clotfelter, ed., *Who Benefits from the Nonprofit Sector?* Chicago: University of Chicago Press. 92–133.

Billings, D. (1990). Religion as opposition: A Gramscian analysis. *American Journal of Sociology* 96: 1–31.

Billingsley, A., and C. Caldwell (1991). The church, the family, and the symbol in the African American community. *Journal of Negro Education* 60: 427–40.

Black, A. E., D. L. Koopman, and D. K. Ryden (2004). *Of Little Faith: The Politics of George W. Bush's Faith-Based Initiatives.* Washington, D.C.: Georgetown University Press.

Blumenstein, A. and A. J. Beck (1999). Population growth in U.S. prisons, 1980–1996. In M. Tonry and J. Petersilia, eds., *Prisons.* Chicago: University of Chicago Press. 7–61.

Boddie, S. C. (2002). One more river to cross: African-American congregations at the dawn of a new millennium. Doctoral dissertation, University of Pennsylvania.

———— (2003). Faith-based organizations and the sharing of social responsibility: Comparing the community programs of African American, interracial, and White congregations. *Social Development Issues* 25: 205–18.

Boissevain, J. (1974). *Friends of Friends: Networks, Manipulators, and Coalitions.* New York: St. Martin's.

Bosniak, L. S. (1998). Undocumented immigrants and the national imagination. In R. Delgado and J. Stefancic, eds., *The Latino/a Condition: A Critical Reader.* New York: New York University Press. 99–105.

Botchwey, N. D. S. (2003). Taxonomy of religious and secular nonprofit organizations: Knowledge development and policy recommendations for neighborhood revitalization. Ph.D. dissertation, University of Pennsylvania, Department of City and Regional Planning.

Brown, B. (2005). *Los Angeles Metropolitan Churches Organizational Profile.* Seattle: BTW Consultants.

Brown, E. (1999). Assessing the value of volunteer activity. *Nonprofit and Voluntary Sector Quarterly* 28: 3–17.

Brown, F. and J. M. Ferris (2004). Social capital and philanthropy. Paper presented at the annual meeting of the International Society for Third Sector Research, Toronto, July.

Brown, G. (2001). *The Consent of the Governed: The Lockean Legacy in Early American Culture.* Cambridge, Mass.: Harvard University Press.

Bruce, D. A. (2002). U.S. Congregational Life Survey: What did we learn about congregations? Paper presented at the annual meeting of the Society for the Scientific Study of Religion, Salt Lake City, October. Also available at http://www.uscongregations.org/SSSR2002-Congregations.pdf

Byrd, M. (1997). Determining frames of reference for religiously-based organizations: A case study of Neo-Alinsky efforts to mobilize congregational resources. *Nonprofit and Voluntary Sector Quarterly* 26 Supplement: S122–S138.

Caldwell, C., A. D. Greene, and A. Billingsley (1992). The Black church as a family support system: Instrumental and expressive functions. *National Journal of Sociology* 6, 11: 21–46.

Canda, E. R. (1997). Spirituality. In R. L. Edwards, ed., *Encyclopedia of Social Work* Supplement. 19th ed. Washington, D.C.: National Association of Social Workers Press. 299–308.

Carey, P. (1978). The laity's understanding of the trustee system, 1785–1855. *Catholic Historical Review* 64: 357–76.

Carlton-LaNay, I. (1999). African-American social work pioneers' response to need. *Social Work* 44: 531–38.

Carpenter, D. C. (1987). The professionalization of the ministry of women. *Journal of Religious Thought* 43: 59–75.

Carroll, J. W. (1991). *As One with Authority: Reflective Leadership in Ministry.* Lexington, Ky.: Westminster John Knox.

Carroll, J. W., B. Hargrove, and A. T. Lummis (1983). *Women of the Cloth: A New Opportunity for the Churches.* New York: Harper and Row.

Castex, G. M. (1978). Providing services to Hispanic/Latino populations: Profiles in diversity. *Social Work* 39: 288–96.

Cavendish, J. (2000). Church-based community activism: A comparison of Black and White Catholic congregations. *Journal for the Scientific Study of Religion* 39: 371–84.

Cerrutti, M., and D. S. Massey (2001). On the auspices of female migration from Mexico to the United States. *Demography* 38: 187–200.

Chambre, S. (2001). The changing nature of "faith" in faith-based organizations: Secularization and ecumenicism in four AIDS organizations in New York City. *Social Service Review* 75: 435–55.

Chaves, M. (1997). Recent changes in women's ordination conflicts: The effects of social movement on intraorganizational controversy. *Journal for the Scientific Study of Religion* 36: 574–83.

Chaves, M. (1999). Religious congregations and welfare reform: Who will take advantage of "Charitable Choice." *American Sociological Review* 64: 836–46.

Chaves, M. (2004). *Congregations in America.* Cambridge, Mass.: Harvard University Press.

Chaves, M., H. M. Giesel, and W. Tsitsos (2002). Religious variations in public presence: Evidence from the National Congregation Study. In R. Wuthnow and J. H. Evans, eds., *The Quiet Hand of God: Faith-Based Activism and the Public Role of Mainline Protestantism.* Berkeley: University of California Press. 1–28.

Chaves, M. and L. M. Higgins (1992). Comparing the community involvement of Black and White congregations. *Journal for the Scientific Study of Religion* 31: 425–40.

Chaves, M., M. E. Konieczny, K. Beyerlein, and E. Barman (1999). The National Congregations Study: Background, methods, and selected results. *Journal for the Scientific Study of Religion* 38: 458–76.

Chaves, M. and S. L. Miller (1999). *Financing American Religion.* Walnut Creek, Calif.: AltaMira.

Chaves, M. and W. Tistsos (2001). Congregations and social services: What they do, how they do it, and with whom. *Nonprofit and Voluntary Sector Quarterly* 30: 660–83.

Chazanov, M. (1991). Mosque has a U.S. flavor. *Los Angeles Times*, 25 January, B1.

Cheever, K. A. L. (2001). Civil rights and the church: The challenge to end religious discrimination while furthering religious values. Paper presented at the 30th ARNOVA (Association for Research on Nonprofit Organizations and Voluntary Action) Conference, Miami, November 28–December 1.

Cherbo, J. M. and M. J. Wyszomirski (2001). *The Public Life of the Arts in America.* Washington, D.C.: Americans for the Arts.

Christiano, K. J., W. H. Swatos, and P. Kivisto (2002). *Sociology of Religion: Contemporary Developments.* Walnut Creek, Calif.: AltaMira.

Cimino, R. and D. Lattin (1998). *Shopping for Faith: American Religion in the New Millennium.* San Francisco: Jossey Bass.

City of Philadelphia Department of Public Health (2002). List of scheduled 2002 clinics. Retrieved February 25, 2003 from http://www.phila.gov/health/units/ddc/fluschd02.pdf

City of Philadelphia Division of Social Services (2002). Children Investment Strategy: Beacons/after-school programs lists. Retrieved February 25, 2003 from http://philasafesound.org/redesign3/as_bcacons1.html#bc

Clarkson, E. (1997). *Promise Keepers' March Motivated by Fundamentalist Beliefs.* Madison, Wis.: Progressive Media project. Also available from http://www.publiceye.org/theocrat/FC_prom.html

Clerkin, R. and K. Grønbjerg (2003). The role of congregations in delivering human services. Paper presented at the Independent Sector Spring Research Forum, Washington, D.C., March.

Cnaan, R. A. (1991). Neighborhood representing organizations: How democratic are they? *Social Service Review* 65: 614–34.

Cnaan, R. A. and S. C. Boddie (2000). *Keeping Faith in the City II: How 887 Philadel-*

phia Congregations Serve Their Needy Neighbors Including the Children and Families of Prisoners. Philadelphia: Center for Research on Religion and Urban Civil Society, University of Pennsylvania.

—— (2001). Philadelphia census of congregations and their involvement in social service delivery. *Social Service Review* 75: 559–80.

—— (2002). Charitable choice and faith-based welfare: A call for social work. *Social Work* 47: 247–35.

Cnaan, R. A., with S. C. Boddie, F. Handy, G. Yancey, and R. Schneider (2002). *The Invisible Caring Hand: American Congregations and the Provision of Welfare.* New York: New York University Press.

Cnaan, R. A., with R. J. Wineburg and S. C. Boddie (1999). *The Newer Deal: Social Work and Religion in Partnership.* New York: Columbia University Press.

Cnaan, R. A., S. C. Boddie, and G. Yancey (2005). Partners rebuilding the cities: Faith-based community organizing. In Marie Weil , ed., *Handbook of community practice* (372–386). Thousand Oaks, Calif.: Sage.

Cnaan, R. A., and F. Handy (2000). Comparing neighbors: Social service provision by religious congregations in Ontario and the U.S.A. *American Review of Canadian Studies* 30: 521–43.

Cnaan, R. A., Y. Hasenfeld, A. Cnaan, and J. Rafferty (1993). Cross-cultural comparison of attitudes toward welfare state programs: Path analysis with log-linear models. *Social Indicators Research* 28: 21–50.

Cnaan, R. A., and A. L. Helzer (2004). Women in congregations and social service provision: Findings from the Philadelphia census. *Social Thought* 23, 3: 25–43.

Cnaan, R. A., and C. Milofsky (1997) Small religious nonprofits—a neglected topic. *Nonprofit and Voluntary Sector Quarterly* 25: S3–S13.

Cnaan, R. A. with J. W. Sinha (2002). *A Preliminary Investigation of a Most Urgent Social Issue: The Faith based Community and Ex-Prisoners' Reentry.* Submitted to Annie E. Casey Foundation.

Cnaan, R. A. with J. W. Sinha (2004). *Back into the Fold: Helping Ex-Prisoners Reconnect Through Faith.* Baltimore: Annie E. Casey Foundation.

Coleman, J. S. (1990). *Foundations of Social Theory.* Cambridge, Mass.: Harvard University Press.

Committee of 70 (2000). Your friendly neighborhood polling places. Retrieved February 25, 2003 from http://www.seventy.org/news/pollingplaces.html

Davis, W. L. (1987–88). Men and the church: What keeps them out and what brings them in. *Journal of the Academy for Evangelism in Theological Education* 3: 46–61.

Day, K. (2001). Putting it together in the African-American churches: Faith, economic development, and civil rights. In P. D. Nesbitt, ed., *Religion and Social Policy* (pp. 181–195). Walnut Creek, Calif.: AltaMira.

DeHaven, M. J., I. B. Hunter, L. Wilder, J. W. Walton, and J. Berry (2004). Health programs in faith-based organizations: Are they effective? *American Journal of Public Health* 94: 1030–36.

de Vaus, D. and I. McAllister (1987). Gender differences in religion: A test of the structural location theory. *American Sociological Review* 52: 472–81.

De La Rosa, M. R. (2000). An analysis of Latino poverty and a plan of action. *Journal of Poverty* 4, 1–2: 27–62.

DePriest, T. and J. Jones (1997). Economic deliverance thru the church. *Black Enterprise,* February, 195–97.

Diaz-Stevens, A. M. and A. M. Stevens-Arroyo (1998). *Recognizing the Latino Resurgence in U.S. Religion: The Emmaus Paradigm.* Boulder, Colo.: Westview.

Dignan, P. J. (1933; 1974). *A History of the Legal Incorporation of Catholic Church Property in the United States (1784–1932)*. Washington, D.C.: Catholic University of America.

DiMaggio, P. and W. Powell (1983). The iron cage revisited: Institutional isomorphism and collective rationality in organizational fields. *American Journal of Sociology* 48: 47–160.

Dionne, E. J., Jr. and J. J. DiIulio, Jr. (2000). *What's God Got to Do with the American Experiment?* Washington, D.C.: Brookings Institution Press.

Dluhy, M. J. (1981). *Social Change: Accessing and Influencing the Policy Development Process at the State and Local Levels*. Washington, D.C.: U.S. Department of Health and Human Services, Youth Development Bureau.

———. (1990). *Building Coalitions in the Human Services*. Newbury Park, Calif.: Sage.

Dolan, J. (1985). *The American Catholic Experience*. Garden City, N.Y.: Doubleday.

Du Bois, W. E. B. (1899; 1995). *The Philadelphia Negro: A Social Study*. Philadelphia: University of Pennsylvania Press.

Dudley, C. S. and D. Roozen (2001). *Faith Communities Today: A Report on Religion in the United States Today*. Hartford, Conn.: Hartford Seminary. Retrieved May 10, 2005 from http://fact.hartsem.edu/Final%20FACTrpt.pdf

Dudley, C. S. and T. Van Eck (1992). Social ideology and community ministries: Implications from church membership surveys. In K. B. Bedwill and A. M. Jones, eds., *Yearbook of American and Canadian Churches*. Nashville, Tenn.: Abingdon Press. 5–11.

Ebaugh, H. R. and J. S. Chafetz (2000). *Religions and the New Immigrants: Continuities and Adaptations in Immigrant Congregations*. Walnut Creek, Calif.: AltaMira.

Ebaugh, H. R. and P. F. Pipes (2001). Immigrant congregations as social service providers: Are they safety nets for welfare reform? In P. D. Nesbitt, ed., *Religion and Social Policy*. Walnut Creek, Calif.: AltaMira. 95–110.

Ebaugh, H. R., P. F. Pipes, J. S. Chafetz., and M. Daniels (2003). Where's the religion: Distinguishing faith-based from secular social service agencies. *Journal for the Scientific Study of Religion* 42: 411–26.

Eck, D. and D. Jain (1987). *Speaking of Faith: Global Perspective on Women, Religion, and Social Change*. Philadelphia: New Society Publishers.

Economist (1995). The counter-attack of God. *Economist*, July 8, 19–21.

Elazar, D. J. (1983). Decision-making in the American Jewish community. In S. Marshall, ed., *American Jews: A Reader*. New York: Behrman House. 201–42.

Ellis, A. (2000). Can rational emotive behavior therapy be effectively used with people who have devout beliefs in God and religion? *Professional Psychology, Research and Practice* 3: 29–33.

Ellison, C. G. (1995). Rational choice explanations of individual religious behavior: Notes on the problem of social embeddedness. *Journal for the Scientific Study of Religion* 34: 89–98.

Ellison, C. G. and L. George (1994). Religious involvement, social ties, and social support in Southeastern community. *Journal for the Scientific Study of Religion* 33: 46–61.

Ellison, C. G. and D. E. Sherkat (1995). The "semi-involuntary institution" revisited: Regional variations in church participation among Black Americans. *Social Forces* 73: 1415–37.

Ethridge, F. M. (1989). Under-reported churches in middle Tennessee: A research note. *Journal for the Scientific Study of Religion* 28: 518–29.

Espinosa, G., V. Elizondo, and J. Miranda (2003). *Hispanic Churches in American*

Public Life: Summary of Findings. Interim report 2003–2, Institute of Latino Studies, Notre Dame University.

Fantasia, R. (1988). *Cultures of Solidarity.* Berkeley: University of California Press.

Farley, C. (2004). *Amachi Year Longitudinal Report, April 1, 2001–March 31, 2003.* Philadelphia: PPV. Retrieved January 20, 2006 from http://www.ppv.org/ppv/publications/assets/167_publication.pdf

Farnsley, A. E., II (2003). *Rising Expectations: Urban Congregations, Welfare Reform, and Civic Life.* Bloomington: Indiana University Press.

Finkel, K. (1995). *Philadelphia Almanac and Citizen's Manual 1995.* Philadelphia: Library Company of Philadelphia.

Fitzgerald, S. (2002). A troubling glimpse into city youths' lives. *Philadelphia Inquirer,* June 20, B4.

Fix, M. E. and J. S. Passel (1994). Setting the record straight: What are the costs to the public? *Public Welfare* 52, 2: 6–15.

Fix, M., W. Zimmerman, and J. S. Passel (2001). *The Integration of Immigrant Families in the United States.* Washington, D.C.: Urban Institute.

Fortune, M. M. and J. N. Poling (1994). *Sexual Abuse by Clergy: A Crisis for the Church.* Decatur, Ga.: Journal of Pastoral Care Monographs.

Francis, L. J. and M. Robbins (1999). *The Long Diaconate, 1987–1994: Women Deacons and the Delayed Journey to Priesthood.* Chippenham, Wiltshire: Anthony Rowe.

Franklin, R. M. (1997). *Another Day's Journey: Black Churches Confronting the American Crisis.* Minneapolis: Fortress Press.

Frazier, E. L. (1964). *The Negro Church in America.* New York: Schocken.

Frederick, M. F. (2003). *Between Sundays: Black Women and Everyday Struggles of Faith.* Berkeley: University of California Press.

Freedman, S. G. (1993). *Upon This rock: The Miracles of a Black Church.* New York: HarperCollins.

Freud, S. (1920). *Totem und Tabu: Einige Übereinstimmungen im Seelenleben der Wilden und der Neurotiker.* Leipzig: Internationaler psychoanalyscher Verlag.

——— (1928). *The Future of an Illusion.* Trans. W. D. Robson-Scott. New York: Liveright.

Fried, S. (2002). *The New Rabbi.* New York: Bantam Books.

Fry, R. (2002). Latinos in higher education: Many enroll, too few graduate. Washington, D.C.: Pew Hispanic Center. Retrieved December 2 from http://pewhispanic.org/files/reports/11.pdf

Fuechtmann, T. G. (1989). *Steeples and Stacks: Religion and the Steel Crisis in Youngstown.* New York: Cambridge University Press.

Gabel, K. and D. Johnston, eds. (1995). *Children of Incarcerated Parents.* New York: Lexington Books.

Galea, S. G., J. Ahern, H. Resnick, D. Kilpatrick, M. Bucuvalas, J. Gold, and D. Vlahov (2002). Psychological sequelae of the September 11 terrorist attacks in New York City. *New England Journal of Medicine* 346: 982–87.

Gallup, G., Jr. (2001). *Americans More Religious Now Than Ten Years Ago But Less so Than in 1950s and 1960s.* Retrieved January 21, 2003 from http://www.gallup.com/poll/releases/pr010329.asp

Gallup, G., Jr., and D. M. Lindsay (1999). *Surveying the Religious Landscape.* Harrisburg, Pa.: Morehouse.

Gamm, G. (1999). *Urban Exodus: Why the Jews Left Boston and the Catholics Stayed.* Cambridge, Mass.: Harvard University Press.

Garland, D. R. (1997). Church social work. *Social Work and Christianity* 24, 2: 94–114.

Gaustad, S. G. and L. E. Schmidt (2002). *The Religious History of America.* San Francisco: HarperCollins.

Geary, D. C. (1998). *Male, Female: The Evolution of Human Sex Differences.* Washington, D.C.: American Psychological Association.

Gibson, P. A. (2004). Religious expressions of African American grandmother caregivers: Social work's role with church communities. *Arete* 28: 21–37.

Glenmary Research Center (2002). *Religious Congregations and Membership in the United States, 2000.* Cincinnati: Glenmary Research Center.

Gough, D. M. (1995). *Christ Church, Philadelphia: The Nation's Church in a Changing City.* Philadelphia: University of Pennsylvania Press.

Goggin, M. L. and D. A. Orth (2002). *How Faith-Based and Secular Organizations Tackle Housing for the Homeless.* Albany: Roundtable on Religion and Social Welfare Policy, Nelson Rockefeller Institute of Government, State University of New York.

Goode, J. (1990). A wary welcome to the neighborhood: Community responses to immigrants. *Urban Anthropology* 19: 125–53.

Greeley, A. (1972). *The Denominational society.* Glenview, Ill.: Scott, Foresman.

——— (1998). Defections among Hispanics. *America* 177, 8: 12–15.

Green, J. C. and A. Sherman (2002). *Faithful Collaborations: A survey of Government Funded Faith-Based Programs in 15 States.* Washington, D.C.: Hudson Institute.

Grettenberger, S. and P. Hovmand (1997). The role of churches in human services: United Methodist Churches in Michigan. Paper presented at the 26th annual meeting of the Association for Research on Nonprofit Organizations and Voluntary Action, Indianapolis, December.

Griffin, S. P. (2003). *Philadelphia's Black Mafia: A Social and Political History.* Boston: Kluwer Academic.

Haddad, Y. Y. and A. T. Lummis (1987). *Islamic Values in the United States: A Comparative Study.* New York: Oxford University Press.

Hall, D. (1998). Managing to recruit: Religious conversion in the workplace. *Sociology of Religion* 59: 393–410.

Hall, P. D. (1998). *Voluntary Associations, Nonprofit Organizations, and Religious Entities: Associational Populations and Ecologies in New Haven, Connecticut, 1850–1990.* New Haven, Conn.: Yale University Program of Nonprofit Organizations.

Hallman, D. (1987). The success of a citizens' coalition in social intervention. In E. M. Bennett, ed., *Social Intervention, Theory and Practice.* Studies in Health and Human Services 11. Lewiston, N.Y.: Edwin Mellen Press. 187–229.

Hardin, G. (1968). The tragedy of the commons. *Science* 162: 1243–48.

——— (2003). The tragedy of the commons. In D. R. Henderson, ed., *The Concise Encyclopedia of Economics.* Retrieved February 22, 2003 from http://www.econlib.org/library/Enc/TragedyoftheCommons.html

Harris, F. C. (1994). Something within: Religion as mobilizer of African-American political activism. *Journal of Politics* 56: 42–68.

Harris, M. (1995). Quiet care: Welfare work and religious congregations. *Journal of Social Policy* 24: 53–71.

——— (1998a). A special case of voluntary associations? Towards a theory of congregational organization. *British Journal of Sociology* 49: 602–618.

——— (1998b). *Organizing God's work: Challenges for Churches and Synagogues.* New York: St. Martin's.

Hariston, C. F. (1998). The forgotten parent: Understanding the forces that influence incarcerated fathers' relationships with their children. *Child Welfare* 77: 617–38.

Lehman, E. C. (1993). *Gender and Work: The Case of the Clergy.* Albany: State University of New York Press.

Leadership Conference of Women Religious (2002). *Women and Jurisdiction: An Unfolding Reality: The LCWR Study of Selected Church Leadership Roles.* Silver Spring, Md.: Leadership Conference of Women Religious.

Levitt, P. (2001). *The Transnational Villagers.* Berkeley: University of California Press.

———— (2002). Two nations under God: Latino religious life in the U.S. In M. Suarez-Orozco and M. N. Paez , eds., *Latinos: Remaking America.* Berkeley: University of California Press. 150–64.

Lincoln, C. E. and L. H. Mamiya (1990). *The Black Church in the African-American Experience.* Durham, N.C.: Duke University Press.

Lindner, E. W. (2002). Personal communication, September 22.

Loewenthal, K. M., A. K. MacLeod, and M. Cinnirella (2002). Are women more religious than men? Evidence from a short measure of religious activity applicable in different religious groups in the UK. *Personality and Individual Differences* 32: 133–39.

Loizillon, A. and M. A. Hughes (1999). *Building Revival.* Philadelphia: Public/Private Venture.

Longres, J. F. and D. G. Peterson (2000). Social work practice with Latino American immigrants. In P. R. Balgopal, ed., *Social Work Practice with Immigrants and Refugees.* New York: Columbia University Press. 65–126.

Longest, J. W. (1991). *The Role of Black Churches in the Provision of Services to the Poor.* College Park: University of Maryland.

Losh, S., C. Fobes, and M. Gould (1994). Ballots, marches, and good works: Religious congregations, community participation and political activism. Paper presented at the annual meeting of the Association for the Study of Religion, Los Angeles.

Lubove, R. (1965). *The Professional Altruist.* Cambridge, Mass.: Harvard University Press.

Lummis, A. T. (1994). Feminist values and other influences on pastoral leadership styles: Does gender matter? Paper presented at the Society for the Scientific Study of Religion, Albuquerque, November.

Maguire, M., R. Foote, and F. Vespe (1997). Beauty as well as bread: Aesthetic considerations in neighborhood planning. *Journal of the American Planning Association* 63 (Summer): 317–29.

Mahler, S. J. (1995). *American Dreaming: Immigrant life on the Margins.* Princeton, N.J.: Princeton University Press.

Manji, I. (2004). *The Trouble with Islam: A Muslim's call for Reform in Her Faith.* New York: St. Martin's Press.

Markkola, P. (2000). *Gender and Vocation: Women, Religion, and Social Change in the Nordic Countries, 1830–1940.* Helsinki: Suomalaisen Kirjallisuuden Seura.

Markstrom, C. A. (1999). Religious involvement and adolescent psychosocial development. *Journal of Adolescence* 22: 205–21.

Martin, E. P. and J. M. Martin (2002). *Spirituality and the Black Helping Tradition in Social Work.* Washington, D.C.: National Association of Social Workers Press.

Maryland Association of Nonprofit Organizations (2002). *Protecting the trust: Revisiting public attitudes about charities in Maryland.* Baltimore: Author. Retrieved December 2, 2005 from http://www.marylandnonprofits.org/html/explore/documents/public_trust.pdf

Massey, D. S. and N. Denton (1993). *American Apartheid: Segregation and the Making of the Underclass.* Cambridge, Mass.: Harvard University Press.

Massey, D. S., R. E. Zambrana, and S. A. Bell (1995). Contemporary issues in Latino families: Future directions for research, policy, and practice. In R. E. Zambrana, ed., *Understanding Latino families: Scholarship, Policy, and Practice.* Thousand Oaks, Calif.: Sage. 190–204.

Matovina, T. (2001). Latino Catholics and American public life. In A. Walsh, ed., *Can Charitable Choice Work? Covering Religion's Impact on Urban Affairs and Social Services.* Hartford, Conn.: Trinity College, Pew Program on Religion and News Media. 57–78.

Mattis, J. S. (1997). The spiritual well-being of African Americans: A preliminary analysis. In R. J. Watts and R. J. Jagers, eds., *Manhood Development in Urban African American Communities.* New York: Haworth Press. 103–20.

Mays, B. and J. Nicholson (1933). *The Negro's Church.* New York: Institute of Social and Religious Research.

McAneny, L. and L. Saad (1993). Strong ties between religion commitment and abortion views. *Gallup Poll Monthly* 331: 35–43.

McDaniel, C., D. H. Davis, and S. A. Neff (2005). Charitable choice and prison ministries: Constitutional and institutional challenges to rehabilitating the American penal system. *Criminal Justice Policy Review* 16: 164–89.

McKinney, R. (2003). *The Clinical Jesus: The Doctor Who Never Lost a Case.* Wilmington, Del.: Sahara.

McPherson, J. M. and T. Rotolo (1995). Measuring the composition of voluntary groups: A multitrait-multimethod analysis. *Social Forces* 73: 1097–1115.

McRoberts, O. M. (2002). *Religion, Reform, Community: Examining the Idea of Church-Based Prisoner Reentry.* Washington, D.C.: Urban Institute.

——— (2003). *Streets of Glory: Church and Community in a Black Urban Neighborhood.* Chicago: University of Chicago Press.

Menjivar, C. (2002). Religion and immigration in comparative perspective: Catholic and evangelical Salvadorans in San Francisco, Washington, D.C., and Phoenix. *Sociology of Religion* 64: 21–45.

Mercer, C. and T. W. Durham. (1999). Religious mysticism and gender orientation. *Journal for the Scientific Study of Religion* 38: 175–482

Mernissi, F. (1993). *The Forgotten Queens of Islam.* Minneapolis: University of Minnesota Press.

Metropolitan Philadelphia Policy Center and the Pennsylvania Economy League (2001). *Flight or Fight: Metropolitan Philadelphia and Its Future.* September. Retrieved December 2 from http://www.metropolicy.org/FlightorFight.html

Michel, J., R. Green, and C. Toppe (2003). Factors influencing volunteering rates by race and Hispanic origin. Paper presented at the annual meeting of the Association for Research on Nonprofit Organizations and Voluntary Action, Denver, November.

Miller, D. E. (1997). *Reinventing American Protestantism: Christianity in the New Millennium.* Berkeley: University of California Press.

Miller, M. M. (1995). Women's authority in the church. *Crisis Magazine,* September, 7–12. Also available at http://www.catholic_pages.com/dir/link.asp?ref=12176.

Miller, P. M. (1978). *Peer Counseling in the Church.* Scottdale, Pa.: Herald Press.

Miller, A. S. and J. P. Hoffman (1995). Risk and religion: An explanation of gender differences in religiosity. *Journal for the Scientific Study of Religion* 34: 63–75.

Mirola, W. A. (2003). Religious protest and economic conflict: possibilities and constraints on religious resource mobilization and coalitions in Detroit's newspaper strike. *Sociology of Religion.* Retrieved January 4, 2005 from http://www.findarticles.com/p/articles/mi_m0SOR/is_4_64/ai_112357732

Mitchell, H. H. (2004). *Black Church Beginnings: The Long-Hidden Realities of the First Years*. Grand Rapids, Mich.: William B. Eerdmans.

Mock, A. K. (1992). Congregational religion's styles and orientation to society: Exploring our linear assumptions. *Review of Religious Research* 34: 20–33.

Molm, L., N. Takahashi, and G. Peterson (2000). Risk and trust in social exchange: An empirical test of a classical proposition. *American Journal of Sociology* 105: 1396–1427.

Monsma, S. V., and C. M. Mounts (2002). Working faith: How religious organizations provide welfare to work services. Retrieved October 10, 2003 from http://www.sas.upenn.edu/cruccs/8 research pdf/workingfaith.pdf

Moore, R. L. (1986). *Religious Outsiders and the Making of Americans*. New York: Oxford University Press.

Moore, T. (1991). The African-American church: A source of empowerment, mutual help, and social change. *Prevention in Human Services* 10: 147–67.

Moran, R. F. (1998). The Latino challenge to civil rights and immigration policy in the 1990s and beyond. In R. Delgado and J. Stefancic, eds., *The Latino/a Condition: A Critical Reader*. New York: New York University Press. 133–42.

Morris, A. D. (1984). *The Origins of the Civil Rights Movement: Black Communities Organizing for Change*. New York: Free Press.

Mullins, M. (1987). The life cycle of ethnic churches in sociological perspective. *Japanese Journal of Religious Studies* 14: 321–24.

Mumola, C, J. (2000). *Incarcerated Parents and Their Children*. Bureau of Justice Statistics, special report. Washington, D.C.: U.S. Department of Justice, Bureau of Justice Statistics, NCJ182335.

Musick, M. A., J. Wilson, and W. B. Bynum, Jr. (2000). Race and formal volunteering: The differential effects of class and religion. *Social Forces* 78: 1539–70.

Nason-Clark, N. (1987). Are women changing the image of ministry? A comparison of British and American realities. *Review of Religious Research* 28: 330–40.

Neighbors, H. W., J. S. Jackson, P. J. Bowman, and G. Gurin (1983). Stress, coping, and black mental health: Preliminary findings from a national study. *Prevention in Human Services* 2, 3: 5–29.

Nesbitt, P. D. (1997). *Feminization of Clergy in America*. New York: Oxford University Press.

Neitz, M. J. (1998). Feminist research and theory. In W. H. Swatos, Jr., ed., *Encyclopedia of Religion and Society*. Walnut Creek, Calif.: AltaMira. 184–86.

Netting, E. F., M. K. O'Connor, M. L. Thomas, and G. Yancey (2005). Mixing and phasing of roles among volunteers, staff, and participants in faith-based programs. *Nonprofit and Voluntary Sector Quarterly* 34: 179–204.

Newman, P. and A. E. Hotchner (2003). *Shameless Exploitation in Pursuit of the Common Good*. New York: Doubleday.

Northwest Interfaith Movement (2002a). *Long Term Care Program Summary Sheet*. Philadelphia: NIM.

——— (2002b). *The Volunteer Ombudsman Project*. Philadelphia: NIM.

——— (2002c). *The Neighbor to Neighbor Project*. Philadelphia: NIM.

——— (2002d). *Fliers for the Neighbor to Neighbor Project*. Philadelphia: NIM.

——— (2002e). *Spirituality in the Autumn and Winter of our Lives: Opportunities and Challenges*. Flier for workshops for Seniors in Partnership Across the Northwest. Philadelphia: NIM.

——— (2002f). *Telling Our Faith Stories: Leaving a Legacy*. Flier for workshops for Seniors in Partnership Across the Northwest. Philadelphia: NIM.

Oboler, S. (1995). *Ethnic Labels, Latino Lives: Identity and the Politics of (Re)presentation in the United States*. Minneapolis: University of Minnesota Press.

O'Connor, E. (1963). *Call to Commitment.* New York: Harper and Row.

O'Connor, T. P. (2002). Introduction: Religion-offenders-rehabilitation: Questioning the relationship. *Journal of Offender Rehabilitation* 35: 1–10.

Oden, M. B. (1988). Stress and purpose: Clergy spouses today. *The Christian Century*, 402–4. Retrieved May 20, 2005 from http://www.religion-online.org/showarticle.asp?title=311, April 20.

O'Donnell, S. M. (1995). Urban African American community development in the progressive era. *Journal of Community Practice* 2, 4: 7–26.

Office of Management and Budget (1978). Directive 15: Race and ethnic standards for federal statistics and administrative reporting. *Federal Register* 43, May 4, 19269

Ogilvie, R. S. (2004). *Voluntarism, Community Life, and the American Ethic.* Bloomington: Indiana University Press.

Oh, H. K. (1989). Study of Korean immigrants' process of socio-cultural adaptation and economic performance in Philadelphia area. Doctoral dissertation, University of Pennsylvania.

Ortega, A. N. and R. Rosenheck (2000). Posttraumatic stress disorder among Hispanic Vietnam veterans. *American Journal of Psychiatry* 157: 615–519.

Ortiz, M. (1991). Good neighbors: Converting commuter congregations to God's agents in the community (electronic version). *Discipleship Journal* 63: 6.

Padilla, Y. C. (1996). Incorporating social science concepts in the analysis of ethnic issues in social work: The case of Latinos. *Journal of Multicultural Social Work* 4, 3: 1–12.

―――― (1997). Immigrant policy: Issues for social work practice. *Social Work* 45: 595–606.

Partida, J. (1996). The effects of immigration on children in the Mexican-American community. *Child and Adolescent Social Work Journal* 1: 241–55.

Partners for Sacred Places (2003). *Urban Houses of Worship and Community Services Endangered: New Sources of Funding and Assistance Needed.* Retrieved September 9, 2003 from http://www.sacredplaces.org/11_End-PSP_Press_Rel.pdf

Perl, P. (2002). Gender and the mainline Protestant pastors' allocation of time to work tasks. *Journal for the Scientific Study of Religion* 41: 169–78.

Perlmann, J. and R. Waldinger (1997). Second generation decline? Children of immigrants, past and present: A reconsideration. *International Migration Review* 31: 893–922.

Philadelphia Area Intergroup of Overeaters Anonymous (2003). *Meeting List—Winter 2003.* Retrieved June 23, 2003 from http://www.oa-phila.org/meetings.html

Philadelphia Corporation for the Aging (2002). *Brochure for the Ombudsman Program.* Philadelphia: NIM.

Pinn, A. B. (2003). *Terror and Triumph: The Nature of Black Religion.* Minneapolis: Augsburg Fortress.

Pipes, P. F. (2001). *Community Ministries Today: Nine Regionally Dispersed Case Studies.* Baltimore: Annie E. Casey Foundation.

Pipes, P. F. and H. R. Ebaugh (2002). Faith-based coalitions, social services and government funding. *Sociology of Religion* 63: 49–68.

Pirog, M. A. and D. A. Reingold (2002). *Has the Safety Net ALTARed? New Roles for Faith-Based Organizations.* Bloomington: Indiana University.

Polakow-Suransky, S. (2003). Boston's Ten Point Coalition: A faith-based approach to fighting crime in the inner city. *Responsive Community* 13, 4: 49–59.

Poole, D. L. (1995). Partnerships buffer and strengthen. *Health and Social Work* 20, 1: 2–4.

Portes, A. (1998). Social capital: Its origins and applications in modern sociology. *Annual Review of Sociology* 24: 1–24.

Portes, A. and R. G. Rumbaut (1996). *Immigrant America: A Portrait.* 2nd ed. Berkeley: University of California Press.

Potts, R. (1991). Spirits in the bottle: Spirituality and alcoholism treatment in African American communities. *Journal of Training and Practice in Professional Psychology* 5: 53–64.

Printz, T. J. (1998). *Faith-Based Service Providers in the Nation's Capital: Can They Do More?* Policy Brief 2, Charting Civil Society, Center on Nonprofits and Philanthropy. Washington, D.C.: Urban Institute.

Putnam, R. D. (2000). *Bowling Alone: The Collapse and Revival of American Community.* New York: Simon and Schuster.

Raboteau, A. J. (1978). *Slave Religion: The Invisible Institution in the Antebellum South.* New York: Oxford University Press.

Reconstructionist Movement (2004). *Perhaps You Belong in a Reconstructionist Community.* Retrieved May 12, 2004 from http://www.jrf.org/recon/perhaps.html

Regnerus, M. D. and C. Smith (1998). Selective deprivatization among American religious traditions: The reversal of the great reversed. *Social Forces* 76: 1347–72.

Rediger, G. L. (1997). *Clergy Killers: Guidance for Pastors and Congregations Under Attack.* Louisville, Ky.: Westminster John Knox.

Reingold, D. A., M. Pirog, and D. Brady (2000). Empirical evidence on welfare reform and faith-based organizations. Paper presented at the 22nd Annual Research conference of the Association for Public Policy Analysis and Management, Seattle, November 2–4.

Roman, J., M. Kane, and E. Turner (2005). *An Assessment of Prisoner Preparation for Reentry in Philadelphia.* Washington, D.C.: Urban Institute.

Royle, M. H. (1987). Using bifocals to overcome blindspots: The impact of women on the military and the ministry. *Review of Religious Research* 28: 341–50.

Sack, D. (2000). *Whitebread Protestants: Food and Religion in American Culture.* New York: St. Martin's Press.

Salamon, L. (1987). Partners in public service: The scope and theory of government-nonprofit relations. In W. W. Powell, ed., *The Nonprofit Sector: A Research Handbook.* New Haven, Conn.: Yale University Press. 99–117.

Salisbury, S. (2004). To raise funds, church art may go: St. Stephen's Episcopal is considering the sale of its treasures to replenish its endowment. *The Philadelphia Inquirer,* February 20, B1, B4.

Sanders, E. C. (1997). New insights and interventions: Churches uniting to reach the African American community with health information. *Journal of Health Care for the Poor and Underserved, 8,* 373–375.

Sarfoh, J. A. (1986). The West African Zongo and the American ghetto: Some comparative aspects of the roles of religious institutions. *Journal of Black Studies* 17: 71–84.

Schiele, J. H. (1996). Afrocentricity: An emerging paradigm in social work practice. *Social Work* 41: 284–94.

Shapiro, J. P. and A. R. Wright (1996). Can churches save America? *U.S. News and World Report* 121, 10, September 9, 46–53.

Shawchuck, N. and R. Hauser (1993). *Leading the Congregation: Caring for Yourself While Serving the People.* Nashville, Tenn.: Abington.

Sherman, A., R. M. Solow, and M. W. Edelman (1994). *Wasting America's Future: The Children's Defense Fund Report on the Costs of Child Poverty*. Boston: Beacon Press.

Sherman, A. (2001). *State and Local Implementation of Existing Charitable Choice Programs*. Indianapolis: Hudson Institute.

——— (2003). *The Community Serving Activities of Hispanic Protestant Congregations*. Preliminary report submitted to the Center for the Study of Latino religion, Notre Dame University.

——— (2004). *Small Groups at a Large Scale*. Indianapolis: Hudson Institute.

Sherraden, M. S. and R. E. Barrea (1996). Poverty, family supports, and well-being of infants: Mexican immigrant woman and childbearing. *Journal of Sociology and Social Welfare* 23, 2: 27–54.

Sider, R., P. N. Olson, and H. R. Unruh (2002). *Churches That Make a Difference: Reaching Your Community with Good News and Good Works*. Grand Rapids, Mich.: Baker Book House.

Sikkink, D. and E. I. Hernandez (2003). *Religion Matters: Predicting Schooling Success Among Latino Youth*. Interim report 2003–1. Institute of Latino Studies, Notre Dame University, South Bend, Indiana.

Silverman, C. (2000). *Faith-Based Communities and Welfare Reform: California Religious Community Capacity Study*. San Francisco: Institute for Nonprofit Organization Management, University of San Francisco.

Singer, A. (2002). *America's Diversity at the Beginning of the 21st century: Reflections from Census 2000*. Washington, D.C.: Brookings Institution. Retrieved April 15, 2002 from http://www.brookings.org/dybdocroot/views/papers/singer/20020402.pdf

Sinha, J. W. (2004) African American Youth and Communities of Faith: Capitalizing on Compassion, at Risk for Greatness. Doctoral dissertation, University of Pennsylvania.

Skocpol, T. (2000). Religion, civil society, and social provision in the U.S. In M. J. Bane, B. Coffin, and R. Thiemann, eds., *Who Will Provide? The Changing Role of Religion in American Social Welfare*. Boulder, Colo.: Westview. 21–50.

Smidt, C. (2003). *Religion as Social Capital: Producing the Common Good*. Waco, Tex.: Baylor University Press.

Smith, C. (1996). *Disruptive Religion: The Force of Faith in Social Movement Activism*. New York: Routledge.

Smith, D. H. (1983). Churches are generally ignored in the contemporary voluntary action research: causes and consequences. *Review of Religious Research* 24: 295–303.

Smith, K. K. (2002). *Manna in a Wilderness of AIDS: Ten Lessons in Abundance*. Cleveland: Pilgrim Press.

Smith, R. C. (2002). Gender, ethnicity, and race in school and work outcomes of second generation Mexican-Americans. In M. M. Suárez-Orozco and M. M. Páez, eds., *Latinos: Remaking America*. Berkeley: University of California Press. 110–25.

Smith, S. R. and M. R. Sosin (2001). The varieties of faith-related agencies. *Public Administration Review* 61: 651–69.

Social Capital Community Benchmark Survey (2001). *Executive Summary*. Retrieved April 11 from Harvard University John F. Kennedy School of Government, Saguaro Seminar Civic Engagement in America Website, http://www.ksg.harvard.edu/saguaro/communitysuvey/results.html

Stark, R. (1999). Secularization, R.I.P. *Sociology of Religion* 60: 249–73.

Stark, R. (2002). *Sociology*. 8th ed. Belmont, Calif.: Wadsworth.

Steinfeld, G. (1999). Integrating cognitive-behavior and thought field therapies within a spiritual framework. *Journal of Psychotherapy Integration* 9: 337–363.

Stone, M. M. (2000). Scope and scale: An assessment of human service delivery by congregations in Minnesota. Paper presented at the annual meeting of Association for Research on Nonprofit Organizations and Voluntary Action. New Orleans, November.

Sugrue, T. J. (1996). *The Origins of the Urban Crisis: Race and Inequality in Postwar Detroit*. Princeton, N.J.: Princeton University Press.

Sullins, D. P. (2000). The stained glass ceiling: Career attainment for women clergy. *Sociology of Religion* 61: 243–66.

Suro, R. (2003). *Remittance Senders and Receivers: Tracking the Transnational Channels*. Washington, D.C.; Pew Hispanic Center.

Suro, R. and A. Singer (2002). *Latino Growth in Metropolitan America: Changing Patterns, New Locations*. Washington, D.C.: Brookings Institution, July. Retrieved October 7, 2002 from http://www.brookings.org/dybdocroot/_urban/_publications/surosingerexsum.htm.

Sutherland, M., C. D. Hale, and G. J. Harris (1998). Community health promotion: The church as partner. *Journal of Primary Prevention* 16: 689–99.

Takayama, K. P. and L. W. Cannon (1979). Formal polity and power distribution in American Protestant denominations. *Sociological Quarterly* 20: 321–32.

Taylor, R. D., L. Jacobson, and D. Roberts (2000). Ecological correlates of the social and emotional adjustment of African American adolescents. In R. Montemayer, G. R. Adams, and T. P. Gullotta, eds., *Adolescent Diversity in Ethnic, Economic, and Cultural Contexts*. Thousand Oaks, Calif.: Sage. 208–34.

Taylor, R. J. and L. M. Chatters (1986). Church-based informal support networks among elderly Blacks. *Gerontologist* 26: 637–42.

——— (1988). Church members as a source of informal support. *Review of Religious Research* 30: 93–202.

——— (1991). Religious life. In J. J. Jackson, ed., *Life in Black America*. Newbury Park, Calif.: Sage. 105–23.

Taylor, R. J., L. M. Chatters, and J. S. Levin (2003). *Religion in the Lives of African Americans: Social, Psychological, and Health Perspectives*. Thousand Oaks, Calif.: Sage.

Taylor, R. J., C. G., Ellison, L. M. Chatters, J. S. Levin, and K. D. Lincoln (2000). Mental health services in faith communities: The role of clergy in Black churches. *Social Work* 45: 73–87.

Thomas, S. B., S. C. Quinn, A. Billingsley, and C. Caldwell (1994). The characteristics of Northern Black churches with community health outreach programs. *American Journal of Public Health* 84: 575–79.

Thompson, E. H. (1991). Beneath the status characteristic: Gender variations in religiousness. *Journal for the Scientific Study of Religion* 30: 381–94.

Thompson, J. D. 1967. *Organizations in Action*. New York: McGraw-Hill.

Tierney, J. P. and J. B. Grossman, with N. L. Resch (1995). *Making a Difference: An Impact Study of Big Brothers Big Sisters*. Philadelphia: Public/Private Ventures.

Toll, J. B. and M. S. Gillam (1995). *Invisible Philadelphia: Community Through Voluntary Organizations*. Philadelphia: Atwater Kent Museum.

Tolliver, W. F. (1993). At the point of need: A model for church-based social services for the ghetto poor. Doctoral dissertation, Hunter College, City University of New York.

Trulear, H. D. (1985). The Lord will make a way somehow: Afro-American Worship. *Journal of the Interdenominational Theological Center* 13, 1: 87–104.

Trulear, H. D. (1998). *From Exodus to Exile*. Retrieved June 10, 2003 from http://www.cpjustice.org/stories/storyReader$652

Tsitsos, W. (2003). Race differences in congregational social service activity. *Journal for the Scientific Study of Religion* 42: 205–15.

Ulbrich, H. and M. Wallace (1984). Women's work force status and church attendance. *Journal for the Scientific Study of Religion* 23: 341–50.

Unruh, H. R. and R. J. Sider (2001). Religious elements of faith-based social service programs: Types and integrative strategies. Paper presented at the Society for the Scientific Study of Religion Annual Meeting, Columbus, Ohio, November.

———— (2005). *Saving Souls, Serving Society: Understanding the Faith Factor in Church-Based Social Ministry*. New York: Oxford University Press.

U.S. Bureau of the Census (2000). *2000 Census Data*. Retrieved October 14, 2002, from http://pasdc.hbg.psu.edu/pasdc/census_2000/Data/SF3/DP1-DP4/05042101.pdf

———— (2002). *Profile of General Demographic Characteristics: 2000, Geographic Area: Philadelphia City, Pennsylvania*. Retrieved March 25, 2003 from http://_fact finder.census.gov/bf/_lang = en_vt_name = DEC_2000_SF1_U_DP1_geo_id = 16000US4260000.html

———— (2001). *The Census 2000 Redistricting Data Summary*. Washington D.C.: U.S. Government Printing Office.

U.S. Department of Justice (2000). *Incarcerated Parents and Their Children*. Washington, D.C.: Department of Justice.

U.S. Senate (2000). *Senate Report 106–404: Departments of Commerce, Justice, and State, the Judiciary, and Related Agencies Appropriation Bill, 2001*.Washington, D.C., September 8.

Vasoli, R. H. (1998). *What God Has Joined Together: The Annulment Crisis in American Catholicism*. New York: Oxford University Press.

Vaughan, J. N. (1993). *Megachurches and America's Cities: How Churches Grow*. Grand Rapids, Mich.: Baker Book House.

Verba, S., K. L. Schlozman, and H. Brady (1993). Race, ethnicity, and political resources: Participation in the United States. *British Journal of Political Science* 23: 453–497.

Voorhees, C., F. Stillman, M. Swank, P. Heagerty, D. Levine, and D. Becker (1996). Heart, body, and soul: Impact of church-based smoking cessation interventions on readiness to quit. *Preventive Medicine* 25: 277–85.

Voye, L. (1999). Secularization in a context of advanced modernity. *Sociology of Religion* 60: 275–88.

Wahba, M. A. and S. I. Lirtzman (1972). A theory of organizational coalition formations. *Human Relations* 25: 515–27.

Ward, C. (2005). Lakewood's gift for Christmas: Mega-church gives symphony big new audience. *Houston Chronicle*, December 8. Retrieved January 10, 2006 from http://www.chron.com/disp/story.mpl/ent/3509942.html

Warner, R. S. (1993). Work in progress toward a new paradigm for the sociological study of religion in the United States. *American Journal of Sociology* 98: 1044–93.

———— (1994). The place of the congregation in the contemporary American religious configuration. In J. P. Wind and J. W. Lewis, eds., *American Congregations*, vol. 2, *New Perspectives in the Study of Congregations*. Chicago: University of Chicago Press. 54–99.

———— (1998). Introduction: Immigration and religious communities in the

United States. In S. Warner and J. W. Witter, eds., *Gatherings in Diaspora: Religious Communities and the New Immigration*. Philadelphia: Temple University Press. 3–34.

Warner, W. L. and P. S. Lunt (1941). *The Social Life of a Modern Community*. New Haven, Conn.: Yale University Press.

Warren, J. T. (2001). *Open the Doors, See All the People: A Guide to Serving Families in Sacred Places*. Philadelphia: Partners for Scared Places.

Warren, M. R. and R. L. Wood (2001). *Faith-Based Community Organizing: The State of the Art*. Jericho, N.Y.: Interfaith Funders.

Weber, M. (1968). *Economy and Society*. Ed. G. Roth and C. Wittich. Berkeley: University of California Press.

Westerkamp, M. J. (1999). *Women and Religion in Early America, 1600–1850: The Puritan and Evangelical Traditions*. New York: Routledge.

Wexler, H. K., G. De Leon, G. Thomas, D. Kressel, and J. Peters (1999). The Amity Prison TC evaluation: Reincarceration outcome. *Criminal Justice Behavior* 26: 147–67.

White, E. G. (2003). *Heaven*. Nampa, Ida.: Pacific Press Publishing Association.

Wilson, J. Q. and G. L. Kelling (1982). Broken windows: The police and neighborhood safety. *Atlantic Monthly* 294, 3 (March): 29–38.

Wilson, W. J. (1991). Studying inner-city social dislocations: The challenge of public agenda research. *American Sociological Review* 56: 1–14.

Wind, J. P. and J. W. Lewis (1994). *American Congregations*. Vol. 2, *New Perspectives in the Study of Congregations*. Chicago: University of Chicago Press.

Wineburg, R. J., F. Ahmed, and M. Sills (1997). Local human service organizations and the local religious community during an era of change. *Journal of Applied Social Sciences* 21, 2: 93–98.

Wood, B. A. (1997). First African Methodist Episcopal church and its social intervention in south Central Los Angeles. Doctoral dissertation, University of Southern California.

Wood, R. L. (1997). Social capital and political culture: God meets politics in the inner city. *American Behavioral Scientist* 4: 595–605.

——— (2002). *Faith in Action: Religion, Race, and Democratic Organizing in America*. Chicago: University of Chicago Press.

Woolever, C. and D. Bruce (2002). *A Field Guide to U.S. Congregations: Who's Going Where and Why*. Louisville, Ky.: Westminster John Knox.

Working Group on Human Needs in Faith-Based and Community Initiatives (2002). *Finding Common Ground: 29 Recommendations of the Working Group on Human Needs and Faith-Based and Community Initiatives*. Philadelphia: Working Group on Human Needs.

Wright-Smith, H. L. (2004). The impact of inner city commuter and community congregations on civic engagement and social action. Doctoral dissertation, City and Regional Planning, University of Pennsylvania.

Wuthnow, R. (1994a). *Producing the Sacred: An Essay on Public Religion*. Urbana: University of Illinois Press.

——— (1994b). *God and Mammon in America*. New York: Free Press.

——— (1998). *Loose Connections: Joining Together in America's Fragmented Communities*. Cambridge, Mass.: Harvard University Press.

——— (1999). Mobilizing civic engagement: The changing impact of religious involvement. In T. Skocpol and M. P. Fiorina, eds., *Civic Engagement in American Democracy*. Washington, D.C.: Brookings Institution Press. 331–63.

——— (2000). *Linking Between Religious Congregations and Nonprofit Service Organizations*. Washington, D.C.: Aspen Institute, Nonprofit Research Fund.

———— (2003). *All in Synch: How Music and Art Are Revitalizing American Religion.* Berkeley: University of California Press.

———— (2004). *Saving America? Faith-Based Services and the Future of Civil Society.* Princeton, N.J.: Princeton University Press.

Wuthnow, R., C. Hackett, and B. Y. Hsu (2004). The effectiveness and trustworthiness of faith-based and other service organizations: A study of recipients' perceptions. *Journal for the Scientific Study of Religion* 43: 1–17.

Yang, F. (1999). *Chinese Christians in America: Conversion, Assimilation, and Adhesive Identities.* University Park: Pennsylvania State University Press.

Yohn, S. (1995). *A Contest of Faiths: Missionary Women and Pluralism in the American Southwest.* Ithaca, N.Y.: Cornell University Press.

Zelinsky, W. (2001). The uniqueness of the American religious landscape. *Geographical Review* 91: 565–85.

Zikmund, B. B., A. T. Lummis, and P. M. Y. Chang (1998). *Clergy Women: An Uphill Calling.* Louisville, Ky.: Westminster John Knox Press.

Zimbardo, P. G. (1969). The human choice: Individuation, reason, and order versus deindividuation, impulse, and chaos. *Nebraska Symposium on Motivation* 17: 237–307.

Zink-Sawyer, B. (2003). *From Preachers to Suffragists: Woman's Rights and Religious Conviction in the Life of Three Nineteenth-Century American Clergywomen.* Louisville, Ky.: Westminster John Knox.

Index

Acknowledgments

The concept for this book began with research grants from the Pew Charitable Trusts through Private/Public Venture (P/PV) to study the role of the religious community in the welfare system at the end of the twentieth century in the City of Philadelphia. I am in debt to their wisdom and insight as to the importance of knowing what is going on in urban America and the importance of focusing on one city as a case example. At one point, when we were short of funds, Bob Buford from Dallas, Texas, listened to our needs and made what he defined as the Buford Foundation's "one and only financial support for an academic research." It was generous support that carried us a long way. Bob, I hope you will find this book and the many academic papers spawned from this research worthy of your support. Support for analyzing the data on Latino congregations was provided by The Center for the Study of Latino Religion at Notre Dame University.

My Dean at the time, Ira M. Schwartz, was most supportive and helpful. I cannot thank him enough for his encouragement and willingness to allow me to do things my way. Even when it seemed impossible to continue with this project, he was supportive and provided me with a research office, graduate assistants, and the means to do my work. His successor, Richard J. Gelles, became a friend and research colleague and gave me space and support for doctoral students even when the research funds dried up.

Other people started me on this line of inquiry. As a secular (nonbeliever) individual who still believes that it is the role of the government to provide social services, I would not have chosen this field of study without many supporting friends and colleagues. Peter Dobkin Hall, now at the Kennedy School at Harvard University and formerly of the Yale Program on Nonprofit Organizations, enabled me to present some of my initial findings at Yale University. He also introduced me to many scholars and practitioners in the nonprofit field who provided me with new perspectives on the topic. My long-time friend Robert Wineburg piqued my interest in this area and provided me with the first research opportunities. We love to disagree and love each other anyway. I have been blessed with his friendship for over a quarter century. We spent many hours discussing and disagreeing over many issues. But I always learn from him, and I hope he feels the same. John J. DiIulio, Jr., is another colleague whom I was blessed to meet and become friends with in the past five years. His intellectual capacity and interest in the topic made him a fun person to talk to and bounce ideas off of. John facilitated the original Pew grant and the support from the Buford Foundation. This book and the study it is predicated on would not have been possible without John's vision and insights.

Diane Cohen and Robert (Bob) Jaeger are codirectors of Partners for Sacred Places, a national nonprofit, nonsectarian organization founded in 1989 to help Americans embrace, care for, and make good use of older and historic religious properties that continue to play a critical role in the lives of their communities. In appreciation of their support, all royalties from this book and my previous books are donated to Partners for Sacred Places.

Special thanks are in order to the people who assisted in data collection. While the authors conducted some of the interviews, many other interviews were carried out by committed and insightful groups of interviewers. As we trained and met many research assistants, only a few stayed with us and completed a significant number of interviews. We include here those who carried out at least 20 interviews each: Wayne Antonine, Johnnie M. Berry, Tina Choi, Dorothy E. Daniels , Nicholas D'Arecca, Jonathan C. David, Carmen and Miguel A. Diaz, Evelyn Echevarria, Loreno R. Flemmings, Rosemary Fletcher, Julie Furj, Sung Kim, Jennifer Litke , Hope Lozano, Ana Marixa Rios-Orlandi, Robert Pritchet, Elsa Ramsden, Mary Rodriguez, Jill W. Sinha, Andrew L. Stahler, Rosemary TenPenny, and Charles F. Tobin. Rosemary TenPenny conducted over one hundred interviews and was the most effective interviewer. Thank you, Rosemary! The task of the conducting interviews was difficult. Interviewers contacted clergy, begged them to be interviewed, spent numerous hours talking to them, and provided us with the richest possible database on congregations in one city. Some of them had only high school degrees while others held Ph.D.s. Some were very religious and some were not at all. To all of them, a hearty thank you.

In order to ask the most relevant questions and make sure that we reached all the relevant constituencies, we formed an advisory board. Its members provided us with numerous good ideas and access to resources otherwise impossible to find. We want to thank them and hope that they will find this book worthy of their support. They are Rev. Luis Cortez, President, Hispanic Clergy of Philadelphia and Vicinity and CEO, Nueva Esperanza; Rev. Linward Crowe, President, Philadelphia Leadership Foundation; Dr. Katie Day, Professor, Lutheran Theological Seminary; Dr. Amin El-Arabi, President, Al-Aqsa Islamic Society; Rev. Richard Fernandez, Executive Director, Northwest Interfaith Movement; Rev. C. Ed Geiger, Executive Director, Metropolitan Christian Council of Philadelphia; Rev. William C. Gipson, Chaplain, University of Pennsylvania; Bishop C. Milton Grannum, Pastor, New Covenant Church; Rev. Robert L. Hargrove, Representative, Church of God in Christ; Rev. Peter Hwang, President of the Korean Ministerium; Rev. Robin Hynicka, Executive Director, Frankford Group Ministry; Rev. Dr. James McJunkin, President, African American Interdenominational Ministries; Archdeacon John Midwood, Episcopal Diocese of Philadelphia; Rev. Henry Nash, Pastor, Grace Community Baptist Church; C.L. Pryor, Pastor, Corinthian Baptist Church; Dr. Verley Sangster, President, Center for Urban Theological Studies; Rev. Monsignor Timothy C. Senior, Secretary for Catholic Human Services; Rev. Dr. Leonard Thompson, Sr., Associate Executive Minister, Philadelphia Baptist Association; Rabbi Brian Walt, Mishkan Shalom Synagogue; Rev. Dr. Dorothy Watson-Tatem, Director, Resourcing for United Methodist Church; and Delores D. Wesley, Executive Director, Center for Urban Ministry.

To coordinate this enormous undertaking, we needed a project director and someone to set the research office on track. My daughter, Ayala Cnaan, took a semester off from college and worked in the early stages of the study. She arranged the databases, the procedures of reporting, and the telephone system. When she decided to go back to school, Rev. Rodney Rogers was hired as project director. He professionally organized the office, set reporting procedures, and facilitated the work of the advisory board as well as the opening of the gates to many denominations and citywide faith groups. When Rodney was offered a more permanent job, Jay Gardner stepped in to fill the void until the project was concluded. Rebecca Krimel worked in the office and helped the project directors carry out their tasks.

Arianne McGinty and Charlene C. McGrew entered most of the data for this project. This was not a simple task. It required patience, thorough understanding of the study, and ability to communicate with the research assistants when data were incomplete or contradictory. It is thanks to them that we have a reliable and workable database. Charlene also helped in editing and collecting information for the book. Andrea Helzer was an intern working with us on planning and organizing the project. Amy Hillier from the University of Pennsylvania Cartographic Modeling Lab helped with setting the figures and analyzing the data using GIS. I gained insight and depth from her help.

Colleagues who critiqued earlier versions made many cogent comments and suggestions that helped improve the quality of this book. The errors are still mine, but they are fewer in number thanks to their detailed and constructive critiques. They are John DiIulio of the University of Pennsylvania, and Edwin Hernandez of Notre Dame University. Rabbi George Stern and Rev. Richard (Dick) Fernandez critiqued the chapter on NIM, and I am thankful to them as they found many inaccuracies.

To all of the above, I am grateful. But, most of all, I am thankful to the many clergy and congregational leaders who took the time to talk with us and provide us with insight and some understanding of the important role congregations play in Philadelphia, and by extension, in urban America. There is no way we could have done this work without those individuals, who generously gave us their time and attention and answered our endless questions. If this book is of value, it is because of their input and careful responses. I hope that they will find some reward for their lost hours by the knowledge gained and by the possible recognition of their important work. I came out of this project impressed with their work, the immense level of job uncertainty, and the number of areas in which clergy are expected to be knowledgeable and competent. Few people in America can be called at any hour of the day or night to counsel a distressed family, carry out a religious service that is meaningful and uplifting, week in and week out, efficiently manage an organization, and also actively care for those in need. I take my hat off to you, and I dedicate this book to your individual and collective sacrifices.